the story of
the
kinks
you really got me

To a great Mum, Ann Hasted,
without whom I wouldn't have written much.

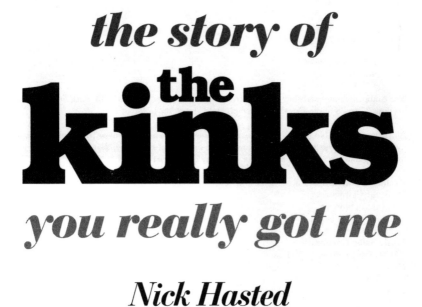

the story of
the
kinks
you really got me

Nick Hasted

OMNIBUS PRESS

London / New York / Paris / Sydney / Copenhagen / Berlin / Madrid / Tokyo

Cover designed by Fresh Lemon
Picture research by Jacqui Black & Nick Hasted

ISBN: 978.1.78038.862.5
Order No: OP55110

Exclusive Distributors
Music Sales Limited,
14/15 Berners Street,
London, W1T 3LJ.

Music Sales Corporation
180 Madison Avenue, 24th Floor,
New York,
NY 10016,
USA.

Macmillan Distribution Services,
56 Parkwest Drive
Derrimut, Vic 3030,
Australia.

Printed in the EU

A catalogue record for this book is available from the British Library.

Visit Omnibus Press on the web at www.omnibuspress.com

Contents

Introduction

"You're gonna find out just how powerful America is, you limey bastard!" It is June 1965, backstage in an LA TV studio, and The Kinks' Ray Davies and a US union official are swapping screamed insults. The American has just likened The Kinks' first US tour to the Japanese assault on Pearl Harbour. Now he is calling them "Commie wimps", and Davies a "talentless fuck", threatening to "file a report" so they'll never sully his country's shores again. Seconds later, the pair trade punches, and Davies storms out. He barricades his hotel door, raging and fearful, thinking of what the Americans did to Kennedy, and Lee Harvey Oswald, paranoid a Mob hit is coming. The Kinks return to Britain soon afterwards, leaving behind a trail of confusion and hatred. By the time America lets them back in, the Sixties will be almost over.

In those lost years, The Beatles and the Stones cemented their American fame, Kinks copyists The Who played Woodstock, and gradually, denied the spotlight, The Kinks' own legend faded. When the great British bands of the Sixties are recalled, they usually come a poor fourth. But while the Stones stopped surprising in 1968, The Beatles blew apart in 1970, and The Who became a bloated self-parody, The Kinks' 40-year career is one of pop's most musically brilliant, contrary and barely known tales.

Founded on the combustible creative core of brothers Ray and Dave Davies, The Kinks have survived regular fist-fights, copious sex with women and men, riots, breakdowns, attempted suicides and a shooting. There have been walk-on parts from the Krays, Andy Warhol and the Queen. More lasting than this is a musical legacy bettered only by The Beatles. In a golden run of singles stretching from 'You Really Got Me' in 1964 to 'Days' in 1968, they invented heavy metal, introduced Indian music to Western pop, became delicate social satirists, flirted with gayness, sang of suburban ordinariness at the height of psychedelia, and crowned the decade with 'Waterloo Sunset'.

Then, just as their peers atrophied, Ray Davies went underground, with a series of unbought, interior albums from *The Kinks Are The Village Green Preservation Society* (1968) to *Muswell Hillbillies* (1971), deliberately buried treasures only now being unearthed. Having invented the rock opera with *Arthur* (1969), he then spent the early seventies writing ambitious concept albums, which The Kinks toured as vaudeville musicals. Triumphantly re-emerging in Reagan's America as unlikely stadium kings, the shock of success made them self-destruct. The Kinks last played together in Norway in 1996.

The cultural juggernaut of the sixties – the Redlands bust and the Stones' rebel soap opera, John and Yoko, the Grosvenor Square riot, Jimi and Janis – thunders on unstoppably today, endlessly referenced and replayed. The Kinks' music exists as a quiet London backwater pub the motorway passed by, where Ray sits in the corner, still anonymously watching and writing. His songs are a sedimentary layer in all subsequent British pop linking Noël Coward to Johnny Rotten, matching how Bob Dylan's revolutionary writing underpins rock in America – where Dave's violent riffs helped spark a thousand garage bands.

Ray is as out of place in 2011 as he was in 1964. But he has, uniquely among his peers, kept on his restless path, trying to describe a world he'll always feel apart from. His destructive need for control has often left managers, labels, journalists and film-makers who have tried to help him and his band depressed and defeated. Like another icon of early sixties working-class rebellion, Alan Sillitoe's lonely long-distance runner, who pulls up short at the finish line to spite the Establishment, even his often wilfully self-inflicted defeats are victories of a kind. He and Dave have never been able to give up, and only occasionally, incompetently conformed. There is a wound in their greatest music, a wish for something better that's been lost, to the past or the future.

It's become a cliché, when writing about America and its art, to refer to the green light F. Scott Fitzgerald's Gatsby sees on the horizon, symbolising the country's unreachable promise. The Kinks' Village Green offers that place in Britain. It's a musical haven for misfits and innocents, where selfish progress can be stopped in its tracks, for the three minutes most Davies tunes play. And just as the doomed romantic Gatsby ended up (like their contemporary Brian Jones) face down in a grubby swimming pool, The Kinks' safe place is braced by awareness that the bulldozers and bullshit, age and decay will crash through anyway. The quixotic courage of Kinks songs is still to insist they shouldn't.

The vibrant, embattled working-class culture the band embody perhaps has less in common with the American home of the blues they spent so much of their lives trying to conquer, than Italy's bawdy humanist films, which accept people with all their self-defeating flaws. No one was more flawed, funny, forgiving and forgivable than The Kinks.

I first met Ray and Dave in 2004; always apart, by then. Dave arrived in a 15th floor central London bar, a high stone's throw from where he recorded 'You Really Got Me' 40 years before. His city was spread out below. "Surprised there's so much left," sniffed the man who backed his brother's Preservation plans, before holding forth with passionate openness even the major stroke that temporarily felled him days later has not extinguished.

The notoriously cautious Ray proved more elusive. For weeks he remained a weary, cagey voice on the end of the phoneline, taping himself even as I did, The Kinks story's Deep Throat and Nixon. I spent an afternoon at Konk, The Kinks' old north London studio, believing he was upstairs recording. A phone call eventually revealed he was a mile away wanting to be alone, the Garbo of Muswell Hill. He had been shot by a mugger in New Orleans the year before, and the physical and psychic injury went deep. But this was also a classic Ray game of brinkmanship and patience. When he relented, he was charming, amused, and bursting with articulate pride in his band. Private demons seemed to assail him, and he kept feeling his shot leg, as if to check it was still there. He was still remarkably open, even about his notorious relationship with Chrissie Hynde (who spoke to me too, and still loved him).

Most of all, the brothers spoke of their childhoods as working-class outsiders, in the north London neighbourhood Ray kept me returning to for years, deepening my understanding and love for their music. I even found the Village Green, where one of the great British stories began.

CHAPTER 1

The Village

The stone archer's bow is pulled taut on the roof of East Finchley tube station. Any arrow that flew would land in the ancient hunting grounds of the Bishop of London, opened by him "for the recreation of the public forever" only late in the Industrial Age, in 1886. Highgate Wood, Coldfall Wood, Cherry Tree Wood and Alexandra Park all still lie to the west of the tube. In a reclaimed, Corporation-owned green between Cherry Tree and Highgate woods, there is an archery range, as if you have quietly slipped back in time to a mediaeval village. Fortis Green Road is a minute's walk north of here, with East Finchley at one end, Muswell Hill at the other and Highgate to the south. Walk a little further east of Muswell Hill and you'll reach Hornsey Art College and the sputtering neon sign of Konk Studios, the home of The Kinks for more than 20 years, now glumly put up for sale by Ray Davies. When I pass it the local cinema, the Phoenix, is offering that harbinger of British working-class revolt of a half-century ago, *Saturday Night And Sunday Morning*. "Step back into the Swinging '60s," promises the poster.

Most of The Kinks' imaginative landscape exists in this small North London kingdom: not much more than a square mile, rarely left by Ray as he has written some of the most odd, funny and heartbreaking songs of the last century. He still lives here. Walk these streets, and you have reached his Village Green, the threatened heart of his England. It was first explored in *The Kinks Are The Village Green Preservation Society*, released almost secretly in 1968, as if it confessed thoughts that were too deep and dangerously fragile.

"It's a combination of places," Ray tells me one day. "It's that green, that little park, Cherry Tree Woods, Highgate Woods, Coldfall Woods, it's part of my growing up experience. That little green is where we played football, and where we stayed till it's dark. That's where a lot of the mystery was. But it could be anywhere. It's all in my head, probably. I spent some time with my elder sister the other day, and we talked about that very thing. A lot of it was our mystery, the stories that we heard. If you sent a car with a camera down Muswell Hill, apart from the buildings being slightly special, it would look like any other town. Some things are best left in the head."

For their thousands of scattered devotees, The Kinks' songs have made these London suburbs as mythic as the Mississippi delta. Many make pilgrimages to the Clissold Arms pub in Fortis Green Road, where a plaque inside recalls Ray and Dave's first gig in December 1960. This used to be tucked in a cosy "Kinks Corner" of the old working-class boozer it had been since the Davies brothers drank there. New American owners gentrifying it into a gastro-pub in 2007 planned to demolish the corner, seeing no worth in relics of a tatty past. Local protests meant there is now a grand Kinks Room, where pints can be sipped on white-clothed tables as old LP sleeves in frames are inspected. Disreputable old regulars sometimes slip in. "I was there trying to track down one of my old schoolteachers," Ray tells me, "and someone in the bar knew where she was. It's right across from our old house – an easy local. I walk around those streets a lot. I love that neighbourhood. It reminds me of the street in New Orleans where I stayed later. Big trees. When my family moved there, it was a village."

Across the road is 6 Denmark Terrace, a narrow, net-curtained corner house. The wider Muswell Hill area's essential gentility has claimed the pub. But it has not yet touched this home. Like the plain Liverpool council house awaiting Paul McCartney's death for its blue plaque and preservation by a National Trust more used to palaces, a new democratic kind of history was wrought here. When I first visit, a middle-aged woman in a suit, one of The Kinks' tired commuters, is putting her key in the door. This is where Ray was born on June 21, 1944, and Dave on February 3, three years later: the source of The Kinks' ordinary art.

"It's so important, when I think back," considers Dave. "I'm the youngest of eight kids, and my mum came from a family of 21 kids. All of a sudden you find yourself in an environment with all these crazy people that are all fighting for space, and it affects your sense of individuality. It was the core that let us survive everything later. My mother grew up around the back of Caledonian Road in King's Cross, and she used to have fist-fights with gangsters in the street. There is a genetic thing there. My mum was my first guru, with her grit and just having to deal with shit, even if it came to blows. There were terrible fragile situations I can think of as kids – not having any money. There was a resourcefulness. It was almost like, when you had nothing, that's when things started to happen. There's that element alive in Kinks songs."

"You'll always be where you're from," agrees Ray. "I remember talking to a friend of mine a few years ago, and at that time I had a posh house. He said, 'You come off like you still live in a terrace.' Most people, if they really stay the way they are, carry that with them."

The brothers' parents, Fred and Annie, were working-class refugees, displaced to the suburbs by the threat of the Blitz: the Muswell Hillbillies of The Kinks' great 1971 album. With a grandmother and six older sisters (most with husbands and kids of their own) crammed into the home or living nearby, at Saturday night parties still more friends and family packed round the piano to drink and dance to music-hall tunes. Characters from future songs caroused there: Uncle Son, Terry and Julie. In colour home movies you can see them all, small, wizened dad's arm around big, fiercely grinning mum's neck. Teenage Dave is part of the uproarious scene, arms flung back as he dances with his black niece Jackie (daughter of sister Peg and a deported African, always loved in this outsiders' tribe). Ray sidles in giving his sideways, uncertain smile.

The two brothers experienced the chaos very differently. "When you were the youngest in the family, it was like a Fellini film – faces everywhere," Dave told Radio 2's Johnny Walker, conjuring the scary, vivid excitement. "I can't explain what my childhood was like," Ray said more coldly in Julien Temple's documentary *Imaginary Man*. "I found it hard to exist in a family with a lot of people in the same house. It was a small house. No disrespect, but I was bored by being in it." He responded by trying to escape as far as he could, walking or riding the bus miles into the West End, a lone observer who always came back. When interlopers visited in The Kinks' first years, some were appalled by what they found. "The house was so crowded that Ray and Dave slept in the front room, with their amps under the bed and gear all around them," said tour manager Hal Carter. Roadie Sam Curtis believed "they came from a very sad home, in my opinion. I felt uncomfortable sitting down in it."

The Kinks' bassist Pete Quaife painted an even bleaker scene to journalist Johnny Black. "I think Ray was ashamed of his upbringing, his mother, his father, the house they lived in – the whole thing. Dave wasn't like that at all. It was just a Ray thing." Ray's conclusion in *Imaginary Man* was more ambivalent. "It was a sense of loving where I was from. But also that I belonged somewhere else, ultimately."

The front room, glimpsed with light diamond wallpaper behind the dancers in that grainy home movie, was nevertheless where The Kinks' first hits were written. "I felt that in some strange way God was always there," Ray wrote in his novelistic autobiography, *X-Ray*. It was where Dave was born.

"I won't go so far as to say that Muswell Hill is a really powerful psychic centre," Dave considers. "But a swami I really respect started in Dukes Avenue in Muswell Hill, early in the 20th-century. I love things like that. We are all much more than we think we are. Maybe Muswell Hill is just as important as the Himalayas. It's where we found a true sort of resonance."

The six sisters were mystical midwives to The Kinks' future. Never interviewed, they are the secret backbone to everything that followed, and a supportive, enduring remnant of a life separate from the band. Rosie was born in 1924, Rene, Dolly, Joyce and Peggy at two-yearly intervals, then Gwen in 1938. Their brightly dressed glamour, embattled strength and femininity profoundly impressed Ray and Dave, in turn adored as the first male siblings. Several sisters carried injuries, evidence of the hostile world surrounding the Davies clan. Peg had a withered arm and damaged hearing, after a stolen lorry careened into her as she played against railings when she was four, back in King's Cross. Rene had a hole in the heart, worsened by the brutal treatment of a Canadian soldier who took her back across the Atlantic as a war bride, from where she sent her mum stoic letters, indicating degrees of abuse. Rosie and her husband, Arthur, would raise Ray with their son Terry in Yeatman Road, Highgate Hill for much of his adolescence, a slightly more aspirational existence.

"That was a big issue with Ray," says Dave, who was partly raised by Dolly. "Even as kids, I think he resented the fact that we didn't have a proper bathroom in the house. My sister Rosie, who he became very close with, had a posher house, a posher bathroom, and a nice car and TV. Ray wanted that middle-class life, I think. And I never did." Dave thinks the model for Ray's familiar urbane adult voice, so far from his unashamed cockney, was another sister. "Gwen talks like that, because she went to grammar school. We had to go in with the scruffs. Gwennie was always the cleverest. She was six years older than Ray, a similar generation."

"It was like being born into a coven of witches," he says of the rest, "because they used to do séances on a ouija board – scared the shit out of me. Peggy – whew! Don't cross her!"

"It was a very highly charged creative environment," he adds, "because my sisters played piano and banjo." The sisters loved dancing in ballrooms and the front room, to big bands, crooners, country and early rock'n'roll. Ray, the co-creator of 'You Really Got Me''s raw savagery, adored Rodgers & Hammerstein, as he would Noël Coward later. The ballrooms' just fading, Thirties glamour was as evocative to the brothers as rock's future shock, as they were influenced by the dreams of siblings of a previous generation. An early *NME* interviewer in 1964 was surprised to discover Ray and Dave in their dressing room discussing Lena Horne, Joan Baez and the Modern Jazz Quartet, and never once mentioning The Beatles. In interviews then, Dave listed his favourite composers as Bach, Gershwin, Berry (Chuck) and Ray. Ray mentioned Glenn Miller. This unique culture to one side of rock, learned from their sisters, would eventually define The Kinks. "We were a little bit behind the times," Ray considered in *Imaginary Man*. "But also privy to stuff that was coming."

"People wonder how The Kinks suddenly changed so much after records like 'You Really Got Me'," says Dave, "but me and Ray always had a host of influences. I wasn't just influenced by Leadbelly – although his riffs were phenomenal, I pulled so many – but Frank Sinatra, Doris Day, Perry Como, Hank Williams, Fats Domino..." Ray meanwhile listened to trad New Orleans jazz at Highgate Jazz Club, and glimpsed Big Bill Broonzy playing folk-blues on TV in a smoky, dark American cellar, a vision of exotic noir cool. "Broonzy to me, because of his incredible size and the way he held his guitar, was the biggest influence on my early childhood," he said simply in *Imaginary Man*. It was over these things that the brothers bonded. "It was easy to work with Dave when we started," Ray agrees, "because we had a lot of records we liked in common, Bo Diddley and blues. For his age he was incredibly resourceful, he knew where to find that music. I loved John Lee Hooker, Broonzy, Hank Williams... it was fun to sit down and play."

The brothers' soon to be notorious rivalry, though, which would make them scrap like wild dogs in The Kinks, kicking and clawing on stage and off, was already simmering. The gap in Ray's front teeth is from a fall when he ran screaming, aged four, from the hated sight of his baby brother. "Ray was probably only happy for three years," Dave laughs. "The three years of his life before I was born."

"I didn't have any problem with Dave being born," Ray sniffs. "I think he may have had a problem with it. I guess that sort of thing builds over the years. I didn't think it would be a problem when I was little. But our relationship wasn't normal, in the sense that I lived with my sister a lot in Highgate a few miles away. So we didn't have that brotherly interaction. Don't get me wrong – we were close. But not as close as probably normal brothers would be. It was only music that really brought us together. That was something where we both said, 'Yes.'"

"There was an automatic telepathy as kids," Dave thinks. "You'd look and laugh at the same thing, and when we got interested in music, that was there as well. It used to surprise a lot of people who'd see us in the studio later, because we didn't communicate very much. But when you've got that going for you, you don't need to talk. It was very quick, all the good stuff, all the ideas – we always had so many ideas. That psychic bond that Ray and I have had has been really important. But it's nearly destroyed us as well."

That telepathy became literal when Dave was 13 and Ray was in hospital. Dave woke in the night panicking, feeling as if he was drowning. He ran into his mum's room, gasping: "Mum, I'm dying. I can't breathe." The same night, Ray had almost died, and needed a tracheotomy to breathe. There is still a scar from it at the base of his throat, and more along his jawline's edge from that teeth-smashing fall, on the side he turns away from photos. He made his childhood a litany of injuries in *X-Ray*, including a damaged lower back when he was 10. The spectre of being crippled haunted him. To this day, a defining fact for those who deal with Ray is his health, seeming to fall somewhere between convenient hypochondria when wanting to be alone, and heroically overcome, genuine agony.

Ray's sense of being an outcast from society, which he would later vent on The Kinks' 1966 B-side 'I'm Not Like Everybody Else', also began in childhood. The night before his 13th birthday, on June 21, 1957, his beloved sister Rene, back from Canada for five years now, who had slept in his bed to keep him company when he was unhappy, and patiently taught him piano in the front room, handed him his first guitar.

"I hope I've inherited some of her character," Ray said to Johnny Black almost in reverie. "Because she was much older, 23 or 24, and I just remember her being stunning looking and really made me feel nice, you know, when she was around. When she used to visit, she bought me records, and bought me cakes and chocolates. She was really nice to me, yeah." To Dave, "Rene was the most artistic one in the family, she could write and paint with both hands. She was a really good pianist."

In Ray's memory, she now played along on the piano as he picked out a tune from *Oklahoma!* Then she defiantly went dancing at a favourite ballroom, the Lyceum in the Strand. Her mother stood watching her walk up the road. They both knew the strain on her heart would kill her. "She died in the arms of a stranger, on the dance floor," Ray said in *Imaginary Man*; dancing, he perhaps embellished in *X-Ray*, to an *Oklahoma!* tune.

"I heard my dad come upstairs, ashen-faced, and he sat on the end of my bed, and I knew what he was going to say before he even opened his mouth, and he started crying, and he said that Rene's dead," Dave remembered in his film *Mystical Journey*. "It was a terrible shock. I felt totally different from the moment before. I grew up suddenly. For the first time I seriously sat up and thought about life after death. I couldn't accept the fact that people died and that was the end."

To me he adds: "I was a happy-go-lucky kid. And I could hear me mum wailing in the background, and a grown man who was old enough to be my grandfather, really, sat on my bed and started crying. I knew that I had to be strong. And I changed that day. Because something transfers energy when you break down like that. It triggers something in yourself."

Dave reacted by tentatively starting spiritual investigations, which would consume him later. For Ray, the rupture was profound. "It was a big turning point," he admitted to Johnny Black. "It would be for any traumatised child. It's your birthday, and everybody's going to a funeral." He reacted by turning in on himself – hardly talking for years, weeping inexplicably, becoming passive, as if he had half-died too. Did he feel any guilt in being handed the guitar he'd longed for in such awful circumstances? "No, I don't feel guilty about my guitar," he says coolly. "I don't have any feeling of guilt about the fact my sister died in the dancehall. It made me enjoy playing the Lyceum when The Kinks played there."

His worried parents sent him to a child psychiatrist in Notting Hill, shameful in the fifties. Ray has said he was discussed like the "queers" in the bus stop toilets. Did people give him a wide berth?

"I don't think my family gave me a wide berth. Maybe they did. Maybe they always have – I don't know. I was just quiet, and moody.

I don't think it was a terrible clinical psychology. I think it was a counsellor for kids who had communication and learning difficulties. Because there were no specialists in that period. Social services were pretty straightforward. You had a bad leg, you got a doctor. You had something wrong with your head, you'd go to a lunatic asylum. It was just a little centre. I just talked, and it was some value. I do remember talking to Dennis Waterman about it, when I was the captain of a showbiz football XI. He was a centre-half, not a very good one. I said, 'Yeah, when I was little, I went to see a counsellor'. People overheard it, and started offering me cups of tea. It's still stigmatised. It was just a counsellor, just a child who was a little bit troubled, and didn't know how to fit in. More than anything else, I didn't know how to communicate. That was something with music that helped me later. I suddenly found that I could communicate with a million people, who felt the same way as I did. That was quite a thing for me."

Has he ever fully come back from that teenage shutdown?

"I think once you get withdrawn or... I don't know whether it's depression. I think when you go in that place, you know when you're getting near it again, but there's never any trick of how to stay out of it. It's just being aware of what dangers are out there for yourself. It happens because I think most human beings are failed creatures. I knew my flaws when I was very young. I think that's probably the edge I had. I wasn't optimistic about anything, but I wasn't going to be disappointed. I wasn't optimistic, but there was something to fight for. I should have joined The Smiths when I was 15," he smiles.

In *Kink*, Dave remembers Ray being taken "up the clinic" when he was 11 or 12, when Rene was still alive. If true, his troubles ran deeper. "I would somehow have to fulfil the role of the older one and keep a lookout for him," Dave decided then. In *X-Ray*, Ray has a guilty childhood nightmare after an early thumping of Dave, who hangs by Ray's fingers from a cliff, "one brother literally holding the other's life in his hands" (Ray can't quite hang on, of course). "I knew that I would always have to protect this interloper," he writes, though he "could never quite forgive him" for trespassing into his perfect, woman-loved life. The boys' private vows to look after each other would fray and eventually be forgotten in the bigger world The Kinks took them to.

Ray and Dave both felt oppressed at their secondary modern school, William Grimshaw (where Rod Stewart was also a pupil), resenting its authority. "Well, the word freedom…" Ray considers. "I was lucky, I grew up in post-war Britain, in a so-called free society. But the Cold War was at its height in my formative years. I was very aware of the Red Threat and totalitarianism, and it never felt far away from me. I grew up with a fear of being crushed as an individual. And I saw it where I grew up and went to school. I wanted to be an artist. The school system was teaching you to be factory fodder, if you didn't have a certain level of exams. The pressure was there, but in a different way to today. It was more like survival."

"I hated school!" says Dave. "No one expected anything of me. I didn't like any of those people who taught me. I had this really beautiful French teacher, and I learned French really well. The next year she left, and I forgot it all. I didn't realise I was dyslexic as a kid. But they used to call it stoo-pid. So that gets your back up, when you think you know more than someone else but can't articulate it, and you think they're full of shit. The school system was really oppressive. That working-class anger came out in my guitar sound. And the beauty was Ray could articulate it lyrically, and I could express it in pure gritty emotion. Those two elements coming together was really important."

That class anger was conscious. Dave read Alan Sillitoe's 1958 *Saturday Night And Sunday Morning* then lent it to Ray, absorbing the cussed snarl of its factory-worker anti-hero Arthur Seaton, with his mantras "Don't let the bastards grind you down" and "Whatever people say I am, that's what I'm not". Sheffield's Arctic Monkeys adopted the latter phrase 50 years later. It could have been The Kinks' career plan. "In the late fifties and sixties, working-class people at least had the chance to express themselves," says Dave, "and they could actually write, and they could actually think – and sing. Look what happened in films. It's funny, I haven't seen [*Saturday Night And Sunday Morning* star] Albert Finney for some years now. [*Billy Liar* star] Tom Courtenay was a mate of ours later, we used to play football with him." Ray educated himself in theatre's Angry Young Men too, beginning a life-long devotion to the challenging, community-based Theatre Royal Stratford East. He and Dave learnt from those hard, realistic, austere fifties rebels, not the next decade's easier, colourful kind. The only authority they admitted was their parents.

"My parents were extraordinarily big influences on both Ray and I," says Dave. "All my mates couldn't wait to get away from home. Well, my mum lent me seven quid, to help me put a down payment on my first guitar. Because she had a vision of a way for us to get out."

"I remember her singing like Mother Courage," says Ray. "Singing songs a cappella. I remember saying to [English folk matriarch] Norma Waterson, you sing like my mum. She had that folky style. Probably some of that rubbed off."

Hornsey College of Art was Ray's first way out. "I could really draw, and I could really write, and that's what saved me," he says. "If I'd stayed in Muswell Hill and got a job there, I would have gone off my head. I knew that very early on, before I even had the band. I knew that there'd be a different path for me. Without the bridge of Art College, I don't think the rest would have happened. I wouldn't have done music. All my experimentation with drugs, I did at college. I cleaned up my act when I became a musician. I remember I was at Art College when I watched The Beatles doing 'Love Me Do' on TV, and thought, 'That's great. I know I can do that.' I owe them a tremendous debt. But being in a band was an accidental thing, it led me astray a bit. I didn't even know I wanted to write songs. I wanted to be in a band to supplement my meagre Middlesex grant, and earn enough money to study guitar in the States."

With the Art College proving frustrating, Ray approached British blues guru Alexis Korner after he played a gig there (when future Rolling Stone Charlie Watts was Korner's drummer). Ray was pointed to a job as a guitarist with The Dave Hunt Rhythm & Blues Band, gigging three nights a week in Soho in the early weeks of 1963. Prostitutes still lined Soho's streets then, and a musician's underground and nocturnal life meant mixing with them and minor gangsters, in a bohemian milieu far from Fortis Green. Ray's voyeuristic creative tendencies lit up. At

18, he was starting to create a life for himself. This was his vision of lost musical happiness as early as 1965 and as late as 1989, when he told Charles Shaar Murray it was "my ideal version of me… No singing, just sitting in a corner playing the guitar like [revered US jazz guitarist] Tal Farlow; walking home to Highgate from Soho and arriving at five in the morning for college at nine." Soon, he was moonlighting with both the Blues Messengers and his brother.

Dave had meanwhile been expelled from school at 15, for being caught by truant officers having sex with his girlfriend Sue Sheehan one lunchtime in the grass of Hampstead Heath. She became pregnant, and they decided to marry, but his mother lied, saying Sue no longer loved him. He carried that wound for most of his years with The Kinks, as Ray did the death of Rene. In his autobiography *Kink*, Dave suggested he had lost a possible life then, for one as a rock star which would sometimes seem empty and mean. "I don't know what that would have been," he says of this phantom path. "I fell in love when I was 14, and we really wanted to get married. It seemed such a natural process. And then we were torn apart. I think my mum had seen so many of her family members end up working on the railways – not that it's wrong to work on railways. But working-class life was a lot harsher then than it is now. I think she thought it would mess up my career. That emotionally messed me up for 30 years. Longer probably. I think it's why I slept with so many people. It made me very resentful to women. Which I didn't realise, being 16."

Only his obsession with rock was left to him, slashed out on an electric guitar. Dave recalls the band that would transform his life growing from duets at home and in the Clissold Arms with Ray, with the later addition of Ray's friend from school and Art College, bassist Pete Quaife, and drummer John Start (soon replaced by Mickey Willett), in winter 1961. Ray remembers it happening after he joined The Dave Hunt Band, in 1963: "Dave [Davies] had a skiffle group at school with Pete. I was aware of what they were doing. I kind of joined that."

Quaife, born in Tavistock in Devon on December 31, 1943, now lived on the Coldfall Estate near Fortis Green. He was a sardonically funny extrovert, almost as intimate with Ray as Dave and a daring, hip dresser who worked briefly for men's fashion magazine *The*

Outfitter. "It all began when I was playing on the corporation rubbish dump at the age of 11," he would tell *Melody Maker*. "Suddenly I reached the bottom of this chute and put my hand on something horribly sharp. It was a spike and went through my hand. Dead gory it was." Learning piano was suggested as therapy. Preferring guitar, he ended up on bass. His tumultuous exit after only three weeks with Ray at Hornsey College of Art showed stubbornness fitting a future Kink. "They said I was a Ted. And I said I wasn't." The discipline of commercial art at *The Outfitter* also disagreed with him. "I looked at myself one day and said, Pete, boy, you've got to get out of this. You're getting bottom-heavy."

Quaife and Dave collected records and outrageous wardrobes together. "Pete was into fashion, and I worked in a music shop in Leicester Square by then," says Dave. "We always used to hang out at lunchtimes and go to these places in Carnaby Street. I used to go to women's hat shops, to wear them just for the shock. The more people were shocked by them, the more you thought you were doing something right. You could just do anything – like Pop Art. *Austin Powers* was dreadful, but it had that superficiality, looking back. It was spontaneous art, in the music and the clothes."

The Ray Davies Quartet became The Ramrods, then, in September 1963, The Boll-Weevils, by now playing primitive R&B, like the Stones and so many others.

Their tale twisted when Willett met Robert Wace and Grenville Collins, upper-class types looking for a group to back the gangling, plummy-voiced Wace's Buddy Holly renditions at society balls in the Dorchester Hotel and country houses. It was a predictable disaster when they left the debutante circuit for an East End youth club, but Ray soon stepped in on vocals, with Wace and Collins as their new managers. Typically, while The Beatles had Brian Epstein, and the Stones hungry PR genius Andrew Loog Oldham, Ray and Dave had rank amateurs. "Grenville was a stockbroker, and Robert came from old money," Dave sighs. "They taught us a hell of a lot. I don't think Ray would have written 'Well Respected Man' without Robert showing him Noël Coward. But from a pure business point of view, they knew zilch."

On October 19, 1963, The Boll-Weevils recorded a demo with session drummer Bobby Graham at Regent Sound studio in Denmark Street. A cover of Leiber and Stoller's 'I'm A Hog For You Baby' showed how lightweight the band were at straight R&B, never a match for the Stones, Animals or Yardbirds. 'I Believed You' (credited to Ray, though Dave claims it in *Kink*) was a more promising, pensively melancholy song about betrayal. The demos were rejected when Wace and Collins hawked them around Denmark Street. But as the newly renamed Ravens' raw live sound won young fans, others glided in, smelling blood. Small-time fifties showbiz star Larry Page became a third manager, bringing in his business partner, cold-eyed Auschwitz survivor Eddie Kassner as the Davies' music publisher. The Ravens impressed top booking agent Arthur Howes as he ate a New Year's Eve Chinese meal in Marble Arch. Shel Talmy, a canny young American who had convinced the London scene he was a short step down from Phil Spector on the strength of a faked CV, became their producer. With Talmy's help a contract with Pye Records was soon eagerly signed (and parentally counter-signed: Dave was only 15). Ray quit Croydon College of Art, where he'd switched from Hornsey. With a royalty rate of 2% (1% in the States), three managers, and Kassner pocketing more than half of Ray's publishing, even by the decade's predatory standards it was a shocking deal. It gave The Kinks a pittance for their biggest hits.

"*Spivs!*" Dave yells at the thought. "It was the old school, fifties spivs still hanging around, sniffing. Sad, but we didn't know. There wasn't really a music industry as such. Everybody was making it up as they went along – getting what we can, because it's not going to be there next year. I was 16, 17. I didn't even think of it as a career, I was so caught up in the magic of it. I signed as we were going along our merry way, thinking everything was going to be all right."

"Our managers were both from the middle classes," remembers Ray. "I made the mistake once of saying they were upper-class. Ned Sherrin corrected me and said, [adopting Sherrin's posh drawl] 'How dare you give those people so much credit? They were a couple of middle-class chancers.' And probably they were. But they were breaking their mould. One of them had been a stockbroker, and wanted to manage pop groups. So it was happening all over. We were all amateurs. We lucked out, we got successful. But you made it up as you went along in those days," he explains, echoing his brother. "There's an element of that amateur, gung-ho quality that I think was good with The Kinks."

Things could have been very different, if Wace had taken up an offer he decided to refuse in 1965, from major Kinks fans Ronnie and Reggie Kray. "Yes, big admirers," Ray smirks. "I think they sent somebody round to Robert's office, and said, 'My boss is very interested in managing you'. I don't know what the outcome was. Probably Robert said, [posh voice] 'Oh, I can't let the band go, but I'll let you join my club.' When I did a new song on TV ['The London Song'] a few years back, the following week my agent got a call from the surviving Kray, Charlie, wanting to talk to me, because he felt great affinity for my lyric, because I mentioned the Kray Twins. When my agent dialled 1471 [to trace the call], it was from Her Majesty's Prison. It was kind of touching in a sense – at that stage, obviously. They were gangsters and in a crooked world, but we got involved in a different kind of villainy. Possibly not as clean cut…"

The Krays were still trying to cut deals with their fellow battling brothers in the eighties, when Charlie knocked on Gwen Davies' door. "They liked us, it worried me," laughs Dave. "They really wanted me and Ray to play them in the movie. I toyed with the idea, but the thought of glorifying criminals grated. You know what Chrissie [Hynde] used to call me and Ray? The Krays of rock'n'roll.'"

The Ravens became The Kinks in January 1964, inspired by the "kinky" leather capes and boots they had taken to wearing, thanks to the increasingly camp and confrontational Quaife and Dave's raids on Carnaby Street. "The name of The Kinks, even now people I think would raise an eyebrow," Ray says. "Because it implies certain things. And people are prejudiced about it." Did he like that suggestive provocation? "Suggestive of what?" he backtracks. "I'm not that smart, I wouldn't even have spotted that. A short name, five letters, we were bottom of the bill and it stood out. The word kinky, yes it's kinky in that sense, it's edgy. But nowadays the word has been toned down, it's part of a general Channel 4 thing. Everything's got to be that way, otherwise it doesn't get on television. Kinky and cheap," he says sadly, of the name that will sit next to his forever. "We thought we'd be doing it for six months, so it didn't bother us."

With Talmy's help, a recording session at Pye Studios with Bobby Graham again on drums yielded the first Kinks single. Little Richard's 'Long Tall Sally' was covered on Arthur Howes' advice, because The Beatles had just played it in Paris. The Kinks' version was pure Merseybeat, the shrieks imitations of McCartney, not the original's atom-splitting roar. Dave's guitar was meek, only a blast of Ray's harmonica suggesting aggression.

Despite Dave and Quaife's limp-wristed goading, Mick Avory, a straightforward, butchly good-looking 19-year-old from East Molesey, Surrey (born on February 15, 1944), became their new drummer. He quit the nascent Rolling Stones after only two weeks because "they were playing in London and it was too far to come", he blithely told *Melody Maker*. The fourth Kink had paid for his drum-kit with two grocery rounds and a paper round. With characteristic deadpan, seemingly unaware absurdity, he realised too late he had no way of getting the drums to gigs. So he strapped the bass drum to his back and cycled. "I'd placed an advert in *Melody Maker* for a rhythm and blues drummer," Avory remembers. "My mum was the one to answer when Robert Wace phoned up. She said, 'He's ever so posh'. I was working at the time in a day job, delivering paraffin. They arranged a meet-up, like a sort of audition, in the Camden Head pub in Islington. I thought they were arty. Pete Quaife was most friendly. Ray was quieter, or more introverted. It was quite a good meeting, the first one. I had to go back, with Grenville Collins asking questions. I went up and played a couple of numbers with them. Larry Page was there. It was pretty well set up, even though we had no idea what the potential was. Would I be able to do a TV show the following day? That was *Ready Steady Go!*, playing 'Long Tall Sally'. My parents preferred me to do that than deliver paraffin."

The Kinks played their first gig on February 1, 1964, at Oxford Town Hall. 'Long Tall Sally''s brief stay at number 42 in the *Melody*

Maker chart and that appearance as unknowns on the year's top TV pop programme showed powerful people were around them now. "*Ready, Steady, Go!* was great," remembers Quaife's then 12-year-old brother David, whom he took along. "Cameras were zooming in on wheels, there were minders pushing people out of the way, girls falling over. That's the first time Dave Davies hit Pete. The presenter Michael Aldred asked Dave a different question from the one he was supposed to. Dave gobbled over his words, and hit Pete because he thought Pete was making a joke about it – a good square one on the face. Ray said, 'You should have let Pete answer.'"

On March 29, they began a package tour with The Hollies and The Dave Clark Five. Damningly reviewed by *NME* on the first night, they soon propped up the bill. Billy Fury's road manager Hal Carter was sent to knock them into old-fashioned showbiz shape, instructing on dance moves, to the teenage Kinks' sneering. "Hal was a lovely guy, very funny, and a real help to us," Dave told Johnny Black. "But the object of Hal being brought in was to turn us into show people, to teach us how to bow at the end of numbers. We got so far as bowing out of synch with each other and called it a day. All the people in the business were from that era when the natural progression was to go from rock to cabaret. But we were relating to people like Muddy Waters and Big Bill Broonzy. These weren't the kind of guys who'd get up and tap dance."

The Kinks were building followings in northern outposts such as Liverpool's Cavern. But the second single from the 'Long Tall Sally' session was Ray's bouncily inane Beatles knock-off 'You Still Want Me'. Play it now, and you'd think this was a band doomed to obscurity, an unread footnote from the Beat Boom of 1964. Released on April 17, it was deservedly ignored. Pye was only obliged to release one more single. The Kinks had one secret weapon to fire: 'You Really Got Me'.

CHAPTER 2

The Riff

Without warning, the rasping, distorted, dirty guitar chops out five notes, again and again, heavier and nastier than anything on a British radio before. A crackle of electricity hangs contaminating the air, then the crump of a drum slams in the song. There's a voice, steadily growing ecstatic, driven so wild by a girl that, according to the singer, "I don't know what I'm doing." A full band is rising behind him, that five-note riff climbing one key then two, but every time the record approaches climax it pulls back. The tease only lasts a minute till there's a muffled groan, as if a man's quietly come. Finally, the singer gasps "Oh... no!" and falls from the mic as a second madman's yattering merges with the guitar's scream, which becomes a wild, clawing solo. "Don't ever set me free," the singer exultantly demands of the girl, sounding as if the trap set by the relentless riff has made him freer than he's ever felt on this earth. Every voice in the room crests in final harmony as the record hammers home, self-contained and complete. Two minutes, 11 seconds, and The Kinks are born.

'You Really Got Me' was a landmark in British rock. Everything depended on it for The Kinks. Dave had created its filthy noise in the Davies' front room in 1963, as he searched for a sound he'd never heard. In *Kink*, he remembered first hooking up three amps with a radiogram.

The badly wired charge flung him across the room, and blew out his mother's lights. Fortis Green had become a place of Frankenstein electrical experiments, as lights in the terrace mysteriously flickered on and off. Dave next connected his green 10-watt Alpico amplifier, bought for £6, to his best amp, a Vox AC30. Still not hearing the sounds pounding in his head, he hacked at the Alpico's speaker cone with his razor, mugging with menaces to extract the jagged result. The "Green Amp" was so cheap and puny it could still hardly be heard over the Vox's hum, at first. Over in Dunn, North Carolina in 1958, Link Wray had punched a hole into his amp with a pencil with similar effect, resulting in his hit record 'Rumble' and the invention of the power chord, on which so much hard rock would depend. An ocean apart, two boys had scarred their equipment till its sound evolved to meet their frustration.

"It's something that I'd been looking for, but I didn't know what it was," Dave says. "I worked on that sound, because I was so unhappy with the guitar sound I had, because the amps you had in those days were just an off switch and a tone control. And I was a great lover of The Ventures and The Shadows and all these instrumental bands that Ray and I grew up with. So I think out of frustration, I got this little amplifier and cut the cone up with a razor blade, not really thinking that it would work. I wasn't a particularly articulate kid. I was a very angry kid, really. And it was a way of venting my emotions. Hearing that sound married up something within me, an anger or rage. It's funny, I still carry a bit of rage with me. Unsolved riddles, emotions still leaking out and bothering me. Nothing gets resolved in one lifetime."

Ray wrote the song that Dave's sound animated in May 1964 (in *X-Ray*, he suggests he wrote an early version when he was 16). He was influenced by the landmark concert film *Jazz On A Summer's Day* (1959), which the brothers had just seen at the cinema, enthusing them with rare sightings of distant American heroes including Chuck Berry and cool jazz saxophonist Gerry Mulligan. Ray later claimed Dave's guitar replaced a sax solo part. "I wrote the first version of 'You Really Got Me' when I was at art school," he explained to Johnny Black. "I had some dental work done and hurt my teeth and had to be fitted with a brace. I lived with my sister Rose. And I bought my first really nice guitar, an Australian copy of a Gretsch, on the HP. I was playing Chet Atkins and John Lee Hooker songs, and wanted to express myself on those F/G chords, more like 'Tequila', if you think of that riff. I was just playing away like that, and I was learning how to play barre chords [with the forefinger holding down all six strings]. That's how the riff came. But the phrase came from musique concrète, and the melody is like a Gregorian chant. It's a combination of that, and odd, snapping rhythms I'd heard, maybe from Stockhausen. I know it sounds weird. I thought I was writing an R&B song. But it's nothing to do with blues. To this day, when I play a G chord I barre it in such a way that it's neither major nor minor. When you sing the melody it's major, when you play the chords it's minor. It's like a bisexual chord. That's the secret of 'You Really Got Me'."

The secret is surely simpler. Ray was playing the jazzy riff of the nascent 'You Really Got Me' on the piano when Dave echoed it with heavy barre guitar chords through his ripped green amp. Ray made the key climb, and then again. They were in their family's front room, as always. The completion of Dave's primitive experiments was the fusing of the radically different brothers in a moment's creative union, as the song's lightning hit. Everything that was special about them began to breathe then. Ray's art found its voice through his brother's wild freedom. "When by accident that guitar sound came my way," Dave remembers, "I thought, 'This is where we're going to go.' It gave a platform for Ray's writing."

The Kinks demoed 'You Really Got Me' on March 18 at Regent Sound Studio. They played it on the subsequent, largely disastrous tour with The Dave Clark Five, as 'You Still Want Me' sank with ignominious speed. The new song was their lifeline. "Our success came from playing that live," Ray says. "When we played 'You Really Got Me' people actually took notice. They realised we had something original." One Saturday night in May, in the dusty ballroom at the end of Southsea Pier, with forts from the Napoleonic Wars still standing guard just out to sea, he felt his first jolt of connection with a crowd as he sang it. In *X-Ray*, he described the moment's consummation backstage as a girl

21

fervently gave him the greatest blow-job of his life. Pye soon reluctantly agreed to the song's R&B attack as The Kinks' third single. If it failed, their chance to escape the narrow lives they had been set would be lost.

In June, in the midst of more gruelling one-nighters across Britain's ballrooms and cinemas, they recorded 'You Really Got Me' in Pye Studios, with Talmy producing. "We thought we'd made a great one when we made the demo," Ray says. "I was in despair after hearing the one we made with Shel." He and Dave both recall it as reverb-drenched and sub-Spector slick – "swamped in echo," Ray told Johnny Black, "and because I'd been on tour, I had a sore throat." Talmy contends it was slower and bluesier than the released cut. The brothers wanted something closer to the raw sound The Kinks heard when they played their lonely one-night stands, and made girls dance and grab them. Talmy, Wace and Collins heard nothing wrong. Now Ray struck the defiant spark which would complete the transformation the Green Amp had begun. A talent for brinkmanship which would become destructively compulsive later made him stubbornly insist on his vision. In Hollywood later that decade, American cinema would turn on the moment Warren Beatty sank to his knees in Jack Warner's office and begged and cajoled an unheard of re-release for his floundering new film, *Bonnie And Clyde*. British rock's course shifted as 19-year-old Ray made his stand in Muswell Hill. "I said to a friend, 'This might be the only [meaning last] record I ever make.'" He demanded to make it again. Pye scoffed at such expensive indulgence, till Ray found an unlikely ally.

"It was really crap," Larry Page, no friend of Talmy's, told Johnny Black. "But Benjie [Pye chairman Louis Benjamin] was insistent that Talmy's version would go out. I said, 'I'm asking you as their manager not to put it out, but put out this other version that we've done' [not yet recorded, in others' accounts]. Benjie said, 'No, I'm sorry, that's the way it goes.' I said, 'OK, I was asking you as their manager. Now I'm talking to you as their publisher, and Shel's version is not going out.' You see, the publisher controls the song."

"Larry said, 'We can stop it by not giving them a mechanical licence' [permitting the record's production], because he was also the publisher,"

Ray confirmed to Black. "To give Larry credit, I think he knew what the spirit of the band was, and what my heart was musically. He had no idea what I'm like as a person. He was a disaster as a manager. But for the small time he was with us, he knew what the band wanted."

"It was a bit of luck, I suppose," Ray tells me. "We took a risk. We were nearly sued by Pye for everything we had, before we had anything. In the end, a sort of compromise was done, we [in fact co-manager Collins] paid for studio time. It was one of the most amazing periods of my life, to be making a record. I got what I wanted."

In the middle of July, The Kinks descended into the basement of IBC Studios, Portland Place. Bobby Graham was still the studio drummer with Avory on tambourine, and another session veteran Arthur Greenslade on piano. They had three hours. Ray asked for a second take of them all playing together as a one-track tape machine turned, and the clock ticked on his future. Ray and Dave looked at each other as Dave invented a violent solo. Ray laughed as he added the vocal track. Screams of pleasure came. "It's like anything that's good like that, that really works," Ray says of the chance they seized. "I saw Jimmy Greaves play football once, and he seemed to have more time when he was getting ready to score a goal than anybody else. Probably the best players do, when the biggest moments happen. When you get in that zone, and everything feels good. We just knew we were going to make a great record. I was hyper-aware. But not just for those two minutes. I was going through a very aware stage. I was aware of everything being right. Of making the right call, being lucky and knowing it, riding it."

Melody Maker had dubbed 1964 "The Year of Reckoning for Trad". But when 'You Really Got Me' was released on August 4, the trad jazz Ray played in Soho had been all but swept aside, as the rhythm and blues-based Beat Boom roared to a crescendo. The Beatles broke America that year, and in July released 'A Hard Day's Night'. Its opening chord, critic Ian MacDonald later noted, rang out like a challenge to their peers, while Lennon and McCartney swapped vocals with complimentary exuberance, as they began to colour in the Western world. Newcastle's Animals reached number one just before them with a slightly bowdlerised, four-and-a-half minute version of the 19th-century brothel lament 'The House Of The Rising Sun'. Singer Eric Burdon sounded more menacingly adult even than the Stones, though Mick Jagger's voice was carnal where Ray's couldn't be. Both bands relied on American covers. "Can you imagine a British-composed R&B number?" Brian Jones scoffed to *Record Mirror*'s Norman Jopling a year earlier. "It just wouldn't make it." The Zombies' July debut 'She's Not There' sketched a lover by her absence, a lyrical conceit worthy of Gershwin expressed with delicate beauty, which followed the Stones and Animals up the reeling US chart. The bare riff which announced 'You Really Got Me' was another jump forward. It was the hardest British rock record yet, written by Ray: prototype punk, primitive metal.

"I've never really liked that term, heavy metal," says Dave. "I think, in all humility, it was the first heavy guitar riff rock record. Just because of the sound – if you'd played it on a ukulele, it might not have been quite so powerful. When I met Jimi Hendrix, he said he thought 'You Really Got Me' was a landmark record. He was really interested in how we got that sound. So I told him."

"'You Really Got Me''s such a pure record, really," Dave concludes. "It's a love song for street kids. They're not going to wine and dine you, even if they knew how to chat you up. I want you – come 'ere."

Its impact was instant, as if its quality was recognised, even needed. The Saturday night before its August 4 release, TV's *Juke Box Jury* and *Thank Your Lucky Stars* both raved about it. The next evening, supporting The Beatles at the Bournemouth Gaumont, Dave's impudently feedbacking guitar on the single silenced even the headliners' screaming, impatient fans. The Beatles' former PR man, Brian Somerville, was hired for The Kinks. Pye called them in to order an instant LP, and rushed to release 'You Really Got Me' in the US through Reprise. In *Melody Maker*, singer Dave Berry, reviewing it in the paper's 'Blind Date' column, understood what he was hearing. He mistook the intro for The Kingsmen, American definers of garage punk staple 'Louie Louie'. "It's fabulous, this one," he said with growing excitement. "I like these records that sound as if they've gone into a recording studio and done what they wanted to on the spot. It's got a good chance of being a big hit. On second thoughts, I'd say it was British."

"The first time I heard 'You Really Got Me' on the radio, I was transfixed by it," Dave told Johnny Walker. "It was an immense event. It's like you're in some sort of hypnotic trance for a few years."

"I found the person I could be," says Ray of his song's success. "When you're walking around north London, not knowing... all right, you're good at art, so you can be a signwriter, or paint posters. I tried to be an artist, a sculptor, made stained glass windows. I wanted to be creative, and I found something. It's not just finding a job, it's inventing a job. And inventing myself. I didn't know what was happening, but the job took me over. I didn't really have to think about it."

"I'd really call myself an apprentice songwriter at the moment," he told *NME* that year. But his ambition was already fierce and defined. "I hope eventually to be sufficiently capable of expressing people's everyday moods, thoughts and emotions in music."

Typically, as his future began, Ray sought out friends and girlfriends from an already sentimentalised past. On September 7, a telegram to 6 Denmark Terrace confirmed 'You Really Got Me' was number one. That night, after a gig at Streatham Ice Rink where the ice melted under The Kinks as they played, Ray was kissed by his dad, who told him he was proud. The month-long high had peaked. Emotional anticlimax followed. "There was a lot of that," says Ray.

Now their lives accelerated. Between the August release of 'You Really Got Me' and leaving for their crucial first US tour in June 1965, The Kinks played 162 gigs from the Royal Albert Hall and Melbourne Festival Hall to the Grantham Granada, and recorded five more singles, two LPs and an EP.

The singles were remarkable. The brothers set out their agenda in the music press that autumn. "We were really surprised when 'You Really Got Me' was a hit," Ray reflected to *NME*, contradicting the certainty he remembers now. "Why wasn't our last disc, 'You Still Want Me'? Because it wasn't any good. We didn't like it much. And we didn't write it. We write for ourselves now." In *Melody Maker*, he added: "When I was at art school, what I got out of it was colour, expression... It's time the groups got wise and did what they want... This is where we're one up because if we don't have another hit for a year, we *will* have another hit. We can't lose because we entertain, and we're always trying to get something different." His "ambition" in *NME* was "to be ahead all the time". To *Melody Maker*'s Ray Coleman, he intimated an agenda beyond himself. "It's an outlet for us. I know it probably sounds corny to say it, but you feel, when you're standing up there, that you want to get something out of your system. Everyone's got it somewhere – the expression, and the need for an outlet. The audience want to express it, so we help them."

The Kinks wobbled on the high wire of how to follow 'You Really Got Me'. For all Ray's confidence, they could still fall now, and be forgotten. The unfinished 'Till The End Of The Day' was held back as too daringly different. 'Don't Ever Let Me Go''s cheeky recycling of 'You Really Got Me''s riff went unreleased. Ray sometimes says the eventual choice, 'All Day And All Of The Night', is his favourite Kinks single. Written in the back of a car days before its late September recording, it proved he and the band weren't a fluke.

It begins with another bare riff, slower and sparer still than 'You Really Got Me'. Again a drum slams in the song. But now Ray's desire for a girl is worldly, adult. He sings with the happy leer of knowing he'll get her, not the teen frustration a hit's let him outgrow. Dave's saurian guitar shadows and stalks him. This time, Ray's encouragement – *"Oh, come on!"* – is gleeful, not desperate. This time, Dave's response is a gremlin's cartoon yowl, and a solo which jerks and clambers into a chaotic climax. Ray remembered Jimmy Page watching Dave play it with his head in his hands, as if his craft had been spat on. In his later band Led Zeppelin's early seventies pomp, US rock magazines routinely assumed Page had played Kinks riffs as a session man. This insulted Dave's instinctive rightness in single after single. "When we're in the studio, I have nothing worked out," he told *Melody Maker*. "Until the red light goes on, I don't really know what I'm going to play." Here he scrambles to a resolution as the record spins, over a jumble of quick, slivered notes, like a surrealist's premonition of needling post-punk technique. 'All Day And All Of The Night' overall is more heavy, more metallic. Reinforced by Quaife's bass, Bobby Graham's drums and the thickened harmonies of Dave, Quaife and one Johnny B. Great, the last seconds ram Ray's desires home. 'You Really Got Me''s prototype had been streamlined and souped up. Released on October 23, it hit number two as its predecessor settled into the US Top 10.

'Tired Of Waiting For You' began blueprints for a new machine. Initially recorded around August 24 but held back, it had started as a pre-Kinks instrumental called 'South', which Dave remembered the brothers playing in the Clissold Arms in 1961. At its heart was Ray, in a vulnerably high voice no one had heard before. Like a promise mesmerically murmured in your ear, he sings: *"It's your life, and you can do what you want"*. A world opens up in that line. Ray says he made it up as the music played. Harmonies make it more hymnal, a quality completed in 'Waterloo Sunset' and 'Days', years later, when Ray and The Kinks' abilities were fully revealed. A beat music heart still pulses in Dave's deep rhythm guitar, wisely added in December. The frustration in the title completes the chorus's lyric, balancing and distracting from its core profundity. A series of small riffing climaxes makes this seem a third bid for sexual release at 45 rpm, another young man demanding his way from a tiresome girl. But in the verses Ray is helpless, stymied. In the chorus's revelatory lines, he is feminine and exposed. The scale of the change was effectively disguised in a hybrid song only half-abandoning the heavy riff style; momentary, something you might have imagined. Released on January 15 1965, it would be their second UK number one.

The Kinks' first, self-titled LP had meanwhile been blasted out between engagements, chasing 'You Really Got Me' into the shops on October 2. With no time to think, its 14 songs leaned on the same R&B covers as their stage show, four more Ray originals and 'Revenge', an instrumental co-credited to Larry Page, joining 'You Really Got ·Me' and two Talmy-suggested – and arranged, and so copyrighted – "traditional" songs. 'Stop Your Sobbin'', inspired, Ray suggested in *X-Ray*, by an ex-girlfriend who wept at his success and how it would harm him, was the only mildly interesting new composition. In this end-of-the-evening, beat-ballroom ballad, he tries to avert the tenderness he knows a girl's cries will force from him in hitching ejaculations –

"*stobbit, stobbit!*" – of his own. In a stifling Ohio suburb it was heard by schoolgirl Chrissie Hynde, 14, who would record it 14 years later with her band The Pretenders, in a future she would for a tempestuous while share with Ray; that's the reason it's remembered.

The Kinks' muscular UK R&B hovered near the top of the charts (then far less important than for singles) for months. Shorn of three tracks as *You Really Got Me*, it reached the US Top 30. Talmy, whose importance has since been downplayed by the band, must have helped the slick, tough tone. "I specialise in getting an American sound," Talmy declared to *Record Mirror*'s David Griffiths. "British recordings struck me as too precise, too perfect...The American sound is more concerned with feelings, even though there might be a couple of bum notes." That sounded right for The Kinks.

The band had every base loaded once *Kinksize Session*, released November 27, topped the EP chart. 'I Gotta Go Now' was the best of three Ray songs, his lulling voice and Avory's ticking drums (trusted outside singles) moodily enacting young lovers separating. On Richard Berry's 1955 'Louie Louie' (a 1963 US smash for Seattle's Kingsmen), Ray luxuriated in the lyrics' mock-epic voyage of a sailor visiting his lover, a more expansive tale than anything he'd written. With easily swung punches from Dave's guitar it approached the pounding purity of 'You Really Got Me', which Larry Page, among others, claims was based on The Kingsmen's record. Dave remembered their love for it instead inspiring Ray's voice. "We played that record over and over," he told Johnny Black. "And Ray copied a lot of his vocal style at the time from that guy [Jack Ely]. I was always trying to get Ray to sing, because I thought he had a great voice, but he was very shy. Then we heard The Kingsmen and he had that lazy, throwaway, laid-back drawl in his voice, and it was magic."

The EP distilled the LP's strengths, which kept them in contention with the Stones, Animals and Pretty Things in the R&B boom. Both were barely relevant footnotes to the band they'd become.

In *X-Ray*, Ray remembers the end of 1964 not as triumphant, but lived in a climate of disgust and fear which would only grow worse. He claims the Stones and Beatles fashionably associated with revolution as the sixties progressed, while The Kinks were affronts to the old order in the fibre of their beings. They might actually have brought revolution about, he writes, and rammed the fact down people's throats. It's true The Kinks' music would become a reproach to conformist and repressive lives. The only other evidence for what he says is the hostile, then dismissive way they would soon be treated. If people were scared by his band, it's hard to know why.

"We didn't have many rivals," he tells me. "Once we got our uniqueness that 'You Really Got Me' gave us, we were a little bit set apart. In this country, they like to know what and who you are, like in the supermarket, so they know what shelf to put you onto. They didn't know whether we were home goods or cleaning fluid. We just had our own shelf. A lot of the time, people evolve – without Elton John, we might not have had Billy Joel. But someone like Joan Crawford, I don't think there was anyone before her. Joan Crawford appeared. And The Kinks, we appeared. Admittedly the name was of the period – it was cued up ready to be taken by someone. But we were the most unlikely bunch to do it. People were like – 'Why you? Why have you been so successful? And how did you make that record? How can a bloke like you write such good stuff?' I suppose, being the way we were, looking the way we looked, people thought this shouldn't be happening. We weren't choreographed. I think the fear was that a band like The Kinks would come along and bring a revolution about, because there was an air of directness about the way that we were. We grew up in a society that had us pegged. Secondary Modern school, and go on to live a certain style of life on a council estate. And I think people were concerned that we broke that mould. That was a lot of what the sixties was about."

Later in *X-Ray*, he mentions a lawsuit derailing the permanent changes he wished to bring about. In a life marked by indecision and funk as often as bursts of brilliance, he couldn't have wreaked such havoc. But what would his revolution have been?

"I was trying to change everything. I wouldn't have been a Stalin-type dictator. I would have tried to change things to make them better. For my world," he says, wistfully. "For my square mile."

An out-take of Chuck Berry's 'Too Much Monkey Business', significantly more unhinged than the LP version, catches the whirlwind The Kinks must have whipped up in obscure corners of Britain in those months, in venues Dave pictures now as "little town hall type places, with old-fashioned stages made of wood, for ballroom dancing – converted for rock'n'roll gigs, and the sounds were echoey, bangy". Footage from the time shows each Kink in close-up as they play. Quaife looks excited, but sometimes drifting off to think about something else. Avory looks reasonably happy to be there. Dave is in a state of permanent ecstasy. Ray appears desperate and panicked.

"Me and Pete took to it like ducks to water," Dave agrees. "We liked the excitement and newness. We'd researched all the music we liked, the R&B, and especially the clothes, the hairstyles. We knew what to do. Mick was like you said." He goes groggy. "'Oh, wow. What am I doing here?' It hit Ray like a sledgehammer."

Ray's equilibrium wasn't helped by Rasa Didzpetris. They had met after a Sheffield gig on May 19, before The Kinks' success. The pretty, petite, sharp-featured convent schoolgirl had entered Bradford as a child with her family, refugees from the carnage that fell on Lithuania in the forties; a war baby in a deeper sense than Ray. She had hitched up to Sheffield with a friend, Eileen, doubtless looking for a bit of fun with a visiting beat group; 'You Still Want Me' can't have been the spur. They went backstage with the other groupies and Ray, 19, kissed her hand with foolish gallantry when the band dropped her at the station. They swapped addresses. On August 13, they met at the top of the steps of Tottenham Court Road tube station for a date. Ten days later, at the house of a friend of Rasa's sister Dalia in Isleworth, west London, the night before 'Tired Of Waiting For You' was recorded as 'You Really Got Me' roared towards the top, they slept together and their daughter, Louisa, was conceived. To the usual fans' cries of "Don't do it, Ray!", they had a traditional Lithuanian marriage in Bradford on December 12. Typically, Dave was fucking Eileen upstairs when he should have been giving the toast. That paternity suit would be dismissed in 1966. In the photos, Ray has a small, hopeful smile. The honeymoon was in Exeter. Ray rented a top-floor bedsit at the Muswell Hill end of Fortis Green, and began married life.

He felt utterly unprepared. Sometimes, he wrote in *X-Ray*, he felt he'd married the wrong girl. Sometimes she looked like a stranger, when he sketched her as she slept in their modest new home. Inside at his worst he felt distant and alienated from events, as if he'd gone into shock. But becoming a husband and expectant father six months after meeting this girl was the least shocking thing happening to him. When they moved into the bedsit, he had no songs left, and the demand and the touring was constant. He wrote to stay sane. Most of the time, anyway, he thought he loved his glamorous young wife. "I'm hopeless around the house," he admitted to *NME*'s Keith Altham. "I put a bulb in a socket at home the other night. Black hand." He was still determined to be the responsible adult he rarely felt like. Most of all, he tried to be good.

"I feel very sorry for Rasa," he told Altham. "It's very hard for her at the moment because she is expecting her first child. I hope we'll have a little girl – I think I'd be jealous of a little boy." He would have four daughters, Dave always the only male rival for family affection. Dave and Rasa's backing vocals merged in most Kinks records of the sixties. He found her a rare catalyst between him and Ray.

'Tired Of Waiting For You' was released as Ray flew away from his wife on The Kinks' first tour outside Europe. A second LP would, it was casually announced, be recorded "during three days when they return". Australasia and expat-heavy corners of the just decolonising Far East were the main destinations. Many Britons alive in 1965 would die without passing Dover. The Kinks would also touch down in America, where Beatlemania was in full cry, and the British Invasion by further Beat groups appeared unstoppable. They refuelled behind the Iron Curtain in Moscow on January 16, and again in Bombay. At his hotel window, in the night-time limbo before they took off again, Ray watched as chanting Indian fishermen hauled in their catch. The sensations this compulsive observer felt when he first left north London for Soho were compounded now. New songs had to be filled with them.

Only Australia really mattered to Ray. Rose, husband Arthur Anning and son Terry had emigrated to Adelaide the year before. She had raised Ray like a mother, and Terry was like a brother. He screamed when they left, as if Rene had died again. It was another dagger in the set world he loved. Ray saw them as refugees from a declining England. They were among a million lured by the Australian government's offer of £10 passage for whites from the Motherland. Mick Jagger, during the Stones' simultaneous Australian leg of their parallel attempt at world conquest, politely met a Kentish aunt in Sydney, and other long-lost relatives. Ray and Dave's reunion meant much more. The family met them in the band's Adelaide hotel, then the planned suburbia, New Elizabeth, for which they'd abandoned Highgate Hill. It would take four years, and the whole of his most impassioned album, *Arthur*, for Ray to say how he felt.

Official dispatches home stayed breezy. "I want to catch a shark with my bare hands," Quaife rang *Melody Maker* to boast. "Everybody looks at us twice here," Ray complained. "They are thinking about our kinky clothes and we are gradually winning them over." Pebbles were thrown at them on the beach and Australia seemed a macho backwater, but the gigs were the usual riots. The Stones tour they shadowed got the publicity, The Kinks staying a half-step behind.

New Zealand was followed by Hong Kong. Ray was in Singapore's Goodwood Hotel, a relic of the "Old Empire" which was starting to fascinate him, when a telegram announced 'Tired Of Waiting For You' was number one in faraway England. Talmy told *Melody Maker* the record was a "gamble" that had "paid off". Ray toasted the comforting news with a waiter. The other Kinks were elsewhere, having fun. They left the Far East by way of Saigon, where American fighter jets escorted them. Probed about the escalating war there by *Melody Maker* in December, only one aspect bothered Ray. "I don't like it because a relative of mine [clearly Terry] emigrated a year ago to Australia and now he's been called up to Vietnam." The bloody place which would define the rock counterculture was a family matter to him.

The Kinks had crossed a reeking river of sewage in Singapore and changed in the stadium's toilets, and as they flew to Manila, Guam, Honolulu, San Francisco and finally New York, a painful blood infection made Ray's foot balloon. He had been away for three weeks now, buffeted through time zones and cultures, always playing to screaming fans. In *X-Ray*, he recalled being frozen with terror in New York. Rather than limp into the heady nightlife in the country whose music had always obsessed him, he locked himself in his hotel room. Dave by contrast had a "girl reporter in my room and we had tea", he told *Melody Maker*, trying not to let the butter melt in his mouth. A house detective found her in the wardrobe and roughly threw her in the corridor, while Dave raged at him. "Trouble was," Dave conceded, "about 50 girls had been trying to get in before."

Avory's humble ambition in *NME* the year before had been "to go to the US to learn the art of jazz drumming and meet most of the jazz giants". He, Quaife and Dave did see Ornette Coleman play in Greenwich Village, but were warned off Harlem by their white Reprise Records hosts. With The Kinks' capacity for carnage, crossing 110th Street may well have been fatal.

Their last, most important professional act before home was to perform on NBC TV's *Hullabaloo*. In career terms, though not human ones, they messed it up. 'All Day And All Of The Night' had followed 'You Really Got Me' into the US Top 10, and they were to tape both on February 12. "They tried to get everyone to do this silly dance at the end of the show," Avory remembers. "They even got [square teen idol and host] Frankie Avalon doing it. Ray had something wrong with his ankle, that was his excuse not to. It's an embarrassing thing to have to do, especially when you're a serious artist. He'd got all these people geeing him up, saying, [Yank accent] 'You can go out there and do anything, and they'll still like it'. So we had a little muckabout together. We did our own dance." They swayed together cheek to cheek like "queers", Ray gleefully remembered in *X-Ray*. David Bowie's mock-fellating of Mick Ronson's guitar onstage was still a decade away. And he didn't dare it in America. It was "too real" for Americans to take, Ray proudly believed, and began a plot "to destroy" The Kinks there. When the programme aired four days later, though, the dance had been cut. Backstage rows over lyrics sung by The Doors and Stones on network TV later in the sixties were etched in rock folklore. The Kinks' bolder stand was wiped. But a combative American precedent had been set.

It was Valentine's Day when they landed back in London. Ray spent one awkward night back with Rasa in Muswell Hill, as a month of culture shocks washed through him. The next morning, as the music press had been promised, "hit-writer Ray" and the band made most of their next album in three days.

It showed. Ray bitterly complained about what he saw as Talmy's slapdash production on the accurately titled *Kinda Kinks*, and the desperate rush of its jet-lagged, hothouse making. He might have looked at the music, the sketched pastiches of a magpie mind.

They were at least sketches towards a new picture. Apart from 'Tired Of Waiting For You' and its B-side, 'Come On Now', sung by Dave as he hustles a girl into hard partying much like his own with Rasa's lusty vocal backing, R&B was mostly, suddenly abandoned. Pretty acoustic shuffles proved Ray had closely watched English folk guitar master Davy Graham during his apprenticeship in Soho basements. Lyrically, absence had focused him on idealising then doubting his new relationship. 'Don't Ever Change' hangs on moments of perceived perfection in a loved one that can't be frozen. 'Wonder Where My Baby Is Tonight' and 'Nothin' In The World Can Stop Me Worryin' 'Bout That Girl' weren't so sure. Unexpectedly whipping out the latter during a Royal Festival Hall gig 45 years later, Ray revealed he'd been 17 when he wrote it. "I suspected she was cheating on me. When I told a friend he said she was. With him. Then, it broke my heart. Now," he smirked, "I can't remember her name."

'So Long' sets sail while typically poring over what's left behind, as he promises to return one day to the old town he loves. "If I thought I could not improve musically, I would give it all up and become a tramp," he mused to *NME*'s Altham. "The idea of tramping around the country with a healthy bank balance in time of difficulty appeals to me." 'Something Better Beginning''s ringing guitars then toll a hopeful new future, in a song which leaves the album in its wake. Like Ray's then-unreleased demos 'There Is A New World Opening For Me' and the pastoral reverie 'This I Know' – another wishful declaration of eternal love, in which he wants the sun to rise to see his girl better – romance also seemed a cover for more supernal longings.

One of two covers, 'Dancing In The Street' was a callow flail at Martha Reeves & the Vandellas' Motown hit. Three months later in Florida the Stones, wrestling with their own version, turned it into 'Satisfaction'. The first of their singles to match The Kinks' force, it leapt past Ray lyrically, and decisively left a band set to catch them in the trailing pack.

Nothing on *Kinda Kinks* matched the focus of each Kinks 45. Only The Beatles, with *Help!* and *Rubber Soul* that year, fussed on LPs as if they mattered more. On its March 5 release, *Melody Maker* still noticed it was "a little scrappy", *Record Mirror* that it fell short of their "usual standards". Though it hit number three, it soon sank.

This slight stumble after six months' sprinting success was then followed by a sprawl to the floor, as the field raced past. Two weeks later, their new single failed. 'Ev'rybody's Gonna Be Happy' is a weird aberration – a record that like the last before they found themselves, 'You Still Want Me', is never played on the radio, because during their hit-making peak it reached only as far as 17, a relative flop by prevailing Kinks' standards. It was a bid for the sharp new soul style which had replaced blues as R&B's meaning in the London clubs where Dave spent his nights, and they had heard first-hand from Motown's Earl Van Dyke Band on a November package tour. Quaife's walking bass leads a tricky, bustling rhythm, the jazzy Avory's debut on a Kinks A-side ("You do wonder what the fuck you're doing there," he notes of earlier, tambourine-shaking sessions). The song's chirpy optimism, though, recorded alongside 'Don't Ever Change' just before Ray's wedding back in December, had a tinny ring. Had all their singles succeeded, Brian Matthew asked when they played it on a BBC session, as it wheezed to number 20 in the *Melody Maker* chart (11 in the BBC's). "This one 'asn't!" Dave piped from the back, not bothered. 'Who'll Be The Next In Line', the more convincing, menacing flip side, was an A-side and garage-band favourite in America.

The week of its release, Tamla Motown's greatest stars – The Supremes, Martha & the Vandellas, Smokey Robinson & The Miracles, Stevie Wonder, and Kinks friends the Earl Van Dyke Six – arrived in north London, at Finsbury Park Astoria. Backstage, Dave was furious to find his band sneered at by "prejudiced" Tamla fans. Motown's Booker Bradshaw wrote to *Record Mirror* from Detroit to personally apologise, thanking Dave for taking Van Dyke and singer Kim Weston "under his wing" and showing them "the good ales" on their earlier trip. The Tamla tour drew poor crowds outside London. But two Bob Dylan albums also made waves that month (The Beatles had been hip to him all year). The Who, who'd supported The Kinks twice in 1964, had debuted with 'I Can't Explain' in January, a Talmy-produced "desperate copy of The Kinks", Pete Townshend would later admit. But their to George Melly "McLuhanite" managers, Kit Lambert and Chris Stamp, next pushed 'Anyway Anyhow Anywhere' as a "pop-art single"; "hard pop". The Kinks' only image had been the dark pink hunting jackets they first wore when they upstaged The Beatles in Bournemouth, and kept on even in Australia's heat. "We imagined ourselves as characters from a Charles Dickens book, and we all think it suits us," Ray explained at the time. "Our drummer, for example. Don't you think he looks like Bill Sykes?" Not only was the old-style R&B they had led becoming outmoded. 1965's speeding pop avant-garde was leaving The Kinks behind too.

The day after they finished *Kinda Kinks*, they were in Manchester for TV and yet another gig. Outside, fans surrounded, pawed and bruised them. The day the album was released, Dave was "pulled about" at a gig in Leyton. When it happened again the next night, delayed concussion meant he was ordered to rest. The moment he was medically allowed, it was back to two shows nightly from Nuneaton to Newcastle. It was as if their "superiors" in Pye and management didn't dare let success's train stop, because it would never start again. They were dumbfounded when Ray put his hand on the brake.

He cancelled a TV appearance in Southampton, then a gig in Tunbridge Wells. He'd had enough of "this shit" and "ran away", he said much later. It caused The Kinks "a dip". "Equating success with happiness led me astray a bit," he tells me. "Success felt quite normal at first. We just thought that the music did it all. We were naive enough then to think that people didn't really attach us to it. But as soon as our pictures were in the paper, we were besieged by fans – the first invasion of privacy." A photo from the time shows a young girl reaching into Ray's car, as he flinches away, appalled. "I thought, being very naive, I could choose to be anonymous if I wished," he continues, "and still have a number one record. I did the best I could not to say much and not do interviews, but then people would speculate. I was a very private person... I still am."

"He was certainly not the kind of person you would say was best-suited to being a rock star," Keith Altham, then of *NME*, tells me. "He always struck me as not having enough armour. He was vulnerable. And consequently, things upset him more than other people. Most of the people I knew who were big stars, like Jagger and Van Morrison and Pete Townshend, when they went on the road, they had a kind of protective screen they put round themselves. Ray was much more open, and didn't seem to have that same wall that he could don. I think there's something of a rock'n'roll Howard Hughes about Ray. You can imagine him wiping his hands after he's shaken hands. There's something obsessive that's part of his make-up. And it's not a good thing to have when you're having to mix with the 'filthy public'."

Promotion for the doomed new single resumed almost instantly. But then Ray, Dave and Quaife physically collapsed one by one. Quaife's fainting (then concussion when he fell), while watching the newest working-class icon Michael Caine in *The Ipcress File* at Muswell Hill Odeon, was a clear sign of nervous exhaustion. Their brains were being rattled with multiple concussions like boxers. None of them could take much more, but still it went on.

Sudden free time had at least allowed Dave and Avory to find a Muswell Hill bachelor pad, after Dave's Mum found him exceeding even Denmark Terrace's rules of hospitality with five girls at once. They pinned signs up on their rooms, like priapic Bash Street Kids – 'Whore's Hovel' and 'Spunker's Squalor'. "Yeah, that was just off Cranley Gardens," Avory reminisces. "That probably wasn't the best idea. Dave used to go off and do his thing. He had this mad mate [*Ready, Steady, Go!* co-host Michael Aldred] and they'd always be extreme or on drugs. I wasn't really into that. I was a drinker. So some of it, I used to stay out of. There weren't too many girls. If it had been nearer the centre of London, it would have been more of a hovel. But working together and living together wasn't a good idea. That's when the bust-up came, and it all fell apart."

The real crash was very near now. The Kinks had always had private punch-ups, Ray and Dave of course most of all. Dave had also taken a handy battle-axe to a West Country hotel reception on being refused a late-night tipple, and several times played wildly on at gigs, bloody shirt shredded by fans. At least once, the blood dripped down his face.

The next few weeks made The Kinks' reputation for aggression and violence (which The Who, as usual, would shortly adopt). "On the road it doesn't wear you out the way it does off it," Ray reflects. "Aggression is good. Dave was 15 when we started, I was 18. When you're that age, sometimes it would spur you on. We didn't consciously say, 'Let's be violent'. It came out of concern, to get our music right and played well. We weren't unduly violent for people that age. Damage to a few hotels. But sometimes when you're trying to get a performance, it's good to get it… right. Sometimes you miss the tension. When you're working with other players, you think this needs a bit of tension, aggression, a little bit of a slap, a kick up the pants, but you don't get it, because everyone's so polite. Most of the best bands… when it's peace and love and they get on very well, they break up after a few records."

Maybe The Kinks couldn't have caused a revolution. But the fear and dislike Ray sensed was becoming real. "People were a bit on edge with us," Avory confirms. "We were not very easy to warm to. We were known as being a little bit aggressive, so people didn't know how to approach you. You get a reputation."

On April 9, the glass-walled elegance of Copenhagen's Tivoli Gardens staged the first set-piece battle between the exhausted Kinks and the world. "I did a press conference the day before," Ray recalls, "and someone said how well-behaved The Rolling Stones and the kids had been a few months before, because there were 200 police waiting outside ready to storm in with truncheons. And I may have said something similar to: 'Well, I like people to enjoy themselves. It's a free world.' And the concert happened, we did one song, and the kids rioted. The police ran in with batons, and we were ushered into this little room. We heard this carnage going on. The kids broke up the auditorium, and we got the blame. The teenagers said we want to enjoy ourselves, and the policemen said we will stifle any attempt to create a riot. It was the first time I'd been onstage and seen the two collide like that. It was terrifying."

"The police were such Gestapo, they were really nasty bastards," Dave remembers, still angry. "The cops were hitting the kids, and they were having a good time, you know, and they were hitting them over the head. What's that thing they always say about America? You can do what you like, so long as you do what you're told. I think that's what triggered me later."

Every window was shattered, every chair matchwood. The next night's gig was cancelled, and The Kinks were confined to the nearby Europa Hotel, the authorities fearing what the mere sight of them on the streets might do. Dave brooded, and gulped down a bottle of brandy with obliterating speed. He hurled it at the bar's ornate mirror, smashing it too. "It's ridiculous and immature," he says, "but it was the only way I could express how I felt." Danish police chased him up and down the hotel stairs in X-rated farce, and bundled him off to jail.

"Nowadays," says Ray, "if a band is successful to the degree we were, they would have a team of bodyguards, and a hotel staff and even a police force who had experienced this before, and knew how to deal with it. We had one guy with us, maybe two, and this was totally new."

"It was frightening, but when I think of it in my head, it's like I saw it all in a movie," Dave told Johnny Black. "I was sitting in the back of the car going, 'Fuckin' cunts!' They put me in a cell, and next day the door opens and Grenville's standing there. 'Come on David, we're leaving.' Just like that, we left. We got back to the hotel, and walked in with Grenville, and it was like running the gauntlet. There was a carpet down the middle, and down the left aisle was all the waiters and the maids, and on the right was the managerial staff, and a guy I nearly punched out the night before, and I had to walk through them to get my things. I turned round and said to him, 'I didn't want to stay in this fucking place anyway,' and they all burst out laughing, Grenville as well with his high-pitched, horsey laugh. It was exactly like a movie." The girl who'd been with him when the police pounded on his door, Lisbet Thorkil-Petersen, would recover to be his wife. Her cousin Biden Paustian would be Quaife's.

Collins' urgency had been because that night The Kinks closed the televised *NME* Pollwinners Party at Wembley's Empire Pool (now Wembley Arena), following The Beatles. "It was all concrete," Quaife recalled to Johnny Black. "It was really out of control and fast behind the scenes, there were crowds of pop stars milling around. Nobody knew when they were going on until about five seconds before. You were suddenly herded through all these corridors and shoved out. And once you got there, you couldn't hear a damn thing. That was possibly the worst performance we ever gave. I remember Ray watching it on TV and everybody was singing out of tune and Ray flipped. He was screaming and yelling and going absolutely nuts blaming everybody. We were all trying to say to him, 'For Chrissakes, none of us could hear anything.' The only thing you could go by was the vibration you felt in your throat." Ray and Dave felt betrayed that, when they came for their award, it was as Runner-up for Best New Group, not the Winner Ray thought they'd been promised. That went to The Rolling Stones for the second time, New again. But the fan-voted results had been published in *NME* in December. Not for the last time, Ray claimed innocence of unpleasant or disastrous facts.

One part of his mind was plotting to free them from the bonds around their career. Another now responded to management pressure to avert their commercial slide by writing a certain hit with smooth efficiency. 'Set Me Free' was almost, but not quite, the last of the heavy riff songs. Dave's opening chords this time were pensive, mordant, the warning sound of a troubled mind to be approached with care. But Ray's intimate, light tone in 'Tired Of Waiting For You' filled more of this inviting but machine-tight, energetic pop song. Like the B-side, the still more insistent 'I Need You', it concerned being shackled by love for an unreliable girl. Lennon's response to such teases in that year's 'Run For Your Life', and Jagger's in 'Play With Fire', were coldly brutal. Ray fell on his knees and pleaded, a young man shamelessly, really in love. Dave's opening to 'I Need You' was a rude, vibrating fart of still rare feedback, a leering insult to recording science. It went to number nine.

Meanwhile, the tour mayhem continued. Dave and Avory's hostility was now more ferocious even than the brothers'. "Mick was good for both of us," Dave accepts today, "because he sat on the fence. It was stabilising for Ray, but it used to get on my wick. I like people to speak their minds."

Avory finally made his views abundantly clear on May 19, at Cardiff's Capitol Theatre. Quaife remembered Dave starting the confrontation the night before in Taunton, Somerset. Dragged from a party and the drink and drugs that were wrecking his mind, Dave fought with Ray, the hotel's night porter, and with a final manic swing hit the retreating Avory's back with a suitcase. Avory's big shovel hands began a solid, regular pounding into the guitarist's body and face, till he was pulled away. With shades shielding his black eyes, Dave took his revenge on stage in Cardiff as 5,000 Kinks fans watched, just after the opening song 'You Really Got Me'. Its solo was doubtless played with special fury. He turned to Avory with contempt. "You're a useless cunt and your drumming's shit," he loudly informed him. "They'd sound better if you played them with your cock." He then kicked Avory's precious bass drum, and sauntered back to his mic. There Avory, legend has it, swung a cymbal at his tormenter. Blood poured from Dave's carved open head as he fell to the floor. Avory, the rush of blood to his own head subsiding, believed he'd murdered him. Running through the crowd and out of the hall, he took a train towards London, surely a hunted man, shrinking into his seat in pink Regency garb. Not something you see every day, I venture to Dave.

"Well I've only got one head," he laughs. "Not many live to tell the tale. Oh, that was outrageous. That was very funny. Though not at the time..."

"It obviously wasn't the way to handle it," Avory now concedes. "It just happened on the spur. It was just a reaction. It was a horrible atmosphere, I could've done without it. I only used a hi-hat pedal, anyway," he explains with scholarly precision. "It wasn't as bad as it was made out. If I'd hit him with a cymbal, obviously that could decapitate someone. It was a hi-hat pedal, and it was an old Premier one, with a rubber foot-plate on it, so it was quite a flimsy thing. The modern-day ones would hurt a bit more."

"I was drugged out for a few days, in a bit of a haze..." Dave says of the immediate aftermath, which the 17-year-old spent with sister Joyce, bandaged and concussed once more.

"It was the top story on the news that night, the Kinks fight," Ray laughs today. "They should have had Mick half in shadow, talking with Reginald Bosanquet! They were making jokes about it. Norman Vaughan on *Sunday Night At The Palladium* said, 'I wanna talk about the big fight. No, not Muhammad Ali, The Kinks.' So it made major news, and Mick was in hiding, because there was a period of time when Dave was told to have him arrested for grievous bodily harm. And he should have done," he concludes merrily. "He should be in prison!"

"I first heard about it when Mick Avory turned up at my front door in Norbiton, and he was seeking refuge from the law," Keith Altham remembers. "He'd come straight off the train from Cardiff. He was really quite shaken. He thought he might've killed Dave. Perhaps he came to me because I was local to Molesey. I was just a bed for the night, which I gave him. I didn't think he'd killed anybody. The way he'd explained it to me, he'd hit Dave on the head and he'd passed out. Prior to that there'd been some offensive behaviour from Dave. Mick was the subject of quite a lot of offensive behaviour at that time, he was the butt of most of the jokes, referred to at one time by Ray as having the personality of a cucumber sandwich. There were a lot of unnecessarily obscene remarks passed to him. I have to say, much as I admire Ray Davies as a talent and a songwriter, he was not a terribly nice person at times. And there was an element in his make-up of a sort of spiteful bully. And that used to occasionally come out with his rivalry with his brother, and it occasionally came out with people that worked for him. And once the dust had settled and Mick realised he wasn't going to be arrested for murder, he went back to sort it out."

In the chaos, future Jimi Hendrix Experience drummer Mitch Mitchell was sounded out as Avory's replacement. "He was sounding out the group, you mean," Avory says. "But he was the wrong kind of bloke. Good drummer. But he wouldn't have lasted with Ray and Dave. He was too opinionated."

Quaife had left Cardiff by train the next morning. "I really thought it was all over for us," he told Black. "I thought that was the end of the band. I wasn't happy in the band anyway, there were so many fights. You didn't know what to say, where to look."

Avory's natural air of dry understatement made the nonsense he was wheeled out to flummox the press with especially hilarious. The melee of boots, instruments and bloody heads had merely been one of road manager Sam Curtis's "dramatic ideas for stage acts" gone horribly wrong, the drummer doggedly insisted to *Melody Maker.* "He suggested an action-packed intro. In the middle part, Dave starts to 'rave up', swinging his guitar around his head, dancing about and all that." As Dave was "prancing about", Avory elaborated, he accidentally "sent my drums flying" and was "clobbered" as he swung his cymbal and stand around his head. "I ran off the stage filled with horror. Sam looked after Dave and we reflected on it all... We were mainly worried that some papers might get the wrong impression..."

Avory's final words were far more heartfelt. "We hope to have some time off before we go to America [scheduled for June 17]. After such a hard tour, we need a rest. We've been on the road a long while. One's nerves do begin to fray."

"They muddied the waters, because they realised it wasn't in their interests to prosecute the situation," Altham says of the subterfuge. "They had an American tour coming up, and it wouldn't have been a good idea to sack your drummer just prior to it. The American tour was more important than anything else. It was hoped it would break the States for them. You're talking about huge amounts of money."

On May 23, two days after 'Set Me Free''s release, Rasa gave birth to Louisa Davies. Photographed with Rasa holding her, both parents look simply happy. Ray is wearing the same suit as at his wedding. You can imagine it next to his pink work clothes in his wardrobe, the adult outfit of a young man trying to grow up. It had been a difficult, painful birth for Rasa. The next morning Ray was in the studio recording demos. Cancelled gigs as Dave inched back to health gave him precious time to appreciate his first child. It was muddied by wondering if he had a band.

He had idly contemplated getting out just before Cardiff. "I'm a collection of loose ends," he told *NME*'s Altham. "I don't want to be a pop star. I think that this is just a part of my life which will come to an end. I should very much like to produce a film. Something dramatic that would convey emotion and reaction." He had Ingmar Bergman in mind. In June, *Melody Maker*'s Chris Welch saw the state of them. "Kink-bashing has almost become a national hobby," he wrote (tactfully not suggesting it seemed The Kinks' hobby too). "They have a dry sense of humour which protects them to a certain extent, but the effects are there. They simmer and seethe, and leader Ray Davies is weary and wary of newspapers and critics." In another Altham interview to dispel "wild speculation about their future", a pale Dave was observed with two girls on hand to carefully comb his hair over his wound. Even so fragile, one was never enough.

According to Page, The Kinks had briefly broken up after Cardiff. "That's what I wanted to do," says Avory. "I thought that was the last word and we can't carry on. I couldn't see meself any way of going back. Dave'd be resentful, and I'd be resentful because he was. We all met in an office. It still wasn't ironed out. But we had to honour our commitments."

Page convinced them of that. "I phoned them up individually and invited them into my office the following Friday at three in the afternoon," he told Black, "not telling them that the others would be there. So they all appear and I decide the best thing is just to steam ahead and not give them a chance to talk. So I started, 'Right, American tour, we open at the Academy of Music, New York...'"

And so the British Invasion's most disastrous campaign began.

CHAPTER 3

Pearl Harbour

When The Beatles appeared on *The Ed Sullivan Show* in New York on February 9, 1964, America changed. "The long, dark Kennedy-death nights were over," Mikal Gilmore, 13 that day, wrote in his book *Night-Beat*. "A nightmare was temporarily broken, and a new world born." But if America's teenagers felt redeemed from the shock of their President's shooting barely two months before, the redeemers themselves had a different perspective. The Beatles feared they might be next, in a nation clearly capable of sudden, inexplicable violence. "We'd like closed-top cars and bullet-proof vests," a nervous George Harrison told *NME* as they toured the US that September. He eventually refused the risk of a San Francisco ticker-tape parade. "It was only a year since they had assassinated Kennedy," he explained later. "I could just imagine how mad it is in America." In 1966, Americans burned Beatles LPs as if they were witches, and after that year they never returned as a group. It was where they shot Kennedy. It was where, 14 years later, they shot John Lennon and, 24 years after that, Ray Davies too.

UK tours then could be anarchic. The thrilling liberation in the footage of girls screaming and lunging at pop bands was mutually dangerous. The Kinks were often surrounded and mauled, and scissors might hack at long pop-star hair. Dave recalls a girl's pelvis being crushed between their coach and the wall on an early tour. The Stones' road manager Ian Stewart heard a girl's back break in the crush at an Ipswich gig. "A lot of them you never heard about," he told writer Stanley Booth. "They were in the local papers the next day, and that was all." But in the States, as in parts of Europe, the outnumbered commissars of British ballrooms were replaced by cops wielding truncheons, hoses and tear gas. The month before The Kinks arrived, the Stones watched frenzied fans beaten off their limo by night-sticks in Long Beach, California, then tear the abandoned car to pieces as they made their escape.

It was a huge, strange country, which The Beatles' bridgehead allowed an almost undifferentiated mass of British bands – Gerry & The Pacemakers, Freddie & The Dreamers and The Dave Clark Five among them – to join the Stones, Animals, Kinks and Manfred Mann in smashing open the *Billboard* charts. In its first months, this US-dubbed British Invasion brushed aside both the saccharine, suffocating pop of Frankie Avalon and his ilk, and the sophisticated brilliance of just blooming soul-pop stars such as Ben E. King. A complacent music industry had no defences prepared. If, in the Invasion's tasteless military language, this was D-Day, The Kinks' tour would be Omaha Beach: a near-fatal setback, under unexpected and withering fire.

Anyone reading *Melody Maker* in early 1965 could track the gathering counter-attack. "The unions have really clamped down over there," John Hawken of Surrey's Nashville Teens told them. "It cost us between $400 and $500 last time to join all the necessary American unions – and you have to pay and repay each time you go." They unhappily signed up to the musicians union, a film union to appear on TV, and a third union for their singers. "They probably ask you the size of your shoes and charge you $1,000 for taking up so much of the earth. It can't go on like this," Hawken bitterly concluded. "The American Federation of TV & Radio Artists," The Yardbirds' manager Giorgio Gomelsky angrily claimed, "are in principle against any foreign artists appearing on TV." "Things are getting tougher for British artists over there," confirmed The Animals' John Steel, returning from a trip where they had a Harlem Apollo show pulled, and only just made it onto *Ed Sullivan*. "They have got it in for the invasion by our groups... Promoters and agents will have to make sure they clear things in plenty of time now. If arrangements are made well in advance and everybody, including the authorities, knows exactly what is happening, then it should be all right."

The administrative chaos in The Kinks' camp meant none of this happened. Dave's injury contributed to the late cancellation of a week of East Coast dates for the US tour originally scheduled to start June 9. A third of the rearranged tour was then scrapped, and three Midwest dates hastily scribbled in just before their June 17 departure. On June 16, they applied for their crucial membership of the American Federation of Musicians.

The contracts the teenage Kinks signed with equal thoughtlessness at their career's start also conspired to hobble them. Firm and steady advice from management was needed. Instead, the tangled implications of their hasty decisions became clear. Denmark Productions, the management company through which Page channelled Ray's songs to its silent partner publisher Eddie Kassner, which took 10% of The Kinks' net income, and Wace and Collins' Boscobel, which paid this from their 40%, were about to begin a draining war for control of the band. Page would also openly feud with Talmy, who had signed an exclusive deal to produce the band at the same time, while The Kinks made their precarious way across America. Page would not last the tour. Wace and Collins didn't even board the plane. The creative team which had pushed 'You Really Got Me' to the top were set to pull the ensnared band apart.

The Kinks themselves were riven with cracks from Cardiff, which one last shove could shatter. "We were all at loggerheads, so it wasn't a good feeling amongst us anyway," says Avory. "Me and Dave had to meet up and talk about it, and be sensible, and it wasn't so bad. But it wasn't a very good atmosphere. And then when things went wrong as well, everyone was agitated. We didn't wanna be there – not for that reason. And Ray wasn't happy."

All Ray longed for was to spend time with his wife and daughter. Page recalls sitting in his flat, wanting his signature on the contract with the main US tour promoter Norman Granz, and watching him let the fountain pen's ink trickle onto the floor. "There's no ink left," Ray innocently exclaimed. "If there's a gold medal for being devious, he'd get it," Page fumes. But the truth of Ray's distress was clear in a song he wrote while pacing at home waiting for news of Louisa's birth, and demoed the next day. 'I Go To Sleep' is a declaration of eternal love to a girl he's been distant from for days, and meets in his dreams. The loneliness it dreads is a tour's long separation. A prestigious recording by Peggy Lee resulted. Ray's demo, picking out precarious, classical piano chords, not thinking he'd be heard, eavesdrops on a worried man.

Almost his last act before he left was to buy an old white semi-detached house in Fortis Green he'd admired since he was a child in Denmark Terrace, yards down the road. Whatever happened, he'd have a home to return to.

"I didn't want to go on [the tour]," he summarises, "because my wife at the time had had a child, and I didn't want to go away from her. And we were ready for a major bust-up in the band – we'd already had one, so we were on a reprieve and it could explode. We were on the verge of breaking up at any point. It was a very dangerous time to send four young guys to America. But our management was going through a terrible crisis, because two managers were splitting up from the third. All our managers ended up in England because, now we know, they were building their own little empires, and, 'Oh, they're on the road, they can handle that'. We were not really represented properly. Which I took a certain amount of grievance at. We were thrown into the lion's den."

The Kinks touched down in New York on June 17 as scheduled. It was almost the last thing to go right. The Moody Blues, who were supposed to tour with them, didn't make it that far, having been denied visas altogether. Still, as Beatle-primed fans screamed at the motorcades smoothly ferrying them between TV and gig engagements, as befitted a band whose first three US singles had hit the Top 10, trouble seemed to melt away. "They were all over us like a rash," remembers Avory. "We were suddenly big stars to them, spoiled and picked up in big limos. We got a police escort, a big reception committee. I thought, 'Blimey.' So this was the big time. It was awesome, really. Everything about America hit us in the face – colour television on 24 hours. Just watching cartoons in the morning. And the skyscrapers made my neck ache, and they had lovely cars with chrome. Everything was bigger and better."

But by only the second gig, in Philadelphia, Page had been briefly jailed for disputing a state tax demanded by a passing union official. Then they drove into the Midwest, the belly of a different America. "It started to degrade into silly little TV shows and smaller venues, crappier hotels," Quaife told Johnny Black. "We did one TV show where they had live cats all over the studio. They'd been given something, because they didn't move. We played in one hicksville country club where the punters didn't even know who we were. We ended up in a plane flying through a hurricane. It shouldn't have been in the air, but nobody cared. It wasn't the tour we'd been promised. It was a total cock-up."

A cultural chasm also revealed itself between a London that at least where The Kinks went was starting to swing, and Peoria and Springfield, Illinois. "There was this feeling that, 'The Limeys are coming,'" remembers Ray. "Once you get out of New York, you're in the Midwest, with people saying, 'What are you doing here?' It's bad enough having Americans play rock'n'roll. What are they doing to our country? And quite honestly, America terrified me. A few years earlier they'd shot a President, and there was this gun culture. It was an enormous place, and... inflexible. I can't explain it but... there was no alternative. What had happened in Britain hadn't happened there yet. And there was no sense of irony, which everyone knows now. It's a place that in many respects was brainwashed. It was as if someone from *Invasion Of The Body Snatchers* had been there. We knew what we were saying to each other, but we were not connecting."

"Mick Jagger, who'd been there before us," Avory adds, "warned they'd go, [in a raucous, sneering Yank accent]: 'Are you a Beatle or a girl?' Silly remarks. Because they all had crew-cuts. They were forward in some things, backward in others." In his notably bilious 1970 interview with *Rolling Stone*'s Jann Wenner, Lennon put it more acidly. "When we got here people were all walkin' around in fuckin' Bermuda shorts... The chicks looked like 1940s horses... We just thought what an ugly race, what an ugly race. It looked just disgusting and we thought how hip we were."

In 1965 in public, The Beatles' press conference irreverence remained cheekily appealing. The Stones, whose first US tour had also been a shambles of bad bookings and showbiz stupidity, had Andrew Oldham on hand to help them play up to their image, and included a reverent recording session at Chess, Chicago's R&B home (and they made sure they played *Ed Sullivan* the next time). The Kinks remained irreducibly abrasive working-class Londoners. Pushed, they pushed back.

"I was quite a cocky kid," says Dave. "I had a bit of bravado. I didn't know what the fuck was going on, just go out there and do it. Get on the pitch and play. But we were surprised at how behind the game they were, how old-fashioned. I don't think people liked us very much. I remember in Detroit going into a coffee shop, and these older people were very threatened by us being in there. If you think of that first Stones tour, they had their hair nicely coiffeured, and they and The Beatles had well-honed PR teams. And maybe we weren't the right materials. We were more rough and ready. We were pretty... messy. Sloppy. America didn't know what to do with us. We didn't know what to do."

"We were more openly of our roots," Ray considers. "The Stones were accepted because they were very smart, and they acknowledged their roots in the culture that inspired them. I was inspired by lots of the same people, but somehow The Kinks thought: 'This started in London, didn't it?' The Beatles had this wonderful twang to their voices, which Americans equate to a Southern accent, it's cutesy. But we were less soft-spoken Londoners in those days, a little bit more, [broad cockney] 'Hello. Where's the sauce then?' It's a lot to do with our inflexibility, as well as on the part of many Americans. We were in their country, after all. But we didn't have any diplomatic training in N10."

The Kinks didn't have to travel long in this hostile terrain to brush against real American evil. "The next job was the Illinois State Armory in Springfield, Illinois on June 23." Quaife told Johnny Black. "We drove up there at night, it was very hot, very humid. There was a thunderstorm, which should have warned me what was in store. We meet the promoter. Now, this guy is a greaseball. He takes us to the theatre for soundcheck, he takes us back to the hotel, then back to the theatre to play, and he takes us to dinner. Afterwards, he invites us all back to his place, says he's got some people coming round, he's got some booze, so we say, 'OK,' and we go back there and stay till about four in the morning, then decide we've got to go. He gets a bit upset about this, says can't a couple of us stay, and we said, 'No,' and we were beginning to get the feeling that there was something strange about this guy. On top of that, there was a very sickly smell about the room. We were all a little bit antsy about this, so we took off to the hotel and that was the last I saw of him. It was quite a few years later that a friend of mine, Doug Hinman, rings up and says that was John Wayne Gacy – the serial killer. We could have ended up as mementoes bricked up in his wall."

Quaife's well-founded reputation among Sixties pop reporters for colourfully unreliable copy may have retrospectively conjured the faint, queasy odour of some of the 27 men and boys Gacy buried under his house, among the 33 killings he was convicted and executed for after his 1978 arrest. Hinman, in his immaculately researched reference book *The Kinks: All Day And All Of The Night*, doubts the band met the most notorious American murderer since Ed Gein. But this then blandly respectable local citizen *was* the promoter of their gig that night.

Ray would be drawn towards such deceptive human extremes in the psychotic commuter of his TV film *Return To Waterloo* (1985), and the Yorkshire Ripper-inspired 'Killer's Eyes' (1981). Told by Black of Quaife's claim, he believed it, as if something had suddenly become clear. "This must be the guy who had the gun in his car," he said. "In my book *X-Ray* he's a nameless promoter. That was the guy, saying he was powerful, knew about guns. He didn't really hurt me, but I was really provoked and verbally assaulted. We were intimidated a lot in the Midwest." The pistol-waving braggart who drives a quaking Ray through Illinois in his "fictional autobiography" doesn't resemble the anonymous Gacy. But this other terrifying figure was, then, real too.

Avory is predictably more sanguine about the physical peril waiting for them. "We didn't go down South. That was almost dangerous then, for some bands. You needed someone to look after you. If you get in the wrong area and say the wrong thing to the wrong person you can come unstuck, they might have a gun on them. Ray found that out [when he was shot in 2004]. But most of the time we got VIP treatment, we were the band all together and we'd get chaperoned – like if we were in New York and I went to Slug's, a jazz club on the Lower East Side where you've gotta keep your nose clean. We didn't get in any real trouble. It was just unions, not gangsters – thankfully."

The American music industry would be more deadly to The Kinks than any serial killer or hoodlum. The group, still "upside down" from Cardiff, Avory says, had suffered the indignities of amateurishly rickety stages in Peoria and Springfield, an onstage power cut in Chicago, and a flight to Reno, Nevada through the sort of lightning-jagged turbulence that finished Buddy Holly. There a pathetically tiny crowd was kept distant from the stage, till Ray called them towards the band, in Copenhagen-style insurrection. More importantly, the poor receipts meant promoter Betty Kaye only offered half their fee upfront, the rest promised after the next night's Sacramento, California show. In response The Kinks allegedly played 20 minutes in Reno and, Kaye claimed, diluted the scheduled 45 minutes in Sacramento with an endless version of 'You Really Got Me'. Page confronted Kaye, suing for unpaid money. Kaye later won the dispute because of the Reno half-show. The band's bad feeling was spreading beyond them. Lingering vendettas were being left in the Nevada desert.

"It was just that whole scene," Avory sighs. "And you think, 'Why were we booked in the first place, for half the gigs?' We'd been thrown in the deep end. America was a bit more together than Europe, but it was still in its infancy, the PAs weren't that big. If you see that film of The Beatles at Shea Stadium, they've got a thin sound and the screams are louder than the band. That's how it was. They didn't mic the drums. If it was a big place, you had to hit the kit harder. I know everyone was the same, but that was our first tour of big places. I don't think we were quite ready for it. We needed to cut our teeth on something else. But if the records are big, then they throw you out in the big time. We were quite good in clubs. Then in stadiums, you couldn't hear anything. I felt lost. I felt isolated. I just used to get despondent, and fed up with it. I felt out on a limb anyway. I only had one foot in the door. And the other on a banana skin."

"The agency we were with had done some dodgy deals with some of the promoters in the Midwest," Ray believes. "So there was a lot of angst going on on that front, and we were still thrown out there expected to do it. And we had a tour manager [Sam Curtis] who didn't really know us. All these factors were contributing."

Ray remembers a more direct portent. "In Chicago, a radio interviewer said to me, 'Any news on who's going to get banned?' There was talk about it."

On June 28 The Kinks landed back in the slick heart of America's entertainment industry, LA. They stayed a week in preparation for their biggest gig at the Hollywood Bowl five days later, taping TV shows and talking to reporters. Eddie Kassner was in town, assiduously selling Ray's songs to Peggy Lee, and less successful acts. Reprise squired them round the Warner studio lot, where they met Dean Martin (who'd belittled the Stones on their first American TV show, and eventually refused a Ray song). Page meanwhile convinced Cher, who with Sonny had joined in Sacramento as their Californian support act, to, like Lee, record 'I Go To Sleep'. The song Ray had written in anticipation of the tour's misery became a roaring success as he suffered it. Page also quietly took a professional interest in Cher. Avory even had time to almost complete the ambition he'd confided to *NME*, to "go to the US to learn the art of drumming thoroughly and meet most of the jazz greats". "I went with Larry Page to see Dave Brubeck at the Hollywood Bowl," he says, "and I met [Brubeck drummer] Joe Morello, a really good technician, an original, brilliant small group player. And I met Shelly Manne on that trip. I was in awe of them." Ray and Dave actually played with one of their heroes, James Burton, guitarist for Ricky Nelson and Elvis, when the American Federation of Musicians required a newly recorded session with US musicians for their *Shindig!* appearance. Dave watched everything he did. The Kinks met another ambition by recording Ray's song 'Ring The Bells' in a modern American studio. The country was giving up some of its riches now. Under endless blue skies, the tour seemed calm.

Then from that blue sky, the British Invasion finally erupted into open warfare. Ray, homesick, isolated and ready to blow, ranted at Page to bring Rasa over. Because she was from Lithuania, part of the USSR, this wasn't easy. Then backstage at a North Hollywood TV studio on July 2, an official from the American Federation of Television & Radio Artists required The Kinks' signatures, and fees – likely the same TV work contract the Nashville Teens complained of grudgingly signing that year. Dave wouldn't do it. The official, Ray recalled in *X-Ray* (where he doesn't mention a union issue), called him "a talentless fuck who was in the right place at the right time". Ray responded with some digs at limp US pop before the British Invasion. His opponent roared as if the Liverpool and Home Counties bluesmen raiding his country really had ripped up its sovereignty. It was just like Pearl Harbour, Ray thought he said.

"We had to sign all these contracts, we refused," he says. "I don't know if it was one particular guy, it was a lot of them. I think somebody called me a 'Commie bastard', and, 'Wait till the Reds run over Britain', all that. I said, 'Oh, don't be so fucking stupid'. Pushing and shoving occurred – nothing as sophisticated as that, probably. Handbags."

A minor punch-up?

"It was a little flourish."

Were you told you'd never work in this town again?

"Oh, we still get that a lot now."

Ray ran from the studio to the safety of his room, wondering who and what he'd offended so far from home. Were these sharp-suited strangers yelling and punching at him gangsters? Assassins? As had happened in the safer context of a Southampton TV show three months before, he'd hammered against his limit of the shit required of him. He put The Kinks' gig at the Hollywood Bowl, an 18,000-seat sell-out with an all-star line-up, on the line, to return to his own way. "I barricaded myself in the Ambassador Hotel – I barricaded the doors up, wouldn't go to a gig one day," he says. "All I wanted to do was go home. They had to break in and get me." Literally? "It wasn't... straitjackets. I was persuaded by our tour manager at the time."

"I'd taken this band from a little pub in Islington to what was going to be the biggest gig of their lives," Page bragged to Johnny Black. Then as he was congratulating himself, he got a call from the *Daily Mirror* asking why The Kinks weren't going on that night. "I'm getting a phone call from England telling me what's happening next door. Ray's excuse was, he was married to Rasa [and wanted her there], and obviously getting a visa was an impossibility. But if it hadn't been that," he says without sympathy, "it would have been the colour of his toothpaste. That was my breaking point. So I spent all day grovelling, while promising myself I'd never do it again."

The Kinks played. Californian kings The Beach Boys headlined (Brian Wilson seething at the Hollywood Bowl's imperfect sound, Avory chuffed it was better than Peoria). The Righteous Brothers, The Byrds, Sonny & Cher, Sam the Sham & The Pharaohs, The Sir Douglas Quintet (with future Tex Mex cult hero Doug Sahm) and Dean Martin's kid Dino and his pals Desi and Billy were all on the bill. Signs of a native revival – 'You've Lost That Lovin' Feeling', 'I Got You, Babe', 'Mr. Tambourine Man', 'California Girls' – rained down around The Kinks, who heard some of their favourite records come to life and gave everything they had. Backstage, as at the Motown gig in Finsbury Park, they felt snubbed, by Beach Boy Mike Love and others. They were like insecure teenagers seeing disrespect everywhere, or else really experiencing it, from nervous young Americans feeling the same way around representatives of pop's new British monarchy.

Afterwards, The Kinks congratulated themselves on a great success. Miraculously, a fur-coated Rasa and Quaife's glamorous girlfriend Nicola landed that night. The worst was surely over. But the next morning, their manager was gone.

"As soon as I heard the first few numbers, I took a car to the airport," Page told Black. "I'd had enough. But what you've got to realise is that I didn't even have to be there. Wace and Collins weren't there. We had tour managers, American agents, the publishers, and we had the record company looking after them, so I was just along for the ride. But it's a good job I was..."

"He mentioned to me that he was going to go," says Avory. "But I didn't know he wasn't going to tell Ray. And then he'd gone, and Ray's gone mad. But his reason really was to go back and clinch a deal with Sonny & Cher, and 'I Got You, Babe'." True or not, Page represented the duo on their European tour.

"After the Hollywood Bowl, everybody pissed off back to England," Quaife told Black. "Just deserted us. We stood outside the hotel, didn't know who to talk to. It was just the four of us. There were still gigs to do, but we didn't even know where they were."

In fact Sam Curtis was still there, along with Page's quickly hired stand-in, local businessman Don Zacharlini. They only had to wait one night for things to get worse. At San Francisco's Cow Palace on July 4, another strong, Beach Boys-headed bill was promoted by Betty Kaye. As in Reno, receipts were miserably low, and only a cheque could be offered to The Kinks upfront. "We got these people coming into the dressing room and shouting at us," Ray claims. "They were saying, 'We don't want you to go on tonight'. I said, 'There's 5,000 kids out there.' 'We've got contract problems with your agent. We don't want you to perform.' I think some of these promoters wanted to show non-performance, so they wouldn't have to pay us."

"By the time we got to San Francisco and the Cow Palace was cancelled," says Dave, "standing in this great huge place with no people in it, the whole thing fell apart. I couldn't wait to get back to England."

By some accounts, The Kinks refused to play if they weren't paid in cash first. They gave a cursory wave to the few thousand in the crowd and left. Their next stop was to play for the military personnel near Pearl Harbour. In their wake, Kaye led outraged Nevadan and Californian promoters and union men in complaining of their "unprofessional behaviour" to the American Federation of Musicians.

"To this day, I still don't know what really happened," says Dave. "There was an awful lack of experience, and incompetence crept in. We didn't know anything about unions. I don't think our management, the third part that was there, realised how powerful unions were. If they didn't like you – if you did something that you shouldn't do – you just couldn't work. It was much more flexible in England. We used to mock [the union] and think it was stupid. We thought we could get away with it."

"The Sex Pistols experienced it years later in a more violent way," Ray considers. The Pistols' 1978 trawl into the South, where they fought with crowds and played barbed-wire-fenced stages smeared in blood, travelling with burly hired rednecks who seemed warders as much as bodyguards, till an already battered band fell apart at an awful San Francisco gig, was a sort of sequel to The Kinks' experience. When a more minor band of working-class brothers, Oasis, aborted a *Rolling Stone* cover shoot because they were bored, and pulled a US tour because Noel and Liam Gallagher had fought, they too lost their chance of stardom overnight. The American music industry has rigid rules for kowtowing to its powers. The Kinks couldn't understand till it was too late, and couldn't stomach it anyway.

They were garlanded in Waikiki. As they made their way up the pioneer north-west coast of Washington state for three final gigs, Ray was surrounded by armed police in Spokane. An outraged citizen had summoned them when the long-haired Limey kissed his wife. Back in Britain, Page was calling the music press to claim the American recording he'd arranged, 'Ring The Bells', would be the next single. Talmy successfully countered with legal proof they could only record under him. The abandoned band seemed to have no say.

When the brothers went home, Quaife and Avory stayed on. Ray later wrote the only thing the tour had been good for was "Mick Avory's sex life", perhaps explaining his sunnier mood. "The sexual thing was always there, the groupies," Avory admits. "But a lot of the time, it was just a bit of fun. In Britain you'd meet up in the theatre. A girl called Anna used to come up from Dartford, play tambourines and she'd dance and strip off. It was a laugh, more than serious sexual contact. When you went to America, the girls were more excitable, and they're up for it, and there's more of them, and you could get them into hotels. In England in those days, you had to send the night porter for some hot milk to get her in. But in America, girls just went to your room and that was it. As long as they weren't underage. So it was freer."

America grabbed him in other ways. "LA really impressed me. I stayed on for a couple of weeks. Don Zacharlini, who owned a chain of supermarkets, showed us around for something to do. We got up early every morning and really enjoyed it. We went to Catalina Island, and Disneyland. I thought, 'This is where I wanna be. I don't wanna go 'ome.'"

For the next four years, The Kinks had no choice. "There were union problems, and there was a bit of a dust-up, and we ended up getting banned," Avory sums up. The AMF blocked them from playing in America. Their career there staggered on like someone who's been shot and not seen the bullet-hole, with US hits till 1966.

"I still don't know what caused the ban, because they were non-specific," says Ray. "It cost us an important part of our career. That cost us the top spot, and a lot of our youth. Because America was the next place to go. At our prime." He laughs sadly. "Coulda been a contender..."

When in 1969 The Who played Woodstock, and the Stones became the British band to finally crash into America's potential for bloodshed at their Altamont gig, as Meredith Hunter pulled a gun then was beaten and knifed to jelly, The Kinks had been all but forgotten.

Back in Britain, they had better things to do.

CHAPTER 4

The Suburban Hit Machine

The crunching gravel path feels like a solid force-field against the outside world. A heavy lion's-head door knocker announces visitors. But walk into the big white semi-detached at 87 Fortis Green, and it's a home. Up the bannistered staircase are the attic rooms where baby Louisa grew up. When she was a little older, she'd sneak into the room where her father's fan mail tottered, and sniff its patchouli scent. More forward girls would gather in the street. Just to the left of the front door off the narrow hallway is the front room with its heavy Georgian shutters, where Ray watched people walk by. In his short story 'The Million-Pound Semi-Detached', he fictionalises a mother exactly like his own who is magically lured here as she nears death, and brought the healing peace he found sitting there. A white piano used to be pushed against the wall. The ceiling is quite low, the wooden floorboards very old. In the back room, French windows open on a long garden which backs onto a patch of green wilderness. In these cosily enclosed, modest rooms, on that piano or his guitar, Ray Davies wrote 'Waterloo Sunset' and 'Sunny Afternoon' and 'Lola' and 'Celluloid Heroes'. Louisa remembers there always being music here. Dave would get the call, to come round and nurture each spark. The Kinks would gather for soft, skeletal rehearsals, as close as they'd ever be. When I stand where the piano was I try and conjure them, and Ray aged 22, pulling 'Waterloo Sunset' from the air in the room, sounding like it had always been there. Sometimes thought to be dissecting the sixties, in songs such as 'Autumn Almanac' Ray anatomised the view from these windows; his suburban neighbours, and the fallen leaves in his private patch of green.

Smuggled onto the B-side of a 1967 single released only in some Continental corners and a US no longer listening, 'This Is Where I Belong' was an ecstatic anthem to the stability of the home he moved into in July 1965. "I won't search for a house upon a hill," Ray sang with triumphant emphasis. "Why should I when I'd only miss you still?" As the Summer of Love approached, he made his stand here with wife and child and hearth and home. Dave's moan of assent as the song faded out showed his fervour for roots too. Everything that mattered to them in the sixties sometimes seemed reducible to a couple of front and back rooms in Fortis Green.

"I stayed in my room a hell of a lot," Ray remembers. "I was young and in love and mopey, and by now I was getting asked to write lots of songs. I was a homebody. That was the knack, I think. That's what confused people that came to see me, especially some of my art friends. They said, 'I don't understand how a guy who lives here can write such great, edgy songs'. But I wanted to stick to this. I thought I lived in the best house in the world. I'd walked past this little semi as a kid and thought I'd love to live there. And I was really happy there, and I wrote great tunes there, and I felt totally in my place there."

Outside his front door in April 1966, *Time* magazine's cover declared his still Blitz-wrecked London was "Swinging... The City of the Decade": the hip heart of the world. "I still felt part of a bigger world and what was happening," he insists. "I went to Carnaby Street when there were just two boutiques there. I used to love going into shops in Swinging London, and I went to a few clubs and I had a good time. But I stayed peripheral. I watched people a lot. I stepped back. Because I'm a very cautious person. And if I get involved in things, I always get into trouble. I'm just an accident-prone, naive fool. I didn't want to get exposed to Swinging London. And when people came up and said, 'Everything's groovy', I thought, 'Well, that's a bit sad, really.'

Because things have to move on. I thought the Swinging Sixties were over in 1965. I was very aware of it being a movement that was going somewhere, and I always wanted the music to be that way."

"Ray was becoming so prolific," believes Dave, "because he'd really found a place in his heart and mind where he could express himself. It was all starting. Ray'd pick the phone up – 'Come round, I've got this idea'. He'd do it on the piano, I'd double it on the guitar, and we've got another song. It was an exciting, spontaneous time. There was a greater freedom we all felt. I remember that sense of freedom, and that we were doing something new, something different from what The Beatles and the Stones were doing. Our advantage over everybody was we had so many ways of doing things. The Stones were always great, but always sounded the same. The Kinks had country influences, and were almost a folk band as well as a heavy riff band. Even then, making another 'You Really Got Me' felt really uncomfortable."

When The Kinks returned from America, resentful, hollow-eyed and defeated, the British pop 45 was approaching its creative zenith. From the summer of 1965 till two summers later, when The Beatles' *Sgt. Pepper* signalled a sea-change towards LP statements, the major bands in Britain and the US pushed the form on every few weeks, challenging the rest to keep up in a relay race with no end in sight. The Beatles seemed to peak with August 1966's 'Eleanor Rigby', which George Melly thought "great poetry... a whole world in 3½ minutes", then topped it themselves with the psychedelic double-A-side 'Penny Lane'/'Strawberry Fields Forever'. The Stones climaxed with their "ultimate freak-out" 'Have You Seen Your Mother, Baby, Standing In The Shadow?' ("We came to a full stop after that," Jagger admitted. "What more could we say?"). The Who blasted out of Ray's shadow with 'My Generation'. Everyone listened equally hard to a resurgent America, where Brian Wilson spent nine months on The Beach Boys' "pocket symphony" 'Good Vibrations', Dylan's 'Like A Rolling Stone' broke the four-minute barrier on the way to six, and the Southern Soul of Percy Sledge's 'When A Man Loves A Woman' joined massive Motown productions such as The Four Tops' 'Reach Out I'll Be There'.

This was "the country of Now", Melly wrote, a chain-reacting pop present like nothing before. The Beat Boom which The Kinks helped launch less than a year earlier already seemed prehistoric as they stepped off their plane (Quaife was nearly arrested for carrying an air-gun, of course). Undaunted and often uncredited, they made some of mid-sixties pop's most crucial leaps forward.

"I suppose I had a competitive streak in me," says Ray. "At school, I liked running and soccer, I liked winning. I didn't know who the opposition was. I was involved in some sort of secret race, to make this record perfect and get it out. There was a certain amount of pressure from the label and management. As soon as a record went down to number 20, they said you've got to have another one or your career is over. But also the pressure was coming from in me. The fact that I could deliver quickly meant that the subconscious back-burn was already fired. You get the block-out syndrome, the focus. I suddenly realised how wonderful it was to be able to focus. I'd never been able to before. Not constantly, 24 hours a day. The shop was always open, like an all-night deli."

The Kinks began this astonishing period with their most hauntingly futuristic record. 'See My Friends'* was actually the fifth of the singles recorded in the ten months between 'You Really Got Me' and the American debacle. Completed on May 3, a couple of weeks before Cardiff, it was held back until July 30 while 'Set Me Free' re-established their commercial momentum. The Kinks knew 'See My Friends' was something else, new and superior. Feedback from one guitar alternated behind a droning second in a hypnotic rhythm resembling a sitar, months before The Beatles or Byrds recorded one ('Norwegian Wood' was taped in October). Heavy bass and drums thickened this into a raga-rock template which fully bloomed in The Beatles' 'Tomorrow Never

---

* The song is sometimes mistitled 'See My Friend' since that was the title on the initial UK single pressing. However, Kassner Music, which owns the publishing rights to the song, specifies the title as 'See My Friends', which are the words Ray clearly sings throughout the track. Most subsequent issues of the song have borne the more familiar 'See My Friends' title.

Knows' the following spring. Tape hiss from the layers of work to get it right added to the hazy feel (in an early take, the fuzzed electric guitar is more obvious, only plucked notes over it even suggesting a sitar). Ray's lyrics' repeated mantra of loss, abandonment and transformation completed a sense of spiritual dislocation. This insidious record's implications matched 'You Really Got Me', as other bands quietly realised.

"I remember one night I walked into a club where we used to hang out, the Scotch of St. James," says Dave, "and Paul McCartney came up to me and said, 'That 'Friend'. Really like that. I should have written it.' You didn't! You can't do everything..."

"We were trying to set up ideas that other people would take on," Ray claims. "'See My Friends' was I suppose an experiment. I had this lovely cheap Framus guitar with rusty 12-strings on it that I played on 'A Well Respected Man' and 'Dedicated Follower Of Fashion' too, and it had this tinny, ukelele-type sound. 'See My Friends' is feedback by accident playing a high octave above my guitar. People thought that was deliberate, and we compressed it [the often maligned Talmy's idea, Ray admits in *X-Ray*], and it sounded really unique. The feedback gave the Framus more elegance, this French horn quality. And the sound helped the lyric flow, the repeating words: 'I can see my friends, see my friends... she is gone, she is gone...' We'd also travelled to India a year before, and I remembered being in that environment in Bombay in my subconscious. I didn't take up meditation. I'm still waiting to see what that's like."

Ray has often told the story of watching fishermen chanting from his Bombay hotel. The fascination with Indian religious thought which soon surfaced in the transatlantic counter-culture had its seeds in records such as 'See My Friends', as well as the heads LSD cracked open. But an August 1964 interview in *Melody Maker* is a less familiar tale. "We're always searching for new sounds," Dave said. "Ray likes Indian music, for example." "Yeah, I like going into Indian restaurants and listening to the records there," Ray confirmed. "I like that drone they've got on them." Dave added: "We've got a drone on our new record ['You Really Got Me'], actually, about halfway through." The consciousness-expansion that shook Western youth had one beginning in a Muswell Hill tandoori.

Some wondered just who the friend Ray had sought solace with *"playing 'cross the river"* was, once *"she"* had left him. "The song is about homosexuality," he later told the *Standard*'s Maureen Cleave. Ambiguity remains in this blurred record about a man on the cusp – of crossing the Thames or Bombay's Ulhas, into a higher state or manly arms. The Kinks anyway attracted gay fans just by their name, even before Ray sang about a 'Well Respected Man' who likes *"fags"* – clearly cigarettes in the UK, a blaring red gay beacon in the US – on their very next release. Drag queen fans the Cockettes later made early seventies American Kinks shows a camp spectacle, and Ray toyed with speculation on his sexuality on stage and record with 'Lola', 'Destroyer' and other songs. Was this not so much because of personal experience, as sympathy with gay people then as outsiders? "I think so," says Ray. "In the period when I grew up, people couldn't understand how I was athletic, and really creative. They wanted you to be one thing or the other. So although it was not a gay or queer issue, it was something I've had a confrontation with, because I wanted to run and paint. People who are really overtly out bother me as much as people who are trapped in the closet. Be yourself. But I've no real judgement on that. It's generally outsiders. Because I'm not sure where I fit in." On stage at the Albert Hall in 2012, he dedicated the song to "a sister who died a long time ago", before singing, "I wish that I'd gone with her." For that night at least, it was Rene who was "gone".

'See My Friends' hit slowly. "At least it's different," *Record Mirror* offered brightly, among a music press still unequipped to analyse rock seriously. The paper found Ray, "quieter than usual", obsessing about its progress. "It's the record," he confessed to the journalist. "The only one I've really liked, and they're not buying it. I put everything I've got into it. The thing I'm most interested in and... well, I just couldn't care less about the others. The last before – I can't even remember what it was called ['Set Me Free'] – nothing. It makes me think that they must be morons." He tried to sound reasonable. "Look, I'm not a great singer, nor a great writer, nor a great musician. But I *do* give everything I have – and I did for this disc." It eventually grazed the Top 10. The interview was the first sign of the strain Ray was under, as his hit production line became personal.

The first song he wrote after America saw Ray finding a fight in the murmuring palm courts of Torquay's Imperial Hotel, just as surely as the Midwest. He and Rasa cut short a week's holiday there after he was recognised by a posh retired Army type, and bluffly invited for golf. Back in their room, Ray seethed at the implied condescension, and checked out the next morning. "I said, 'I'm not gonna play fucking golf with you,'" he claimed years later. "'I'm not gonna be your caddy so you can say you played with a pop singer.'" The towing away of Pete Townshend's treasured American car on the orders of his new Belgravia neighbour the Queen Mother that year inspired 'My Generation', and a Chelsea woman sneering at a posh car he surely hadn't earned at traffic lights later in the sixties confirmed his spitting rage at the ruling class. The lower-middle-class Jagger's February B-side 'Play With Fire', an elegant threat to an heiress slumming in Stepney, had announced the attitude.

The Imperial's West Country gentility, it would become obvious over the years, was greatly appealing to Ray. But his working-class pride was pricked. His response, 'A Well Respected Man', introduced British pop to the character study and satirical sketch. Owing nothing to Dylan's already highly influential Ginsberg and acid-inspired style, it was more Noël Coward, Somerset Maugham or Peter Cook. For the first time it set out Ray's own lyrical world.

The record opens with the harp-like strum of a minstrel beginning a fairy tale. Harder, martial drums and acoustic guitar like the relentless chug of a commuter train drive its dissection of a man on a treadmill. The Man's respectable stockbroker job is a hypocritical veneer for his ogling the girl next door, while his slutty wife makes eyes at tradesmen behind his back. He's an ageing mummy's boy waiting for daddy's money, and Ray's voice rises in sneering upper-class affectation at his slashing lampoon's climax.

"Looking back there are landmarks," Ray considers. "The beginning of the lyrical stuff was 'A Well Respected Man', which was a song that nobody asked me to write. It was something that I'd observed on holiday, and the first time I actually stood back from what I was. Before that everything came from boy-girl teenage angst. 'Well Respected Man', that's a watershed because I started singing about other people. Something is turning, evolving."

Those around them baulked at this as a single. But the EP *Kwyet Kinks*, collecting it with three more largely acoustic songs, hit number one after its September 17 release, and was one of the year's best-sellers. Dave's 'Wait Till The Summer Comes Along' was his first significant song, a country ballad in the rawly open-hearted style which already characterised his voice and life. Ray's 'Don't You Fret', among aggressive acoustic guitar storms which showed it was still The Kinks playing them, secreted moments of still serenity, and some of his truest words: "Make a new pot of tea/Make my favourite dish/Do the things that I remember/ That'll make my dearest wish." The tea their mum always had ready for them till the end of her life, the comfort of memory and familiarity: these were the domestic touchstones with which Ray changed rock. In America meanwhile, 'A Well Respected Man' was a single, and reached number 13. The Beatles had made its youth sick with Anglophilia. This was their first really, exotically English vinyl fix.

The deli wasn't open all the time. In November, with the next single needed and another album to fill, Ray, who'd been seriously writing for barely more than a year, hit his first wall. Wace whisked New York pro Mort Shuman (writer with Doc Pomus of Elvis and Drifters hits) round to Fortis Green for a night's mentoring. "Lose the wife and kids," Ray remembered Shuman advising, as the veteran looked round his dream home. More constructively, he suggested a retreat to writing's simple pleasures, creating a song around favourite chords. Ray wrote 'Till The End Of The Day' that night.

It returned to old Kinks verities. Released on November 19, it updated the heavy riff for the sharper, soul-powered times and rose easily to number six. Ray sang in the voice of a hip young man who feels resurrected every time the sun rises, a perfect Mod hungry for experience, having the endless time of his life. Perhaps he was secretly thinking of the morning ecstasy of pushing his baby's pram round Muswell Hill. But Dave's strangled, high-tension solo and he and Rasa's sunburst harmonies made this pop to blast its subject from bed.

The B-side let him know what happened next. In the middle of the sixties youthquake, Ray asked, 'Where Have All The Good Times Gone?' It was his most brilliant gambit. This song's conformist raver thinks his youthful energy is how it will always be, in a decade where life is suddenly easier for the young and novelty and optimism are endlessly replenished resources of a special generation, who'll somehow be under-30 forever. Bright, daring clothes, each month's new pop wonders on transistor radios, money in the pocket: what a thing it is to be alive in 1965. Then one day, he looks around to realise he's gotten old. Those years of possibility are in the past, and he can't claw them back. McCartney's 'Yesterday' mourned a love affair, but when this boy begs for that day to return, it's his whole careless life he's lost. It's gallows humour, aimed at people who don't realise they're going to die. Ray was 21.

"We'd been rehearsing 'Where Have All The Good Times Gone?'," he remembers, "and our tour manager at the time, who was a lot older than us, said, 'That's a song a 40-year-old would write. I don't know where you get that from.' But I was taking inspiration from older people around me. I'd been watching them in the pubs, talking about taxes and job opportunities."

Did he ever feel youthful?

"No. I guess I felt at my most youthful in the early eighties, when I was playing the stadiums and jumping around. But as a young kid, I was very, very serious. I was an older, wise child, they call them now. I know this is a weird thing to say, but I think I was saved because I had a really bad back problem then. It could have been really serious. So I could relate to people with that kind of mobility issue. And I was aware of feeling older. I played soccer, I ran. But that injury instilled something in me. I was aware when I was young that it's not always going to be this good. And so that made me write in a more mature framework."

The song reserves its affection for "Ma" and "Pa", who never had the fallen raver's easy life – who "didn't have no money but always told the truth". These are its heroes: the generation written out of the Carnaby Street dream, like Fred and Annie Davies, whose values are more permanent. "I wrote for what I called the great generation, my parents' generation," Ray declared, looking back in *Imaginary Man*, "who lived through world wars and the depression. I wrote for what they stood for, what they believed in."

"When The Kinks became successful," he says, "we were in that Technicolor, Swinging London, but the home was still a black-and-white documentary, and I didn't see much changing. And my family didn't expect it to. They'd not given up aspiring. They were concerned with living. Whereas Dave and I were concerned with this whole social movement, and so we were... not at odds with them, but it was great to go back to the family parties when we were really successful, because it was a great leveller for us. I think one of the reasons The Kinks survived so long, especially through that early period of violence and lawsuits, is because of my mum making me a sandwich and saying, 'Eat that and shut up'. I feel bad for other people who didn't have that, like The Beach Boys. But they're in California. That's another world."

'Where Have All The Good Times Gone?''s clambering riff and Ray and Dave's gleeful singing deserved the A-side many now think it was. The Kinks' best album so far, *The Kink Kontroversy*, anyway repeated the single's mood swing when it followed a week later. It begins as a diary of their American misadventure. Dave plays the wailing riffs he'd absorbed from James Burton in Hollywood on 'Milk Cow Blues'. 'Gotta Get The First Plane Home' and 'When I See That Girl Of Mine' move a lonesome Ray back to Rasa with jet-set speed, his love for her declared again in the gauzy ballad 'Ring The Bells'. 'Till The End Of The Day' closes the A-side.

Again, bad, hilariously misanthropic news is waiting on the flip. Hard times, rain and depression assail humanity but, "What's the use of worrying because you'll die alone," Ray advises, indifferent, in 'The World Keeps Going Round'. 'I'm On An Island' is a relatively jaunty calypso about lovelorn self-exile. After 'Where Have All The Good Times Gone?', 'It's Too Late' is then followed by Ray having Dave pensively wonder 'What's In Store For Me', and if he should just get old, beaten and tired now. 'You Can't Win' is a glorious finale, Ray and Dave telling the listener how things really are: "Times are pretty thin, and you can't win." As they left their callow R&B style behind, this was a real London blues. Beneath the jet-black realism was an amused defiance, growing from the working-class knowledge that you're never likely to get out from under. And with that illusion disposed of, you can get on with bloody-mindedly trying. Another chink of Kinks philosophy fell into place.

Also on the A-side was Dave's first defining song, 'I Am Free'. It's a promise to himself never to be a disposable cog in society's machine. Tolling guitar and piano ring him into a better, wide-open reality, but as would always be true, he asks someone, surely Ray, to join him. The 18-year-old from the teeming Davies clan wanted to be free, but not alone. "All society controls people," he says of the song. "You have to get a certain grade at school, fall in line, and there's this thing within me that keeps saying, 'I am free'. Society's built on lies. It sounds naive, but you only truly function if you follow a spiritual logic." Did that freedom also show itself in chucking a bottle at that lovely Copenhagen mirror? "Course it did!" he laughs. "It's both. It's breaking things, pushing forward, when you're too restrained and you can't move. I don't like this, I'm uncomfortable, I want to get out of this – I am free. It's different when you just destroy everything. But that was a part of the rage, particularly of working-class people. We'd never had a voice, prior to '64. We were down there – we couldn't do art."

The Kinks continued to tour, as 1965 turned into 1966. With America off-limits they focused on fervent European fans. "We've had some bloody great riots," Quaife proudly informed *Record Mirror* from West Germany, where Sam Curtis was hit by a hurled bench. On one Stockholm trip, they'd barely left the airport before their driver had a heart attack and almost piled into another car. They returned to Copenhagen without incident in September 1965, and Dave even had a quiet date in Tivoli Gardens with Lisbet. But somewhere between there and an unlikely week-long residency at a Reykjavik cinema, they mislaid their drummer. "He's got no money and we are hoping he will join us," Brian Sommerville told the press, as if discussing a stray schoolboy. "If he contacts the promoter there he will be all right." Avory found his way home, but after the band refused to play an "unsuitable" Copenhagen gig a year later, the Scandinavian Musicians Union also banned them. Deposed fascist dictators sometimes seemed more internationally welcome. Even their return to Cardiff on November 27, 1965 saw Ray winch down the safety curtain on his own band when his mic-lead broke. "Every time we come to South Wales there's a fiasco," he said, which was too geographically specific. Most noticeable in 1966 was the previous insane schedule's slowing, with gigs peremptorily cancelled or grudgingly played.

Back home, Dave lost himself in the tumult of "Swinging" London, making up for his brother's reticence. "Those first three years were like being in a permanent state of euphoria," he says. "It was the energy of being that young, and in tune. I had some money. I was so used to growing up and we never had anything. It was like London was in black and white before, in '64, and in the fifties. Even though my sisters wore those fifties-type clothes that were bright, and pre-empted a lot of the fashion." The sisters again were an example, almost a premonition for the brothers' adult adventures. "They were of a slightly different generation. But they had some of the spirit that was in the sixties, the way Gwen looked towards the weekend, when she used to go out with her boyfriends at the local dancehall the Athenaeum, where me and Ray and Pete did one of our first gigs. It's Sainsbury's now. People tend to over-glamourise things – especially the sixties. But it'll never happen again. It was a period of time that was choreographed perfectly, by destiny."

Though they sometimes railed against the ruling class on record, Ray and Dave took advantage of the experiences of mixing with them the decade allowed. In a 1966 Sunday supplement spread photographing that year's great and good, Dave stood in the back row with boxer Terry Downes. Roman Polanski, Brian Epstein, Susannah York and David Hockney were scattered among eminent politicians, judges, clergymen and lords, all of the latter forgotten now.

Dave, who once said he was "put on this earth to shag posh birds", had become comfortable with the upper crust at the debutantes' balls the band played backing Wace. "They did look down on us at first," he says. "'Robert, could you bring those lads along?' But we soon mixed in. There were a lot of things going on behind the scenes, a breaking down of the old class system, and it was art and fashion and music that did it. I talked to Polanski. I thought he was gay. A bit fragile – a budding Oscar Wilde. There were a lot of people then who were affected, and thinking they had to fall into a certain role play for the time. And camp was coming in. Hockney was very camp. You can see the way he looked – very deliberate, with his glasses, trying to be fashionable with a jacket and Chelsea boots, but he didn't quite have it right. People were trying on characters. It was like a masquerade. What masks fit the best?"

Dave's own camp clowning when The Kinks had begun accelerated now he had the cash to really raid Carnaby Street. "Robert [Wace] saw the potential of the way I looked," he says. "Robert would say, 'Dave looks a right dandy. You could wear a flowerpot on your head [which, in one ill-advised hat, he pretty much did].' And that gave me confidence. I'd get a lot of ideas from my girlfriends – back-combed hair, and make-up, slight use of lipstick. Of course I knew a lot of models at the time, and we'd exchange ideas about how to look. 'Oh, that's cool – let me try...' A lot of the girls I met used to be really envious of the natural shadow I had over my eyelids, and I have really long eyelashes, so they would make me up with eyeliner to highlight those features. Me and Pete loved it. After a photo-shoot, everybody else would wash and change. We'd go straight up the pub, or a club. Sometimes it got a bit hairy. Even in the business, we were disliked."

Ray claimed a song on the next album, 'Dandy', was inspired by Michael Caine in *Alfie*, and *Saturday Night And Sunday Morning*'s Arthur Seaton. His affectionate warning about the escalating perils of girls – "three's a crowd, and four you're dead!" – was plainly aimed nearer home. Dave had moved north from 'Spunker's Squalor' to Cockfosters. Really, though, he lived in the Scotch of St. James and Cromwellian clubs, with their mock-baronial swords and suits of armour, discos and 4am licences, and the former's roped-off, raised section for Stones, Kinks and Animals, and the models who hovered round them. "I must go home... I haven't been home for three days," *NME*'s Keith Altham found him mumbling. And it was those women he'd been with, so many, as if he wanted to get to the end of them. *Kink* includes many hilarious and enviable encounters. But he also remembers waking after a drink and purple hearts blackout, to the shame of a beaten, scared girlfriend still next to him in bed.

"Growing up around so many beautiful sisters was important, because I always felt comfortable around women," he says. "But what happened with Susie when I was 15 challenged my whole outlook. I started to see them as sex objects rather than as women who I could share deep passions and sensitivity and being in love with, which me and Susie weren't allowed to express. So I thought, fuck 'em, most of 'em. You get into a really aggressive, macho mind-set. It's such a fine line between anger and sex. My sexuality was anger, arrogance, you will like me, come on. To be fair, women liked me. Because I didn't care if they didn't."

Dave's experiences tumbling through London weren't confined to voraciously fucking women, but men too. Think of how he grew up, even with the guiding hands of his sisters, and his life then can be seen as a great sexual adventure. The heirs of Arthur Seaton, once they'd cracked open class's constraints, made freer, braver spiritual and physical leaps than anyone but themselves had imagined. It was Ray who wrote of being discussed like "the queers at the bus-stop", and whose dad worried about him because his hands were feminine compared with Dave's; Ray who would tease about sexuality in song. But Dave was not only dressed and beautified by women, but loved men with touching openness.

"It was still illegal," he remembers, "and being called The Kinks – people used to come up, [effeminately] 'Do you live up to your name?' 'Well, we might do'. Me and Pete used to have a field day. You look at some of the pictures and the poses – it was such a wind-up. We'd rather be at home watching the Arsenal. But it was important, because I think it helped... sensitivity. The dressing up and the more intimate things didn't bother me. It's still self-expression."

Dave's closest male relationship was with *Ready, Steady, Go!*'s co-presenter Michael Aldred. Aldred had an ill-fated spell sharing

"Spunker's Squalor" with Dave and Avory, violently snapping when Dave tumbled in half a night late with another man, and a romantic meal in the bin. "Dave's main preoccupation is the diverse pursuit of happiness," Aldred wrote in *The Kink Kontroversy*'s liner notes, adding, with attractive perceptiveness: "But he, too, swings between the extremes of frustration, elation and black boredom." "We had a really great relationship," Dave says, "until he caught me going out with some chicks. And I thought, we can do what we like, can't we? He was in love with me. I wasn't in love, but I loved him."

Dave's explorations were shared by the Stones' Brian Jones. "We had, not a menage a trois, but a triad relationship," he says. "Whenever I'd go to Paris to see this girl, Brian had been too. We had a mutual fantasy about being together. We only found out via the girl. And sadly, we left it too late. I had a lot of respect for Brian. He gave the Stones sophistication, he had a unique way of thinking, and a camp, sensitive vibe. A terrible tragedy."*

"If I hadn't had that relationship with Michael," Dave concludes, "I might have wondered if I'd ever been gay. I realised that I wasn't. But I had a very important relationship from it, realising the needs of another man in a totally different way from what I'd grown up with. That really taught me a lot, about how to interact differently with men. But it made me realise how much I adored women. Investigation, innit?"

The investigation almost got out of hand after a Kinks gig in a Rutland village on August 20, 1966, when the promoter, a retired Army type named David Watts, proved considerably friendlier than Torquay's 'Well Respected Man'. As the night wore on, Ray, observing Watts' smitten affection for Dave, took the major aside and offered to sell his brother, if Dave could have his house.

"I just wanted to unload him," Ray explains between smirks. "I thought I was doing the right thing. This chap was so enamoured with him, I thought maybe I'd found him a good home. The poor guy was married at the time too, I think. It was just a joke, really. But there was an element of good thinking there. Go this route, at least look

---

* Jones died in mysterious circumstances on July 3, 1969.

after yourself. See that you're looked after. But, we were drunk. There wasn't a bill of sale..."

"That says such a lot about Ray," laughs Dave. "That feeling of, I don't like him, I don't want him around me, really – but I wanna make sure he's all right. So fuck off, but you've gotta be all right.' He's always been like that. David was a lovely guy, but I was just sending the whole thing up."

'David Watts' on next year's *Something Else...* album, and its hit 1978 version by The Jam, immortalised him. "I have fond memories of David Watts," says Ray. "After the famous encounter, we didn't see that much of him. He turned up at a few gigs. I went up to try and find out where he was, and he'd died. David Watts was one of the Empire's great characters. He went to the opera with Marlene Dietrich. He was one of the great sports. Again, he was the sort of chap who was out of place."

Mostly, Ray observed Dave's adventures from afar. It makes me think of Boris Karloff's elderly scientist in Michael Reeves' 1967 film *The Sorcerers*, who vicariously enjoys Swinging London's youthful sex and violence through a telepathically controlled raver. Ray explored his feelings on the situation in another *Something Else...* song, 'Two Sisters', about a young housewife and her careless sibling. "Dave made up for both of us, he was the youthful, fun-loving one," Ray says. "'Two Sisters' is quite accurate, in the sense that one had all the freedoms – one brother stays in, and the other goes out and has fun. And one resents the other for the ability to do it. But in the end, look what I've got..."

Ray's unfashionable efforts to be a responsible husband and father in a secure suburban home, putting food on the table by writing songs, is admirable. But does he feel he lost out by leaving the sensations of the era to Dave?

"I found my work, and stayed out of all that," he says. "I felt odd when people came up and said, 'Oh, let's go out, man. Let's get... groovy', or whatever they used to say, 'No, I'm all right, actually. I'm fine. You do it, and I'll write about it.' It was more like that. Almost journalistic. And I guess I feel bad that I missed a lot of that. If I had involved myself in any of it, I probably wouldn't be here today. Maybe I shouldn't be... I don't know about that..." He's talking in 2004, on a bad day. He blurs the sentence's potential darkness by completing it. "Maybe I shouldn't have been so guarded and secretive and so... suburban. But not really suburban. My ideas went too far for that."

Ray's symbolic distance from hip sixties London was shown when The Kinks' Pye radio plugger Johnny Wise remarked to Johnny Black about once meeting him for lunch "all the way up to The Spaniards in Hampstead" (barely 15 minutes by tube from the West End). But London came calling when a fashion designer invited to a Christmas 1965 party at Fortis Green sneered at Ray's sweater. With typical Davies pluck, he had a punch-up at his own party. He wrote 'Dedicated Follower Of Fashion' afterwards, fusing this experience with Dave's for The Kinks' next single.

"I was young enough for it to be vengeance," says Ray. "I typed it all out on a typewriter first draft in white hot anger, and I sang exactly those words. 'Dedicated Follower Of Fashion' was meant to be really angry. Luckily it turned out to be funny, because Mick was playing the drums [Avory's supposed ineptness is a regular Ray theme]. There's a wonderful song I keep meaning to finish called 'Don't Talk Down To Me'. You can write those endlessly. But the way to get your own back is to write another successful record. The more beautiful it is the better. That's the real smack in the face."

Dave explained its musical genesis to *Melody Maker*. "We both think George Formby's brilliant in a sort of social way and that's how Ray got the idea – from listening to George Formby records. It's not really a commercial sound – more a social attitude." The single's opening chords were again sitar-like, after which Ray's Framus's ukulele-style strings impersonated Formby's dinky strum. Quaife claimed the frustration of finding that sound made Ray tip a tape-reel on the studio floor and set fire to it. A martial beat drummed the Dedicated Follower and his absurd "Carnabetian army" to the next boutique.

"This doesn't sound like the same group who recorded 'Till The End Of The Day'," *Melody Maker* puzzled on its February 25 release, but "a humorous, jogging, Joe Brown-type semi-comedy... send-up of the fashion-conscious mods." Guest reviewer Pete Townshend was kinder. "Fantastic. I like Ray Davies because he's married and he's still hip." He was more sympathetic too to the song's subjects. "Good luck to 'em. I used to be one myself. Down the East End, they've all got new suits." When asked, Dave drawled: "I don't talk about clothes – I wear them. I'm a dedicated follower of my own fashion."

The *MM* had come around by the time its March 26 cover announced: "Trend-setting with the new 'social observation', The Kinks have the Top 10 sewn up..." The band was steadily evolving, as the satire trialled on 'A Well Respected Man' now targeted the scene 'Where Have All The Good Times Gone?' undercut, and the unhip "ukulele" was, like the "sitar", embraced. But the report ended by noting: "Ray Davies is still in bed with influenza." It was much worse than that.

Like a puppet whose strings have been snipped, Ray returned from a short European tour to collapse at home on March 8. Flu and nervous exhaustion were diagnosed. The pressures he had been under since 'You Really Got Me' were finally too much. They'd been ratcheted up by the poisonous fall-out from The Kinks' decision to sever themselves from Page and Kassner. Page's perceived desertion from America and conflict of interest as both co-manager and co-publisher were mentioned as catalysts. Extremely low royalty rates and Dave being 15 with no legal advice when their parents signed for them added to their case. Writs from Kassner and Page had briefly held up 'Till The End Of The Day''s release, claiming "breach of contract" and "conspiracy". Ray was meanwhile taken by Wace and Collins to sign with Belinda Music's boss Freddy Bienstock in Savile Row, a self-made respected man whose manner and lifestyle Ray deeply admired. His songwriting royalties were put in escrow by a judge till the conflict was resolved. It would be 1970 before he knew if he was free. A demo for a film that was never made, 'All Night Stand', caught his misery: "All these people on my back/ 10% of this and that."

Now he feverishly retreated to Fortis Green, wildly lashing out at family members from his sweat-soaked bed when they tried to help. Dismayed to see himself on TV, he put it in the oven. Was the pressure he put on himself to keep his hit machine turning 24 hours a day the main reason for his breakdown? "I don't know if it was a breakdown," he says. "I went to sleep one day and woke up a week later. I don't know what that is. I went through a lot of emotional problems because the management thing was coming to a head, there were disputes everywhere. It was an awful time in that respect. But you had to keep writing through the angst, which isn't worth it. I pushed myself a lot. I still do. My brain was intelligent enough to say, 'Go to sleep'. Which it did. It gave me a nice rest. I look back on that as a happy time. There's nothing like being ill with a record in the charts. The heat's off, for about five weeks."

In a daffy move that never happened to another major band, The Kinks were meanwhile shipped off to fulfil a week-long tour of France and Belgium, with a vaguely Ray-resembling Muswell Hill mate, Mick Grace, replacing him on guitar and Dave singing, in the hope fans wouldn't notice. "That was worrying," deadpans Avory. "It's difficult when a guy who writes all the stuff, and people know what he looks like, and he sings it all, isn't there. Lots of fans there would go [puzzled French accent]: 'That isn't Ray'. So that wasn't very satisfactory. We did a French television show, and that was a farce. Ray's singing the song on the record and Dave's pretending to be him, and we're miming. They said, 'It's all part of the contract.' Grenville went in the studio with the director and said, 'The boys don't want to do it. We're only here as a gesture.' The director started babbling away in French, and Grenville said [and here Avory adopts a clipped accent, raising an interrogatory eyebrow a bemonocled Terry-Thomas should be beneath] 'I understand every fucking word you're saying, but I won't speak your filthy language. De Gaulle won't speak English, so why the hell should I speak French?'

"That was the difference between Grenville and Robert," he considers, of the two managers now left in charge of them. "Robert was funny because he did upper-class twit things. Grenville was really funny, a hooray Henry sort of bloke who came out with great one-liners. Grenville was about 6' 5", and so was Robert. But where Robert was very thin, everything was big about Grenville. Everyone smoked then. But he'd have a box of cigarettes with hinges on, which he'd open and say [effete Leslie Phillips voice]: 'Hello, would you like a cigarette?' And the box was in a greatcoat with big pockets."

Back in London, Ray deteriorated. On March 17, he ran out of his front door and didn't stop for six miles, till he reached Brian Sommerville's Denmark Street office and tried to punch him. Then, weaving through Soho's alleys escaping police once again trying to arrest a Kink for assault, he hid in Eddie Kassner's office. Kassner was as pleasant as could be expected, till Wace and the doctors spirited their charge back to bed. Funny in retrospect, it sounds a frightening day.

"Total waste of energy when I missed," Ray says. "He ducked, and hit his head on this table. It was a bad shot. But the cops and robbers chase afterwards was worth the price of entry."

How did it feel to be in his head that week? "About the same as it feels now. Pretty strange. I don't know what I was running to or from, in that state. The band was doing a tour without me, and it was during that tour that I think Brian accused me of being a traitor and not getting on with it. The problem was not being able to tell people what's going on in my head. I don't know what was in my head. Total confusion. Artists' care and needs were not taken that seriously in those days. There were no clinics to help you. Well there were. But there were white suits involved. And I was just completely washed out and drained, and tired, and a bumbling fool. The sods don't know they're doing it, but they do treat you like a machine – management, friends, record companies. 'Oh, you can do it', you know. But the old brain says you need a good sleep."

Lennon/McCartney and Jagger/Richards survived the sixties mentally unscathed. But of the great solo writers competing to keep their hit factories running at this fiercely competitive time, with only their own minds to fall back on, Pete Townshend, Brian Wilson and Bob Dylan snapped too. "It's good to have someone to bounce off," Ray accepts. "I did have the band. Dave was always supportive – at that point. I always listened to Dave. But it was all, I think, on me. When they were on tour when I was sick, I didn't realise how important the other three were to me. I didn't have them, and I felt isolated. But at some point someone has to deliver the record. It's like the old saying in *The Hustler*. 'I know you can beat him at pool. But will you?' That's the difference. It's that judgement. I was more tuned in and honed then," he sighs, as if the days of breakdowns were a better time. "It beats you up after a while."

Continuing to write also saved him. "It did let me keep my sanity. I got 'Sunny Afternoon' after that. And a few good songs for the next album – songs like 'Fancy', a little ballad about being misunderstood, in a world where no one can penetrate me and understand me."

"I'm mentally too strong to have a nervous breakdown," he claimed in *Imaginary Man*. "I can pull myself together." Perhaps this depends on your definition. "Ray was full of demons and hobgoblins and what was going on in his head must have been horrible," Quaife remembered to Johnny Black. "I had the guy in my arms crying, several times, trying to explain what he was going through. I think I understood him, which made me quite unique. Eventually, though, he'd always just draw back and go into himself again." In *X-Ray*, Ray calls the collapse "just one of a series of 'mind overloads'", though the first to affect the band. "I admire Syd Barrett for walking away," he said in *Imaginary Man* of Pink Floyd's ex-leader, whose own delicate mind was scrambled by acid and pop pressure, and beat Ray's Denmark Street marathon by making his final retreat from London to the safety of his mum's Cambridge home on foot. "I was on the verge of doing something like that. But by this time I had a young family to support, so I kept on working." There was more to it, a steel stability that came from an inner drive to succeed that the bosom of his Fortis Green family nurtured, but didn't create. "As soon as the gun goes, I don't stop till the finishing tape. It's the way I am. It's the way I trained myself to be." There would be worse collapses in future. But Ray's nearness to his own nerves also made The Kinks' music more fragile and true.

"I couldn't really understand what a nervous breakdown was," Avory concludes. "Because I'm not taken that way. I'm a more basic person than him. But Ray recovered from it, and we went on."

During his "sleep", Ray had grown a drooping Zapata moustache (soon chopped). He had also recuperated musically, he explained in April interviews to announce his return. "My first interest was classical music," he revealed to *Melody Maker*, "and while I've been ill I've been listening a lot to Bach. Other things listened to were Glenn Miller,

Frank Sinatra." Miles Davis's bossa-nova-based *Quiet Nights* (1963) was another touchstone. "It sort of cleaned my mind out and started fresh ideas," he said of this time in bed listening to soft and old music.

The Kinks only played four gigs in April. They were finally being left alone. As a sunny spring began in Fortis Green, Ray wrote songs in the morning, played with Louisa in the long back garden, then lay in a darkened room in the afternoons. The fever of the last 18 months was breaking.

Those new ideas soon came into focus. "I hope England doesn't change," he said, under April *Melody Maker* headline "RAY – THE PATRIOT KINK". "I hope it doesn't get swallowed up by America and Europe. I'm writing a song called 'You Ain't What You Used To Be.'" The Kinks' long abandoned hunting jackets had spoofed the country's image, and they'd taken its suburbia into the charts by echoing Coward and Formby. But this was the first time Ray identified the band with England. Being banned from America ("It must be Our Man Flint after us," he confided to the *MM*) was starting to change him. These English interests would soon deepen, and come to define The Kinks.

Their past meanwhile kept them notorious. In a May *MM* interview, Ray claimed that ever since Cardiff, promoters assumed they were drunk, winking knowingly when the band said they weren't, and cleared valuables from the dressing rooms to stop the band thieving them. "Somebody told me they'd heard Mick Avory was in the Hitler Youth," he said, a bit carried away. "He's from *Molesey*, not *Mosley*. We are all hooked on LSD of course, and Dave is a junkie... and we're supposed to hit women disc jockeys." This reputation as comical, clever thugs was overwhelming their real achievements. Another *MM* feature, "SOUNDMANIA!" listed the sonic innovations sweeping through 1966, the fad for Indian sounds included. 'See My Friends' wasn't mentioned.

The Stones' brilliantly stage-managed bad behaviour had made them such risqué society darlings that even when they were genuinely persecuted in a series of 1967 drug busts, bishops and the editor of *The Times* queued up to praise them. By contrast, the accidentally controversial Kinks, and their inventions in this period, were increasingly ignored. "The Kinks stood aside watching, with sardonic amusement, the pop world chase its own tail," George Melly wrote in his brilliant contemporary history of the scene, *Revolt Into Style*, "and they turned out some of the most quirky intelligent grown-up and totally personal records in the history of British pop. Their trouble (or perhaps their strength...) was their non-conformism, their refusal to join the club. They were and are hugely underrated in consequence." Dave has a blunter view. "There's a thing they say in America – you can't say that because you mean it. Being tongue in cheek was more acceptable than being honest."

The British public still loved them. 'The Taxman's Taken All My Dough' was their next single's first title. "This really follows on from 'Well Respected Man'," Ray told *Melody Maker*'s Bob Dawbarn. "It's the Man after he's lost his money. I wrote it some time ago to pay off some tax." He had the awareness to dodge the solipsism of 'Taxman', George Harrison's response to the returning Labour government's supertax on the rich. Instead, retitled 'Sunny Afternoon', it conjured a comically indolent, roguish aristocrat, languidly resting on the lawn of his requisitioned country house with a cold beer for company. His romantically impractical tax-dodging scheme is to sail over the horizon. Peel away the fictive layers and he's still Ray, sipping that beer in his suburban back garden with the sun warming him, moaning about money with a disarming, crooked smile.

A descending bass-line representing the fallen toff is the hook ("Actually, I play it on guitar, finger style," Quaife told Johnny Black. "Bloody difficult, actually"). Session keyboard player Nicky Hopkins' harmonica-like melodica adds to the verses' comically archaic twenties atmosphere, recalling mansion house parties and a more recent craze. "It's almost trad," Ray said. Listen to it again, though. What makes the record optimistic are Rasa and Dave's most beautiful backing vocals. They come in with Ray's first word, *"ooohs"* like birdsong in blue sky. At the end, they join him singing *"in the summertime"*, Rasa and Dave so high and feminine it sounds like Ray duetting only with his young wife, hoping for a nice day.

'I'm Not Like Everybody Else' was the B-side. Ray offered it to The Animals and others, and finally gave it to Dave to sing. It's a snarling rejection of domesticity and uniformity, an outsider's threatening confession. On an alternate take, Dave sounds close to psychotic, a growling voice you wouldn't want in your ear. It was the polar opposite of 'This Is Where I Belong', as if a side suburban Ray had repressed was rising up.

"'Sunny Afternoon' is the last in a trilogy of numbers which I wrote all at one time," he claimed to *NME*. "The other two were 'Well Respected Man' and 'Dedicated Follower Of Fashion'." The former was written a year earlier, but as Ray was praised for and wrote more socially adept lyrics, a need for themes and statements was also growing. "They didn't get 'Sunny Afternoon'," he says of those around him. "I said please. I was right with 'You Really Got Me' and all the others – just put this out in five weeks, the sun's coming out. Pop music should be an immediate response to the world."

It was released on June 3. Their maligned label believed enough to put them on a breakneck promo schedule to knock The Beatles off number one. On June 30 they were topped, after only two weeks. Their new single 'Paperback Writer' was only a glib, late attempt at Kinks-style satire anyway. Ray had raced past them. On July 30, with 'Sunny Afternoon' still in the charts, England won the World Cup. "I wished that I had a machine-gun, so that I could kill us all and it would stop there," he wrote in *X-Ray*. "But we had to go to Exeter for [a] concert." In Ray's front room, The Kinks stayed gripped till England's extra-time win, then like any engrossed sports fans watched the presentations too, reaching the inaccessible West Country ten minutes before the gig's midnight curfew. "The promoter kicked Ray up the arse," laughs Dave. "We're only ten hours late, what's the matter with you?"

Pete Quaife wasn't there. Even at this new pinnacle disaster struck, coming back from a Morecambe gig as 'Sunny Afternoon' was released. "To get away from The Kinks," Quaife told Johnny Black, "I used to drive with the equipment roadie, Jonah, Pete Jones, who lived next door to Ray and Dave [when they were at Denmark Terrace]. I fell asleep. Then so did he. I woke up when there was this almighty jolt and a crash and I remember thinking, 'Why the hell have we stopped on the motorway?'" They had crashed into a stationary truck, throwing Jones through the windscreen. "I tried to open the door and it fell off. I thought, 'It's not supposed to do that, surely.' Then I realised what had happened. He was pretty badly injured and I had a broken foot and concussion. We both ended up in hospital in Warrington. I've still got the scars." Quaife had begun to feel sidelined by Ray's increasing studio control and perfectionism, and worn out by the band's violence. His friend Jonah's smashed pelvis and horribly battered face haunted him.

"While I was in hospital, I had time to reflect on it all," he said. "Dave and Mick came to see me. Dionne Warwick dropped by as well. But Ray didn't come and I thought, 'You bastard.'" John Dalton, ex-bassist for The Mark Four, replaced Quaife on tour and TV as he sat wounded and brooding. Naturally, one of Dalton's first acts was to be thrown into the clink for the night by an irate promoter in Fascist Spain. Quaife quit the band on September 11, resigning his share from what had become a limited company on September 30.

In November, he unexpectedly returned. In *Kink*, Dave mentions persuading him back with a casual phone call (leaving Dalton to become a coalman). But Quaife's brother David Melville-Quaife, then a 14-year-old living with Pete as he recuperated at their parents' house, remembers things very differently. "The car crash didn't affect him," he says. "It just gave him a month to sit around and think about things. It had started off with them driving in the same van to gigs. And then he used to go on his scooter, when it was local. That was more of an excuse to be away from them afterwards, when everyone was arguing. He'd take me along whenever he could to local gigs, as moral support. And then when it was a long tour, he used to actually get in the equipment van with Pete Jones, and not in the car. And that's when he had the crash.

"It was Ray who persuaded him back. When Ray was speaking to dad, it was almost blackmail – like offering money. It wasn't nice. And my dad being an ordinary London bloke, with his own grocery shop, he could see through people. And Ray actually got thrown out of the house – not physically, but he was told to go. It's difficult for me to say exactly how Ray seemed, because I was a lot younger. But I thought he was a little bit rotten. A little bit threatening. I didn't know exactly the words he'd said, but from Pete's reaction afterwards, I could see he was scared, and a little bit shaky. I really don't know why. But I think that was part and parcel of the breakdown he was starting to have. He was scared of everything." So Quaife came back. But it wasn't the same.

He'd almost finished their fourth album *Face To Face* before he quit, anyway. "I want to link up every track with additional sounds and musical interpolations," Ray had informed *NME*'s Altham in June. "We've got thunderstorm effects, bongos, a metronome, and Mick plays 'Whistling Rufus' on a shepherd's pipe." Avory's vocal debut (like "late Bernard Bresslaw" enthused Ray) on 'Lilacs And Daffodils' was also tantalisingly promised. Waves lapped on the shore before 'Holiday In Waikiki', and Grenville Collins' impossibly posh phone voice began 'Party Line'. But Pye refused Ray's other ambitions. Instead, *Face To Face* was notable for diversity and imaginative arrangements. "With album tracks in those days there was a sense of freedom," Ray explains. "You didn't have to make a two-and-a-half minute success [as with singles]. And maybe we were a little bit freer than we should've been. *Face To Face* is a collection of songs I'd just recorded, rather than an album. Each on its merit. No need to make it bigger than it is."

Top session keyboard man Nicky Hopkins, prominent since *The Kink Kontroversy*, is omnipresent on rippling boogie-woogie piano and harpsichord; 'Session Man''s demolition of hack musicians' attitudes couldn't have been about him. "PSYCHEDELIC – IT'S THE NEW WORD" *Melody Maker* informed its readers around that time, and 'Fancy' was a rare Kinks return to the thick sitar drone 'See My Friends' pioneered. But where George Harrison's similarly trance-like 'Within You Without You' on next year's *Sgt. Pepper* offered egoless nirvana, Ray in meditation mode toughens his shell. The most affecting song, 'Rosie Won't You Please Come Home', was his first about a real relative (other than Dave). He sings in a querulous, elderly parent's voice, pathetically offering to bake her a cake if she'll only return – "your room's clean, and no one's in it." It's a blatant letter to Australia, where Rosie and Terry never wanted to go, crying all the way as they followed Arthur's orders. Her young brothers' plea must have pierced her.

The most remarkable song was 'Rainy Day In June'. Thunder survives to introduce it, rain lashing as Ray peers into his suburban garden and imagines demonic forces at work in the foliage, supernaturally exaggerating the bestial struggles for survival there. 'Too Much On My Mind' survived from his therapeutic songwriting as he'd recovered, a look inside a disintegrating head. "I could have written that 10 years before," he says. "And I could've written it yesterday." 'Little Miss Queen Of Darkness' is, like 'Dandy' and the next single's B-side, 'Big Black Smoke', a Swinging London cautionary tale. Ray had explained his disapproval back in 1964. "The kids are getting to be so unoriginal – they've just become a mass," he told *Melody Maker*. "They think that if they go out and get stoned on Purple Hearts they're part of the scene. I'm not a prude or anything...but..." He twitched at his net curtains, Concerned of Muswell Hill. But the songs were funny and sympathetic, 'Big Black Smoke' especially a modern London folk song, complete with Dave as town crier: the first suggestion the city would be their subject.

Released on October 28, *Face To Face* did much less well than *Well Respected Kinks*, a budget compilation of singles and scraps Pye had knocked out the previous month. It was a pattern the label would repeat, to The Kinks' increasing disgust.

They finished 1966 with 'Dead End Street'. 'Where Have All The Good Times Gone?''s reality check was on the A-side now. It directly described a reality of grinding poverty, cold-water flats and short rations, for people who ironically sing, "We are strictly second-class." "We are moving through a period now that is just like the Depression," Ray told *Melody Maker*. "Every night now there seems to be a documentary on TV about miners." In fact, welfare support was growing and the gap between rich and poor being deliberately narrowed by Harold Wilson's policies. But that was no comfort on the bottom rung 1966's pop cavalcade otherwise forgot.

The pill was sweetened by what Ray called "a rotten sort of trad jazz sound". The lead instrument on the new single from the makers of 'You Really Got Me' was a woozy trombone, allegedly by a pissed session man found in the pub. An earlier version had been "too cold" without it, Ray said. Talmy hadn't wanted to change it, he would later contend. So when Talmy dislocated his shoulder in a freak accident and had to leave the studio, Ray took over. "I think the last thing Shel was involved with was 'Dead End Street'," he claims. "I wasn't happy with the version he did, so we did another overnight. After 'You Really Got Me' we had an understanding with Shel about how the records should sound. But the second album disappointed me. He let some bad double-tracking go. He was probably under pressure. I'm still waiting to do a new vocal on 'Sunny Afternoon'. I don't think the first take quite cut it. You couldn't really tell The Kinks what to do in the studio anyway. As soon as 1-2-3-4 was over, they were playing. There was no mystery to it." Ray included a muddy, tromboneless take on 2008's *Picture Book* box-set to prove his point. He claims Talmy never knew his version had been replaced, which seems hard to believe. Talmy vigorously disputes the whole tale.

What mattered was Ray had decided he had to go. Sommerville had resigned after the attempted assault, Page and Kassner were out in the cold. The paternalistic support group that had been around them since 1964 was being dissolved. "I'd like to own the group," Ray told *Disc & Music Echo*'s Penny Valentine. "I want to run them by myself. There's too many people at the moment." 'Sunny Afternoon''s success had also let Ray finally negotiate better royalties from Pye, and a new US deal with Reprise. Bienstock gave him his own publishing company within Belinda, Davray.

The breakdown which had left him apparently helpless in bed had resulted in a manic burst of assertive strength. It was a pattern he would repeat, as if every collapse or failure had to be compensated for with redoubled zeal, greater control, superhuman activity. He actually seemed to gain power from sickness, hibernating and storing energy when he looked half-dead. He wouldn't be written off. He couldn't stop.

The Kinks made a black-and-white promo film for 'Dead End Street', roaming Kentish Town dressed as undertakers with a corpse that leaps from its coffin. It was meant to substitute for the grind of gig and TV appearances. The BBC thought the film was in bad taste so didn't show it. The single still sailed up the Top 10. It was their third big hit of an eventually golden year.

Mick Avory, Pete Quaife, Dave and Ray Davies strike a pose, publicising The Kinks' second, flop single 'You Still Want Me' in April 1964.

In the red hunting jackets which defined The Kinks' early image, on ITV's *Thank Your Lucky Stars*. Ray's discomfort on stage is clear.
(DAVID REDFERN/REDFERNS)

'Yesterday Man' singer Chris Andrews between Dave and Pete on the *Ready Steady Go!* New Year's Eve special, 1965. (DEZO HOFFMANN/REX FEATURES)

Pete, Dave, Mick and Ray. Ray: "If you think of The Kinks as a little business, Mick was the one who stabilised as best he could, Dave went out to the clubs, Pete Quaife was the PR guy, always very nice to people in the industry. I was the quiet one who did the writing." (BRUCE FLEMING/REX FEATURES)

Mick leaves the safety of home in East Molesey, Surrey, for a wild life on the road with The Kinks. (PICTORIAL PRESS)

Dave with lawyer David Sarch (left), and Grenville Collins, an inexperienced but affectionately remembered co-manager. (MIRRORPIX)

Picture Book. Dave photographs the band, styling themselves by now. Mick wears one of his two identical pairs of black shoes. (GAB ARCHIVE/REDFERNS)

Ray looks appalled as a fan reaches towards him. Sensitive and introverted , he found fame intrusive and debilitating. (LEBRECHT)

Pye Studio No. 2, where most Sixties Kinks music was made. Dave: "I love the partition in the middle. It's symbolic – we're together, but there's a barrier." (LFI)

A pensive Pete Quaife. He became increasingly disillusioned and worn down by the sometimes violent and chaotic nature of life in The Kinks. (CHRIS WALTER/PHOTOFEATURES.COM)

Dave trawled women's clothes shops for the most outrageous clothes he could find. He had his pick of Swinging London's models and actresses.
(PICTORIAL PRESS)

Dedicated followers of fashion. Ray, by now influenced by Noel Coward, perfects his feyly quizzical look. (CHRIS WALTER/PHOTOFEATURES.COM)

Ray was an all-round sportsman at school, and he and Dave skipped gigs to play football or watch Arsenal into the Seventies. Along with music, it bonded the brothers. (PICTORIAL PRESS)

Ray marries Rasa Didzpetris at St. Joseph's Church, Bradford, on December 12 1964. (MIRRORPIX)

Ray and Rasa with their first daughter Louisa, born May 23, 1965 at Alexandra Hospital, Muswell Hill. Ray would try hard to be a good family man. (MIRRORPIX)

Clowning at the airport. For all the carnage, life in The Kinks was sometimes great fun. (MICHAEL OCHS ARCHIVES/CORBIS)

"We knew what to do, just with our body language," Dave says of The Kinks then. "We were like a football team, where you don't have to look up to know where the other player is. I played a lot of football in me younger years, and I played with [Spurs great] Danny Blanchflower [in a Showbiz XI]. He'd say, 'Run', and the ball would land at his feet. It's important that me and Ray used to play football together. You focus on the same thing, and learn those interpretive skills. In those early singles, you plug in your amp and then you plug into the drummer – and 'Oh shit, this is great.' What you're playing is secondary in a sense. You're running on instinct and passion, mixed together like something fibrous. I think if you listen to those records, you can't analyse it, because it wasn't analysed in the first place. They're a phenomenon, really."

CHAPTER 5

Waterloo Sunset

Ray Davies was in Van Morrison's Belfast flat when he first heard the record which dominated the Summer of Love. *Sgt. Pepper's Lonely Hearts Club Band* indicated a turning tide towards mystic whimsy and psychedelic rock. It was joined by radical debuts including *The Velvet Underground And Nico*, Pink Floyd's *Piper At The Gates Of Dawn* and *The Doors*. The hip singles which chimed were Procol Harum's 'Whiter Shade Of Pale' and The Beatles' 'All You Need Is Love'. The new rock mainstream was drifting away from The Kinks. The hippie counter-culture bloomed around them on both sides of the Atlantic, with the hope of upending the straight world, and, in the US, avoiding conscription into Vietnam's bloody jungles. Their own personal counter-culture in 1967 fought for Fortis Green's verities; restorative cups of tea after a hard day, not LSD to unpick its existence. "I didn't listen to it all," Ray says breezily of The Beatles' magnum opus. "I was just passing through. It was all right. I knew I'd put out the best song of the year, so it didn't matter to me."

Sgt. Pepper sounds like a brilliant sonic artefact now. The Kinks' greatest song, 'Waterloo Sunset', is a spell cast every time you press play, drop a stylus, or hear a snatch of it on a radio as you wait in a shop. It has made millions contemplatively pause around Waterloo, a busy urban area to which it has given a sacred glow. The place already had that resonance for Ray. Previous Kinks singles had moved from roaring teen desire to satires about others. Personal feelings more complex than being in love had been tucked onto B-sides and albums. Though only he knew it, 'Waterloo Sunset' drew on Ray's past, spilling fragile memories.

Even if you don't quite grasp the lyrics, you catch the narrator's condition. He is a lonely, wounded animal who doesn't dare leave his room, scared by the restless flow of the Thames and the crowds "swarming like flies" around Waterloo tube. Even the cold spring air is too much. So he contents himself with watching the young lovers Terry and Julie, and the beauty of the sunset from his window. "And I don't feel afraid," he sings, staring at and holding onto the view of his "paradise". The comfort the record finds for this understated pain is one reason hearing it can feel like healing.

"I didn't think to make it about Waterloo, initially," Ray says. "It came to me as being not the death knell, but a statement about Merseybeat. But I realised the place was so very significant in my life, and it's always best to write about what you know. It's not nostalgia for me. It came from good and bad feelings. I was in St. Thomas's Hospital when I was really ill [when he had his tracheotomy aged 13], and the nurses would wheel me out on the balcony to look at the river. I used to go to Waterloo every day to go to college as well. It was also about being taken down to the Festival of Britain with my mum and dad. My dad took me by the hand and said something very poignant. I said, 'What does this mean?' He said, 'This is the future.' It was a fifties version of what the future was. I seem to recall they had a very strange tower."

The Skylon tower did give the 1951 Festival, which would later grow into the concrete canyons of the South Bank Centre, a science-fiction edge. There's a short film made at the time, Derek York's *Festival*, in which a working-class kid playing with his mates on a bomb-site gets one of the free tickets the Festival's organisers floated over London inside balloons. He has a tiring day cheekily cadging food and rides, before returning home to be thumped by his mum. It was revived for a 2010 screening at the South Bank's National Film Theatre, in a compilation of shorts called *Bow Bells And Waterloo Sunsets* (though every film predates the song). In the black-and-white footage, the concrete South Bank is almost unrecognisable as it gleams with possibility. Ray's dad didn't imagine it.

"I've thought about it a lot," he continues. "It's also about the two characters in the song, and the aspirations of my sisters' generation before me, who grew up during the Second World War and didn't have all the advantages I had growing up in the sixties. I used their character. It's about the world I wanted them to have. That, and then walking by the Thames with my first wife, and all the dreams that we had. Her in her brown suede coat that she wore, that was stolen." He laughs quietly. "And sometimes when you're writing and you're really on good form, you get into that frame of mind and you think, I can relate to any of these things. That's when you know it's something good."

"Everything was right for it," he said in a TV interview at the time which seems to describe a visionary state. "If I stopped writing, I went out, and I went past buildings that reminded me of the song. Everything happened. I saw rivers and things. And I had to do it."

"I've got a sense of researching myself," he says now. "It's my way of dealing with emotional content. Maybe it's something I learned through art school. Rather than absorb all the ideas, let them flow out, and some sort of sense comes out of it. It's certainly the case with that song. 'Waterloo Sunset' works on many levels of memory, but not consciously. It's a subconscious thing at work, on a level that none of us know about. That comes through in the record, that's what people pick up on. But if you listen to the words without the music, it's a different thing entirely. People go on about the song – I love the song, I always loved it the first time I played it and finished it. But no-one else in the world knows what that was like. So why talk about it? It's the record, actually, and being able to make it myself. And I took care, because I knew what I had."

The Kinks have strong, sometimes diverging memories of making their delicate masterpiece. "It was just in a chord state, at first," Ray says. "I remember I bought a little mini-grand piano, and I wrote it on that. What was missing was the sound, the arrangement. I probably didn't play it to Dave till we were in the studio."

"Ray introduced us to it the front room in Fortis Green," says Avory. "That's where we heard all his songs. He played it on the piano, and we'd get the general tempo, and a feel for it. Dave thought of a riff, then I played the rhythm in semi-quavers on a high-hat to accompany the intro – dang-danga-dang-danga-dang. Then when it goes into the song, you do the right thing together. You have to be careful with songs like that. They're not bashed-out rock'n'roll. They're quite subtle. Anything that stands out too much takes away from the mood. But at the time we were working quite well together, and it fitted into place quite easily. Everyone thought about their own part, conscious of what the others were doing. That's the way we did things then. We mixed more socially, so we were closer together as people."

"How things used to work," says Dave, "was that Ray often got ideas sitting around the upright piano he had, like the one in my mum's front room. Often Rasa would be there too, and we'd exchange ideas. I think a similar thing happened with 'Waterloo Sunset'. Pete was there, too. The first time I heard it, it was a verse and a chorus. The first verse was the important one." In Dave's memory, everyone chipped in devotedly. "It was Pete who came up with the 'sha-la-la' bit. I think the descending bass-line was his too. Apart from the vocal lines and the guitar riff at the beginning, I think the arrangement evolved from playing it. It was Ray's song, of course. But we were all so in love with its atmosphere that every embellishment contributed to the outcome. That unity of spirit is very important to songs like that. The Kinks had that then, without question. When we got in a room with each other, we were charged with ideas. It was an unconditional, inspiring creative situation. Me and Ray were very close. When Rasa and Pete were with us, there was a great bonding. We all loved each other."

Shel Talmy maintains this was the last Kinks single he produced. "I think the last thing Shel was involved with was 'Dead End Street'," demurs Ray. "I think his getting credit was more to do with his deal with the record company [no producer is named on the single's label]. 'Waterloo Sunset' was mine, I think. Alan MacKenzie engineered it for me. Those staff guys at Pye contributed a lot, because they knew what The Kinks wanted. They knew where to put the compressors."

"Shel was a vibe person," Dave says. "But I don't think he really understood what we were doing. Ray was protecting his song from getting damaged by him, like it was his child." Avory agrees. "'Dead End Street' didn't really work with Shel's style of recording. He over-produced it. On the more subtle things he wasn't so good. Ray took over after that."

"Visually, I knew exactly what I wanted it to sound like," the former art student says of his first production. "It's like the singer Laura Nyro said: 'I can draw what I want something to sound like.' Sound and images work together. It works on that level for me. The song has a lot of emotional depth to it, and I wanted the sound to echo that depth. That's why I took care." The days when whole albums would be done in three days were suddenly gone. The song drew out Ray's perfectionism.

"I did the back-track over the course of two or three sessions," he continues. "I did it in Pye No. 2, a smaller studio, while making an album. I did it on the end of sessions. I said, 'Let's go back to that, and do the next bit', and gradually built it up. I tried it out at the beginning with Nicky Hopkins on keyboards, and it felt too professional. So I put it down with bass, one of those old Fender acoustic guitars, drums, and piano I played. I kept it as a band track. I think it's one of the last real band's tracks we did. All the effects went down as we recorded it. Then I went on a separate day and put Dave's guitar down. That was a rarity for us then. It went down first usually with the back-track, because it was a guitar-driven band. But I wanted a certain part. It's one record where Dave really sat down and we worked together as a team, and he played what I wanted him to play."

"We were looking for a sound for the guitar line," Dave says, "and Alan MacKenzie came up with this fifties idea – that Elvis echo, with a triplet tape delay. It was a lovely feeling of liberation, hearing that echo on my guitar. Something big, inside a little idea. That Danson guitar playing one note at the beginning is the glue that holds it together, like when football managers talk about a side's spine. When you've got that backbone, you've got a chance. I love the counterpoint, where the bass and my guitar go down as the song rises. It's like tunes I loved as a kid, that went up and down like snakes and ladders – it's sad, but you know it's going to erupt into something good. The way Bert Weedon would dampen off the string at the bridge, getting that little plucking noise, Chet Atkins too – we combined all those things. In situations like that, where you don't have a lot of time, you draw on everything you've learned. And my mum and my sister and Uncle Frank are in it too.

"It didn't have a bridge, at first. I added that inspired by the shifts in Frankie Valli & The Four Seasons, those fifties pop songs. 'Waterloo Sunset' was derived from an earlier time musically, with bits of the fifties – that 'sha-la-la'. Inspirations from our childhood, in current metaphors for what was happening in 1967."

A third session began with Dave, Rasa and Pete recording ethereal backing vocals. "I've been doing it with a choir recently," says Ray, "and a lot of the ideas in my head were choir-like." Dave remembers his closeness to those he sang with, neither of whom he's seen in years, or will again. "Rasa was a great Mamas and Papas fan, and always fancied herself as a singer, and she was good. We just sang along. It was very organic. It would be lovely to be able to work like that now. I was a great fan of Jo Stafford. My sister Dolly had a lot of her records, and I used to listen with my mouth open. She had that lovely, soft tone I admired. Having Rasa there, that female vibe, softens the attitude of the song. It makes it warmer."

Then Ray added his backing vocal. That just left his lead vocal, and lyrics he hadn't shown a soul. All the music had been made without anyone else having a clue what they were playing was about. It was so personal, he was frightened they would laugh. "A lot of the time after that," Avory says, "he'd just play the chords on the piano so the boys could learn them. Even if the words were completed, he'd rather keep it to himself. It wasn't ideal. But because we had empathy, we could do it."

"The song was all written out in longhand, there were no bits to fill in," Ray says. In *X-Ray* he remembers polishing those lyrics obsessively at home, till they were "like a pebble which had been rounded off by the sea... perfectly smooth." "They didn't hear my lead vocal until the very last moment," he confirms. "I felt very precious about it, because I really didn't want to rewrite this. I had it all set in my head. It was all definite."

"When I first heard it I thought it was about some pervert in his mac having a wank!" Dave jokes of the lyrics' voyeuristic perspective and sad claim that "I don't need no friends", which so clearly describes teenage Ray in his hospital bed, and perhaps Fortis Green's adult outsider. "No... it's a song about isolation and detachment, and not wanting to be a part of the world. That was often a sub-plot with The Kinks. Because as a band we never really fitted in. It's that feeling we had in a lot of our stuff, that it's them and us. It wasn't just Ray's observations. It was us looking outside at a harsh world, and trying to pick out the bits of it that were beautiful and inspiring. Because a lot of it was ugly and frightening. The warmth of the record comes from our empathy with the characters and the music, and the friendship we had with each other. A lot of the feeling I get from listening to it is of safety. I felt very safe in the music, and in the picture Ray was trying to paint. That what's happening outside isn't as important as what's happening inside us, when we're together."

"I could've written it now," says Ray. "It's the detachment from the person singing it – the subject matter – that I find interesting. I'm on the outside of the narrator's experience. Identifiable, but in the distance. I'm not the focal point. I wasn't aware I was doing that. It is a voyeuristic lyric. But it's not about a seedy voyeur looking out of his window. He just knows that what he's looking at is an idyllic situation, and he won't be able to fit into it. So he's staying away."

Terry and Julie cross the Thames to "paradise" in the last verse. What does Ray think is waiting for them there? "It's like one of those Cartier-Bresson pictures," he says. "You see the two people and that's their love caught for eternity. Regardless of what happens to them later in their life, that's the moment they were in love and it exists forever. 'Waterloo Sunset''s like that."

"It's a song about two people going on a journey to a better world," he told Radio 2's Johnnie Walker, on a darker day, "but for some reason

I stayed where I was and became the observer. I did not cross the river, they did, and had a good life, apparently."

"When you are born south or north of the Thames, there's a totally different feeling on the other side," Dave says, of lyrics which could just be about north Londoners getting home. "It's a border, a change, crossing bridges and water – going over to the other side. It's a wonderful moment that you can't really analyse. The Thames does things to you, especially when you've lived in London your whole life."

"It paints a picture of a journey he used to make," says Avory. "And it's a scene that everyone sees when they walk across Waterloo Bridge. Lots of people have said to me they always think of that song when they do." The simple beauty of that low, tree-lined view across the river, with St. Pauls to the right and Parliament to the left, is universally loved by Londoners. It's hard to know now if 'Waterloo Sunset' enhances how we feel, or helped create it. Born in 1967, I've never looked without hearing the song. "How you feel about the view," Ray advises, "depends whether you're going to jump off the bridge."

The identity of the two young lovers crossing the river is one of the sixties' piquant, enduring mysteries. Terry and Julie were thought to be Terence Stamp and Julie Christie, glamorous young stars together that year in *Far From The Madding Crowd*. Ray says Terry was his cousin, of course. Dave thinks the song's secret code is even more personal. "I've always thought Ray meant him and Rasa. Ray's never been very good at emotional things. He projects them onto characters in songs."

Does Ray think so many people respond to the record partly because it draws from such a deep well of his emotions and memories?

"I think so. I don't remember my emotion as I wrote it. I didn't feel that precious as I did. Because the lyrics were fine, they did the job. Looking back now, they could be better, I use the same rhyme a couple of times. But I guess it's the way you tell 'em. It's like putting together a jigsaw puzzle. Because the record had faults, sonic issues. The vocal isn't mixed very high, it peaks through, you can just hear the words trickle out. Even the bass is quite pulled back. It's all very delicately played. Nice touch playing from Avory. Because Avory was a wrist player, the old-fashioned way of playing drums. People forget that element, on this and 'Sunny Afternoon'. It's ambient-sounding, and minimalist. It all fits together. It exceeds the sum of its parts."

'Waterloo Sunset' was finished on April 13. "I still remember pulling the fader down for the fade-out, and just getting that right," Ray says. "In those days engineers wouldn't let you touch anything. Alan let me. It was the first one I could actually have my hands on. We still have the masters somewhere. I'd like to get the tape out and see what I'd do now. Probably stick it in ProTools and give it more beef. But that would have totally destroyed it.

"Because," he concludes, "that record does something else. It triggers people's imaginations, as well as what they're actually hearing from the gramophone or radio. It puts people into a world. Like most things that have been around for a long time, it sounds commonplace and inevitable now. I was there when it was played back the first time, and it sounded like nothing like it had ever been done. Now I think of it, 'Waterloo Sunset' was all in the air," he says, suggesting the visionary again, "waiting for someone to put it together. Whereas 'Days', for instance, all came from me."

Ray was still reluctant to let it be heard. In *X-Ray*, he claims he considered not releasing it at all. "It was very personal," he says. "I still get a personal feeling from it. But once it goes out there, it's everybody's." Instead, he took an acetate home, and for a few days pretended he had made it for his family's private pleasure. Its first audience comprised niece Jackie and Rose, who was visiting from Australia and spent every second she could with Ray.

"That time playing it at home to my sister was magical," he says. "They said... nothing! Jackie was quite a critic – she still is very critical of what I do. But it's when they say nothing they think it's a really great record. I think they were moved. I know Rose liked it."

It was released on May 5, as spring turned to summer. It was held at number two by Sandie Shaw's banal Eurovision Song Contest winner 'Puppet On A String', The Tremeloes' bland 'Silence Is Golden' and, signalling the change the summer would bring, The Beatles' 'All You Need Is Love'. In America it didn't chart, and remains largely unknown.

The ban was finally killing them. "Maybe they did us a favour," says Dave. "Because the music turned a corner."

"It's the best record you'll ever make," *Disc & Music Echo*'s perceptive singles reviewer Penny Valentine rang Ray to tell him, and it was. He has re-recorded it twice. On *The Kinks Choral Collection* (2009), it's the song that's least changed by the addition of the Crouch End Festival Chorus, though even this local north London choir sound too professional compared with Rasa's innocent keenness. On *See My Friends* (2010), Ray is joined by Jackson Browne, proving it can survive on its acoustic guitars and harmonies.

His only substantial postscript is his short story 'Waterloo Sunset', in the eponymous 1997 collection. Here, petty crook and painter Fox, dying of cancer, eyes so sick the view from his window has an Impressionist blur, discovers he is a character in a story, and wanders along the Strand and Embankment in a sort of death-dream. He crosses Waterloo Bridge and then starts back, lingering at a spot by the river where he is told people stand to watch their whole lives flow by. The river stops, a flash freezes him inside the song's imagery, and he's freed. "You'll capture the picture in your own imagination, and there'll be a space in it for you," he's told by a man waiting futilely at a bar for "the man who wrote 'Waterloo Sunset'", who will not cross the river. More prosaically, Fox was first nicked when the song came on the radio and distracted him in his get-away car. The policeman whistles it as he puts on the cuffs.

That's just how the record works. A friend of mine remembers being unhappily back in London in the early nineties after years abroad, feeling lonely and different. Walking past the old County Hall, she looked up-river and wished she lived there. The London air was turning into the song's "chilly, chilly" early spring, and as she saw Waterloo Bridge she sang it in her head. At that moment, a hip, different-looking courier cyclist, an unusual sight then, passed her whistling it too. It was the first time she felt there were people in the city with whom she might connect; that you could be different but understood, like the characters in the kind song. When a boyfriend around then gave her flowers from the stall where he worked at Waterloo Station, she thought of Terry and Julie.

That's the everyday impact of this beautiful London folk song and pop record. You might get something like it from a Beatles song, but not from the Stones or The Who. It's why The Kinks are loved.

"It's not a question of being loved," Ray says. "I just knew, within the terms of what I was doing, that I couldn't have made it better. I'm not saying it changed the musical landscape of the world. But in the world that I inhabit, it did all the right things. It's a very innocent record. I'm proud of that. You can't beat innocence."

CHAPTER 6

The End of the Golden Age

"I had achieved everything I set out to do creatively and I was 22 years old," Ray wrote in *X-Ray* of the spring when 'Waterloo Sunset' took The Kinks to their high water mark. His prodigious near-peer Peter Cook had reached the same dizzy peak aged 28 in 1965, with Broadway, the West End, nightclubs and television at his feet. It left Cook bored, drinking and idling his way through his final 29 years on the embers of his satiric genius. Ray responded by rejecting the previous standards of The Kinks' success. The rest of his career would be a sometimes extreme over-reaction to the early pressures and shoddy deals they had been victim to. He determined to take complete control, and write entirely personal songs which weren't intended to be hits. This made the next two years a period of almost fatal disaster, which the band wouldn't wholly survive.

Not much seemed wrong as, to general astonishment, Dave's first solo single, 'Death Of A Clown', raced past 'Waterloo Sunset' into the Top 10. Early in 1967, Dave had had a moment of unpleasant clarity in the wrecked aftermath of yet another party. The hedonism suddenly seemed hollow, surrounding him with strangers' pasted-on smiles, all of them expecting 'Dave the Rave' to do something outrageous. He was brooding on this first comedown from his sixties high the next day, when his sometime Copenhagen sweetheart Lisbet told him she was pregnant. In a distanced frame of mind, he guessed he might want to marry this girl he loved and settle down. The wedding happened secretly in April in the small town hall in Fredericksburg, Denmark, with no other Davies present. Dave bought a house in Cockfosters, ten minutes up the road from his family. Quaife secretly married Lisbet's pregnant cousin Biden Paustian around the same time.

Dave was sitting in his mum's front room a bit later, feeling inadequate and out of balance, disappointed with his life. It was a still morning in Fortis Green's backwater, made for reflection. Playing the battered brown piano on which 'You Really Got Me' had been written three years before, he picked out a "silly, simple tune", he remembered dismissively in *Kink*, and phrases poured into his head. 'Death Of A Clown' was how he felt about himself, a chastisement to live differently. The parties and omnivorous sex hardly slowed. But Dave finished a Dylanesque lyric of carnival surrealism, with a trainer frantically searching for his runaway fleas and lions who have impotently lost their roar surrounding a sad, drunken clown.

Dave's direct tune and gruff voice were matched by The Kinks' rough acoustic treatment in the studio, with Nicky Hopkins' barrelhouse piano, and Ray singing in the background like a boozy hick. Though Dave said at the time that "Ray wrote it", according to both brothers' books all Ray added was a wordless, short bridge, and the striking intro, picking out the tune with the glistening, harp-like treated sound of the strings inside the studio Steinway. Unlike Dave, who gave similar service countless times, Ray got a co-writer's credit.

"We thought it was just a little song we could stick on an album," Dave told Johnny Black. "I was a little bit depressed at the time and Robert [Wace] in his smooth way said, 'Maybe we should put this out as a single. Ray says he really likes it.' Robert would tell me things Ray had said that Ray wouldn't tell me himself. He would tell me the positive things."

Released under Dave's name on July 5, it hit number three, joining 'Waterloo Sunset' as one of the songs of 1967. Though he was seizing control of The Kinks' career, Ray didn't yet know which direction to take it. In May he'd publicly contemplated following Brian Wilson's example in sending the band on the road while he stayed in the studio, announced he was working on a solo LP and planned to "exploit" Dave more. He kept talking about leaving The Kinks, wondering what more they could do. The lure of films, theatre and panto (an unlikely dream since the previous year) distracted him. "Once you've had a number one record you can only repeat yourself," he'd told *NME*'s Keith Altham that December. "You go on *Top Of The Pops* and stand there and sing the song. We wanted a challenge – something different – which is why we did the 'Dead End Street' film." To *Disc & Music Echo*'s Penny Valentine, he listed more specific dreams. "I write a song and think how much nicer it would be to make a three-minute film of it instead, to show people what I really mean. I want to make a proper film, anyway. They keep offering me the chance to make film music, but I'm not Benjamin Britten or anything. And... I really want to do *everything* myself. To have my own idea, film it, write the score, produce, star..." His song 'Groovy Movies' was part-satire, part-fantasy: "Sometimes I think I want to better myself/...Sometimes I think I won't make it playing in a rock'n'roll band/ Sometimes I want to be a big-shot director and try to make the world understand/ By making groovy movies..." But he couldn't just quit. "I'm worried about Dave," he told Altham. "I might leave the group, but I want Dave to be financially and emotionally secure first."

Dave's solo success seemed an opportunity to send the younger, prettier brother out to be the pop star, lifting the commercial pressure Ray had started to resent from his writing. For a moment, a different future seemed to present itself: a rebalancing of power, allowing Ray and Dave artistic liberty and happiness.

All Dave really enjoyed of his solo career, though, was the gold-braided coat he wore on *Top Of The Pops*. "I always liked Charles II's clothes," he says, "because they were so elegant. Robert introduced me to a theatrical costumiers, [Monty] Berman's. And directly I saw that Charles II look with the bell-shaped three-quarter length coat, I fell in love with it. Because they'd carried that on in the Edwardian period, they had those lovely three-quarter length drapes that the Teddy Boys copied to a certain extent. My uncles were Teds, they were everywhere round Muswell Hill. Flick-knives, and a fag hanging out of the mouth, jiving to bebop, boogie and trad jazz, I used to love all that style. And then I just walked into Berman's, and saw this coat. Oh, it was a beautiful style. I tried to buy it, but they wouldn't sell it. I had other things similar that were made to look like it, but it was never the same. You put something like that on and it's snug, and you take on a persona straight away." Dave the dandy had his eyes and eyebrows darkened with make-up too. He seemed a more obvious and natural star than Ray.

But this unexpected, almost accidental solo career confused The Kinks (who played on this and subsequent "solo" tracks) and made Dave sick and unhappy. He cancelled TV shows at short notice, withdrawing from the single's success. Two more of his songs joined 'Death Of A Clown' on September's *Something Else By The Kinks* album. 'Love Me Till The Sun Shines' seems a plea for an unconditional but loving one-night stand, Hopkins' organ adding a Stax-goes-down-the-Cromwellian air. 'Funny Face' is more mysterious. Aggressive guitar blasts alternate with sepulchral reverence. Whether it's a wedding or funeral service isn't clear, as Dave sings with soprano purity: "I see you, peering through frosted windows/ Eyes don't smile, all they do is cry". Something's wrong and doctors are involved, for a girl or a baby, which Dave is locked out from, as if in a bad dream. His much delayed second single, 'Susannah's Still Alive', told everything to those who knew him. It was about an ageing spinster, drinking and dreaming of a young boy she'd die without seeing again. Now he'd tapped into his subconscious to write more than occasionally, Dave's lost life with Sue and their daughter pounded to the surface. The frosted glass in 'Funny Face' is the kitchen window of Sue's family which he'd tried to glimpse her through when they were torn apart in 1962. 'Love Me Till The Sun Shines' begs a ghost girl who's already gone. He sings, "Oh, Susannah's still alive..." desperately.

"That's because those feelings were never really resolved," he says. "As an adult, I still carried them. It's a sad story, really."

Does he agree that, just as Rene dying when Ray was 13 is the wound he carried through his Kinks career, the loss of Sue when Dave was 15 is his?

"Yeah. Rene had a big impact on me too. But with Sue it was life-long feelings that I suppressed, and had great difficulty coming to terms with. And I had a child that I never saw. In later years, I found out that my mum used to see Sue in private, and that infuriated me. I remember once she showed me a picture that she had kept from one of her secret meetings with Sue, of [their daughter] Tracy when she was six."

And of course he'd have wanted to be in that room?

"I was just so angry," he says quietly, tired and exasperated. "It's like I never came to terms with that. When I first got married, I had four boys, and Lisbet always thought she would have a girl. She knew in the back of both of our minds that I was having a problem."

The girl you should have had?

"Yeah. It was a big deal."

'Susannah's Still Alive', as direct and rambunctious as 'Death Of A Clown' despite its secret subject matter, was released on November 24 and reached number 21. 'Lincoln County', an even more infectious and upbeat country tune, followed nearly a year later on August 30, 1968, and flopped. The idea of Dave as a solo star and second front for The Kinks in the charts had already died. Desultory efforts were made towards an album into early 1969, before being quietly dropped. The tantalising results were scattered across B-sides and compilations. A last single, that January's 'Hold My Hand', might as well not have been released. Sent to Germany to back a glimmer of chart action on a TV show, Dave's performance, stupefied by strong hash and the draining effects of a prostitute's industrious blow-job in his dressing room, typified the sorry tale. In *Kink*, he blames an insultingly cramped studio booked by Pye for his cold feet at going alone. But the man who would later feel his self-expression being crushed by Ray felt lost when it was offered. Barely out of his teens, he let the chance slip through his hands.

"When I felt the record company pressuring me to make an album, I felt the naturalness of what I was doing was being lost," he says. "I thought, ''Ang on. It all seemed so easy up to this point. Now they're demanding that I do something...' I'd pick up a guitar and I couldn't do it. 'Write a song.' 'What do you mean, write a song deliberately?' Ray honed his craft around learning how to write about things like a brief. But that took time. And I didn't like working like that. I wanted it all to be natural and instant and spontaneous. I felt right up to that point everything we did flowed right – the songs, the parties, the people you met. That first three or four years was like being characters in a hit musical. And making an album was daunting, because being pressured meant it didn't feel genuine. Sometimes I felt terrible. Some of the songs that came out of those album demos, like 'Crying', 'Do You Wish To Be A Man?', are all symbolic of feeling: 'Oh, fuckin' 'ell, I don't want to grow up. I don't want to do this when I don't really want to.'"

Did he not want the responsibility of songwriting and a solo career because of the adult life it might lead to?

"Maybe you're right. And also, growing up in a big family, I found the band was like an extended family – working with Ray, and Pete was like a brother, and then the audience loved you and you loved them back, so that was like a new family as well. I'd been lifted out of the group as a focal point. After a while I preferred it to be a group. It felt more comfortable to me. Because being in The Kinks was just like being at home. And I had such fabulous feelings about growing up there."

Meanwhile, The Kinks had finished 1967 in apparent triumph. *Something Else By The Kinks*, released September 15, was now bolstered by two massive hits, 'Waterloo Sunset' and 'Death Of A Clown'. Ray was also finding his writing's real subjects, again avoiding a Summer of Love irrelevant to everyone he knew. 'Lazy Old Sun' toyed with the fashionable psychedelic style, with tabla-style drums and celestial harmonies. But it was prosaically cosmic, simply looking at the sun in wonder. Like the three songs on *Face To Face* about property worries ('Most Exclusive Residence For Sale', 'A House In The Country' and 'Sunny Afternoon'), songs such as 'Two Sisters' and 'Situation Vacant', about a newly married man who loses everything chasing his mother-in-law's aspirations, had adult concerns. Dave's slow, short riffs shadowed the tunes, crucial but no longer central. Only Ray's sly parody of their Rutland friend 'David Watts', the "gay and fancy free" golden schoolboy the girls want but somehow can't get, sounded like the sharp pop Kinks of '66.

Something Else is a genteel album, about civilised, ordinary pursuits spread across the classes. It sounds inconsequential, but becomes quietly profound. The last time I listened to it, my favourite song wasn't 'Waterloo Sunset' but 'Harry Rag'. Named for the rhyming slang for fags, it's about the restorative pleasure of cigarettes. The caved-in old woman wheezing her last who "curses herself for the life she's led, and rolls herself a harry rag and puts herself to bed" and the bloke having a smoke with the last penny left by the Revenue ("Bless you, taxman!") lead the defiant gaspers. Ray's vivid enjoyment of foolish indulgence climaxes irresistibly: "Ahh, the smart young ladies of the land, can't relax without a harry in their hand", with which "they boast and brag, so content because they've got a harry rag". You can picture them puffing, fags between fingers, pointing and darting into mouths as they hold forth. Ray sounds like a rustic, confiding folk singer, and the band play a music-hall knees-up, except that's too grand; they could be down the Clissold. "Eng-land!" squeaks Dave on the fade-out, still giddy with the World Cup. America and its R&B sounded more than an ocean away as they sang. When someone yelled for it at a 2010 gig, Ray happily busked 'Harry Rag' at the Royal Festival Hall.

'Tin Soldier Man' could be about a boy parading toy soldiers up the street, or civil servants marching to work in the morning, and either way feels like the sunlit, thinly populated and untroubled city street of a fifties children's book. 'End Of The Season' is a twenties-style cut-glass-voiced complaint from a cricketer adrift in gentlemen's clubs that have lost their sheen "now that Labour's in"; and most of all because his girl's far away on a yacht in Greece. 'Afternoon Tea' sounds like Ray himself, still sitting at the cafe where he met a girl who went away. The details are tiny, the words wistfully, archaically polite: "You take milk, if you please/ I like you talking to me because you ease my mind." 'Waterloo Sunset''s B-side, 'Act Nice And Gentle', had pleaded for "some civility". *Something Else*'s miniatures create a gracious but endangered world. Ray's kind words can't make her stay.

""All for peace and quiet's sake"" Ray murmurs happily, quoting 'Situation Vacant'. "Nicky Hopkins was on keyboards. I like the dynamic on that record, he let it build. It is a funny album. I remember a good friend of mine asked, 'What's the new album called?'" He gives an offhand shrug. "'Something else.' No pretension, but I like that. Another one…"

Its sales were disappointing, scraping in at 35. A couple of months later, a second random Pye compilation of As, Bs and EP tracks, *Sunny Afternoon*, made number nine. About a quarter of a million already owned 'Waterloo Sunset', and weren't encouraged by Pye to think of The Kinks as the new, *Sgt. Pepper*-led phenomenon, an albums band. They were becoming outmoded. Ray's frustrated reaction was quietly building steam. Still, October brought yet another massive hit, making their status as one of Britain's biggest bands seem secure.

Shel Talmy, who'd worked on some of *Something Else*, was gone, contract lapsed, or at a negotiated end. "I enjoyed picking and recording excellent songs," he emails me of his time with them. "But my experiences with the band – except Pete, the only one I was close to – and their handlers during and after recording was less than stellar." Ever since, Ray and Dave have downplayed Talmy's importance to a sound which changed deeply and immediately in character without him. But in 1971 Ray, never really wanting anyone to leave, once he'd got rid of them, told *Melody Maker*: "I would like Shel Talmy to produce us, because I really enjoyed working with him."

The first Kinks single officially produced by Ray, 'Autumn Almanac', was deceptively ambitious. Its intro of acoustic guitar and biscuit-box drums is followed by eight discrete yet flowing phases, in three minutes. "It's got lots of little facets," Ray agrees, "it's like a little play. I like that song because it's story blocks that all seem to fit together. That's a nice bit of work. It's comfortable, it feels good, and I've got through it. That's the best part of writing songs. It's like jewel-making. When I was in art college, I wanted to be a good craftsman, and it's great to build a song like a little box. I was experimenting with backward tapes, and the melody in the beginning reverses in the middle. It's called mirroring, but I didn't know that."

'Autumn Almanac' is also Ray's ultimate if ambiguous tribute to 87 Fortis Green. As he's often recounted, it was inspired by his hunchbacked gardener Charlie, of whom he'd been frightened as a child.

His contentedly mundane expressions – "Better get the leaves up" – as he raked Ray's lawn now seemed enviably wise. So 'Autumn Almanac' begins as a dawn overture to his dewy hedge and the insects inside it, pausing to again praise tea and cakes in hymnal tones and, in a pop first, bemoan his chronic bad back. Having set hits in the English summer and "chilly" spring, he relishes the crunch of leaves now summer's "all gawn". But the song then keeps going, as ordinary Ray adopts a nasal voice to list unbreakable weekly rituals of Saturday football, Sunday roasts and summer holidays in Blackpool. Avory pounds like cutlery-clutching fists on the table demanding dinner and a trombone's brass announces Blackpool. Then it fanfares a quite different verse, as Ray praises "my street" (the song's original title), which he says he'll never leave. That proud promise darkens in implication as he explains, "All the people I meet/ Seem to come from my street/ And I can't get away/ Because it's calling me..." Drums and siren voices get louder, coaxing him back to his suburban heaven. "Yes," he keeps saying as the song fades out, insisting he means his pact with conformity. But like a desperate cry for help scrawled by a hostage on a window, the suggestion remains that he's trapped by a community he can't get away from, as if in some science-fiction nightmare.

'I'm Not Like Everybody Else', Ray had written. Now, after another year in his dream home, he desperately wanted to believe that he was. He was trying to fall back into the ordinary life he'd grown up in. Subsequent songs such as 'Uncle Son' also deeply admire real people he knew and their values. But while he was too much one of them to be a rock star, he was also too different to truly belong, or want to. 'Autumn Almanac' was his failed, heartfelt effort to be normal.

"I'd like to have no brain," Ray says, "and not have the hunger to do this, and be ordinary. I think I'd like to be part of a community. I'd like not to want any better, to be happy with my lot, and say, 'That's great, I've achieved a lot in this limited little bubble I live in. And... here's my Autumn Almanac.' 'I'm Not Like Everybody Else' is somebody who's aware he's in that suburban bubble – but at the same time, they will not beat me. They will not stifle me, I will still have a voice. It's not total rebellion. It's maybe realising that to be accepted you have to stifle that voice a bit, and not speak up. It is a terrible inner conflict. I do long to be the ordinary guy, and I applaud the ordinariness of the world, and the trivia. I love that. But maybe I'm not trivial enough."

'Autumn Almanac' got to number three. But even now as his band seemed at a new peak, worries nagged at Ray. "I remember doing 'Autumn Almanac' on *Top Of The Pops*," he says, "and thinking to myself, 'I'm too old to do this.'" He was 23. "Because I was tired. I wanted to do more interesting things. I loved the song. I just felt that pop hadn't moved on. You had more underground music, and the West Coast explosion in America [where bands such as The Grateful Dead were making San Francisco's Haight-Ashbury district rock's new epicentre, overflowing with teenage drop-outs and drugs]. The next phase was coming, and I was getting itchy feet with pop in Britain. And the ban on going anywhere near the States, which I can't emphasise too much, was kicking in and eating away at us. My only regret was that we couldn't be out there to show what we could do live. A lot of it in '67 and '68 was who could get out there and tour, and make the impact. And it was in the hands of bands like the Stones, and Cream and Jimi Hendrix and The Who, who were coming back megastars. You think, 'Aw, these people are doing really well.' And I thought, 'I don't think it's ever going to be any different for us.' So we're stuck here. We had the rest of the world. But it was not America. I was worried that we'd get left in this weird English place."

1968 then dismantled all the success they'd had. On January 12, *Live At The Kelvin Hall*, a recording of a Glasgow gig from April 1 the previous year, was belatedly released after being out, and ignored, in the US and Europe in August. It was already a time capsule of a lost pop age, as Glaswegian girls scream indiscriminately through Ray's game try at 'A Well Respected Man', portraying the weird anomaly of a band playing increasingly thoughtful material during a hormonal rite. The girls lustily roar "I've got a big fat mama trying to break me!" for Ray during 'Sunny Afternoon' while Dave howls through 'Milk Cow Blues', in a near-nine minute R&B medley with 'Tired Of Waiting For You' and the *Batman* theme, and tries out a nicely lazy blues solo on 'You Really Got Me'. The screams don't sound like the elevating hysteria of *The*

Beatles At The Hollywood Bowl, released as even more of a relic (though a holy one, because it was them) a decade later. Though quick overdubs were probably done, it stands as surely deliberate reportage from Ray (the "Musical Director") on the roughly played, chaotic appeal of a typical Kinks show when they were teenage pin-ups. Finding it in a second-hand record rack in Essex in the dog days of 1975, Charles Shaar Murray gave an even more belated and amused rave review of the "classic white punk singing" and "out-of-tune collapse-ending" of "a great documentary album, a great *what-goes-on* album". In 1968 it sounded, and made The Kinks seem, ridiculous.

Worse, there was no modern live experience to compare it to. Between December 1967 and April 1968, The Kinks played four gigs. The contrast with the heedlessly shattering schedule they were forced through by management in 1964 and 1965 was deliberate. After Ray's 1966 breakdown, and his careful removal of all the people who had told The Kinks what to do, what he now chose was to sit at home and write. Then, refusing the rushed recordings of the Talmy/*Kinda Kinks* years, he sat in the studio with the band, for as long as it took.

The friends he respected as peers now weren't other pop stars, but Ned Sherrin, the urbane writer-producer behind *That Was The Week That Was*, and Ray's old art school teacher, TV face of 1966 and *Private Eye* columnist Barry Fantoni (for whom Ray wrote a flop single, 'Little Man In A Little Box'). His only public work in the first months of 1968 was a weekly topical song he wrote inspired by the pages of *The Hornsey Journal*, to be sung by Jeannie Lamb on the BBC satirical show *At The Eleventh Hour*. He was living the quiet, creative life of the respectable songwriter Sherrin saw him as. He was also laying the foundations for what started as his long-promised solo album, but by 1968 had become a Kinks task. An unreleased 1966 recording, 'Village Green', and Dylan Thomas's poetic play about a rustic idyll, *Under Milk Wood*, were said to be the inspirations. And in between, on Saturday and Sunday mornings, Ray and Dave played football in the park. As Dave has said, except for special moments making music, this was where they were closest. The tradition continued into the Seventies. If Arsenal were at home, they spent Saturday afternoons watching them. Playing another bunch of gigs around Britain bored them. They cancelled far more dates than they played, and whole foreign tours, with contemptuously little notice. After they bailed out of an Australasian tour with Dave Dee Dozy Beaky Mick & Tich (unpromising enough, in the sixties peak year of angry Western revolution), Arthur Howes also left them. They had always liked the booking agent. Howes taking them on, they said in their first interviews, was their big break. But there was nothing more he could do for them. They couldn't be bothered with the mechanics of being successful.

While The Kinks sat around bemoaning the damage the ban was doing to their American careers, they were carelessly demolishing their standing at home. Beneath 1967's calm surface of hits, promoters and fans had enough of being let down. Dave didn't help when, quizzed by *Disc & Music Echo*'s Bob Farmer on their serial no-shows, he mentioned "football matches" as a factor. Wace later admitted he had to beg new booking agent Harold Davison (who seconded them to Barry Dickens) to take them on.

Before that, they found themselves on a twice-nightly April package tour with new teen stars The Herd and The Tremeloes, amongst others. It was an ignominious return to the now anachronistic kind of pile 'em high bills they'd played with The Dave Clark Five, four years before. *Disc & Music Echo* watched them at a quarter-full Walthamstow Granada with sympathetic dismay. There hadn't been many girls still really weeping and screaming at pop acts when they'd played the Kelvin Hall in 1967. The last few tired yells came here, and mostly at The Herd's handsome new star, Peter Frampton. The reviewer noted Ray's boredom and forced smile and that the band, not untypically, were "instrumentally rather dire". At least "Dave was very chuffed to be working again." The short, hit-packed, sometimes inept show hadn't changed since their suddenly gone glory days. As the tour dragged on, they realised how far and fast they'd let themselves fall. "The worst thing about that period," Ray claims, "was our suits. They weren't even velvet, but felt – pink, blue, green, all different colours. They looked awful. And they were really expensive."

They also had to play with the sinking certainty of their first flop single since 'Everybody's Gonna Be Happy', three years before. 'Wonderboy', out on April 5 a day before the tour started, was very different from that rhythmic experiment. A seemingly casual, rushed choice as the follow-up to 'Autumn Almanac', it's unlike anything else by the band.

In *X-Ray*, Ray says he wrote it after his marriage to Rasa showed its first cracks, and he conducted a chaste, on one occasion impotent, near-affair with an ex-Royal Film School teacher called Georgie, to whom he confided all his fantasies of cinematic and poetic success, and shared drunken, hopeless kisses. In its aftermath, he and Rasa (not knowing his secret longings) were trying for a second child. Downing a bottle of vodka one night after she had gone to bed, Ray decided he wanted a boy, and wrote 'Wonderboy' to his imaginary son. The song was a "parting gift" to Georgie, and a "cry for help" from a man not knowing if he was "sane" as he wrote it. If the story is true, the alcohol may explain its uniquely tongue-tied and inarticulate optimism. He's trying to say that two loving people looking at each other can be as meaningful as anything, that life is what you magically make it, not a solid thing of "work and plunder". But his strangely squeezed, thin voice on record doesn't sound quite serious, and half the harmonies too verge on parodic. He is trying to say, and believe, more than he can. "Life is lonely," he repeatedly concedes, as its stumbling, disjointed end fades out. "It's not a song, it's a vision," he said much later. It's the fascinating sound of him reaching out for and falling short of one, a sloppy grope towards something supernal. Putting it out as a single showed how confused he was.

Ray and Rasa had a girl they named Victoria that Christmas. The record sold pitifully, reaching number 37. In his favourite restaurant down the Kings Road, Aretusa, John Lennon reputedly demanded it was played over and over. What he heard in its strangely moving grooves, we'll never know.

"It did well, 'Wonderboy'," Ray says. "It reached the peak of what I expected it to. A creative person should be allowed to fail. It was a comparative failure."

"It's a great record," Dave says loyally. The thought that he might soon be reduced to the life on the railways his mum had feared for him, as their success fell away, didn't faze him. "I don't know why it didn't bother me, but it didn't. Because I thought the record was really great. So maybe we know something they don't know. I must admit, I had such a great faith in Ray's writing ability that I thought so long as we were OK, it was all going to be OK. If I could go up the pub and have a pint with me dad and talk about football, and have a game of shove ha'penny with his mates, I felt like everything was all right."

It might sound like working-class nostalgia now, but that's exactly how Dave spent afternoons in Fortis Green. His old playground of Carnaby Street boutiques was less forgiving. "Come back when you have a hit record," he remembers one owner telling him, when he tried to take some coats on credit. "I went there three months before and it was, 'Oh, try this on, oh, take it, don't worry about it,'" Dave says. "He wanted to see it on TV, you see. How crappy and superficial people are. It was surprising. But still amusing."

Avory, too, was worried. "It was so reliant on Ray writing the right number," he says. "We felt we'd missed out in America. And then if you're not making hits in England, you feel like it's waning. You don't quite know where you're going to go."

Other old certainties were falling from The Kinks. With Rasa pregnant (from around the time 'Wonderboy' was written), Ray decided to sell the dream home where he'd had almost all his success. Ignoring the wisdom of several of his songs, he arranged to buy a most exclusive, mock Tudor estate in Borehamwood, Hertfordshire – a county just north of London popular with commuting professionals. Two of his sisters had told him he should move somewhere suiting his status, he later said.

Quaife's disaffection was also returning. In January he'd played with a cast on his wrist, after yet another explosion of violence. The music press were told he had fallen at home. "It was Dave," says Quaife's brother David. "It was quite bad actually. He came up from behind and hit him with objects. I know that Pete put his arm up to protect himself and he got hit by something, I don't know what it was. It was the face first of all. He was in the hospital for a week. He said to everybody, being the nice bloke he was in those days, that he fell off his scooter. That was a goddamn lie, because it was me driving the scooter around then."

In June, Quaife deliberately missed the plane to an Irish gig, twice. He walked straight through the plane as the others boarded then, having been picked up from his north London home by Rasa, stopped her from driving him to the next flight in time. It was a form of passive resistance.

In May, as Ray worked The Kinks remorselessly to make their next single sound the way he heard it in his head, Quaife had made his disgust plain. Ray and Dave both remember him scrawling 'Daze' on the empty tape box awaiting that song, parodying its real name.

"I was drawing this little man," was Quaife's version, quoted by Doug Hinman. "Ray kept me in the studio so damn long I was beginning to lose my mind." To Johnny Black he added: "I remember trying to stay awake making 'Well Respected Man'. It was so boring [even then]. I had no input whatsoever. If I said anything I was ignored. I know I'm not as good as Ray Davies, but I am a creative person and I do have ideas." The perfectionist studio control Ray had fought so hard to grasp, and the lack of anything else for his band to do as their live work died, was breaking The Kinks.

In retrospect, he saw that as the subject of their last big hit of the sixties. Dave had the opposite reaction. "I remember when I heard Ray start playing 'Days' round the piano, I was really full of emotion," he says. "'This is great. We've got to do the bridge, the harmony.' It made me feel like it didn't matter if anybody didn't like it, because we were together."

The record begins with crashes of acoustic guitar and shivered cymbals, a sudden sound like waking up from a dream. Ray's failed, sad affair was still in his mind as he sang, "Thank you for the days." His voice, which "trickled out" on 'Waterloo Sunset', murmurs at first. But as he sings his life's been stolen by a fleeting love, the music gains galloping urgency, and his voice firms with hurt feeling. A minute into this miraculous hymn for loss, Ray hits that emotion's hard wall: "I wish today could be tomorrow/ The night is dark, it just brings sorrow/ Let it wait." He tosses the last line away, angrily denying time's cruel course. He won't willingly let go of his final moments with someone he loved. He won't hurry to be alone in the world. Then for the rest of 'Days', he gives in. The Kinks' playing opens like a sunburst, really celebrating and thanking what's gone. "Believe me", he keeps saying as he claims he's not frightened, and finally you do. There is a catch in this song waiting to hook anyone experiencing loss, and help them. It applies to an affair's end, or deeper despair. But finally, 'Days' feels triumphant. Ray drags the memories with him out into the sunlight, saying that through this, nothing is lost.

To Nicky Hopkins' biographer Julian Dawson, Ray wrote: "It has that strange emotion to it; it was obvious I was saying goodbye, not only to a house, but to a way of life, a time, an inspiration; Nicky's part [on piano and Mellotron] gave 'Days' a mysterious religious quality, without being sentimental." To me, he chooses this meaning: "'Days' is a retrospective point of view, which it could be argued is saying, 'That period is ending'. What I was really saying is that what I first felt when 'Autumn Almanac' was coming to pass. The Swinging Sixties were over. There was a TV producer called Johnny Stewart who did *Top Of The Pops*. And he put us on the last *Top Of The Pops* of that decade and insisted that we sang 'Days', because he felt it was an anthem for the end of an era. So I wasn't alone in the way I felt. By then the game was up for England, as far as music was concerned. America had taken the industry back. And that wonderful period of fertility from '63 with The Beatles emerging to '66 with 'Sunny Afternoon' was coming to an end – the great pop golden era. As a movement, as a period, that was the magic time."

'Days' was released on June 28. It got to number 12 and stuck around for months, arresting their free fall. Ray's *NME* confidante Keith Altham reported: "The current hit pleases him quite greatly because it proves The Kinks could come back after a dud single like 'Wonderboy', of which he says: 'It should never have been released. I didn't want it released. We did it as a favour to someone!'" He'd said much the same after 'Ev'rybody's Gonna Be Happy'.

The same day the single came out, another entanglement was removed. At Westminster's Court of Appeal, Denmark Productions Ltd. v Boscobel Productions Ltd. was finally resolved. An initial ruling by Judge Widgery the previous June against Denmark's attempt to cling on to The Kinks was reversed in technicalities, but not effect.

The case was full of telling and sometimes hilarious detail, as Lord Justices Winn, Harman and Salmon and the two parties' QCs took a dim view of the band's haphazard affairs. Among the "numerous hangers-on" required by pop groups, Harman explained in dryly relating their history, "in December, 1963, they came under the notice of one Wace, himself only about 21" and, with Collins, "anxious to manage pop artistes. Neither of them knew the first thing about how to conduct such an activity." This was why they placed 10% of their steep 40% management fee from the band's earnings to Page, who "in the early days anyhow, [did] the lion's share of the promotion activities"; Wace and Collins busied themselves with "the book-keeping". When the contracts were signed, "none of The Kinks was of age".

The contracts between The Kinks and Boscobel [Wace and Collins] and Boscobel and Denmark [Page and silent partner Kassner] on February 12 and 26 1964 were "lamentably clumsy", Hinn chided. But in the latter's vital clause 6, Harman quoted, Boscobel "assign to [Denmark] all their rights of placing any and all" Kink-written music. "Mr. Page and Mr. Kassner set great store by clause (6)," he said with meaning. "It was not directly profitable to [Denmark] but enabled them through Mr. Page to channel all the compositions of Raymond Davies through the Kassner publishing organisation which was what Mr. Kassner wanted since it was a source of great profit to him... Mr. Page said that without that right 10 per cent commission would have been unacceptable." In other words, management was a means to get the publishing. "The Kinks were a great success; their earnings rocketed from nothing to £90,000 per annum" subsequent to which, they were still being paid £40 a week – "... and it was significant that Mr. Page's remuneration for that activity [from Kassner] was largely increased in August, 1964 [when 'You Really Got Me' was a hit]." Co-manager Page's interest in placing publishing was, Boscobel's side complained, a "secret commission" unknown to the band.

Harman moved on to the cataclysmic tour of America. Quoting the findings of the original judge, Widgery, he brought out significant facts: "Kassner, in particular, was in favour of the venture because it would enhance his publishing profits." Page, meanwhile, "was anxious to go...

having possibly in his mind that he might pick up other business there; that was in fact what he did, as he was entitled to do... It was agreed between him and [Wace and Collins] after some discussion that he, rather than they or some nominee of theirs, should perform this most important task." Wace and Collins, it transpired, had argued for the tour manager for the previous Australasian trip. The band would only go with Page.

"Things did not go at all smoothly and the tour was afterwards described by Mr. Page in a trade paper as having been a disaster, but," Harman sunnily concluded, "[Judge Widgery]'s impression was that on the whole it did not go too badly."

Page's subsequent leaving of The Kinks in LA without telling Ray was the crucial moment. "He gave as his reason that that would only produce an outburst of temperament by that young man... the whole group held an indignation meeting on the airfield." Widgery had "found that Mr. Page left for some private reason which he had not revealed."

Judge Widgery had originally ruled that this abandonment amounted to "frustration" of Denmark's contract with the band, so terminating it. Denmark's QCs, Alan Campbell and Michael Kempster, colourfully scoffed: "[Denmark] would never have contracted on the basis that their entitlement to their earnings could be jeopardised by the temperamental whims of a teenage dance-band." Boscobel's QCs Robin Dunn and Andrew Bateson reached the opposite conclusion from the same unimpressed character assessment: "If a man is put in charge of temperamental artistes who have enormous earning power but who know little of the world and are still immature infants, he is not entitled just to walk out on them without giving any reason."

Winn concluded that the "clumsy" contracts of 1964 meant there had never been a direct bond between the band and Denmark, only an expectation from the latter that The Kinks "would continue to accept" their subcontracted management position. "Once he had destroyed the confidence formerly reposed in him by The Kinks [by leaving them in LA]," Winn concluded, "Larry Page was no less disabled from performing the contract... than if he had... died."

Though Denmark's appeal was allowed, they gained only a few more dusty days of their 10%, which was to be paid on The Kinks' gross earnings between June 30 and September 14, 1965. Boscobel paid half the very large court costs (£10,000 just on the initial trial). Both sides' appeals to the House of Lords were rejected on October 9, 1968. Ray's object when he stood seething on that LA airfield three years before, wanting rid of Page who, it was said several times in court, he'd developed a "hatred" for, had finally been achieved.

Little else had been. This was a draining and revealing legal sideshow to the real business which had attached itself to The Kinks' music, as was clearly recognised by the Lord Justices.

"I gather... from what [Denmark Q.C.] Mr. Campbell has said," Salmon noted, "that the plaintiffs are not very interested in the 10 per cent, or in... damages either. What really concerns them is (a) the right which they allege they acquired under their agreement to place all songs and lyrics written by The Kinks, and (b) the injunction by which they seek to enforce that right." No court would do so, as those rights had since late 1965 been granted to Belinda, later renamed Carlin. "I can understand the anxiety of Mr. Kassner on this score," Salmon nevertheless continued. "He is one of the two shareholders in [Denmark]. His American music-publishing corporation might have made large profits out of Ray Davies's songs and lyrics." Harman concurred that placing Ray's songs was "the prime object of Kassner", though Denmark's case couldn't help him.

Kassner's separate claim to continue as Ray's publisher carried on remorselessly till 1970. It was a continuing drag on Ray's mental resources and mood. His songwriting royalties since the start of the dispute remained out of his reach. He had not yet been paid a penny for 'Waterloo Sunset' or 'Sunny Afternoon', and wasn't sure he ever would be. His discomfort in the posh, cunning world of courtrooms where the murky showbiz deals of Denmark Street had led him scarred his subsequent attitude to deal- and money-making. He'd later write an album excoriating everyone involved, and the whole music business's tainting grubbiness, snapping off the hand that half-fed him.

But Ray's own conduct, as brought out in the trial, bore some examination. The Kinks had signed "a contract with us on much the same lines as the last," Boscobel had told Denmark on September 14,

1965. So Page's removal hardly improved the onerous management percentage on all their work. However, Harman said, of that 40%, "in [Ray's] favour at a later date [after February 1964] royalties on his compositions were released from the scope of the agreement." At an early stage, he had ensured that his earnings as chief songwriter, already the most potentially valuable part of The Kinks' career, would be even greater compared to his bandmates, still presumably paying 40% on all their work. It would of course take a broad view from a young man to see this as unfair.

The question of whether The Kinks still had a career remained open. The Herd package tour was just the first indignity. They had spent the fortnight before the release of 'Days' playing Swedish "folk parks" – not the open-air rock festivals they'd pictured, but funfairs through which kids wandered licking lollies. In *Kink*, Dave remembered wondering if this was how it would end. 'Days'' success (still a steep drop from the previous year) changed little. Though no one knew it, it marked the end of their golden run of hits. They'd never recover from this year in Britain. And they hadn't yet sunk to the bottom. In October, the creators of 'You Really Got Me' were booked into the cabaret circuit of Durham's working-men's clubs. They played as respectable working-class men uninterested in rock came from upstairs casinos to sit and eat their chips.

"It was panicky management, and we changed our agent, and they sent us to play clubs up north – Stockton-on-Tees and places like that," says Ray. "We played so loud scampi and chips rattled on the plates. It was... not degrading. But I thought, 'There's got to be something better than this.' I didn't cope very well. Thank God we had to do two different shows at two different places at night. Because I'd never have got through it. I didn't sleep very well. I never have been a good sleeper. I was raring to go in a new direction, and these people thought in their limited point of view, let's get as much out of the old direction as we can, before it dries up."

"He went through a very strange space at that time," says Dave. "It was like a singles machine, The Kinks: 'Write another one. Go on, just one more...' I think the album we were making that year was the first time we actually did something we wanted to."

"Some people thought we were on our way out," Ray admits. "It was a 'gathering storm and coming through it' period. They wanted us to keep the singles coming, which would have been death. That's why I stopped it. That's why I did the albums that followed. The first run of singles was a wonderful time, and I wouldn't have changed it for the world. If I don't have anything else in my career, I've got that, and I'm really proud of it still. But it became an albatross in the sense that you become typecast. I felt it was time to shift my writing from pop singles, and do something bigger, with more depth. To trigger off thoughts in people, so it's something intuitive, and more than just what's on the plastic."

And so The Kinks disappeared into the Village Green.

CHAPTER 7

God Save the Kinks

"Maybe it's an artistic death wish to put something out like that," Ray says of *The Kinks Are The Village Green Preservation Society*, the album almost no one heard but which now defines his band. "It was a culmination of all these years of being banned from America. I wanted to do something English. As I've said, I somehow thought our music came from nowhere, and didn't have influences from America, and there was also lots of music hall and classical standards and English music in The Kinks. With *Village Green*, I wanted to write something that, if we didn't get another chance to be a mainstream, contesting band, if we were never heard of again, this is where we came from. This is what we like, and who we are.

"I think the innocence was beginning to be corroded, and swept away," he says of his emotional terrain when he wrote it. "That was evident. The record was a belligerent stand against all the things I felt were eroding me. Every good band has a time where they sit back and think about what their future's going to be, and make a crossroads record. Wilco did it a few years ago with *Yankee Hotel Foxtrot* – a record nobody wanted, least of all their label, which went on to be their most successful. *The Village Green Preservation Society* was a bunch of songs that I put together where I didn't care about the commercial outcome. I just wanted to write about the stupid things that I liked. My competitive edge wasn't burned out. I repressed it. I was angry. I said, 'I'm deliberately not going to be successful this time.' I'm going to write about what I like. It was a final stand."

It had begun as Ray's lone stand, and first solo album (there wouldn't be one of those for another 38 years). "That was because I wasn't sure if they would come along with me," he says. "The band were a hard band with a cutting edge, inspired by R&B. And I came in with songs which related to none of that. But after the first few tracks, it became a band record."

"I'm glad we went in that direction," says Dave. "It's such a turning point in our career. Because all the things we aspired to were driven by American music. When you really listen to 'You Really Got Me', although it sounds unique, you can sense The Ventures in there somewhere. But with *Village Green*, we had to turn in on ourselves, because we couldn't go to America. And it makes you look at what you've got around you. It was an introverted look from Ray's point of view. And from mine, it was a digging in, with feelings of love and support and passion that built a foundation for Ray's writing. He toyed with it being a solo record, but we were stronger doing it together. He was going through a lot of torment at the time, and without people there to help and support you, sometimes you get tired. But then, without the breakdown he had in 1966 and the other pressures he was under, he might not have thought of anything like *Village Green*."

The album marked out the territory where The Kinks would make their stand. You can flip open the pages of the *London A-Z* and trace your finger over the woods and greens in N2 and N10 which form the physical Village. Listen to 'Village Green', the song the album grew from, and its church and steeple and Sunday school will come vividly into your mind if you walk down a lane between Fortis Green and East Finchley tube station, and pass a church primary school which feels so peaceful and secluded, London melts away.

The record was really born in 87 Fortis Green, in rehearsals in Ray's cosy back room, with his garden stretching out behind. Most of the songs grew organically there through late 1967 and 1968 ('Village

124

Green' went back to November 1966). "We started to rehearse a bit more and work things out with *Village Green*," Avory remembers. "You'd think of an idea, and: 'Ray, he likes that.' You feel a bit lifted. So we had a little hand in arranging the stuff. When we used to rehearse there in the back room, it wasn't like the same set-up we had on stage. I had a little bass drum thing, and it was all fairly quiet, low-key. You could hear each other better. The band would jam there, and he'd record everything and think, 'They seem to play that kind of groove well together' and pick bits out and work it into the song. Because he was always working on songs. He probably had a theme of what he was going to write about. But it could be manoeuvred around as far as the music went. And it proved a better thing to do. Because you were more together, and when you went in the studio you knew what you were doing more. Rather than say, 'Here's a song, make the best of it, because the time's running out.'"

Quaife too tended to remember the album's making as an interlude of creative peace. "Either Ray was not feeling too well or he was very tired, maybe it was the court case," he pondered to Andy Miller in Miller's book about the album. "But all of us managed to get in ideas and put them over and do them, which was amazing. During rehearsal *and* recording. Just for that little period he lightened up a lot."

"In a way I feel I've left the business," Ray had told Keith Altham at the end of 1966, and as the album came together in batches of unhurried recording sessions at Pye, the band barely bothering to go into the wider world and play live, letting their commercial fortunes ebb till they could hardly return, this became almost true. Ray's songs were fragile barricades round his mind, trying to keep out everything that was disturbing it. The deft imaginative harmony of the music they made conjured a place of safety, with tremors of danger.

The album's initial centrepiece, 'Village Green', was inspired by Dylan Thomas's evocation of a day in a rustic Welsh idyll, *Under Milk Wood*, and Ray's disgruntlement on noting the modern metal casks his ale was being pumped from in a Devon pub. Nicky Hopkins' harpsichord gives a cod-mediaeval mood to its tale of a young man who leaves the village green to be famous and, regretfully nostalgic for its clean air, simple people and his youthful love for Daisy, foolishly goes home again, to find her upwardly mobile and married with his old rival Tom, the grocer's boy now in charge of the expanded grocery. The village's old-world charms have become a tourist attraction for camera-clicking Americans. Undaunted, he still dreams of talking with Daisy about the Green they remember.

Though the album includes a song called 'Animal Farm', 'Village Green', as Andy Miller has also noted, strongly evokes another Orwell novel, *Coming Up For Air* (1939). In it George Bowling, a 45-year-old insurance salesman, is overwhelmed with dismay at his fading married life in West Bletchley, a once rural, built-over suburb, and by London's rush hour, the Americanised modernity of a milk bar and its ersatz wares, radios that keep playing the same song and a country being concreted over; his complaints could be Ray's, his eroded suburbia, Fortis Green. In a drunken reverie, he slips back to the time he was happiest, aged seven in his Oxfordshire home village at the start of the Boer War, when everything in England started to go wrong. Orwell makes you smell and taste this arcadia where in memory it is always summer, places you deep in its "sleepy dusty hush", makes you ache for this simpler England we all think was just before our time. Like the Green in Ray's village there is a centre to this imaginative landscape, a secret pond with a giant fish, a place of wonder watched with the afternoon-long intensity of a child. George half-knows this is delusion as he falls into it. Still he goes back to the real village, and has his memories trampled by its sordid reality, hardly made worse by World War Two's nearing shadow. Ray's midlife crisis came when he was 20 years younger than George, of course.

The ambiguity of Orwell's clear-eyed satire of cosy English dreams is betrayed by the deep feeling with which he conjures them. Ray maintains this realistic edge, but out of personal need goes much deeper into his remembered bolthole. The short distance this will get him in reality is shown in the second song, 'Do You Remember Walter'. Thinking of meeting an old friend who at school had shared his plans to "fight the world so we'd be free", he knows that now they'd have nothing to say. "People often change/ but memories of people remain," he comforts himself, as he does in 'Days' (meant for but left off the album). The gap time can open in a life also chills 'Picture Book', which catches both the jauntiness of family days out, and how unreachable photos' "memories" eventually leave those "days when you were happy/ A long time ago." A seasick sway of piano, bass and tambourine reinforces Ray's horror of photos in 'People Take Pictures Of Each Other', because "you can't picture love that you took from me." He's soon queasily begging: "Don't show me no more, please..."

One of the simplest songs, 'Sitting By The Riverside', has its balmy picture of Ray drinking wine with his girl darkened by hysterical hurdy-gurdy keyboard swirls speeding out of control, then stopping as if nothing happened. Ray asks to "please" keep him "pacified" so he can shut his eyes, nature's lapping river a tranquiliser keeping bad dreams down. The chugging, harmonica-powered blues, 'Last Of The Steam-Powered Trains' is by my count the only rock song to declare "I live in a museum, so I'm OK". 'Animal Farm' offers a stronger refuge, a country shack where people and wildlife live simply, and Ray and his girl can make that last stand, against a half-mad world built to kill dreams. His singing shows his relish for the fight. But 'Big Sky' portrays the indifferent cosmos looming over the Village. Its God-like figure is briskly unsympathetic to the screaming children he looks down on, because he's depressed and "dead inside". There's more comfort in 'Phenomenal Cat', which begins with an irresistibly impish tune on a flute like the start of a cartoon, and lures you into a fairy-tale world of unlikely wisdom, decorated with Goons-like helium, nonsense voices. 'Wicked Annabella''s phased guitar feedback sounds like a normal 1968 rock nightmare, but it's a cackled fairy tale about a witch waking demons in the woods.

"You asked once," says Ray, "if I was ever youthful – maybe this is the youth I thought I missed. 'Do You Remember Walter' was directly inspired by a close friend of mine who met me once I'd had success, and we didn't really know each other any more. So there are elements of reality. But the Village Green itself could be the youth that I wish I'd had, after which I would have been something else. Probably it's saying goodbye to youth, as well – that I'm a grown-up person now, and these are my childish thoughts about steam-powered trains, and playing cricket in the thunder and rain – what it was like, before I forget about it. Before I lose my memory. The record's about childhood, really. Lost childhood, but also just being a kid, and the naiveté. Being naive was something I found I needed to touch upon again."

The Village Green also seems a mythic home for Ray, like the Black Hills longed for in the later *Muswell Hillbillies*. "That's a thing I've always been searching for," he says. "I've never been pinned down to a home. I've always been on tour in a sense. I've never unpacked. The grass is always greener on the other side." Though he's thinking mostly of his later life, in 1968 he was preparing for an unhappy uprooting to a mansion in Borehamwood, where the record's last few songs were written. "It was somewhere I could actually say, when you lose everything else, when the world's got too much for you, at least close your eyes and think of this. Everybody's got their own personal Village Green, that's my theory. To some people it might be a hobby, or a band that they like. I had nothing to really inspire me except my own work. So I looked to my own work to find a refuge."

The Kinks Are The Village Green Presevation Society is arguably the first rock concept album; a Ray-written equivalent to something like Sinatra's uniformly melancholy *Only The Lonely* a decade before. "It's not a storyline, it's an emotional thread," Ray confirms. It's all the better for the looseness of a concept which allows in the sly 'Starstruck', his fourth cautionary tale about a party girl (swiftly following 'Wonderboy' B-side 'Polly'), with the cocky twist that she's starstruck by him.

The song that drags everything together into a triumphant shape it wouldn't otherwise have is 'The Village Green Preservation Society'. It's an anthem to endangered English experience, to the small details of life that get lost, that no one official will ever miss. It's The Kinks turning themselves from the R&B punks of four years before into a scrappy National Trust for the preservation of Desperate Dan, draught beer and strawberry jam, small shops and variety. Donald Duck is equally part of an English childhood, while the moving wish to save brave George Cross winners shows this isn't just childish business. The epic, evocatively parochial lists it encouraged in later oddball English rock writers did the same, as with Lawrence of Denim's inclusion of the IRA's deadly Birmingham pub bombings in his otherwise kitsch seventies reverie 'The Osmonds' (1992). It's the opposite to England's official, imperialist anthem. 'The Village Green Preservation Society' is an almost hopeless resistance song, against remorseless forces called progress that don't care how we feel, or that we might like something that's in profit's way. It's against office blocks and skyscrapers, but it isn't only reactionary. "Preserving the old ways from being abused/ Protecting the new ways for me and you," goes the chorus. The next line is sung with a realistic shrug: "What more can we do?" And the last with quixotic defiance: "God save the Village Green".

"I guess the title song is a juxtaposition," says Ray. "It contradicts some of the other material. It's to be sung as a chorus. It's a bunch of people singing it in a pub. And probably they're in a Conservative stronghold." Dave recalls: "I loved the opening few bars of that song, the optimism. Our bonding gave us a strength: "We are the Village Green". It was like, 'We're impenetrable. We might not have a lot, but you can't kill us. You're going to have to *shoot* us.'"

In some ways, the album fitted in very well with the rock music of 1968. The mood was of retrenchment and rolling back, after the psychedelic apogee of *Sgt. Pepper* had tipped by late 1967 into the flaccid indulgence of The Beatles' *Magical Mystery Tour* film and the Stones' *Their Satanic Majesties Request*. Dylan had signalled the sea change when he returned like a prophet from the wilderness after a year away with the austere *John Wesley Harding*. His old backing group The Band made the crucial switch with *Music From Big Pink* in August 1968. This alchemic brew of American roots music immediately influenced the Stones in time for their resurgent November masterpiece *Beggars Banquet* and the next year's countrified *Let It Bleed*, and The Beatles moved to 'Get Back'. Up in Muswell Hill, in a suburban house called Fairport, Fairport Convention had *Big Pink* "continuously on the turntable", their old bassist Ashley Hutchings tells me. In 1969, they drew on their own roots to found English folk-rock with *Liege & Lief*. They knew The Kinks, and could have found inspiration much nearer than The Band's Woodstock home.

Finally, though, *The Kinks Are The Village Green Preservation Society* didn't fit. Most bands returned to a more indulgent, freeform version of American blues-rock fundamentals in 1968. Ray retreated inside himself, and found comfort in English things. He made The Kinks stand for something unfashionable: the conservation of emotionally valuable objects, the halting and questioning of progress. He tried to stop pop's forward motion. He had left the "country of Now".

If there had been any chance of the album getting a fair hearing, Ray sabotaged it himself. 'The Village Green Preservation Society' was recorded on August 12, finishing the 12-song album scheduled for September 27 release. In Scandinavia, France, New Zealand and Italy, the presses rolled and this album reached the shops. In *NME*, Keith Altham wrote a rave preview (though he privately thought much of it "risky" and "twee", he told Andy Miller). Then Ray halted production, and began writing more songs. That October, The Kinks endured their tour of working-men's clubs. The 15-song version Ray finally delivered to Pye in November had removed 'Days' and 'Mr. Songbird' (about how songs can save you), and added 'Big Sky', 'Animal Farm', 'Sitting By The Riverside', 'Last Of The Steam Powered Trains' and 'All Of My Friends Were There' (the hilarious anxiety dream which now ended the album). There were further delays, as Pye demanded a single. Ray, the album's significance clearly growing all the while in his mind, refused, and insisted on a stage show of his concept. The last line of the professionalism The Kinks had been dismantling along with their career throughout 1968 was breached. Now, Ray wouldn't even let them release a record. Wace quietly withdrew from managing the band for a few months, mortified.

Village Green finally slipped out on November 22. Despite later myths propagated by Ray, it wasn't entirely ignored by the music press. *Melody Maker* and *Disc* praised it highly. But any momentum or label goodwill it might have built had already been fatally holed. It didn't chart anywhere in the world. Dave Davies' solo album, though all but completed, was abandoned soon afterwards. Their one-time rivals The Beatles and Stones bestrode the world with the 'White Album' and *Beggars Banquet* that Christmas. The Kinks had reduced themselves to rumoured releases of phantom records. They'd made a last stand no one noticed.

"It was a very selective release, or should have been," claims Ray. "But the companies I was with at the time were geared up to sell hundreds of thousands." It sounds, though, as if there was an element of cock-up in its vanishing. "There's an element of cock-up to most things that we've done. In a sense, it did everything that I wanted it to do. There was an element of, 'We totally understand why this isn't going to be successful.' Everybody thought that. John Peel did. Even John's producer Bernie Andrews said, 'I can't understand why I like it so much, and yet it's not successful'. And you couldn't say that about many records."

It was the first album for which Ray assumed total control. He's often said he shouldn't have been allowed to make a record then. "Maybe if I've taken the devil's coin to make music in an industry..." he tries to explain. "If I want to write a book, I should write a book, don't make records. I tried to make poetry with records – in sound effects, and harmonies. It was a secret novel, or a secret record, that people find for themselves. I'm not out to impress anybody. It's a bunch of demos of a record to be made at a later date, by a band who could articulate the material, and turn it into something more... majestic. Other bands had their pet projects, and somehow made them into records. But we made a record that really shouldn't be listened to by anybody. Or certainly not played on the radio. That was not my intention. They're like folk tunes, in a way. There's an old saying with folk music, on the sheet music: 'To be played intimately, as if among friends.' That's the direction for this record. When people think about The Kinks, they still think about that album. And most of them haven't heard it."

"It was a prophetic album," Dave concludes. "It was the nineties when people thought, 'Hang on, we can't rip all the buildings out, they actually look all right', and then it was a bit late. The destruction and architectural misery of London in the sixties was like someone bombed it. You don't throw away everything that's old. There are a lot of old things you want to keep, that add towards our future culture. *Village Green* epitomises what Ray was starting to realise about observing the world and people around him. And it galvanised us. It gave us the emotional strength to do the next thing. It's a big undercurrent of energy that supports that period. Because everybody thought we were out of fashion, out of touch. People just did not know what to do with us."

The Beatles had turned themselves into Sgt. Pepper's Lonely Hearts Club Band by donning colourful marching-band costumes for an extravagant sleeve by pop art designer Peter Blake. *The Kinks Are The Village Green Preservation Society* was declared in calligraphy so tiny you had to strain to read it in the LP racks. It looked like just another Kinks album. Only on the back sleeve could you find the title song's lyrics, and an evocative photo of the band strolling through the long grass of Hampstead Heath on a sunny summer morning. In this patch of north London wilderness, Quaife walks slightly apart from the rest. But he was happy. "That was one of those days when everyone got on great," he told Andy Miller. "I could take you there now and take you where we walked. Down by the lake, over the bridge..." As much as Ray's songs, it's The Kinks' harmoniously creative playing that makes *Village Green* if not their best album, then the only one as perfectly balanced as their great singles. David Melville-Quaife confirms his brother's happiness making it. "He *loved* it. He was crazy about it. Dad was good at electronics and had built us a gramophone – he built a television from scratch, too, before anybody else had one. Pete was so pleased about that gramophone, and he used to sit cross-legged in the afternoon listening, after coming back from the studio with a demo disc. *Village Green* he was just enthralled about. It was the last time he wasn't told what to do."

The credits at the bottom of the back sleeve stated: "I am Raymond Douglas Davies – guitarist, keyboard player and singer". This lost the band another ally. Nicky Hopkins, whose keyboard contributions were crucial on this and every album since *The Kink Kontroversy*, never worked with them again. "I did about 70% of the work on the *Village Green* album," the normally mild-mannered Hopkins told a US interviewer the next year, "and not only did they leave me off the credits, but they put Ray Davies down on keyboard. I was so mad; I'm just not into The Kinks... Ray Davies is such a mixed-up person. He's unbelievable!" He later claimed he hadn't been paid for the sessions, that the band were "greedy bastards", and Ray in particular was "so tight his arse squeaks when he walks". In Julian Dawson's biography *And On Piano... Nicky*

132

Hopkins, Ray vaguely writes they "couldn't find" Hopkins the next time they wanted him. Trying to use him again in 1988, Ray felt "his voice was distant and lacked commitment". After Hopkins' death in 1994, Ray was warm in his tributes to a man who had felt less valued by him in life: "I say to every... keyboard player, 'Can you play like Nicky Hopkins?'"

A far more serious loss followed. In January 1969, Quaife told Ray he was leaving the band for good. He was prevailed upon to stay for the recording and promotion of their next single, 'Plastic Man'. Ray's refusal to provide Pye with 45s during the standoff over *Village Green*'s release meant this came nine months after 'Days" by now fading success, on March 18. It was a bouncily inane novelty tune, with a fantasy lyric about a conformist who's fake right down to his plastic gums. Like 'Mister Pleasant' – a 1967 European A-side and number two hit in Holland, wisely relegated to the B-side of 'Autumn Almanac' – it sullied 'Dedicated Follower Of Fashion''s tradition of rapier satire with blunt cynicism. Ray's lyric denied its target individual humanity and so lacked any. It was a dispirited half-try at a single, their worst since before 'You Really Got Me'. The B-side, 'King Kong', echo-drenched heavy blues eerily anticipating T. Rex, was better. Generally good reviews showed this caricature of Kinks pop now matched the public perception of them. It limped to number 31. On March 31, Quaife quit The Kinks.

"The original band was phase one," Ray equably reflects to me, one day in 2004. "The double-winning team was broken up. You have to sign some new players. The team is still as good. And you go on to win other things. But it's not the same team." He showed more resentment of Quaife's decision to Johnny Black in 2000. "Pete got everything out of it that he wanted to get out of it really early on," he said, asked to respond to the bassist's feeling that he'd been treated like a session musician. "He got on TV. Met a few interesting people. Some people got into it because they wanted a piece of the swinging whatever it was, and then it became a job and they didn't like it any more. Pete was one of those guys. I was the guy that had to come up with the songs. Not that other people weren't entitled to, it's just that I got the pressure to. And I'm sorry, but he couldn't do it. And I knew how I wanted the records to sound. Whenever I wrote songs and thought about the band, I thought of him," he said, softening for a moment, "and I still think of him as the bass player, so he's always in my mind. To say that I wouldn't let him say anything is nonsense. I just don't think he had anything to say. He never turned up for recordings in a nice frame of mind. We were all under stress, but Pete was a true Swinging Sixties person. He lived the times and he enjoyed it, but my duty was to deliver a little bit more than that. I was writing songs that people thought were important. And the band I was, and still am, proud of. Pete walked away from the band as such and just went for the success. My loyalty was with the firm."

"I thought it was a bit sad when Pete left," Dave tells me in 2004. "I thought he just lost the thread. I think the car crash really messed him up, seeing a close friend of ours from school, Jonah, mushed up like that. I think that really freaked him out. He had a lot of psychological problems, Pete – which didn't help, being between me and Ray. It was the three of us who started the band up, coming from the same school and a similar background. He was integral at the beginning. It was more difficult and weird for Pete than it was for me, the way things went. Ray and Pete were in the same class, and Ray was always a very good athlete. And there's this picture I've got of Ray in the foreground, winning the 200 metres or something, and you can just see Pete in the background. That kind of thing grated, I think. I suppose I didn't help, because I wanted my space as well. Me and Pete became closer than me and Ray. So much happens in groups that's like families. I would love to know what he really thinks.

"But I didn't mind Pete leaving," Dave reflects. "It would have been worse if he'd tried to stay. I didn't have any emotions either way. I was sad initially. But there wasn't any lingering, 'Oh fuck, don't do it...' Maybe it was natural for Ray to move into a different creative place, and Pete didn't understand it. I think Ray missed Pete more than I did. Andy Pyle [the mid-seventies Kinks bassist] actually bore a resemblance to Pete. Ray's terribly sentimental. He can't let go of anything."

"I'm still coming to terms with it," Ray says to me in 2012, of losing Quaife from The Kinks. "Because Pete didn't say much. Near the end, when I seemed to be more important than him, he backed away. But we were quite close friends. I think Pete had more aspirations. We were from a similar area, although Pete was from the Coldfall Estate," he considers, showing the subtle borders in his postage-stamp north London kingdom. "Interesting thinking about Pete, Pete was born in the West Country, I think his mother was evacuated. So there's a slightly different bearing on the way he was. But there was a unifying factor – and I can exclude Mick on this. I think Dave, Pete and myself, we were us against the world. And Mick came along, and I think shared some of that philosophy, but he's still basically his own man. He plays golf, for heaven's sake!

"Pete left for a few reasons," Ray concludes. "He got married to this rich Danish girl, and was alienated from being our mate, because I wrote the songs and people were more inquisitive about me. But primarily he was scared of the business things going on around us. Pete was spooked by all the business people we had to meet. He was terrified, I think – he had what I call Noel Redding syndrome, people pursuing him with one lawsuit after another, and he was terrified most of the time. I'm not sure what of."

"The real reason my brother left the band was that Dave Davies punched the shit out of him," Melville-Quaife tells me bluntly. He's referring to the beating a year before which left Quaife's wrist in a cast. "I have a son called Dave and I sent him to visit Pete in Canada in the early eighties, and he explained to my son what happened. It was Dave Davies, he hit him really, really hard. I know this, my son would not lie. Pete had been keeping it back all that time. We never did know how he broke his wrist. He just wouldn't talk about it. That was the straw that broke the camel's back."

In Melville-Quaife's memory, other hurts had gnawed at his brother. "At least a year before the accident, the way the band was paid changed. They had been doing a four-way split, Ray was dividing it up. Then after that, it was, 'We'll do it this way', and he started just getting 40 quid a week – it might have been a week, it actually might have been every 14 days. I know he was earning less than me dad, who ran a grocer's shop. I believe Mick Avory was on that as well. Pete kept

135

asking to see the accounts, and he wasn't allowed access. That really upset him."

As a musician too, Quaife felt more genuinely demeaned than Ray realised. "When they came out with 'Session Man', he just sat in the front room and cried his eyes out," says his brother. "Because that's what he felt like. It was disgusting. He was really upset that he was not recognised, and was not allowed to do anything. In the bass guitar club, he was really good. In the beginning, he just wanted to get the good music out, and be different, and be recognised for what you are. He didn't play traditional bass-lines, and it was easy for him to do, and he thought, 'Why hasn't anybody else done it?' With the bass he played on 'Milk Cow Blues' on the live album, I remember John Entwistle from The Who coming round and saying, 'Show me how to do that.' And then gradually, his input was taken out. He'd come back from doing a track, and find it was completely different on record. It was horrible for him."

The sometimes abusive grind of life in The Kinks, which Ray and Dave seemed to somehow thrive on and of which his broken wrist was a culmination, also wore the bassist down. "They used to call him Crutch," says Melville-Quaife. "He used it on an email and took it as a joke in the end. But at the time, that wasn't very nice. When I first visited him in Denmark after he moved there, he said, 'Here, you can have this.' It was one of his old stage-jackets. And in the sleeves was written, 'Crutch you cunt'. At his funeral in 2010, Mick Avory asked me to read this out: 'Sometimes we would make cruel jokes about him. But he would just shrug it off, and rise above it.' I know Mick was doing his best when Pete died to make up for that. It must have been tough for me brother, being beaten up all those times. He got the verbal beatings and the mental beatings as well. Those last two years in the band were absolutely terrible for him. Because he wasn't built for that sort of thing. He didn't want to cause anybody any pain. If there was an argument, he would walk away. If me mum and dad told him off, he'd just sit down, grizzle a little bit, and then go up to bed by himself. It's one of my biggest memories. He did not like friction."

As Quaife had changed his mind once, it was understandably hoped he'd do so again. "Ray kept popping up there saying, 'Why don't you come back', and Pete said, 'I can't.' I think Ray offered him a bit more money as well. And there was something about him being under contract, and them wanting a year-and-a-half back from his money but he said, no, sod it, I'm going. The damage had been done by that time, because he'd been through so much. Constantly bullied, I suppose you'd call it now. In those days, it was accepted. He'd been having a breakdown before and after deciding to leave. It was going on for some time. You could see him getting worse and worse. In the end, when the pressure was still on him to stay in, my dad could see that that was it, Pete had to get out. It was final. He just couldn't do it any more. He was in such an emotional empty state. It was difficult to get information out of him, because it had hurt him so bad. He was the same as me. I'm a manic depressive, after being in the Army for nine years. I think being in The Kinks then affected Pete similarly."

Had he shown signs of that manic depression before things went wrong in the band? "Definitely not. He was the most happy-go-lucky bloke you've ever seen."

Leaving the group relieved him, to an extent. "He brightened up a lot," his brother remembers. "He started up another group, because it was the only thing he knew, and he had to get cash in the house. He was left high and dry, literally cut off from one week to the next by The Kinks." Ray and Dave's sense of betrayal during a commercial crisis for The Kinks mounted when, the week he left them, Quaife was pictured playing with a new band, soon named Mapleoak. They gigged with little success around Birmingham and Denmark. Quaife left them in April 1970, claiming their drug use put him off. "It was a mistake that he got into that," says his brother. "It was the first thing that came along. It did help, because he loved playing."

As The Kinks' career continued, life for their ex-bassist deteriorated further. "He got a job hanging Esso signs up at petrol stations, to make ends meet," his brother remembers. "So he went back to Denmark with his wife, who I don't think liked not being married to a pop star. It was a very rich family, and her father wasn't very nice. He said, 'I've got a job for you at this new restaurant I'm opening. The head waiter can show you the ropes.' That's a *long way* from being on the stage. Divorce proceedings started almost immediately. Then he got a little bedsit, because he was told by the family never to visit his one-year-old daughter again. That was too much for Pete. I'd booked a flight to see him in the summer holidays, and then there was a telegram to say they were separating. It was a shock to us all. Mum was really worried. It was the first time he went missing, for two or three months. He had a habit after that, when things got too bad, he'd just disappear. No one would hear a word from him. For a couple of years, once."

There would be upturns, and further tentative connections with The Kinks in the future. Talking to journalists and fans, Quaife clearly kept fond memories of their first years. "It was a dream come true," says Melville-Quaife. "When they were playing in small gigs, and my dad sometimes drove the band, even then the Davies brothers were kicking off. But it was good fun in those days, it was fantastic. He loved it. I remember he got driven back from a policeman's ball in a black Mariah at two in the morning. He came walking up the stairs, trying to be very quiet, took his trousers off and the 30 shillings he earned that night fell out of his trouser pocket on the floor and woke everyone up. He was supposed to play rhythm guitar, but the Davies brothers got guitars first. I remember him saying lots of times that that was the best thing that ever happened to him. Because then he could get on with doing the bass-lines that he wanted. I enjoyed it, when everything was going good. On my summer holiday, Pete would take me round on tour for company. Dave was always blown out of his head, Ray was aloof, and Avory was into girls. It was a real education. But things changed."

The Kinks turned from Quaife's greatest pleasure to a trauma. In 1970, he left the music business behind. Perhaps this was why Ray, even in sympathetic interviews, thought his old schoolfriend was a "true amateur" and "not a great music lover". By contrast Quaife told interviewer Martin Kalin in 1998: "I don't even have to see a rock band. I was watching a classical orchestra on TV and I realised how much I still miss it." Melville-Quaife thinks Pete quit from thwarted love. "It was a struggle afterwards," he says. "He enjoyed doing what he was doing, it's all he trained for. And there was no other chance ever in his life to show what he wanted to do – that was ripped away from him. Denny Laine used to say, 'Go on, play bass with us', Eric Clapton [apparently] asked him to join [what became] Cream. I had the idea that he could do it. But he didn't. I think it was a traumatic thing, going back into a studio and starting again, because he was scared of getting hurt again. And so when he got older, he had to do other jobs to survive."

It sounds like Quaife would have loved to continue as a professional musician, but was too broken to do so. "That hits the nail on the head. He was actually devastated by what happened all those years ago. It sounds stupid, but it's the only way I can put it. The effect it had on him was terrible. Pete would just start crying, he couldn't get over it. He was hurt mentally quite badly, which lasted all his life. It really did him, absolutely. It must have hurt an awful lot. It's just a bloody shame."

Melville-Quaife was in his mid-teens as the band turned sour, very young to remember the exact chronology of events decades later. His emotional truth, though, and the lifelong effect of particular incidents, seems clear. No one in The Kinks ever ended up face down in a swimming pool. But their chaotic career did have a victim. In the next few years each of them would take that role, to an extent. Quaife fell hardest, and least culpably. The fond music business legend of the battling Davies brothers wasn't so funny if you got too close.

There was a fascinating hinterland to The Kinks' music at this time, written to order by Ray for *At The Eleventh Hour* and then another TV show, the sitcom *Where Was Spring*: songs such as 'Did You See His Name?', a haunting two-minute tune about shame resulting in suicide, and 'Where Did My Spring Go?', in which Ray's obsession with ageing reaches its hilarious conclusion as his faculties fail him one by one, and he goes to the grave railing against the tiring sex and rain-soaked school runs that hurried him there. These commissions were joined by a much more ambitious one from Granada Television at the end of 1968, an experimental play with The Kinks' music about the fall of the British Empire. There was vague talk of Ray working with John

Betjeman. Novelist Julian Mitchell eventually provided the script, which characteristically channelled this grand theme through the fate of Ray's brother-in-law: *Arthur.*

Rehearsals for Ray's new songs began in his new Borehamwood mansion's big back room. Rasa had given birth to his second daughter, Victoria, at a nearby hospital on Christmas Day 1968. Still bravely fumbling to be a family man, the dinner he had been cooking for Louisa was burnt to a crisp when he returned. He was already finding the leaded windows and grand Tudor trappings undercut by its drafty isolation. Quaife worked on some early music, but on his exit the band barely broke stride. Avory was told to whistle back John Dalton. "He was the sort of bloke I was used to knocking about with," Avory says. "We found a level straight away. He was down to earth, same as me. Pete was a nice enough bloke. But he was more in a fantasy world." Dalton had been jailed by Franco's police in his first spell with the band. On his fourth gig back they barely got out of Beirut, after a dispute with an irate promoter.

As Ray and Mitchell worked on *Arthur* through the spring, the title character became a generation older than Ray's relative. This Arthur is a First World War veteran whose life through a century of imperial decline is recalled during a visit by his son and daughter-in-law before, tired of Britain, they emigrate to Australia. "It was an interesting dynamic," Ray says. "I wrote a song, then the scriptwriter was on at me and the producers, and then the band saying, 'Come on, we just want to make a rock record.' It was my first experience of working with what other people wanted to say and wanted it to be. I still wrote it and presented my stuff. But I wanted it to encompass the bigger picture."

Ray must be thinking of later, more intransigent concept albums that The Kinks resented. They loved *Arthur.* "*Village Green* felt delicate and difficult to make," says Dave, "because it was getting into a new area for us. I always liked *Arthur* better. It made me feel we were being recharged again. It was a new direction. It was also sonically very good, because I think we used the first 16-track tape recorder ever [in fact 8-track]. We could isolate the sounds better, they were thicker, ballsier. *Arthur* was a really important time."

"When Ray went into the concept stuff," Avory remembers, "the shapes of songs, the tempos and rhythms were different, so it was always interesting. I wasn't really a rock'n'roll drummer, I was from a jazz background, so the more subtle things suited me better. We developed a style together. I've never really thought we were a rock band as such. I liked *Village Green*, but I felt he could have done something better on some of the tracks. The production on it probably wasn't up with what was going on at the time. *Arthur*, that was a good album. Because I knew where it was coming from. It was fairly personal. Ray had found something to write about, nostalgia, and his family."

"With *Arthur* I wanted to say something about an injustice I felt was happening," Ray says of the themes he and Mitchell developed. "The Arthur I was writing about was working class. He was my relative, and I lived with him and his wife, my sister, for several years. And all I would hear at dinner was how they'd been betrayed. But for joining a band, I might have gone to Australia, like they did and so many of my schoolfriends had, just because they could buy a better house for an amount of money. I was grateful I'd found something that could keep me living in England, and keep me fed and that I could thrive on. Because of my family situation, I saw how a lot of British people went abroad and got a bum steer. It changed their whole lives. In our case the family was broken up.

"What happened to them is not a lot, really," he continues. "They got a nice house, a nice job. But it was a profound loss. Because after my first sister died, Rose was the one that was closest to me, and she didn't see all the fun stuff happen. She saw me as a serious schoolkid with lots of problems, then she went to Australia, and suddenly I'm a songwriter on the television, selling lots of records. And my nephew Terry went to Australia, and he would have shone in the sixties and seventies. He's done OK where he's gone. All I'm saying is: it was a sense of loss to me. Because I was selfish about it – probably still am. I wanted the whole unit to stay together. But life isn't like that."

Arthur Or The Decline And Fall Of The British Empire is The Kinks' most angry and epic record. It was lavished with real orchestral parts instead of the cut-price Mellotron effects Ray had mostly relied on before, suiting the ambition of the coming colour TV production. He sings in a voice he never used again, seemingly tape-slowed and slurred at times, both affected and impassioned.

'Victoria' begins in a world of village greens, unquestioned class oppression and the imperial stability of the Victorian era's end where "I was born, lucky me..." This celebratory-sounding anthem, with its breezily propulsive bass and guitar and cresting chorus, came across as a good old-fashioned Kinks single when it was released as one in October. The frustrated rage which powers *Arthur* becomes clearer with the threateningly tense martial drum-roll introducing 'Yes Sir, No Sir'. Ray's voice ranges from Dalek-robotic to the high-flown purity of the officer sending the masses to war, and horsey, twittish guffaws as Ray and Dave spoof the upper-classes' real rationale: "Give the scum a gun and let the buggers fight."

'Some Mother's Son' stands alone in The Kinks' career. It's a song about the trenches, again starting quietly, with harpsichord and acoustic guitar. Ray finds heartbreak in the carnage particular to him. His young soldier is peering at the sun and thinking of games he played as a child. He hears a friend's voice, and dreamily turns, and at this moment has his brains blown out. What makes the song so intensely moving is its flash to the same moment back in Britain. There, mothers wait for their children to run home from school. This wasted corpse who won't ever come home was such an innocent boy, and in his mother's mind always will be. Ray's voice keeps swelling with the song, tottering on a hysterical edge. Probably Mitchell's script helped his dramatic control. But his uncharacteristic fury burned from within. "*Arthur*'s better than *Village Green* because the stories were about real people now," says Dave. "'Some Mother's Son' was such an impassioned piece of music because it's based on my mum's brother, and the stories that we'd hear about these family members that died in wars."

'Drivin'' releases us to a Sunday country car jaunt along a route the Davieses might take, past Barnet church to Potters Bar, free for a few precious hours from Denmark Terrace's debt and rent collectors. 'Mr. Churchill Says' skips forward to the time of air-raid sirens and Vera Lynn. Its satirical tone as Churchill's speeches brainwash the working classes to go back to war for the bosses uncertainly crashes against descriptions of corpses in Blitz-burned houses, and the pride in saying to Hitler: "Do your worst, and we will do our best." The swaggering 'Brainwashed' takes the argument forward to people after that war, enslaved in Ray's mind to social security and the state, under the thumb of the same authorities as in 'Victoria', who are letting the Empire they fought for fall away.

"It wasn't just the working classes who felt that," Ray says. "It was the leisure classes. A good friend of mine was an officer on a ship and got taken prisoner by the Japanese. He was middle class, went to university, and had more to come back to. He stayed away. He never came back. He told me that we needed to win the war, but he hated what was left for us all, not just the working classes. I don't remember the war, but I remember that sense of betrayal. On tour, we sang to a generation who could still remember the adherence to authority in those songs from National Service, where you gave up the right to be a free man. I was part of the generation after that. I wish I hadn't missed it, in many respects," he adds unconvincingly, "because we weren't fighting any wars."

Then there's 'Shangri-La'. The elegantly sung first verse congratulating Arthur as he sits back in the dream home he's spent his life working so hard for makes you expect a quiet hymn to suburbia. But the trap he's unwittingly set for himself by carefully climbing his small ladder of success redoubles 'Autumn Almanac''s claustrophobia: "You've reached your top and you just can't get any higher...You can't go anywhere." The chorus unleashes barrages of brass and strings. By the second verse the achievements allowed to this "little man", the indoor toilet, rented TV and radio, mortgage and daily commute, look tawdry, just more ways to keep him in his place. The Kinks crash in with the brass in the second chorus. The third verse's aggressive acoustic guitar intro – verses have their own intros in this epic – could be The Who, as it lists houses identifiable only by proudly affixed names, because they all look the same. The brass is driving the song on and Avory's smashing his cymbals, before a return to peace and slippers on by the fire, with the new emphasis of this Shangri-La's hollowness. The final chorus blasts through the five-minute barrier. *Village Green* was meant for playing "intimately... among friends". 'Shangri-La' tries to find the limit of how big a song can be.

Ray's stated inspiration was the "designed community" of Little Elizabeth near Adelaide, where he'd visited Arthur, Rose and Terry on The Kinks' 1965 Australian tour. But walk up the street to 87 Fortis Green, and most of the houses have names too. "'Shangri-La', that was a bit of a bitter song," he says. "I don't know whether I still feel good about it. I like the technique. But the sentiment sometimes bothers me, because it's contempt for what I am. It's thrown at myself. I am that person. I have a kind of guilt feeling about it. But it had to be written. By that time I was developing the script with Julian, and it fitted the theme."

Two songs speak directly to Ray's self-exiled family. On 'Australia', he adopts the working-class accent that peeks through in early TV interviews, before he was quite polished. The brass and harmonies are pure Beach Boys as they sketch the Australian dream for the English, of surfing, sunny Christmas and a clean, crime-free life. Its rambling instrumental breakdown is the first four self-indulgent minutes of Kinks music, worryingly like the "progressive" solos infecting rock in 1969. Perhaps meant for the film's incidental score, it's one of several misjudged moments on a not wholly controlled album. The closing song, 'Arthur', also finishes in loose gospel exulting. But when Ray and Dave keep singing, "Oh, we love you, and want to help you", films and records are forgotten. Like 'Rosie Won't You Please Come Home', this is a private message to a distant relative. Dave remembers being in tears as he sang it. Even Ray was racked with emotion.

"That lyric in 'Arthur', 'Arthur, you think the world's passed you by... maybe you were right all along'," Ray reflects, "was an acknowledgement that maybe he had to go on his path. Arthur heard the record before he died. He said, 'There were some good things about England. You picked up on too many negatives'. At least I got some feedback from him. There's a sense of loss in that song too. A sense of, you're never going to see one another again."

The lead-up to *Arthur*'s release proved The Kinks' commercial freefall. 'Drivin'', an odd, stopgap single in June, was their first not to chart since 'You Still Want Me' in May 1964. To the band's amazement, 'Shangri-La', the grandest of all their singles statements, did no better in September. The Kinks no longer warranted special dispensation to get a five-minute song on the radio. *Arthur* followed *The Kinks Are The Village Green Preservation Society* to UK chart oblivion on October 10. It had been kept back, waiting for the constantly delayed film which was the ambitious project's whole point. In December, with director and cast finally ready, Granada refused the budget. *Village Green* was an album almost no one heard. *Arthur* became the soundtrack to a film that was never made. The Kinks were surely cursed.

Even *Arthur*'s status as the first "rock opera" was, it's often noted, dashed when film-caused delays let The Who's *Tommy* sneak in first, helping save their own stuttering career. This argument is flawed only by *Tommy*'s release on May 23 1969, when *Arthur* was still being recorded, and its script incomplete. More striking is the similar interest in Pete Townshend's story of a traumatised pinball wizard with what he's called Britain's "post-war geography", and the unhealed scars suffered by his parents' wartime generation, relocated, like *Arthur*, to the First World War. At the end of the sixties, Ray wasn't the only one looking back at where he came from. Rock's self-importance by 1969 was bound to lead to such attempted cohesive statements, whoever got there first. Townshend and Ray would both keep trying to repeat the trick, long after everyone else gave up. "I *exalt* Ray Davies, and also Dave Davies," Townshend anyway said, talking about *Tommy* to *Uncut*'s Simon Goddard in 2004. "People in America talk about 'The Beatles, the Stones, The Who'. For me it's 'The Beatles, the Stones, The Kinks'... I certainly wouldn't have presumed to compete with The Kinks."

'Victoria' reached number 33 in December; a bit worse than 'Plastic Man', a bit better than 'Wonderboy'. It was their last record of the sixties. Dave looks back on this fraught end to the decade fondly. "There's a song on *Arthur* called 'Young And Innocent Days'," he says. "It's got a similar feel to 'Days' and it's about losing everything. When I got up to the microphone to do the harmony, I just felt everything was going to be all right anyway. Like do your worst. It encouraged me. It maybe goes to show how little value there is in commercial success.

OK, so you can send your kids to posh schools and get a Rolls Royce. But what is the value of the experience that you're having?

"It goes back to my song 'I Am Free'," he says, gathering steam. "It's important not to lose that spirit. Because that was a period when everybody was making a lot of money. The Beatles were buying mansions in the country, the Stones and Eric Clapton. And it defeated itself a bit. It was almost like these people who came from similar backgrounds to me had lost the fight. They'd just become part of the Establishment, part of society as it wants them to be. Money is part of the conditioning. We never really became that rich – because we were ripped off so badly, which was horrendous. But then we had peaks and valleys – you'd have success and then you'd have nothing. Which makes you live and think differently about what's going on around you. You can't get lost in a castle. There are certain periods of The Kinks, the reality check moments when things go wrong, that remind you why you're there, and how you got there."

As if to prove Dave's point, in October Ray moved back from his unhappy mansion to his semi-detached Fortis Green Shangri-La.

Ray, who sang the decade out on BBC TV with 'Days', has mixed feelings about the period some in Britain don't seem to think he outlived. "Anyone who was fooled by the sixties would think it was a time when everybody in society could mingle," he says. "One of my managers, one of the stockbrokers, said, 'You know when this is all over, everybody will revert to type'. And he was right. It's like when a war's over. All the soldiers come back, and they put their suits on, the middle-class man and the upper-class one, and they all go back to what they were before."

The Kinks' future lay in a forgotten place. They had vanished from America and its charts long before The Who completed their ascension as unassailable rock stars at Woodstock in August. But the countless "mud people" The Band's Robbie Robertson described playing to in that field (a distaste shared by Townshend) also now had an underground press serving their needs. Here, The Kinks had scattered loyalists preserving their flame: writers such as Paul Williams, who in June 14, 1969's *Rolling Stone* reviewed *Village Green* in impressionistically articulate language as yet undiscovered by the British music press. Referencing Erik Satie, Stephen Crane, Howlin' Wolf and Maurice Sendak, sharp observations were arrived at through the dopey haze, as he noted Ray's songs were about "not necessarily joy but the reaction to joy... one suspects it's not just that he's capable of a certain detachment, but also that he can't escape that detachment, it's the way he's always known things." He took a run-up to his conclusion via their last US hit, 'Sunny Afternoon', "one of the songs of the century... one of the highest feelings man has yet recorded in art... It's so far down, and raises me so far up... I'm thinking only genius can hit me this directly... I've never had much luck turning people onto The Kinks. I can only hope you are onto them already. If you are brother, I love you. We've got to stick together." Such writers understood where The Kinks' music had gone, sympathised with and portrayed them as beloved underdogs, and wrote to the Woodstock Nation.

"Even though we were not allowed to tour America," Ray reflects, "the peace movement took the album up, when it eventually came out on Reprise. There was a certain element that thought it was anti-war. Americans interpreted the *Village Green* as being something that Americans should cherish. In a strange, misconceived way, they took it as something of theirs, albeit in a very cult way."

While Pye's boss Louis Benjamin ran an increasingly outmoded singles-churning machine, The Kinks' US label, Reprise, had also changed. Its visionary boss Mo Ostin made it the first American major to treat rock not as a distasteful but profitable fad, but the music industry's engine, made by artists who would make more money from the new fans filling Woodstock if their visions were respected. Randy Newman, Van Dyke Parks, Jimi Hendrix, Van Morrison, The Grateful Dead, Joni Mitchell and Neil Young were major acts for Warner/Reprise by 1969. Ostin read and valued the underground press. Though *Something Else* and *Village Green* reputedly sold only 25,000 between them in the US, *The Kinks' Greatest Hits*, released to cash in on 'Sunny Afternoon', had sold steadily. Their potential as a hip cult could now be tapped.

Ray spent several weeks in Hollywood during 1969, producing an album by The Turtles. "Ray stayed at the Hollywood Hawaiian Hotel and drank a lot of beer and liked to read *Playboy* a lot. Just an average guy," the band's Mark Volman unobservantly concluded. While Ray was there, he negotiated the end of The Kinks' American ban. "When we signed a letter apologising, I didn't even read it," he says contemptuously. "I couldn't really say, 'You've got to redraft it'. Just get this *ridiculous* situation over with." Visas were suddenly granted.

On July 3, Ray and Wace met Reprise executives and rock writer ally John Mendelsohn in LA to plot the comeback. The rallying cry sent to the underground press was: 'God Save The Kinks'. An 18-track career summary, *Then Now And Inbetween* was mailed to reacquaint them. Maverick ad writer Stan Cornyn cooked up a typically outrageous press kit which Brian Sommerville would have jumped off Waterloo Bridge rather than sanction. Meant to ramp up an anti-establishment rep, it included the unfortunate mock-headline: "English Rock Group Arrested on Rape Rap". Ray vetoed planting actual stories in the press.

The Kinks' supporters responded, *Rolling Stone* deciding only two *Arthur* reviews would do. Greil Marcus's named it "the best album of 1969", showing "The Beatles have a lot of catching up to do". *Tommy*'s great success, far from harming The Kinks in the States, had created a critical hunger for rock opera, letting Marcus declare that *Arthur* proved "Pete Townshend still has worlds to conquer".

On October 17, the British Invasion's last, battered battalion touched down in New York. They met the unrecognisable new world of rock tours like Japanese soldiers stumbling blinking from the jungle. The Village Green's safety was far away. It was America which would alternately save, define and almost destroy them for the rest of their careers.

CHAPTER 8

On Broadway

A merica at the end of the sixties was a very different nation from the one that had evicted The Kinks in 1965. Then, as it mourned an assassinated President, The Beatles' ebullience was dragging the country out of the constricted culture of the fifties. But in the meantime, it had suffered a series of regular body blows. The year 1968 began with the Viet Cong's shockingly effective Tet offensive, while the massacre of civilians in My Lai by US Marines showed the human and moral cost of the failing Vietnam War. Bodies of leaders who'd promoted hope dropped with such numbing regularity they might have been at the front line: Martin Luther King, Robert Kennedy, Malcolm X. There were race riots, the worst in the home of Motown's Sound of Young America, Detroit, which were enflamed by US paratroops, and a police riot that bludgeoned hippie protestors and dissenting delegates at the Chicago Democratic Party convention.

When The Kinks played LA in November 1969, Charles Manson's gang were being rounded up after committing brutal murders in the Hollywood Hills, where previously benign young rock and movie stars were holed up, armed and paranoid. The killing at the Stones' Altamont gig in December symbolically cancelled out Woodstock. Nixon was President, rousing the "Silent Majority" into violent counter-demonstrations against anti-war protesters, whose Weather Underground fringe began a doomed terror campaign. The hippies' 1967 San Francisco wonderland Haight-Ashbury was a seedy drug ghetto. In nearby Oakland, the Black Panther Party was at war with the police. To many, it felt like a new Civil War. There was a ragged exhaustion in the country. The Kinks had missed another sixties party.

"Because I'd had horrible experiences in America a few years earlier," Ray considers, "it was no surprise to me that all this news was coming over here. I watched it not with relish, but as if I was justified in my fears that it could erupt like that. The first time we went to the States, I wasn't aware of many coloured people, African-Americans, because it was ghettoised. So when Black Power happened, I wasn't surprised at all. I wasn't shutting myself off when we were making records like *Village Green* – I was very interested in what was happening. They were still in this war, and they were going through their first phase of guilt when we first went back. I remember playing the university in Portland, Oregon when they had the first lottery for conscription."

The Kinks played New York's Fillmore East two sets nightly, on October 17 and 18. Years of desultory and occasional European gigs were no preparation for the opportunity they'd wanted so long. Screamed at in 1965, now crowds were seated, often stoned and serious. Dave was crippled by nerves, moaning, "I can't remember the fucking lyrics!" during 'Death Of A Clown'. *Billboard*'s review observed that "Davies' lyrics were obliterated by the roar of the volume and further plundered by the group's musicianship".

"When we went back," Ray explains, "America had the Fillmore and San Francisco and the drug culture, and it was a different world. They put us in the Fillmore East, and we'd never played with monitors before [which allow musicians to hear themselves, and became standard as PA systems became louder]. It was a big learning curve. [Fillmore promoter] Bill Graham was the driving force who'd taken American rock out of the school hop and turned it into a serious, adult art-form. We didn't even call it a soundcheck, we called it a rehearsal. Our first tour had been in big halls, 20,000-seaters in Philadelphia and the Hollywood Bowl. This time we were starting at the bottom."

"We did virtually start again when we went back over there," says Dave. "We didn't even know what to put in the set. We tried sixties hits, *Village Green* and *Arthur*. We did the college misery tour, and built up a cult following." Avory remembers the return positively. "Even though we hadn't been saturating them with tours, we had an underground following, and they were aware of what we were doing. Of course we couldn't play big places. But we played nice, well-attended gigs. I think they liked it because we were very English, and that's what we portrayed to them, the English nostalgia. You only had to speak and they were, 'I love your accent... oh, say something again'. That was very common. We had a good time, and we were helped by the record company."

To Ray especially, American success was crucial. Like Muhammad Ali's campaign to regain his unfairly stripped heavyweight boxing crown in the same period, The Kinks took more punishment than they would have in the prime years they had lost, but wouldn't concede defeat. Would they have carried on, without that American prize? "No," Ray says. "That was our quest. We wanted to go back there, and reclaim what I felt had been cruelly snatched from us. It's very difficult to do that. It was an upward journey. It took eight years."

The effort was all the more stubbornly great because of The Kinks' human weakness. The Stones and for a while The Who had the stamina and drive to conquer countries. But while Avory was enjoying the open goal his accent gave him with America's young women, and Ray sat in hotels working with management and media, Dave became the next Kink to break down. After only two weeks away from home, he entered a terrible darkness. It would last three years, and almost consume him.

On Halloween, The Kinks supported The Who at Chicago's Kinetic Playground. In the long dull hours afterwards, Dave took a girl he didn't want back to his Holiday Inn room. He wrecked the place in a fury, then ran amok in the corridor and punched through a glass exit sign. Blood poured from his badly cut knuckles. Unable to play guitar for a week, the next few gigs were cancelled, and he flew to Denmark to rest with Lisbet and his son, Martin. It could have been typical Dave wildness, like the time a few days before when he'd admirably called an obnoxious Boston DJ a "useless fucking cunt" on air, and taken a swing at his head. In fact, the depressed sense of uselessness in his hedonistic life which inspired 'Death Of A Clown' was clamping down on his brain. He drank constantly, and tried Angel Dust in New York. This was the period, as the fag-end of the sixties turned into the seventies, when a half-decade's heedless partying made corpses of Jimi Hendrix, Jim Morrison and Janis Joplin. Dave the Rave's reserves of endorphins were surely shot away. He was left terminally low.

In the sleazy Hollywood Hawaiian Hotel, before eight important shows at the Whiskey A Go Go, he swayed through days and nights of drugs, rosé wine and languid hungover sex with a girl called Norma he had picked up for the week. She handed him his first LSD pills. As it took hold the hairline cracks in his mind split. The objects in his hotel room lost their solidity, reality becoming malleable, no longer there to hang on to. The girl looked like a lizard frozen motionless on their bed, as if he was recovering truths from prehistoric cells of his cortex. He soared to revelatory highs. And he wept, utterly overcome. In the following days, he kept drinking and downing sleeping pills, trying to fix his mental state. But something in his brain had broken. "I found that important LSD experience opened up something that I wasn't ready for," he says. "It suddenly threw me into a place of isolation, that I didn't have the equipment to deal with."

In *Kink*, Dave remembers being onstage the first night and playing a second out of sync with The Kinks, as if there had been a slight slippage in time. He walked off halfway through, and retreated to his hotel, ready to give everything up if he could somehow repair himself. He slept for two days, but still crept through the Hollywood Hawaiian's corridors feeling like he was made of bone china. He was deeply disappointed with his brother when Ray coolly told him they should continue the tour. Given all it had taken to get back to America and Ray's preference for work over stimulants, his dim view of Dave's quick collapse is understandable. Doug Hinman's meticulous diary of The Kinks' lives, *All Day And All Of The Night*, finds no shows missed, and Dave even leading the singing at their first Whiskey gig. Dave at least wanted to run away.

"I never really liked performing in front of people," he says. "There were times when I wished the ground would open up, especially the early seventies. Too zapped out, man. Totally zapped out. It can be a pretty miserable life, being a writer or musician. Look at Ray. It tends to be undervalued, because of all the drugs and the partying – the Ozzy Osbourne rock'n'roll thing. That's just glamourising the misery, really, trying to make it funny." He brightens. "Although it is funny. It's hilarious. But it's not as simple as that. And when you're on tour, nobody gives a shit, everybody wants to make money. With the drugs, it was a very dark spiritual time for the business. There was very little happening musically, and a grey, dark energy around."

Dave's mind didn't go back as it had been before. He was suffering what he calls in *Kink* a "spiritual death", a "shedding" of previous beliefs as the extreme, apparent insights the acid's shock triggered repeatedly flooded his brain. "I had important psychic experiences at that time that really helped me move forwards, realising I'm a spiritual person, and not just fodder," he remembers. "But in the meantime I'm still trying to play and we're round the world going crazy, and trying to pretend everything is all right. I was having panics and anxieties – 'What the hell am I doing here?' There's a recognisable consistency to these states of mind, from other people I've spoken to since who've experienced psychic phenomena – people hearing voices. It's not necessarily just chemical imbalances in the brain. It can also be opening up something. But it's confusing. It was awful."

Dave didn't look for psychiatric help, worried they'd find the years of drink and drugs had caused permanent brain damage. In a grim irony, when I reminded him of this in 2004, it was only days before his stroke. "I didn't go for help because I was too paranoid!" he laughs. "The brain damage thing popped up a lot in that period. Maybe this is the end? When you're in that place, there's no way you can get out. Because if you tell someone, 'Ah, that's what they want you to do...' It's a really powerful, disordered, bad frame of mind. I didn't trust anybody. When you've been in that horrible place, and you meet someone else who has, they know. There's a connection, and less distrust. It's a hypersensitive state."

153

"Dave had a nervous breakdown?" Rays says when I mention this collapse to him, suggesting it's the first he's heard of it. "A quiet one? I didn't know you could have a quiet nervous breakdown. I guess people do actually, thinking about it. I was going through a lot of stuff. I always felt he was very strong in that period. But then possibly he did have a breakdown."

Dave was left terribly lonely in The Kinks as they battered their way back into America. "I don't know how Ray felt. He was going through a different kind of turmoil, with his family. And maybe me and Ray were incapable of helping each other. I don't think the other guys realised what was going on, and it didn't help that I didn't. My body and my mind were changing, and I didn't know what to do about it. I could see my future going in a completely different direction. The bottom line was, I have to do this myself."

The childhood interest he'd taken in spiritualism after Rene's sudden death became an anchor for Dave to cling to. "As a younger man, I loved horror stuff – Vincent Price and The Ravens [the early Kinks name taken from a Price/Karloff horror film], these images of the occult. I was interested in this whole area of metaphysics. People grow, people's values become different. Because it isn't just a material world. Although a lot of people would like us to think it is. And our lives have growth periods, like nature. We shed leaves, they die and grow again. And I was going through a period where I had to embrace this new stuff going on inside me. But I felt like I was being tormented for even daring to think about these things. My father was very sensitive. But he came from a background where you didn't talk about that. It was all right for the women to do a bit of Ouija board, and read tea leaves like my mum. But guys weren't doing that stuff in our family. When I'd get home, I'd go to Foyles and get a book on astrology, and psychics. I think what pulled me through was that I very seriously took up yoga. I used to go to spiritualist groups, hoping no one knew who I was. I found astrology a very potent tool. It really helped me, that investigation. But it was an awful time. I still had to play the game of what people expected me to be."

Despite the wounded man unnoticed in their midst, The Kinks' performances and reviews picked up during nearly two months in the States. They flew home in December with their cult reputation enhanced. Though *Arthur* just missed the *Billboard* Top 100, 'Victoria' hit number 62. The door was ajar, and more tours were eagerly scheduled.

Avory was the next to sicken. His hepatitis cut a February 1970 East Coast run short, and pushed West Coast and West German legs back to May. Ray completed his acting debut in a BBC1 *Play For Today*, *The Long Distance Piano Player*, in Keighley, Yorkshire in March. Then he began work on the next necessary step in The Kinks' commercial resurrection: a new international hit single. In *X-Ray*, he remembered his dad goading him to take on the world with one song again, in the pub on Christmas Day.

'Lola' announces itself with an intro as arresting as any since 'You Really Got Me': a heavy clang of acoustic guitar letting you know that, for just a moment, the old Kinks are back. "I wanted to write a hit," Ray told John Wilson on Radio 4's *Master Tapes*. "It wasn't just the song. It was the musical design. It wasn't a power-chord song like 'You Really Got Me'. It was a power-chord beginning. It needed a special acoustic guitar sound... sonorous, growling, with an attack to it. There's a macho swing to it, a stride, for all its questionable content." He hunted Charing Cross Road for the acoustic instruments the return to hit-making required: a Martin guitar similar to one he'd seen his idol Big Bill Broonzy use, and a Dobro, with its loudly resonant metal base for the strings. "I tracked the Martin three times, slightly out of tune, so it resonates. Then I got the Dobro out... The first phrase was simply something for [1-year-old daughter Victoria] to sing along to – la-la, la-lah... I added the transvestite stuff later." The Kinks only knew the chorus when they recorded it. Dave recalls creating the chord sequence that was 'Lola''s "foundation" in back room rehearsals at Ray's house: uncredited then, or as his brother reminisces now.

The first verse could be a folk song, as Ray takes us down to *"old Soho"* as a naive young man enters a romantically described club where the champagne tastes like coca-cola (because, of course, it's a clip-joint). A touch of organ and electric guitar toughen things up, and when the virginal youth realises his beautiful dancing partner with the "dark-brown voice" isn't all he had thought, staccato, punched-home lines describe the violence of the revelation, as he pushes "her" away, before accepting his fate. In his huskiest voice, Ray's declaration that "I'm not the world's most passionate man", but he knows he's a man "and so is Lola", is both warmly humorous and casually accepting. The single fades out with a grand coda matching the chorus's infinitely addictive chant of Lola's name with a sound like sheet-metal vibrating. December's massive, coda-heavy 'Layla' by Eric Clapton as Derek & The Dominoes surely took notes on 'Lola'. Released on June 12, it hit number two in the UK, The Kinks' biggest single since 'Waterloo Sunset'. Helped by an appearance on *The David Frost Show*, their first specific US TV slot since 1965, it went to nine there.

'Lola''s effortless androgyny effectively set up the early seventies, months before Bowie lolled on the sleeve of *The Man Who Sold The World* in a dress, and more than two years before his breakthrough as Ziggy Stardust let him publicly toy with bisexuality. A quieter pioneer, Dave Davies, could still be seen cruising Greenwich Village in his girlfriend's dress and make-up in 1974, delighting in the look on the drunkenly lecherous Avory's face when he realised who he was eyeing.

The exact inspiration for 'Lola''s teasing narrative remains a mystery. Avory's familiarity with the transvestite bars of west London, where, Ray recounts in *X-Ray*, his resolute but affable butchness was always welcome, provides one possibility. "We used to know this character called Michael McGrath," Avory recalls. "He used to hound the group a bit. Because being called The Kinks did attract these sorts of people. He used to come down to *Top Of The Pops*, and he was publicist for John Stephen's shop in Carnaby Street. He used to have this place in Earls Court, and he used to invite me to all these drag queen acts, and transsexual pubs. They were like secret clubs. And that's where Ray got the idea for 'Lola'. When he was invited too, he wrote it while I was getting drunk. All The Kinks were a bit versatile. It was something different, back then, drag queens and stuff. As far as the general public were concerned, they weren't really enlightened. We never had any followers that were normal. We just thought it was fun. Because they are usually funny people aren't they. With the patter they've got."

"It was a real experience in a club," Ray says (a posh Paris one, he sometimes suggests). "I was asked to dance by somebody who was a fabulous looking woman. I said 'no thank you'. And she went in a cab with my manager straight afterwards. It's based on personal experience. But not every word."

Though the chronology is a little off, others have suggested a date with Warhol Superstar Candy Darling. "I didn't have a date with Candy Darling," Ray says. "We just went out to dinner. I knew it was a drag act. But the thing about Candy is, when she died, she was lying in state in St. Vincent's Hospital, so that everybody could see how much she looked like Marilyn Monroe. Then the stubble started to grow, and the mortician hadn't done a good job. But I like the way that even in death, someone can have their dreams."

Warhol's Factory crowd in the years after his 1968 shooting by Valerie Solanas, which he never wholly recovered from (an early sign that artists too were targets of the assassinations unleashed in the sixties), offered a radically different hang-out for The Kinks in New York. "We used to go to Max's Kansas City," Ray remembers of a club also favoured by the city's bohemian fringe. "That's where we bumped into Holly [Woodlawn], and Jackie Curtis, and Andy Warhol. That was funny. We did a thing called *A Home Movie* on 16mm, and we shot a lot of footage down there. Warhol was a great act. He had the tenacity and guile to actually carry through ideas other people would have thought too outrageous. That was his ploy. And he was very good at generating his own publicity, unlike me. I admire that."

Ray was comfortable with this new set. "Why don't you ask me what sort of men I like?" he teased Candy when she co-interviewed him for Warhol's *Interview* magazine in 1972, before informing her that "in north London pubs... perfectly straight labourers like to get drunk and see a good drag show".

Mary Woronov's memoir of the Factory, *Swimming Underground*, describes its denizens as bitchily asexual vampires huddling together at night, frightened by straight, daytime New York. This tribe of fantasising outsiders amused and relaxed Ray. "They seemed a bit more sincere about their desire to be famous," he says. "The people I knew in

England at that time were so hungry, and so obvious in their ambition that I didn't find them attractive to be around. There was something kitsch and brazen about the people at Max's. They knew what they wanted, and it was funny. You don't make real friends in places like that. And everybody knew that. There's nobody you could count on. Candy Darling was a kind of friend. But in cliques like the Factory, it's the satellite people who are dangerous, the ones who want to be part of it and hang round the back, waiting for people to go. The people themselves are so involved in their own presence, they haven't got time to be dangerous."

Back home, *The Long Distance Piano Player* was screened on BBC1 on October 15. Ray reputedly called a rehearsal that evening so the band wouldn't see it. It was directed by Philip Saville, also responsible for Bob Dylan's dramatic debut on British TV, *Madhouse On Castle Street* (1962). The writer was Alan Sharp, a late-blooming Scottish member of the working-class authors who had come up with Alan Sillitoe and John Braine. This was his last work before leaving for Hollywood, where he wrote some of the key films of America's paranoid early seventies comedown, including the haunting post-Watergate conspiracy thriller *Night Moves* (1975), directed by Arthur Penn and starring a doomed Gene Hackman.

More pertinently for Ray, this took him back to the grey world of hard working-class rebellion he and Dave had discovered when they shared their paperback of *Saturday Night And Sunday Morning*, at the dawn of the sixties. The title even nods to Sillitoe's *Long Distance Runner*. Ray plays Pete, scheduled to play piano non-stop for a marathon four days and nights, in a Salvation Army hall in a small Yorkshire town of cobblestones and terraces. It could almost have been written by Ray, so closely does it shadow his own state of mind. He is driven on by heartless manager Jack (*Saturday Night* veteran Norman Rossington), in a Sisyphean musical endeavour symbolised when he dreams of pushing a piano uphill, then being crushed by it. As he sits playing, he talks almost to himself of a lost childhood friend, Charlie Field, and a fox he saw running free, as if in a stray acre of the Village Green. His loving wife complains to Jack he's "making a spectacle of himself, making himself ill". Pete acknowledges that his "endurance is a dangerous thing", but says "I can't think of anything I'd rather do". He responds to Jack's goading, as Ray does to his inner, driving demons: "Have you ever tried anything yet and not been able to manage it?" Turning his wife away, he says: "It's not that I don't want help. But I've got to do it on my own."

Ray needn't have stopped the other Kinks seeing it. He only occasionally remembers his Yorkshire accent. But he has soulful, distant eyes which cloud over or affect a dangerous, damped-down look, and a disconnected smile. His long hair flops over his bowed head before he finally barks his rebellion at his manager. The radio catchphrase of music-hall star Sandy Powell "Can you hear me, mother?" and fragments of Shakespeare come through gritted teeth, as if channelling Olivier in *The Entertainer*. Typically, he underacts. "It's a great portrayal," says Julien Temple, later to direct Ray many times, "of a musician having a nervous breakdown."

Ray wrote songs for projects by similar talents in this period: 'Nobody's Fool', the theme to the great bittersweet 1971 TV series *Budgie*, starring Adam Faith as a semi-criminal working-class loser, and written by *Billy Liar*'s Keith Waterhouse and Willis Hall; and the theme to the Ned Sherrin-produced National Service war film *The Virgin Soldiers* (1969), its lyric replaced over Sherrin's objections. "I was happy anyway," Ray said, thinking of the musicians Hollywood's resources had allowed him for the sweeping march he'd written. "Because I had my brass band, and I had it to treasure forever." Ray's peers were working with British cinema's newest visionaries; Mick Jagger starring in and writing a song for Nic Roeg and Donald Cammell's *Performance*, while The Who's *Tommy* would soon be filmed by Ken Russell. In October 1970 The Kinks signed up to make the soundtrack for *Percy*, a comedy about a penis transplant directed by *Doctor In The House* auteur Ralph Thomas. Professional managers, incredibly, were involved.

October also saw Ray finally remove the most tenacious of these he'd felt controlled and ripped off by in the sixties. He settled with Eddie Kassner out of court, paying him, from some accounts, £30,000 and agreeing a reduction of his already tiny writing royalty on every hit up till 'A Well Respected Man'. Ray wrote in *X-Ray* that with a young family to support, and Kassner's threat of endless appeals, he couldn't risk losing. Bizarrely, his royalties since 1965 were only now released.

The Kinks were back in the US in November, belatedly following up 'Lola'. On November 27, they released a new album, *Part One: Lola Versus Powerman And The Moneygoround*, which mercilessly exposed how fraught Ray and Dave were both feeling. More than any other Kinks LP, it was confessional and confrontationally raw. The album was recorded during the spring and summer at Morgan Studios in Willesden Green. John Gosling, a classical music student whose audition keyboards had ended up on 'Lola', became a fifth Kink. With his wilderness prophet hair and beard, he was nicknamed Baptist.

As its long-winded title suggested, *Lola* was a concept album. Much of it directly savaged the music business. 'Denmark Street' was a very different London song, advising that you "follow your nose" to Soho's street of music publishing, where Kassner was based. 'Top Of The Pops' hilariously satirised the success that might follow, just as 'Lola', the next song on the album, gave The Kinks another taste. Stoned reporters asking about their influences, crazed photographers shouting "Shot of a lifetime", Gosling's holy organ as a record reaches number one, and the ripe Jewish accent (Ray parodying Kassner, presumably) of an agent promising "real money" make it the cynical biography of a hit. 'The Moneygoround' then details The Kinks' actual contract, naming "Grenville" and "Larry" while prancing piano follows Ray's money as it's chiselled off around the world by publishers "for a song they've never heard". "On the verge of a nervous breakdown/ I resolved to fight right to the end," Ray declares (though at the last, he gave in). The song reeks of betrayal and stress.

"That's when they were starting to make us conform to a business," says Ray. "That album is fairly accurately about what people give up to conform to the Establishment, the music industry. Some of that album had a – not bitterness, but awareness that we were going through this struggle to get royalties, and all of us had families, and we wanted to do well to feed them. And so we had had to bite the bullet and go in with these people like Allen Klein, who can get you a better deal. But the payoff is, you sign the contract with the Devil. And you go on these tours and you have to make back the advance. It's the Devil's coin. And the payback comes. And suddenly, it's all corporate."

The album makes this alienation very personal. 'This Time Tomorrow' begins with the roar of a jet plane ascending. In his seat seven miles high as the sun disappears behind him, Ray looks down at the clouds. He is adrift. Gosling's steady organ maintains the sensation of cruising, and heavy strums of acoustic guitar defy his fears. But he doesn't want to touch down. "I don't know where I'm going," he cries fearfully. "I don't want to see". He is worse off than the sad but comforted voyeur of 'Waterloo Sunset'; he isn't hidden from the claustrophobic rows of houses far below, but can feel the people in them "looking up at me". The elder Davies was also losing his moorings.

"I felt that I'd lost contact with my family," Ray says. "Because I'd been in a pop music bubble for five years, and I didn't know the people around me any more. 'This Time Tomorrow' was about transience, and an ephemeral world. Clouds, and where do we play tomorrow, and what am I doing as a person tomorrow? It's a floating song, and I was floating into a different era. Going with the flow for a while, until I work out where I want to be."

Ray still lived in Fortis Green, still sometimes drank in the Clissold with his dad. But a song slipped onto *Arthur*, 'Nothing To Say', was perhaps an early warning of how this was starting to feel: "I'll have to go soon, because I'm getting bored/ So far, Papa, I've got nothing to say". "It's a song about growing up and growing out of things, seemingly," says Ray, looking back sanguinely today. "But the miracle of what we are and how we function and life itself, is that we think we run away from something, and then suddenly, decades later, you say, 'I don't want to lose it. I want to recapture it.' On the same album there's a song called 'Young and Innocent Days'. You've left, you want to get out of there, you're frustrated, suffocated by an environment and saying, 'There's nothing to say, I want to leave here, you're brainwashed people.' And in a moment of quiet and calm, you think about the innocent days that have passed and gone by."

In 1970, the strain of keeping faith with the ordinary working-class people he lauded and felt his family to be, but had never been wholly comfortable among, was becoming too much. Behind his own suburban front door, marriage with two kids was losing its thrill. *X-Ray* mentions mutual affairs. He could no longer completely deny he was a rock star. "You're going along thinking you're still the same as a person," Ray says, "and then you stop at a crossroads, you turn round and you say, 'Fuck it, I'm different!' And it's happened. You've gone through the sound barrier. You've progressed to that level where you think, 'Who am I?'"

'A Long Way From Home' shows what Ray is scared he's lost. He mourns "the runny-nosed and scruffy kid I knew", and derides the adult who's replaced him, the picture of success in his hand-made overcoats. He's rich but no stronger, older but no wiser, because he's far from his home, and no longer recognises his past. 1972's album *Everybody's In Show-Biz* returns to these sentiments in 'Sitting In My Hotel'. "If my friends could see me now..." Ray sings sadly, high in his rented room, watching the world through his window untouchably far away. He prances round the room "like some outrageous poof", watches TV till the morning in quiet depression, and reflects on his foolish pop star life. His friends, he knows, would ask "what on earth I'm trying to prove".

"'A Long Way From Home' is a little ballad I wrote," Ray says. "It's one of my fondest memories of that time. You're dressed in fancy clothes, you don't know yourself any more. You've drifted away from the source of what you started doing. Our environment had really helped our music. With the exception of stuff like 'You Really Got Me', all the best early Kinks songs that I wrote took place within a mile of where I grew up. It all related to the neighbourhood, and people we knew. And by that time, I think we had lost the plot about where we wanted to go with our music. We'd lost our roots musically, and we were drifting away from Muswell Hill. By the time we got to *Lola Versus Powerman*, I was still living in north London, Dave was. But the empathy with our surroundings had gone. And we were going to America – a larger landscape. It wasn't such a cosy world for us any more. The song 'Powerman' evokes that feeling, with the discords coming down in the middle section. It was the crumbling of a world."

Though Ray felt his working-class roots tearing free of Fortis Green's soil, he didn't betray them. *Lola Versus Powerman*'s most simply affecting song, 'Get Back In Line', is about a working man wondering if he'll be picked for a day's labour by the union, here just another authority figure. The sun over his head shines or goes in on the whim of another's decision when, in a plaintively sung, beautiful detail, "all I wanna do is make some money/ and bring you home some wine".

As with his anger at the British Empire's collapse on behalf of those who fought for it, you can question the enemies Ray picks, and his answers. But the consistency of his radicalism lies in the song which opens and closes the album, 'Got To Be Free'. Its envy of the wild freedom of "a flea or a proud butterfly" with the title for a chorus offers no political solutions, and can sound trite. Unless, that is, you're feeling under the thumb of another's authority which seems it will never let you be. Then the song starts to be a manifesto for walking out of the door in the morning with your self-respect, and firming dreams of change. "Stand up straight," Ray tells himself, "let people see I ain't nobody's slave." He's crazily sure of this individual revolution in attitude: "It won't be long/ Because we are right, and they are wrong."

Dave provided 'Rats', hard rock describing exploitation as a queasily bad trip, with parasitic rodents breeding in the heat and crawling on his back; and 'Strangers', one of the best songs he's written. It finds him on a mentally post-apocalyptic path, his time and world obliterated, torn between fury and an ecstatic love of life. But a generosity of spirit wins through Dave's torment, in lines like his brother's about taking his girl some wine when, looking at everything he owns, he decides "we'll take what we want and give the rest away". He feels he and the one next to him on his lonely path have become strangers, but reaches out to carry on: "we are not two, we are one". Over basic acoustic guitar and Gosling's piano and spiritual organ, the lyrics take Dylanesque symbolic twists. It is the unhidden crack in Dave's voice, the way he gasps for words as he sings with an open heart where his brother would artfully modulate, which gives it emotional power.

"'Strangers' is really about, 'I'm going into the new'," Dave says. "You might think it's nutty, but why can't we work it out so that we can go there together? That's what was going on inside me. If you want to be schizophrenic about it, maybe I was saying it to myself, on one level. 'I know you're fed up with that life, why don't you come with me?' But I was also saying it to my brother, and people around me. I know things are changing, but can't we still move together? Do I have to just cut certain friends off, because they think I'm a nutcase? Because that's how I was brought up. You don't just care about what you're doing. How do your actions affect the people you love, and have supported you? I was always of the mind that, if things change, we should take things we love with us."

'Strangers', 'This Time Tomorrow', 'Sitting In My Hotel', 'Long Way From Home' and another lovely Dave song on *Everybody's In Show-Biz*, 'You Don't Know My Name', all seem at least partly sung from one Davies to the other, when both were feeling lost, but couldn't say why to their brother's face. The private family communications of 'Rosie Won't You Please Come Home' and 'Arthur' had become even more movingly intimate. Ray and Dave are reaching towards each other in these songs.

"I think so, and it was unspoken," Dave says. "We're so different, and we were starting to go on two different paths, and there was a love thing that always held us together. And without that, there would have been no Kinks. There would have been none of this in '71, or 'Lola' or anything. A lot of really powerful foundations of relationships are built on a special kind of love. That kind of love that is so tangible that you're connected as if it's an iron bar."

These few songs on a couple of little-regarded Kinks albums are, along with the record made between them, *Muswell Hillbillies*, and the idea of the Village Green, the emotional heart of their work. There is a tenderness in them which comes from truly expressed pain. At their weakest, Ray and Dave leave themselves most open. As with 'Days', these songs are there when the listener needs them.

"That's one thing I always liked about working with The Kinks," says Dave. "There's so many periods of fragility, and things going wrong –

and yet you still do it. It's almost like seeking out the imperfections, the things that are behind everything. There's a power in imperfections that we tend to miss."

Lola Versus Powerman contained a second big UK hit, 'Apeman'. It was a more playfully extreme expression of 'Got To Be Free''s desire for a simpler life, Ray dreaming of getting away from a worrying world of pollution, nuclear peril and the rat race, and going back to swinging naked from the trees. This funny calypso sung in a Caribbean accent had just enough faint edge to make it more than a novelty. The promo film shot on Hampstead Heath, where the four original Kinks had last wandered for *Village Green* photos, was almost better than the record. Puffing a cigar and with shirt wide open, Ray leads 1970's extravagantly Afghan-jacketed band past beeping cars into the wilds, where Gosling, in full gorilla costume, sweeps him into his arms and scarpers. The Kinks act like the Goodies. Gosling still had his gorilla mask on for his *Top Of The Pops* debut when, as in the film, his fellow Kinks can hardly contain their grins. Dave reveals in *Kink* their accident-prone new boy had fallen off the podium as the camera swung towards his now vacant stool.

"It was Grenville who thought we should use a piano and keyboards. So John Gosling joined thinking that, 'Hey, man, I've hit it big!'" Dave laughs. "We very quickly brought him down to earth. He was Lola for that song, and then an ape." 'Apeman' hit number five, seemingly signalling a new run of hits. But being back on *Top Of The Pops*, which Ray had just ruthlessly satirised, didn't excite Dave either. "I know it sounds silly, but it never bothered me when we weren't in the charts. When you have a big emotional support network, you feel that you can do anything anyway. In fact, when 'Lola' was a hit it made me feel a bit uncomfortable. Because it was taking us out of a different sort of comfort zone, where we'd been getting into the work, and the writing and the musicality was more thought about. It did have that smell of: 'Oh, blimey, not that again.' I found it a little bit odd, that period. And then it got odder and weirder."

Avory has happier memories. "I enjoyed the success we had with 'Lola' and 'Apeman'. We probably didn't make the most of it at the time. I always liked 'Lola', I liked the subject. It's not like anything else. I liked it for that. We'd always take a different path."

The Kinks' third US tour of 1970 ran through November and December. Ray had to fly back to London to re-record a line in 'Apeman' when Reprise executives noticed pollution seemed to be "fucking" more than "fogging" up his eyes. This delayed its US release till the week after they returned home, which is perhaps why it stalled at 45.

Like the 'Apeman' film, the tour showed the year wasn't all misery for The Kinks. Avory fondly recalls the carnage when they were unwisely given time off in LA. "I think one of the most outrageous things," he says, ticking off a mental list, "was when we were staying at the Hollywood Hawaiian Hotel, quite near Hollywood Boulevard, where there were joke shops. We used to like dressing up, and that night Dave was a New York cop, I was a clown, Baptist was a hood, and Dalton was a cop. We all had simulated guns. Baptist had this carbine repeater Tommy gun. And we went to see James Taylor. The representative of our record company was a bit way out, saying, 'Oh man, this is great, but you've gotta be really quiet when James comes on.' And James Taylor came out, and Dave saw him coming down the stairs, and shot 'im. I dunno what he thought of that. It was quite a loud gun. Probably thought he had been shot. They got rid of us, but let Dave stay. We went off to the Whisky A Go Go, and terrorised that place. Stupid behaviour, really. I remember trying to do a back flip. I couldn't do it sober. I fell on me 'ead."

The next morning, Grenville Collins, the increasingly frayed and irate manager who accompanied them in America, called a crisis meeting. Ray, who'd innocently spent the evening watching *Fellini's Satyricon*, listened, frowning. "Grenville said, 'This has got to stop,'" says Avory. "'It can't go on like this. It's going all round the town that you're imbeciles. You're supposed to be a serious band.' Just as he was giving us a lecture, Baptist came in through the door. He'd just been down the joke shop. He appeared in a Viking helmet with a Viking horn, and blew it. Everything he'd said just fell on the floor."

The following year, 1971, began with a UK tour on the back of their renewed success, their first since the disastrous package and cabaret bookings of 1968. It included, incredibly, their first London gig in four years, showing how much more important America had become. They returned to the US in March. The same month the *Percy* soundtrack was released in the UK. The full horror of the Hywel Bennett and Britt Ekland-starring sex comedy which spawned it had already limped out of cinemas. Ray reputedly stormed from the premiere when he saw how his music had been butchered.

The penis transplant plot perhaps loosely inspired 'God's Children', a protest against science interfering in man's unchanging nature. Like 'Animals In The Zoo' and 'The Way Love Used To Be', it was a prettier variant on 'Apeman''s desire to run back to the wild. On 'The Way Love Used To Be', Ray sounds particularly strained and out of time as he again seeks somewhere "we'll belong". Movie world strings and brass give some grandeur even to a kitsch run-through of 'Lola' (whose chart-topping position was the only reason *Percy*'s producers had called him, Ray wisely suspected). 'Moments' was, in retrospect, the plea nearest his heart. It portrays a fading love affair – ecstatic moments, and "the moments of stress that we'd better forget", a line thrown away lightly, by a man hoping to get away with it. There's an unusual quaver in Ray's soft voice, a familiarity with the woman he addresses as "love", and awareness in the lyrics that despite his apologies, he somehow can't change. He and Rasa slow danced to it in the front room as their life cracked apart. Even the song's hope is faint.

The shipwreck on which these lovely songs were sunk was quickly obvious. A 'God's Children'-led EP put the best on a life raft in April, with a personal letter to reviewers from Ray. It was ignored, as was the 'God's Children'/ 'Moments' single Reprise released. They refused the album.

Ray valued the latest brush with the film world *Percy* had given him. But the fiasco it made of music over which he'd taken perhaps foolish care, following Pye's signal failure to promote *Lola Versus Powerman* (released the same day as 'Apeman' but not charting, in stark contrast to its two singles), convinced him The Kinks needed more clean breaks with their past. He and Wace shopped around in America for a new label. Perhaps unwisely, they signed a lucrative five-year contract on

November 12 with RCA, a label which, though it had Elvis, constantly struggled to make the rock impact Reprise specialised in. They paid over the odds hoping The Kinks, with Bowie and Lou Reed, would change that in the seventies. "We left Pye Records because we could see that they were not listening to our pleas to do albums, and sell albums," Ray explains. "That's why I stopped it. That's why I tried to do my albums, the theme records that followed. It's a whole different mind-set for those albums in America." The new label offered a priceless enticement they would live to regret. "The key deal point with RCA," Ray explained to Radio 4's John Wilson, "was that they had no creative input."

Pye claimed they were still owed albums by the band, who eventually had to buy themselves out of their contract. Ray had personally compiled a premature valediction of the Pye years. *The Kinks* (soon dubbed the "Black" album for its forbidding sleeve) was a 1970 double-album starting with 'You Really Got Me' and ending with 'Days'. Journalist and fan John Mendelssohn put together the more ambitious and successful *The Kink Kronikles* double for Reprise in 1972. Thanks to a seemingly minor clause in their 1966 Pye contract, which the spurned label ruthlessly exploited, their catalogue was also spliced together on random, almost endless compilations for the next 30 years. The band, anxious that new work should be heard, were understandably furious. Still, one of those shoddy compilations, *The Golden Hour Of The Kinks*, was the first Kinks record I bought. It randomly shuffles songs from 'Louie Louie' to 'Shangri-La', emphasising the dazzling range of achievement. The 20 tracks on its overloaded grooves always signal summer to me.

CHAPTER 9

The Unabomber of Rock

The Kinks' RCA years started promisingly. "There was a lavish launch in New York, and a lavish party at the Hyatt House [in LA] as well," Ray remembers. "We all thought it was funny. Because the band never took anything seriously. On my own, I probably would have taken it a little bit seriously. But not with the characters I had."

Warhol, Lou Reed, Alice Cooper and transvestite theatre mavericks and Kinks super-fans The Cockettes attended the New York party at the Playboy Club on November 18, which cost a then huge $10,000. Reporters from *Melody Maker*, *NME* and London's *Evening Standard* were also flown in and put up at the exclusive Plaza Hotel for three days, adding considerably to the expense. But The Kinks' fortunes hadn't really changed. "On the second night we all went to The Kinks' party," remembers Chris Charlesworth, there for the *MM*. "During the course of the three days in New York I repeatedly asked if I could interview The Kinks but the request was turned down. I discovered that on the last night we were there they were playing a gig in upstate New York, but they couldn't organise me attending that either. I thought this was absurd. I'd come all this way, and all I could report was a few lines about a knees-up. Here was an opportunity for me to do a big spread on The Kinks in *MM* – circulation 200,000 in those days – and nobody was interested. Also at The Kinks' party were Moon and Entwistle from The Who, on the eve of a tour, and their manager arranged tickets for me for the next day. So I flew down the East Coast with The Who and they got a big spread in *MM* and The Kinks missed out, even though they'd paid for me to go to the US in the first place. In hindsight, this was symptomatic of all that ailed The Kinks in those days. No one in charge to make snap decisions that would help them."

This soon became literally true. Grenville Collins, increasingly exhausted by The Kinks' behaviour, and according to Dave having just married an heiress, amicably quit once the new deal was signed. On December 30, Robert Wace resigned in a bitter row with Ray, who had asked him to reduce the management fee, now he was the only manager left. "The problem [of exiting]," Wace sighed in Andrew Loog Oldham's autobiography *Stoned*, "is that you create these people and then, sooner or later, you get fed up with them or they get fed up with you, and then the bugger of it is that you can't go on stage and play the guitar. I mean, they've got the residual."

The last of the odd group of men who had gathered round the teenage Kinks in 1963 was suddenly gone. Ray thought they were no longer needed. The Kinks could manage themselves now. He at last had total control.

The first RCA album, *Muswell Hillbillies*, suggested what he might do with it. The crosswinds as The Kinks leaned towards America, while Ray and Dave felt dislocated and adrift, for a moment blew them back to north London. The working-class resentment at oppression in 'Get Back In Line' and 'Got To Be Free' was magnified and explored. The apparent last stand Ray had made in *The Village Green Preservation Society*, when he found refuge in childhood memories kept safe in his head, became more urgent and solid. His mind and body were now explicitly at threat from his urban environment and the "people in grey", the authorities who knock on working-class doors. As he felt himself being uprooted, he dug his heels in. *Muswell Hillbillies* is an album of almost hopeless defiance.

Its world is laid out on its gatefold sleeve. A sunny London afternoon dimly lights the dusty, high-walled Victorian solidity of the Archway

Tavern. The five Kinks stand drinking at the bar. Only the flat-capped Avory's yellow scarf and white trainers make him stand out as he holds a pint. Dave's eyes are closed, glass already empty, leg bent as he leans on the bar, looking like a man who's forgotten how to give a fuck. Ray stands straight, and looks unreadably into the camera. A man not much older than them turns from his paper to stare suspiciously. The Kinks look incongruous in a local pub where the Davies family regularly drank. That was why Ray felt himself leaving this society. But it also made him fight for it harder.

"Because it's on an island," Ray said of choosing the pub location in the BBC concert documentary *The Kinks At The Rainbow*, "and when I do interviews which give me more than two columns, I can talk about it being like England." To me he says: "*Muswell Hillbillies* was an attempt to get back to where we were from. We were out of our depth, and when I get out of my depth I try to find somewhere that's reasonably like home. It's safer there. Somehow it works as a record. I think maybe the artwork pulled it together."

The Kinks At The Rainbow was filmed at the Archway Tavern a few months after the September 1971 photo-shoot, and the man giving the apparent interlopers at the bar a filthy look is interviewed. He cheerfully hopes to get "free drinks" from the exposure. Like the smartly turned-out old man of Fred Davies' age who sings the music-hall song 'Lily Of Laguna' to Ray, he clearly does accept The Kinks. But Ray's humble, quiet and down-turned eyes as the old man sings look something like shame. He is utterly respectful, but can't quite fit.

Muswell Hillbillies' wider context is also laid out in the film. "It was about people being moved out from places like Islington, to places like Harlow," Ray explained, "and being taken away from where they belong." The record was first of all about the Davies family, and the relocation of Fred and Annie from inner-city Islington to middle-class Muswell Hill. Though Dave says this was from fear of the coming Blitz, the theme of forced relocation and demolition of homes permeates the songs. In the inner sleeve, The Kinks stand outside an apparently bombed-out and condemned Victorian terrace, fenced off with corrugated iron, such a feature of the early seventies. The film takes

Ray to a similar neighbourhood not far from where he played growing up. "Now it's a desert," he says. Casting an eye over a block due for demolition, he decides it "looks pretty sturdy to me". The film cuts to the house being smashed, and his comic dismay.

"That was all in response to the demolition of the Caledonian Road, North End, and the Dartmouth Park Hill estate, which has now replaced all those places you saw us standing against in that album sleeve," Ray says. Caledonian Road is a short walk from the Tavern, North End in Hampstead, near the Willesden studio where the album was made. "It's not that it's my constant quest. But it's something that shouldn't go unnoticed, in a distant time, when people bother to actually listen to music, and some of them might pick up on this. Which is my own cataloguing of where I'm from, and what's become of it. Things that are gone, and things that are there."

The extremity of Ray's rebellion is laid out in the opening song '20th Century Man'. It's the whole century he's resisting: its massively destructive technology, from the napalm then burning up Vietnam to the H-Bomb, and the Welfare State he thinks has stolen his privacy and lets grey officials walk through his front door. He misses the green fields of William Blake's 'Jerusalem'. "I'm a 20th century man/ But I don't wanna die here," Ray sings, and, still more quixotically in 1970, "I don't wanna be here." In the 21st century, he still opens shows with it.

The tremors you can feel shaking *The Village Green Preservation Society*'s idyll are full-blown mental cracks now. 'Acute Schizophrenia Paranoia Blues' finds the street outside too much to deal with: "I don't trust nobody/ but I'm much too scared to be alone". In '20th Century Man' even his mother doesn't understand him, as he tries to hold his sanity together, or else, if he blows, there'll be bloodshed: "Don't want to get myself shot down/ By some trigger-happy policeman". In the companion song that begins side two, 'Here Come The People In Grey', a man about to be unwillingly relocated plots to live in the fields in a tent, with a shotgun to protect his bare peasant's fiefdom from the police. Desperate people who can't cope with the demands on them have taken such measures. In Forest Hill in south London, a tramp

172

built a hut for himself in a small patch of ancient wood in the eighties, and carved out a letter-box with his address on the fence, declaring his domain to the postman. No one knows if he died in hard freedom, but the letter box is still there.

This was the kind of absolute liberty Ray sympathised with. To Ray, the Welfare State, a glorious post-war bulwark allowing working-class survival and safety in most eyes, is just another way to snare you. In 'Uncle Son', trade union bosses and the generals who sent cannon fodder like Arthur to the trenches are essentially the same: "They'll feed you when you're born/ and use you all your life".

"I remember writing a little scenario for '20th Century Man'," Ray says. "It was just a madcap idea for a movie. This guy was like a suicide bomber at the end of a building that was going to be knocked down, and he said, 'If you're going to knock this place down, I'll just blow myself up.' That sort of mentality. A bit like the Unabomber." This was the attitude Ray was also now taking with his music, his own business and bosses, as *Lola Versus Powerman* showed, inseparable from a wider struggle. "Yeah. I'll go down screaming with my career and I'll make a statement – and maybe people in the future might learn something from it. Totally mad, really," he says, not thinking so.

Ask Ray where his fear and hatred of the "people in grey" and authority come from, and he goes back to the fifties. "When I was young, I was subject to fear," he says. "I knew to fear the knock on the door. It was the Cold War, and there were stories of another place in Europe, where people had their rights taken away. And maybe my household discussed that sort of thing. We didn't have political debates. But I grew up thinking if there's a telegram or the phone rings or there's a knock on the door, it's bad news. And often, it was. I wasn't rebellious. But authority was treated with suspicion. And going for a few times to the unemployment office with my dad, for a day out, and relatives who were talking about losing their jobs, I sensed it." 'Get Back In Line' comes from this, of course. "I listened a lot as a child. I didn't really play with my other peers, I listened to the adults, and maybe that's the key to how I picked up a lot that frightened me. Simply because it was happening to those people. And it stayed with me. And I don't think these people in grey have gone away in our so-called free and – what's the word? – transparent society."

Ray sings in many accents, from cotton-mouthed bluesman to shabby-genteel English. What's most striking, especially on the original vinyl, is the way his voice often almost vanishes, like a man walking out of a bar letting his last point drift off behind him. He is dislocated even on the record. He refuses even to be heard. "It's a, 'I don't care if you hear this or not'-type vocal," Ray considers. "It's sung into the guitar. If you want to hear this, listen over and over. Which is silly…"

The transatlantic, trans-class limbo Ray felt himself falling into in 1971 is built into *Muswell Hillbillies*' title, and its bare blues, jazz and country music of almost purely American roots. The use of early sixties Kinks tour-mates The Mike Cotton Sound meant though that, in Ray's words, it was pub jazz. And the love of country music, he notes, "came from my sister". It was a schizophrenic way to try getting back home.

"It briefly reconnected me," Ray reflects. "My home was I think still there. Although personally I was detached from it. My relationships were not the same with my family. And 'Muswell Hillbillies' meant it was a step across the water to America, acknowledging the hillbilly in me – the lyrics that say 'Take me back to the Black Hills that I've never seen'. Using an American sound and references, 'Oklahoma, U.S.A.' is about a working-class woman growing up in Islington. It's cross-breeding, cross-cutting back and forth between two different worlds, a parallel universe, and *Muswell Hillbillies* was like that. The conceit of that record was that there are hillbillies even in London, but we don't know it. And perhaps I'm like that."

I suggest the whole album could be folk songs from the Archway Tavern. Ray, as he did in that old documentary, wants to think the whole country could be found in that pub. "It was in the Archway Tavern where I first saw anti-British activities," he says. "Burning the flag, and a lot of other stuff. I used to take Barrie Keeffe there, who was a writer friend of mine, and Barrie went on to write *The Long Good Friday* [which in 1979 presciently combined rugged individualist old-school London gangsters, Docklands demolition and redevelopment, and IRA terror]. So it did, in a strange way, open the door into what was going to happen in the seventies. When I wrote that album, the war had already started in the North [of Ireland], the troops had gone in. '72 was when it really kicked in, Bloody Sunday. I was aware of what was happening politically. It wasn't a record without some sense of place or time. It's a very political record."

Ray's constantly whirring mind, bored by repeated facts, sometimes layers new insights onto old events as he's questioned about them yet again, time and place bending as he works at the meaning of a past which still lives strongly in him. Barrie Keeffe met Ray in 1977, and had his revelation in (probably) the Archway Tavern the next year. Which doesn't mean Ray's wrong. Maybe the contrails from *Muswell Hillbillies* and its symbolic locale really did linger into *The Long Good Friday*.

"I was about to write *The Long Good Friday* when I was knocking about with Ray," Keeffe recalls, "we used to socialise quite a lot, drinking and that. And the inspiration did come with Ray – I'd never remembered who it was, but that's right, we went to one of those North London Irish pubs, and they did burn the Union Jack on stage, and they were coming round with a collection, and Ray said, 'Don't give away your English accent.' 'Fuck me, it's protection, it's protection...' And in the traditional gangster film there's got to be an enemy, usually another gang, which I was fed up with, it's so predictable. That suddenly became the IRA. I found out they ran a lot of Belfast on protection and terror. And that spark came from that night with Ray in that pub. I wonder if I've ever thanked him for that? He'd ask for royalties!"

"I'm really uneasy about talking about these old albums," Ray anyway suddenly adds. "After a while, songs should exist in their own right. Maybe that's why I'm more specific about the political stuff, because maybe one day people will see, that's what he was talking about. So it's clear..."

That politics is very personal. Most of *Muswell Hillbillies'* second side is about members of the Davies clan. The closing anthem 'Muswell Hillbilly' sees slum clearance as a totalitarian state "solution" to the working class, stuffing them into "identical little boxes" like a prison camp. Ray declares, "They'll never take away my cockney pride", and that pride's expressed through family and friends. 'Oklahoma U.S.A.' is about his sister Rosie who he "used to watch walking to the factory," he explained before singing it with heartbreaking feeling at the Albert Hall in 2012. Walking home from the pictures where she's watched *Oklahoma* (the escapist musical which soundtracked Rene's death), she picks up the paper on the way back to her decrepit house, head still free. The beautiful piano melody and utter sympathy in Ray's voice repeat 'Got To Be Free''s need for a greater escape from work's drudgery, or else "what's living for?" Apart from celluloid dreams of America, the only havens this record offers are its constant humour, and the Davies panacea, 'Have A Cuppa Tea'. Their mum and grandmum both had pots constantly brewed. As Dave's acid-blasted mind tore at him in those days, mum had a cup ready as he walked through the door. Sometimes, for some people, it is their only comfort.

'Here Come The People In Grey''s protagonist plots a "one man revolution". 'Uncle Son' remembers a railwayman, staunch socialist and union man who died of T.B., and believed in real revolution as if it was Heaven. "He loved with his heart/ He worked with his hands," Ray sings of him. "'Uncle Son' is about our political system, which hasn't changed much since I wrote it," he says. "There's a guilty feeling in it. It goes back to the same world as 'Long Way From Home', and expresses the way people are used by political parties – going back to my root working-class feelings, acknowledging the working class. Because growing up, Muswell Hill wasn't really a working-class area. But I was very aware of the political parties, and the payback they took from us."

Rosie Rooke, whose "alcoholic bloodshot eyes" are the first image in 'Muswell Hillbilly', was Ray's mum's best friend, a busty, glamorous and tragic figure of his childhood. There was a cruel undertow to a tale he'd heard of Rosie and Annie. "They were walking around Islington market when they were about 15," he told Radio 4's John Wilson. "My father picked up a bundle of horse manure and threw it at her, and knocked her hat off." It was the pretty hat of a woman who wanted more.

"A good reason for doing these songs is to celebrate those people," Ray concludes, "because a few of them aren't with us any more. And short of the people who love them still, and at family get-togethers talk about them, I like that some of those people are there for all time – so long as people want to hear the songs."

Muswell Hillbillies is about Ray and Dave's family as working-class refugees tossed about by the state. But it's also about Ray as a refugee from that family, about to try his luck in the real Black Hills of America. Guiltily, he was leaving the dreamers with no choice behind. "It was a kind of warning to me, and now it has happened," he says. "With families, and a sense of place, it happens to us all – they explode, they go on to different places, families become fragmented, then get together at Christmas and have terrible fights. Going to school in the fifties, I was aware that a change was happening, and that it was inevitable. When you're older, you can see it coming, though you're not quite sure what it's going to be. It's still happening, the world will continue to evolve, and crumble around us. I'm trying to understand why."

Muswell Hillbillies was released on November 24 in the US, two days later at home. "Return of the working class hero" was the tag-line in RCA's ads, referencing John Lennon's 'Working Class Hero' the year before. Raised by his aunt in the sort of lower-middle-class suburban semi-detached Ray only bought as a star, Lennon overcompensated in his great song's grinding anger. When he moved to New York in 1971, Lennon would embrace the more facile revolutionary posturing dabbled with by the even more middle-class Mick Jagger, who had "loved" the violence at 1968's anti-Vietnam War protest outside the US Embassy in Grosvenor Square, then written the superficial 'Street Fighting Man', and the more surreal and grandiose rebel fantasy 'Salt Of The Earth'. Ray's ideas on revolution and class were much funnier, and realistically embraced the probability of failure. Not bowing or denying who you are was the most you could expect. He underplayed *Muswell Hillbillies* as a "comedy album" in *Melody Maker*, partly true, while also proudly saying he'd made "a more definite statement on this LP than ever before". The real revolution he claims The Kinks could have caused in the sixties was never more explicit than *Muswell Hillbillies'* maniacally absolute, half-defeated insistence on a better world.

Though the US rock press were primed to love them, reviews of this latest unexpected new direction were mixed. The album's coalsto-Newcastle Americana underwhelmed *Rolling Stone*'s Metal Mike Saunders, who complained "it's such a drag to hear the routine 1971 country slide guitar rot turn up on a Kinks album", though most of the record sounded like British music-hall to him anyway. RCA's extravagant publicity campaign and repeated touring still only let it graze the US chart at 100, slightly better than *Arthur*. "Wouldn't a new hit single help?" *Melody Maker*'s Chris Charlesworth asked. "Yes, but I am not looking forward to going through the mechanism necessary to get a hit single," Ray answered. "The stuff I am writing at the moment is album material. I just don't like all the problems associated with singles, promoting them and things, because people think that's all you are doing. I don't think there are any singles on *Hillbillies*." '20th Century Man' was one in the US, stalling at 106. There was no single, or album success, in the UK. Ray's terror at repeating Pye-era indignities torpedoed the commercial chances of The Kinks' greatest album.

"Having just signed that big deal with RCA, it was not the ideal record to bring out," Ray accepts. "Although they loved it, actually. It got awards and things. It was me also saying, 'I won't be anywhere as good at another job, so I'm going to make the most of it while I'm doing it, and take risks. I think I'll be writing until the end, and it's the body of work that will be important.' Rather than saying this is a bunch of singles. That I got lucky with..."

Dave loved the album. "After the sessions, Ray and I used to go back to my house and listen to the tapes together," he told Peter Doggett, "coming up with suggestions for what we could do next. It was a really special time. It was probably just about the last time Ray and I did that." But though Dave felt comfortable in the studio and at home with his children (a second son, Simon, had been born in June 1970; Christian would follow in April 1972), he couldn't tell his adult family about the voices in his head, alienating him too from his surroundings. On *Muswell Hillbillies*, his supportive harmonies and electric guitar were suddenly minor elements. *The Kinks At The Rainbow*'s concert, filmed at Finsbury Park's Rainbow Theatre on January 31, 1972, shows a dramatic shift in the band's balance. Ray, diffident on stage when they began, has never been so camply flamboyant. Dave, masked by a defensively thick beard, shrinks into himself, hardly moving and hardly there. Ray even slides on his knees playing guitar on the closing 'Set Me Free', as if becoming his brother, whose paralysed husk stands behind him. "We don't really have any problems now," Dave says in the film of their relationship. "We've all grown up together." A punch-up would be preferable to his meekly passive voice. A live photo from 1971 shows his eyes wide with desperate intensity, mouth set, looking unconnected to the hand playing his guitar.

"Oh God," he says, looking at it. "That scares the living shit out of me. Because I'm going through hell. When I see that picture, it throws me right back into the place I was in at the time. Because internally and spiritually, I was going through an immense transformation. I was getting into mystical things. And yet I was still in that world of get up there and play the hot riffs. Playing every night, drinking, sex, the rock'n'roll life, the usual. And I found it really difficult to cope with these two worlds. So I was stuck in the middle, and I felt stranded. There are other things that are more important than smashing away on a guitar on stage. My world was becoming a lot bigger, broader, deeper, and I was searching for a means to connect with it. I felt like there were very few people I could communicate these ideas to. I was 24 in '71. Pretty young."

1971 had been punctuated with cancelled tours because of Dave's condition: Australia in January, Austria and West Germany in March. Time off in LA in April was marked by a further despairing descent into a mescaline and red wine binge, a too brief stay in hospital for overwhelming depression, and a wiped week of US dates. The Australian gigs postponed to June gave Ray and Dave what would prove their last chance to visit Arthur. They were otherwise a draining fiasco of blown amps and surly crowds.

In America, though, which had loathed and overwhelmed the old Kinks, they could do no wrong. Before a prestigious date at New York's classical venue the Philharmonic Hall on March 30, Ray unwisely joined the band on tequila in the plush backstage bar. Maybe from mixing with medication for pain from his childhood back injuries, even a pint reputedly goes to his head, in marked contrast to his bandmates, named the Juicers by bemused Americans. Mid-gig, a legless Ray fell towards Dave, who stepped out of his way as he crashed into speakers which tumbled to the floor. Encouraged by Dave, much of the crowd invaded the stage. The *New York Times*'s Mike Jahn found the spectacle "sordid", noting dozens standing at the front throughout, "smoking marijuana and turning to shout obscenities at anyone who asked them to be seated", and "several hundred" onstage by the end. "The sound of crunched microphones could be heard. One man walked up the main aisle spitting into the seat."

US reviews routinely mention inaudible vocals, distorted sound, and behaviour where "professional" isn't the best word. At a Maryland gig in September 1972, Dave was too drunk to stand. During the song 'Alcohol', Ray skidded on some spilt beer and was knocked out cold. He returned some time later, Dave recalls in *Kink*, concussed and head bandaged like a mummy, to sing 'You Really Got Me'. "After the show, Gosling was so upset and distressed that he ran from the building crying," writes Dave. "Our tour manager chased him and slapped his face to calm him down. He was like a hysterical child. Afterwards I drank myself into oblivion."

But this reputation as unpredictable, shambolically smashed eccentrics enhanced their cult. And when everything kicked in, the early seventies Kinks were uniquely great. Ray's sudden addiction to camp showmanship fed off American crowds who loved him for it. Two March 1972 Carnegie Hall shows, taped for the live half of the August double-album *Everybody's In Show-Biz*, caught his peak. "The whole of the front row were drag queens," he told Peter Doggett. "All of the Warhol crowd were there, people like Jayne County and Holly Woodlawn. They were in the front, all standing up...They were the only people I could actually see." White-suited and bow-tied, he responded with more high camp and androgyny. Hits were edited from the album in favour of vaudeville tunes such as 'Baby Face' (growled in the style of Louis Armstrong), and five transformed *Muswell Hillbillies* tracks. Singing 'Muswell Hillbilly' there, he impersonates Johnny Cash. 'Alcohol', a darkly funny cautionary tale on the album, is a strung-out

Victorian melodrama introduced by Ray aping W.C. Fields, and sung with a beer bottle balanced on his head. This replaced anything from the sixties as the set-piece showstopper in America.

"I wanted to lighten things up a bit," he says, "with the bow ties and the flares. I guess people thought, 'Oh, this is vaudeville time'. There was more to it than that – I was still looking for an alternative to the guys in red suits. I was looking to build a band of new personalities, and get their music across. We used a lot of Dixieland horns. We really revelled in that time."

Much of *Everybody's In Show-Biz*'s studio half is a writing challenge akin to the Hancock episode about the boredom of an English Sunday where absolutely nothing happens. Eight songs are about the repetition and disillusion of life on the road, summed up by the closing line of 'Motorway': "I never thought I'd travel so far to work". 'Here Comes Yet Another Day' adds to 'Sitting In My Hotel''s document of the loneliness Ray was dragging himself through for their American comeback. The john in that song is a loo in another, his Atlantic crossing still incomplete. As on the live sides, Gosling's imaginative keyboards and trad brass replace Dave's guitar at the sound's heart. 'Unreal Reality', in which Ray stares at LA's silver-painted girls and infinite skyscrapers and no longer even trusts his sense of touch to tell him what's authentic, sounds like a small echo of Dave's struggle.

Emotionally convincing and funny as the album is, Ray had meant it to soundtrack a film of their March tour. He'd wanted a *Muswell Hillbillies* TV movie too. "RCA did not understand I wanted to make videos and films in 1972," he says indignantly. "I said, 'This is one of the most important things you'll ever get involved in.' I taped the meeting, I've still got the tape – they said, 'We want you to make music, we're not in the entertainment business.' Mind-boggling lack of vision."

RCA did indulge Ray with film for his 16mm camera. The frustrated director who hadn't been allowed on a film course at Hornsey Art College (pushing him towards pop) let his friend Laurie Lewis shoot The Kinks at restaurants, hotels and gigs, in grainy natural light. Aside from tantalising glimpses of an animated Ray, Lou Reed and pale-faced

181

Warholites in the video for 1988's 'The Road', the footage still moulders in Konk. *The Colossal Shirt*, made in London in 1971, was among Ray's other 16mm experiments. The most widely seen was the promo for 'Supersonic Rocket Ship', a wistful calypso inspired by Concorde which hit number 16 in the UK in May. The long-suffering Gosling was fitted with wings while Ray, dressed like one of the Kaiser's generals, bossed him around his back garden.

Hollywood as a place fascinated Ray. *X-Ray* mentions his affair there with a Southern redhead named Savannah, who stripped at the Rat Trap, where the men held flashlights for intimate inspections. At 1970 or 1972's end, depending which clues you believe, Ray spent three weeks living with her on Hollywood Boulevard.

"I soon fell out of love with Hollywood," he says, "when I went back and had to live there for a little while. It was a cheap rental place. It was Christmas, New Year time. It's not a nice place, with destructive people. It was all very Nathanael West, *Day Of The Locusts*. I could see all that coming down – Fitzgerald's *Crack-Up*. I could see how that easily could happen to me. So I got out of it. It's different to Soho. It wears a veneer... it's like it's got this filter over it, it all looks pink. I think it's more decayed than Soho, morally, and the people accepted it. I couldn't see any definition between good, bad and ugly. Whereas if you feel threatened in Frith Street, you think, 'Can't go down there tonight, it's a bit dodgy,' in Hollywood, you're welcome everywhere. It could have been the Scientology House. It could have been a bar. It's going back to that alien look when we first went to America – a lot of people had that blank expression. So I soon knocked that on the head."

Why did he go?

"Just to finish off some business, really. And write a few more songs. And I was finishing off a screenplay that never got made."

The screenplay, *Darrel And Becky*, was about two failed dreamers on Hollywood's fringe, wishing they were stars but destroying each other. In a version that appears in Ray's 1997 book *Waterloo Sunset*, everyone looks like a forties star when the light is kind. The scabs and sores show when their luck fades. Would-be writer English and Rat Trap stripper and would-be actress Rosa appear in porn films when they need to. The seedy apartment building with a pool where they stay was doubtless Ray and Savannah's. English writes a song about the people he tramps the Boulevard with, and pins his hopes on getting it to the English band having a party at the Hyatt House, whose singer looks just like him. Jealous anger, despair, and fame based on mutable identity and sexual exploitation power the story, called 'Celluloid Heroes', after a song that tells it far better.

'Celluloid Heroes' climaxed *Everybody's In Show-Biz*. It was Ray's first American reward, moving from 'Oklahoma U.S.A.''s Islington fantasy, to those soiled by walking the actual streets under Hollywood's sign. It also left working-class life to consider his own stardom. Soft piano and acoustic guitar shadow his delicately heartfelt vocal at first, but after more than six minutes, the song has become an underplayed epic. It finds heroism in movie stars' images, and the flesh and blood pain which creates them. Reducing them to their stars on Hollywood Boulevard's Walk of Fame, trodden on by new hopefuls, their lives' resilience is made more moving. "If you covered him with garbage, George Sanders would still have style", Ray sings of the silky English charmer who killed himself with an overdose that April, while the human tragedy of Marilyn, who "should have been made of iron or steel" but isn't tough enough to tread on, is caught in a couple of lines. There's suffering if you find fame, and just as much if you fail. Ray finally wishes he existed up on the screen, because everywhere else pain and death await. Victoria's approving smile at its melody as she lay on his Fortis Green floor encouraged the lyrics of his Hollywood song.

Everyone knew it was a Kinks classic to stand with anything they'd done. Ray chopped it under five minutes for the American single's November release, leaving it at over six in Britain, then hacked its length there for a second try in January, as if demanding a recount. It stubbornly refused to chart, leaving the next 40 years' playlists clear for Elton John's monstrously saccharine Marilyn tribute 'Candle In The Wind', and The Kinks' early seventies greatness largely buried. "It was probably our biggest non-hit hit," Dave told Peter Doggett. "It was a really dramatic piece in its own right, and it also seemed to be a sort of allegory, summing up a lot of what was going on in our own lives." It didn't matter. "DJs didn't care about the content of the song. They just said it was too long to play on the radio."

This period ended for Dave in his own lonely American place. In the tacky blandness of a New York Holiday Inn in August, after two triumphant Kinks shows with The Beach Boys, the demonic voices rattling around his head for the last three years took gleeful charge. Unable to go to anyone else's room for help for fear of what they'd say, Dave looked at the inky, rain-streaked high window. "You can never go back to the way you were," he remembers the voices taunting him in *Kink*. "It's too late. Jump." He put his head in his hands, weeping, and prayed for help. Linda, an old girlfriend passing on the off chance he was in and just qualified as a psychiatric nurse, knocked on the door.

"That was a big, big turning point," he says. "It could have made or broke me as a human. Because I came very close to jumping out of that window in New York. I know it sounds really corny, but I was helped spiritually at that time. Someone came to the door at the right moment, and I believe in that now. Omens, and that things don't happen by chance. If a plane's going to crash, and for one person on it it's not their time, it won't."

Dave gave up hallucinogens, took up vegetarianism, and intensified his spiritual quest. He saw the ghost of his possible future six years later, at Hollywood's Hyatt House. "It's very weird," he says, "because I met Keith Moon a few months before he died, and he seemed totally different. And I was with my new girlfriend, and we wanted to do stuff, but I felt he was saying, really [in a scuzzed-up voice], ''Ave a pint, Dave, go on...' All that. I was helped, but I think Keith had gone too far down that road. Makes you think, doesn't it?"

Back in Britain, Ray began 1973 working furiously on a major new project. He would be the next to fall.

CHAPTER 10

"The Kinks Are Dead"

There was a thunderstorm on Sunday morning at the White City dog track, with monsoon rain so heavy you couldn't see the stage at the Great Western rock festival held in its bleak, mostly empty concrete stands. Such was its severity a canopy broke under the weight of water. The 10,000 crowd – a quarter of the number predicted for this unhappy, chilly event – were waiting for the headliners, Sly & The Family Stone. It was at this gloomy spot where Ray Davies had decided to finish The Kinks.

"I just want to say goodbye and thank you for all you have done," he said at the end of their set. A DJ had already cut in with the Stones' 'Satisfaction' on the PA, drowning out the full text of his retirement speech. "It would have ended with 'The Kinks are dead, I am dead,'" he wrote in *X-Ray*. As he was led away, he wished he had died. "What," *Melody Maker* saw a watching girl ask her friend, "was that all about?"

The crisis in Ray's life had taken half a year to reach this climax. At the end of 1972, The Kinks were booked to play the Theatre Royal, Drury Lane, as part of celebrations to mark Britain's entry into the Common Market on January 1, 1973. Ray seized on this high-profile gig in the heart of London's theatre district as a chance to resurrect *The Village Green Preservation Society* as the musical he'd often dreamed of.

With only a month before the show, he barely slept as he obsessively composed and rewrote songs, and worked on the stage presentation at a fevered pace. His already strained marriage creaked further.

Only five new songs made the show, on January 14. A brass band and chorus, a set modelled on Vauxhall's licentious pleasure gardens (shut in Victorian times), and projected family photos, film and stills of sixties figures visually enhanced Ray's vision of a just-lost England. The music press raved. He had pulled it off. But musically, his new concept remained a small part of the regular Kinks set list. There was still so much work to do. A new album would have to be written straight away. A BBC *In Concert* filmed the following week shows much of the music The Kinks played with this line-up. It also shows the thin-lipped, gaunt state of their singer. He was already looking like the awful photos taken of him at White City, six months later.

In February, The Kinks went back to their late sixties routine of weekend gigs and weekday recording, as they began what would become *Preservation*. At the same time their own studio, Konk, was being built in an old biscuit factory in Hornsey bought with RCA's lavish advance. When Ray returned home one April morning after yet another US tour, and crashed, jet-lagged, into bed, Rasa wasn't there. When he awoke, he'd missed her. Feeling miserable and sitting up in bed watching the snooker show *Pot Black*, he eventually went out and found her in a Chelsea club with male friends. Ray started telling them the plot of *Deep Throat*. In the ensuing melee, his skull was cracked with a pot plant. In June, a finished double album of Ray's grand project sounded flat and disappointing to him. The Kinks started recording the songs again, at a half-finished Konk. On June 20, his 29th birthday, he came home to an empty house which would stay that way. In *X-Ray*, he remembers the note his wife left in place of the two daughters she took with her. "I've gone, please contact my solicitor." Dave came round that night. He saw Ray sitting at the window of the front room which had so inspired him, looking like an abandoned child. Ray saw a rat in the 'Autumn Almanac' garden.

On the 29th, the first UK single from *Preservation*, 'Sitting In The Midday Sun', was released. The song re-imagines *Village Green*'s 'Sitting

By The Riverside', where its protagonist, soon named The Tramp by Ray, is found. *Muswell Hillbillies'* disaffection from society also resurfaces – "who needs a job when it's sunny?" Ray's latest pleas for languid relaxation with "no purpose or reason" came as usual from a restless, work-addicted mind which found peace only in such lyrics. Flutes and Beach Boys harmonies maintained the song's idyll. The promo film shot three days after Rasa left shattered it. Ray's upturned eyes, usually controlled and unreadable in those days, plead and accuse. His forehead keeps crumpling in frowns. The brave smile he finds to fit the words lasts seconds, replaced by a man swaying, pursing his lips and running his hands absently through his hair, in front of a camera when he looks in desperate need of a psychiatric ward. More likely, he needs help only Rasa can give him.

Two days after that, the White City gig was announced. Ray wrote in *X-Ray* he accepted it so he could invite Rasa and their daughters, thinking a great show, and his farewell to The Kinks, would win them back. He also believed she thought his musical success was running dry, the reason he suspected Quaife had left too. He couldn't seem to grasp that not every relationship was mercenary, or filtered through his work.

His sister Gwen came to his house to try to comfort him, and Dave and Joyce went to Bradford to fruitlessly reason with Rasa. But just as Dave had to deal with terrible mental agonies while on a hotel-bound rock'n'roll tour of America, Ray really only had his own resources to draw on. He mixed champagne and Valium at futile parties like wakes. A few days after making the promo film, his devoted assistant Marion Rainford* found Ray in the bath, overdosed on tranquillisers. His stomach was pumped at Whittington Hospital. The *Preservation* recordings continued.

Ray's relationship with Savannah hadn't survived her coming to London to strip. But a friend of hers, Roxy, came to stay, and nursed him through till the White City show. In *X-Ray*, he remembers that

* Rainford had worked as The Kinks' publicity agent at the prestigious Tony Barrow International PR company in Hanover Street, but eventually left TBI to work exclusively for The Kinks.

when the supporting acts in the grim show overran he sat on Shepherd's Bush Green, watching that Village Green's edges being developed with the tacky urban commerce familiar today. Of course, Rasa and the children hadn't come.

Backstage, the atmosphere was horrific. Roy Hollingworth, a friend of Ray's on the staff of *Melody Maker*, heard rumours of his retirement buzz around the artists' bar. Marion Rainford had wondered if Ray would show at all. Hollingworth found her standing protectively outside his dressing room. "He's in a dreadful state. Christ, he's in a dreadful state," she said. When he came out, he definitely was. "Ray looked frightening in dark glasses," Hollingworth wrote, "for the sun wasn't shining. And limp under an overcoat. His face looked harrowed and worn. And his hair, usually shiny, was dark and tangled. But he smiled and touched those he knew." LA music biz security thugs hustled Ray's friends away from him, clearing the stage for the real star Sly Stone and his retinue of 40. Ray and The Kinks were dismissed as drunks who couldn't play. "It was a bastard day and a bastard festival. Damp and friendless White City," Hollingworth summed up, in the heat of that Sunday's emotion. "The vultures picked the stage." He saw the sky turn orange and felt the wind blow as The Kinks hurried on. The *MM* writer heard Ray say, "I'm fucking sick of the whole thing. Sick up to here with it." Avory smiled uncertainly, and kept playing 'Waterloo Sunset'.

"Ray hadn't been married that long, and he had a couple of kids, and them leaving was a disruption for him. He's probably used to it by now..." Avory says, alluding to Ray's two marriages since. "It puts you all on edge, when you know there's something like that going on, and you know he's not right, and, what's he gonna do? Is he just gonna walk off? I don't know what he'd taken. He'd probably had a few drinks. But he was very depressed, obviously. Everyone was walking on eggshells. And then he went up and did the show in the normal way, and he announced, 'That's it. Thank you and goodnight. I'll see you in the next life' sort of thing. He'd given up."

"Nightmare," Dave says of that day. "I was there in body, but I really didn't wanna be. I tried to do what was expected of me. People like that persona and I'll give 'em what's still left of it. The whole event was eating me up. I hated being on that fucking stage. And to be honest, it's such a hellhole to be, I probably didn't realise to what extent Ray was going through his own hell. It sounds unbelievable that we both would be in that place at the same time, but we were. And you can tell by the way he grimaces in the photos that day – he really can't cope.

"When he came back on stage after the show to announce he was going to end it all and kill himself, and the PA wasn't even on, how farcical can you get?" Dave laughs. "'What's that prat talking about?' Very funny. And very sad, poignant – tragic. It nearly ended up a big tragedy, because at the end of that day, I had to go to hospital after they pumped Ray's stomach out of all the stupid shit he was taking. I didn't know he was taking shit all day long, because he was going to kill himself. The ultimate drama queen. Woe is me..."

Ray had got through all the Valium his doctor had prescribed. Ken Jones, their tour manager since 1969, was driving him to the Highgate office where Rainford worked for The Kinks, and had moved Ray to keep him from the horror 87 Fortis Green had become. He detoured to Whittington Hospital to have Ray's stomach pumped a second time, from a far more serious overdose. Dave soon arrived to help. When Ray left the hospital, his heart pumped so much it almost killed him. He moved in with Dave and Lisbet physically nursed him back to health. *X-Ray* gratefully mentions Lisbet but Ray erases his reliance on Dave, as if his brother wasn't there. "When Rasa left, it was like a chasm had opened up for him," Dave says in *Mystikal Journey*. "She was a really important catalyst between me and Ray." Though he was by now starting to feel estranged from his brother, Dave bought records and played them to Ray: his first, rarely admitted love – classical music (Mahler's Second, 'The Resurrection'), and Chuck Berry. After a while, Ray picked up his guitar, and the brothers started to play. It could have been 1963 again, everything before them, and Rasa not yet gone.

"The three weeks that followed were awful," Dave remembers. "But in a way, because he was so fucked up, it gave me strength. Someone's got to do something. A lot of this younger/older brother syndrome goes backwards and forwards – it's complicated, for fuck's sake. It still is, sadly. But I think it's important for people who want to know about this stuff that everything's not a Hollywood, glamorous movie picture. And all these negative emotions are equally as important."

Ray went with Dave's family to Denmark for two weeks in August, the first time they'd holidayed together since the sixties, when their dad would come too. Even now he kept writing, while the outside world was left to wonder. A more high-profile RCA artist, David Bowie, had announced his retirement onstage 12 days before Ray. But it turned out he only meant Ziggy Stardust. Ray's rock'n'roll suicide was almost literal.

"He feels that tours and concerts have split his married life," Rainford told Roy Hollingworth. "Ray is in a state of despair. The Kinks don't believe what he's saying. I don't believe what he's saying." Gosling was shocked to hear his livelihood being tossed away with no warning. Avory was, as always, *laissez-faire*. "You're never quite certain when people do that," he considers, "because they are temperamental, they go up and down a lot. I was surprised – but knew Ray was apt to change his mind. You can't take everything he says as gospel. I thought I'd give it a while, and see how it goes. I wasn't really convinced it was all over. We'd done too much to just disappear. But I was disappointed that it was going that way. You're not working as a team while all that's going on. But with two brothers, The Kinks always blew hot and cold." Hollingworth's impassioned report and open letter to Ray showed how on a precipice it all seemed, to those who'd seen the white-faced singer close up that Sunday. "Nobody will press you to stay," he wrote. "Those who love you will let you make whatever decision you wish to make." Then thinking of the music that would be lost, he contradicted himself: "Think again, Ray. Think again."

Later in August, Ray returned to work on *Preservation* at Konk, still very far from well. "We all had to pretend like nothing had happened," Gosling told Neville Marten and Jeff Hudson. "Ray was doing weird things like walking around with glasses with no lenses in." It took a roadie to puncture the tension, peering at Ray and politely asking: "Are those for reading or long-distance?" Gosling doesn't think Ray was ever the same as before.

On August 28, Ray wrote to the press, reversing his retirement. "Several weeks ago I wrote a letter to the world; it turned out to be a letter to me. But I do feel that I made a decision, whether motivated or not, to change the format of the band. The White City was not a happy place to say goodbye. The sun was not shining, my shirt was not clean...The Kinks are close enough now to be able to work as a team in whatever they do and anyone who thinks it is only my back-up band is very much mistaken. On stage it's like Leeds United – all teamwork. In the studio there are still things to extract from The Kinks on an artistic level. Whether or not it turns out to be commercial remains to be seen."

I ask Ray if he had been worn down and made fragile by working so hard in that period; and if, at White City, he shattered. He pauses. "I was shattered. The White City gig was I think just a personal problem. I just felt that all the advice I was getting from the world and advisers and people was coming through in my songs. I'd already said that to myself: 'Somebody tell me something new.' I just wanted to get out. I just wanted to take a year off and go backpacking. It's not an unusual thing for someone to want to do. I felt trapped by the job I was doing."

It's been said he tried to commit suicide that day. Did he mean to succeed? "Err, I don't know if I... I can't remember, to tell you the truth. It's all so long ago." His voice goes weak. "Is that OK?"

What did he find worth hanging on to in that period? "Not a lot," he says coldly. "Nothing. I felt bad about playing my hits, I felt bad about writing new stuff, people felt it wasn't as good. I didn't really want to hang on to anything."

Inevitably, between Rasa leaving and White City, Ray's misery had inspired a gorgeous Kinks song. 'Sweet Lady Genevieve' is an apology to his wife. Ray rides in on a pistol-crack drum, explaining he's come back to "Genevieve" (queen to his "vagabond"). He lists his faults and foolish acts. "But," he brushes them aside, "that was so long ago..." Gosling's organ glides through a verse which hangs suspended like a dream, as it takes us back to the hot summer evening Ray first drunkenly seduced Rasa the schoolgirl Kinks fan. "Forgive me, please... put your trust in me," he sings, his shaking voice belying the surging melody. "Oh, love me..." At the end he demands: "So will you come back to me?" But he builds his roguish untrustworthiness, the fact he won't really change, into the song that's supposed to convince her he has. He can't help himself as he writes the truthful end to his marriage. Once you know why his voice is overflowing with apparently happy but unstable feeling, 'Sweet Lady Genevieve' becomes almost unbearably moving. When it was released in September, its crafted, deceptive pop joy deserved to be a hit. If Rasa had heard it on the radio every day, what might she have felt? But The Kinks' suicide as a singles band had been successful.

"It's sung by a not wholly good person, which is nice," Ray reflects. "It's sung to my wife, at that point, acknowledging that it was all over. And not sure who was leaving who. And not feeling wholly good about yourself. I love the character I wrote it for, The Tramp. All these characters are a bit of me. That's what's so interesting about it, to me. And he was a sort of a vagabond. 'Guys, don't worry, everything'll be fine' – and you know it's not, but you still get carried along by their promises of a better time. You know it's going to end in tears. You know from the things he says that he's not going to change. I could do a whole album about that…"

Preservation Act 1 was finally released in November, with the intended double album's *Act 2* still unfinished. It was slightly delayed by the death of Rose's husband, Arthur, in Australia, finishing a grim year. The back cover, shot at the end of August, shows The Kinks, their horn section and female backing singers as an ideal, smiling community, sitting under a leafy tree in sunny Highgate. But Ray is still wearing the red–flowered white shirt from White City, and the kneeling Dave's eyes aren't right yet.

Written and recorded under awful pressure, its music successfully balances the Village Green's rustic refuge, and the new dark forces threatening it in what would grow into Ray's grandest concept. 'Morning Song' is a beautiful prelude of choral voices and strings. 'Daylight' then introduces a more densely populated Village than in 1968, set in an uncertain period when men train for the Empire Games (the British Commonwealth Games since 1970) and boys like Captain Scarlet. 'There's A Change In The Weather' identifies a storm on the Village's horizon. 'Money & Corruption/I Am Your Man' introduces the slippery, pseudo-socialist Mr. Black who claims he'll save them from corrupt wide-boy dictator Mr. Flash, well played by Dave, who plans the Village's demolition and profitable redevelopment.

So much for a plot splicing *Muswell Hillbillies* and *Village Green* themes. But *Act 1* shares some of *Village Green*'s loose emotional concept, letting in individual songs such as 'Sweet Lady Genevieve' and 'Sitting In The Midday Sun'. 'One Of The Survivors' (a US single in April) reintroduced Johnny Thunder, the only conventional rebel in 1968's Village, a bike-riding rocker based on Brando's *The Wild One*. Now he's overweight and his sideburns are grey, like the ageing Teds on seventies streets, but he keeps riding and listening to his Elvis and Jerry Lee records.

The idea is really caught on the third wonderful song Ray sings as The Tramp, 'Where Are They Now?' Ray looks around for the Swinging Londoners, the Beatniks, the Mods and Rockers and most especially the Angry Young Men and protest singers and wonders, "Where on earth did they all go?" He wishes the best for Arthur Seaton as much as his creator, Alan Sillitoe, and that *Don't Look Back In Anger*'s Jimmy Porter "has learned to laugh and smile". He hopes things worked out for the original working-class heroes he grew up reading, while gently mocking how time works on youthful ideals, and slips rebels back into the crowd. "It's like *A Clockwork Orange*," Ray thinks, "where are the friends, the rebels, the droogs? They're all violent together, but when he comes back after trying so hard to be altered by the pharmaceutical industry, he confronts one of his old rebels, who's become an authority figure, and he gets the shit beaten out of him. I hope that doesn't happen to me. I want to be not just rebellious, but to have something to aspire to."

Ken Barnes' largely positive *Rolling Stone* review shared a general view that getting to grips with *Act 1* without *Act 2* was "intriguing and confusing". Ray seemed to agree, sanctioning an extremely low-key release which barely registered even in the US (where it made 177 in the charts; *Everybody's In Show-Biz* hit 70). In October, doing interviews to prove he was still in one piece, he told *NME*'s Andrew Tyler: "You know, I'm still only five years old... I don't want to be any more... I'm able to communicate on a very basic level. I know what food I like to eat. I've got two pairs of shoes – one for on and one for offstage and when they wear out I buy another pair. I'm reasonably all right. I've got enough teabags and maybe I can start writing again, which would be a good thing." In November, Ray took The Kinks into Konk for *Act 2*. Aside from some UK gigs, they kept working in their new Hornsey home till March 1974.

I make perhaps my last visit to Konk in 2011. The neon sign outside is switched off. "Investment/Development Opportunity" a sale sign entices, of the place where *Preservation* was made. The former factory is a dark grey concrete block built onto one of a street of narrow, turreted Victorian houses. When the front door swings open, the banistered staircase points up into darkness, and old-fashioned landings with faded blue carpet that might lead to a cheap bedsit. A ping-pong table is still set up in the lounge. The snooker table baize is holed, the orange sofas faded but comfortable. There's an alcove where the bar would have been in this abandoned playground.

In the studio where so much of the rest of this story took place, a small, old framed photo of Morecambe & Wise has been left. I sit talking to Mick Avory behind the big old recording desk. Through the glass, a piano waits. In Konk's rambling corridors, tape-to-tape reels and blocky grey machines, the debris of Kinks recordings, are stacked. After Dave built the studio up from nothing in 1973, he prided himself on its state of the art equipment. As recently as 2006, the year's hottest new band, Arctic Monkeys, came here for some B-sides, Ray's ears still ringing when he met me that morning. But a slick super-studio doesn't suit The Kinks, even if the world still wanted such things. Konk in its apparent last days is homely, down on its luck, and feels like a shipwreck from the time it was built, Kinks history tangible in the air. Avory and I shiver, the notoriously stingy landlord having turned the heating off. As I take a last look, Ray flits past, scarf flung behind him like Rupert the Bear. He shuts the door firmly, half a lifetime's work here still not done. He had hoped Konk would be a hang-out for artists, like the Factory where he loved seeing Warhol. Avory remembers its heyday rather differently.

"It looked more like a pub than it does now," he recalls of the living area downstairs. "It was fairly dimly lit, had the flocky sort of wallpaper and loungy furniture, and a snug. So it was quite cosy. We made it like a games room, with the snooker table. Then when the bar was built, we made it like a club. There were various members from around the surrounding district. Graham Chapman from Monty Python was one, and Bernard McKenna, the scriptwriter – they were all friends that knew each other through the Python team. They used to come along and play snooker, darts. It was a little place they could go. That was a good little phase.

"We tried to leave the bar alone till we'd finished our work," he continues, of the social club where 13 Kinks albums were made, "but there were always games of snooker going on, when we had a break. We'd play Ray at snooker, it was a little retreat then. The bar here, that really determined how long you were going to carry on drinking. Ray always kept a clear head. But we had an engineer [Roger Wake, who signed up for *Schoolboys In Disgrace* in 1975] that could drink several pints of cider, or Guinness and cider, or bitter and cider, it was strong stuff. And he used to be mixing in here, and he could carry on and not fall asleep somehow. He was a big guy and could handle it. I used to go and get him the pints."

Ray often had cause to regret combining his studio with a pub. As he was the licensee, Hornsey police station regularly called to inform him "we've had some complaints" about the latest bawdy lock-in, and demand entry, no matter how exotically faraway he might be touring. Ray, though, made it clear when playtime was over.

"We used to call him the Headmaster. I think that's what inspired him to do *Schoolboys In Disgrace*. He has got that presence. You can't join in everything with him. Because he's not someone you can take the piss out of. There was always that sort of distance there. You had to just deal with it."

Avory spent other early seventies afternoons far from Konk, in the afternoon drinking clubs of Soho. "We used to go out on binge interviews," he remembers. "It'd be, 'Oh, meet me at [Soho pub] De Hems at 1 o'clock'. We'd meet long enough to get trashed, the pubs used to close, and then we'd say, 'We didn't really do that interview, did we?' And he'd say, 'No, don't worry, [confiding voice] I know what you would've said.' And then we'd go to a club in Denman Street, because you'd got the taste by then. There wasn't anyone there that you'd recognise. The CID, it was their watering hole. All the Flying Squad."

When Ray had an album on the go, did he have to know where Avory was – every Kink on call at all times?

"No – we weren't on a lead! Didn't have cameras following us, like you do now. You used to do your own thing. Long as you didn't do anything really outrageous, like that fight in Cardiff."

While Avory was out drinking with the Sweeney, Ray worked doggedly on *Preservation Act 2*, a full-scale musical play for Granada TV, *Starmaker*, and produced an album, Claire Hamill's *Stage Door Johnnies*, the first release for yet another major project, The Kinks' own label, Konk Records. He'd left Fortis Green utterly behind when a judge gave Rasa (now living in south London) custody of their children, moving to a large house in Effingham, Surrey, less than a manor but with grounds and liveable outhouses. Migrating south of London, Ray hoped Louisa and Victoria might visit him more easily. In fact, Victoria would see little of him for some years. Though he would retain a Highgate house, and first Ken Jones then Gwen and her family moved into 87 Fortis Green, giving him access to his Shangri-La into the nineties, Ray seemed finally to have torn up his roots. For the next decade, Muswell Hill and the Village Green would almost never be his subject.

His friends, he'd understood in 'Sitting In My Hotel', would gently ask "what it is I'm trying to prove", and "what it's all leading to?" as he sat alone writing songs for "old time vaudeville revues". This was only the start of a manic, near-superhuman working jag which would produce two further concept albums, and accompanying, touring multimedia stage shows in two years. It would be easy to believe this was a workaholic's outsized compensation for losing his wife and children, a hole so big no second could be left to consider it. It's more demonstrably true that Ray can only find any mental peace by working, no matter what the further cost to an often already battered body or mind. And so this is the only way he could go backpacking, and leave the old job he felt "trapped" by behind. As he wrote in the letter that signalled his return to action, there was to be a change in "format" for his band. He had killed the old Kinks on that White City stage. For all the many faults of what followed, it is one of the most remarkable efforts of sustained, individual creative will in rock history.

Preservation Act 2 was released in the US on May 8 (to coincide with a short tour), and back home on July 26. During its protracted making, the 19-track double album had outgrown the balanced and sometimes beautiful world of *Act 1*. *The Village Green Preservation Society* itself, the oasis of everything The Kinks stand for, had been concreted over by a crude overspill of songs. Its shrinkage is shown when the final battle between Mr. Flash's debauched regime of spiv capitalists and Mr. Black's sanctimonious socialist rebels rages "outside a small village somewhere in the Northern Zone".

"It is connected to the Village Green," Ray explains, "in that it's the next phase, it's what happened to these people when they got older. And Mr. Flash came into prominence, and his dictatorship was replaced by another regime that seemed it would be helpful to the country until it got in power, and then controlled the people. It had a bit more going for it than just a string of ideas. It was about corruption, really. I guess adults can be corrupted, then their innocence is gone. We tried to do a narrative record, [future *All Creatures Great And Small* star] Christopher Timothy was the narrator. I remember saying to Dave, 'If we're going to keep doing stuff, I'll write what I want to write about.' I just wanted to write a political record. Mr. Flash is a political-cum-vaudevillian character. And there were a lot of new fans in America who felt that resonated with their government, which was Richard Nixon at the time."

In *X-Ray*, a future, fictionalised Ray, sitting in the dusty ruins of Konk, hopefully asks his interviewer if *Preservation* is on the school curriculum. The younger man keeps to himself that it's considered a minor subject. The work Ray put most into and had most hopes for as an artistic breakthrough is widely considered a clunking failure, barely heard and best left buried. Enviously watching the latest revival of Pink Floyd's own bombastic concept double album *The Wall* being globally televised in 1990 from Berlin, as if it somehow caused the Wall's fall, Ray actually started re-recording *Preservation* for reissue. "It's my lost lifelong project," he confessed, "the thing that I constantly find myself going back to, like Rembrandt kept painting his self-portrait."

If you take *Preservation* as a serious political work with instructive themes to stand alongside a novel, then it is a failure. The Tramp's potted history of the 20th century, 'Nobody Gives', focuses on the 1926 General Strike and Hitler's Holocaust, and puts a plague on left and right wing. Though dreamily supportive of the people, Ray's distrust of collective endeavour offers them little help. The grounded incitement to individual revolution in *Muswell Hillbillies*, where you could feel Ray's anger at the crushed hopes of people he knew, and were let into the condemned homes where they lived, was lost in generalised big ideas.

Musically, the invisible art of a 'Waterloo Sunset' is replaced by tangible effort as Ray heaves constituent parts into place in a giant but unfinished structure. One of the more successful songs, 'Artificial Man', takes directly from Kubrick's 1971 *A Clockwork Orange*, as Flash's savage individualism is cleansed into a new antiseptic, mentally controlled reality. But *Preservation* itself often feels artificial, the construction of a single overworked mind. Where Dave cameoed as Flash in *Act 1*, Ray now takes almost every part, switching from Flash to Black, even playing some of the women. He'd do so in the stage show too, changing costumes in a manic one-man musical. It's tiring to listen to at first. Imagine how its broken composer-star felt. "It was a very real-world time for me," Ray says. "But that was a complete fantasy world."

The two combine on the Dixie jug-band ballad 'Mirror Of Love' and 'Nothing Lasts Forever', a crooned, claustrophobic but heartfelt take on 'Days', in which Flash/Ray is abandoned by a lover. His undying love, though, will keep her memory locked in his mind. Against the odds, the finale 'Salvation Road' also finds stinging, defeated emotion as the New Order crushes dissent and The Tramp is moved down the line. "Oh, there you go," Ray keeps bitterly rasping, one of those clichéd phrases of acceptance – like "that's just the way it is" or "just move on" – we're fed as trusted values are torn up by invincible corporate powers. It leaves the improbable impression there's something to this lopsided work.

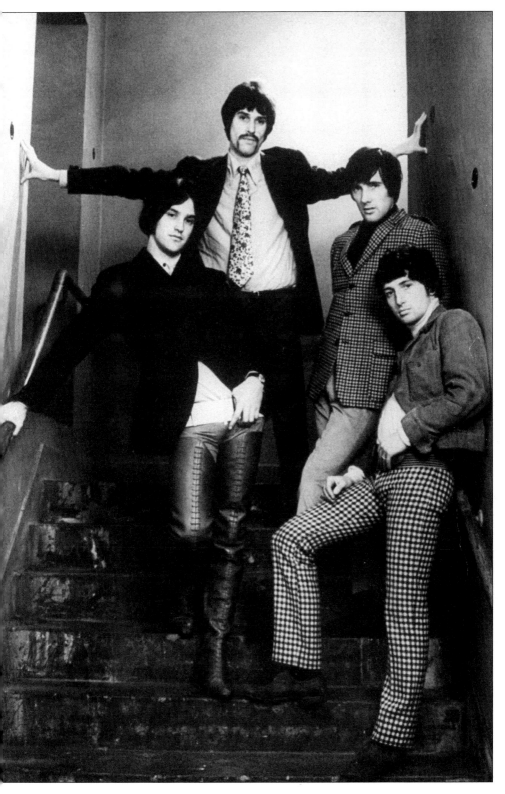

ay with the moustache he wore in the wake of his March 1966 breakdown, when the relentless need to write innovative hits got too much. In the ubsequent break, he wrote 'Sunny Afternoon'. (TERRENCE SPENCER/TIME LIFE PICTURES/GETTY IMAGES)

Pete with the scooter on which he'd tool round Muswell Hill, giving him his reputation as The Kinks' king mod. (CHRIS WALTER/PHOTOFEATURES.COM)

Another day, another TV show. Ray's taking the lead now. (LFI)

John Dalton (right) replaces Pete Quaife on bass. He'd filled in once before for 'Dead End Street' in 1966, and was a stabilising, skilled presence from 1969-76. (PICTORIAL PRESS)

Pete Quaife with Michael Juhlin on stage as Juhlin & Quaife in Copenhagen, July 1972. Quaife left The Kinks in a distressed state, had an unhappy time in Denmark, and soon quit music for good. (JORGEN ANGEL/REDFERNS)

The Kinks at the Roskilde Festival, Denmark in 1972, at the time of *Everybody's In Show-Biz*. Keyboardist John "Baptist" Gosling (second right) has become the fifth Kink. (JORGEN ANGEL/REDFERNS)

Gosling in his early role as the band's willing joker. Dave plainly isn't all there, or trying to hold his brother up. (BARRIE WENTZELL)

hn Gosling. He'd leave the band in 1978, frustrated at the endless indecisive hours Ray kept them in their new studio, Konk. (BARRIE WENTZELL)

ve down the pub. Behind the smile he was feeling wretched, and in '72 contemplated suicide. (BARRIE WENTZELL)

Ray soon after 1971's *Muswell Hillbillies*, his great statement on his working-class roots and hostility to pointless progress. (BARRIE WENTZELL)

Ray distraught at White City stadium, 1973, after Rasa left him. He announced his retirement on-stage, and overdosed immediately afterwards. (BARRIE WENTZELL)

The demon alcohol: Ray in camp showman mode, at the height of The Kinks' cult reputation in the US as unpredictable wild men. (IDOLS)

erybody's a star. Ray takes his identity-crisis concept album *A Soap bera* to the stage in 1975. (PICTORIAL PRESS)

Dave without much to do as Ray's concept album period continues. (FIN COSTELLO/REDFERNS)

e Kinks make a rare Seventies trip to *Top Of The Pops.* (RON HOWARD/REDFERNS)

The Kinks in character. Ray as Mr. Flash prepares to lead his half-willing band in the *Preservation Act 2* LP's touring vaudeville musical.
(GAB ARCHIVE/REDFERNS)

Ian MacDonald's *NME* review ruthlessly exposed it. Taking sideswipes at Pete Townshend's *Tommy* and *Quadrophenia* (released the previous year), he found "rock operas" doomed to failure, hobbling rock's "music of untutored impulse" with a narrative form requiring "songs that have been objectively created and slotted into the nearest hole" and "the artistic strain of... the unfamiliar dimension of Theatre." *Preservation*, "the longest rock opera so far and, paradoxically, the least ambitious" was "the first really clear-cut victim" of this obstacle to "extended rock composition". Macdonald's kicking is forensically aimed. "The story itself is quite calamitously simple... the words are a shade on the schlocky side... there's no *penetration* within any of the individual songs." And the music? "There's hardly any here." He allowed the dim possibility that a promised live version might add something. "As it is *Preservation Acts 1 and 2* stands as an Awful Warning to those rock songwriters with aspirations towards a misconceived notion of the artistic permanent."

Preservation Act 2's cover and inner sleeve, though, tell a lighter, more likeable tale. Ray sits as Flash, pallid in white make-up with an insipid smile, wearing a multicoloured dressing gown and a hat borrowed from Roy Hudd. He's modelled his super-villain alter ego on the music-hall comic hero of both Davies brothers, Max Miller. Dave looks delighted as a switchblade-stroking, sharp-suited spiv, Avory's a gangster brute, Gosling a lascivious vicar, Dalton a ranting Che type. Take *Preservation* as a primary-coloured panto with radical but humorous political intent, performed by English music-hall troupers in the costumes on its sleeve, and it starts to work. As I sat around one afternoon at Konk vainly waiting for Ray, to keep me amused Dave's son Martin, then with the family firm, dug out some Betamax videos of their US shows at this time, unseen for 30 years. They prove that when Ray finally wheeled the *Preservation* stage show which was its real point to America in November, this is exactly what it became. The tapes' mixture of silent-movie style black-and-white footage shot around Hornsey, with Ray ranting on a balcony as Mr. Black, shoestring theatre sets, music hall and rock'n'roll performance is a revelation.

The ambitious *Quadrophenia* shows Townshend hauled on tour in late 1973, which had The Who trying to explain its themes as they went along and taped musical effects apt to misfire, show the amateurish, Heath Robinson nature of these long-abandoned ventures by performers wholly untutored in the forms they were braving. Testing rock's potential, they mostly found they'd exceeded it. Townshend's cherished, unrealised 1971 project *Lifehouse*, a dystopia somewhat similar to Ray's, had simply defeated him. Bowie also abandoned a *Ziggy Stardust* rock opera in 1973. But reviewers and audiences of *Preservation* on both sides of the Atlantic (it rolled up for a weekend at London's Royalty Theatre in December) generally agreed. This was far from the often turgid album. With showman Ray to bring it to life, his grand folly was funny, entertaining, and actually worked.

The American premiere, at Colgate University in frozen, tiny Hamilton in upstate New York, played to a "mostly blitzed-out college audience sprawled all over the floor of a basketball court", underground paper *Good Times'* Kris DiLorenzo reported. The slide and film projectors, lighting and 14-piece band (a four-man brass section and six backing singers now swelled and overwhelmed The Kinks) took 12 hours to set up. As they would for the next year or so, The Kinks supported themselves, getting the old singles out of the way. 'Waterloo Sunset', Ray told the crowd, "was from the days when we used to make hit records. Now we don't need to." DiLorenzo saw Ray charismatically inhabit Flash and row with himself, up on screen as Black. She found problems in the music and staging, and worried: "Ray sings, dances, acts and clowns his guts out...[but] can't be expected to be onstage the entire time at the same intense energy level...[he] can't carry the whole shebang on his skinny shoulders." That misunderstood him. In New York, an unimpressed *Village Voice* also felt the whole edifice would collapse "the next time Davies left the stage". But the *Boston Globe* more typically called it "a remarkable achievement", while the *Buffalo News* reported crowd boos and hisses for the villains, enhancing its "vaudevillian atmosphere with a crazy, good-time fondness". Back in London at the Royalty, the music press adored the show, *Sounds* stating its "combination of rock and theatre has rarely been used to such direct effect". For *Melody Maker*, its "simplistic morality tale of the struggle against a villain to preserve something sacred... deserves a long run in a large theatre."

"The problem," Ray says, "was I had a band, and it was not an appropriate project for a band to do that wanted to reactivate a conventional career. That's why I was at odds with The Kinks, because I took them in a direction they're on record as saying they weren't comfortable going. I know when we did it at the Royalty Theatre, my agent said, 'You should take it and turn it into a show.' I said, 'No, I've got to do another album. I'm in a group.'* But I should have work-shopped it, down the Edinburgh Festival. And if it hadn't been... not encumbered by the band, but I could have worked on the story a bit. It was destined as a project not to completely succeed."

"I would have liked to be a songwriter in the forties," he told *Circus'* Scott Cohen. "I would have liked to have lived at a time when I could have said, 'I'm working on a new project,' and could have taken five years to do it." He was similarly wistful to *Crawdaddy*'s Greg Mitchell. "I'd like to work on a musical outside The Kinks and outside me as a performer. I'd like to stay around in New York and just get a show together. I should do that really, but I keep getting involved in these silly contracts." The under-rehearsal, overwork and crazed schedules he had railed against in 1965 though were no longer the fault of the times. This was how Ray had taught himself to survive. "I like to be happy but – I'm just one of those people – I've got a streak in me," he told Mitchell. "I don't know what it is... but I get really unhappy all of a sudden. I want to walk and be alone and not see anybody. The only way I can get out of it is to get up and start working. What is frightening is when you can't even work and you just stare at a wall... I don't like sitting around."

Ray wasn't in the greatest shape as he made *Preservation*, or the further concept albums, *A Soap Opera* and *Schoolboys In Disgrace*, which rapidly followed. "I never am!" he laughs, truthfully. This period, more than

* In fact Ray did work on a theatrical version of *Preservation*, apparently abandoning it because of The Kinks' schedule. "We could have gotten Michael Caine to play Mr. Flash," he sighed.

Village Green, is when he's often said he shouldn't have been allowed to make records. "I should have been locked up," he agrees. "I thought then the record industry was over. Too much money, getting too corporate. There weren't enough good down-to-earth wide boys exploiting you." It looked like a concerted bid at commercial suicide, at least less harmful than his actual attempt.

But were the records he made what he wanted them to be?

"No! Sonically, I guess they were OK. Success-wise, they didn't reach it. But that was never the primary concern. Because I wanted the piece to stand up. Elton John and Rod Stewart were selling out mega-concerts and getting gold watches from the promoters, and I felt it was all becoming a bit serious. And I wanted to experiment. It was almost like a fringe period, instead of mainstream Broadway. We turned into a fringe band."

Claustrophobic as he felt inside the old confines of his job as a songwriter in a band, did he want to leave rock behind altogether then? To escape into theatre or television? "TV's always interested me, film has always interested me. But being a theatrical writer's never really appealed to me, although I've done it. To create your own space, and create your own style... and... there's nobody like it," he says, reaching for what he was seeking. "And I think The Kinks were like that at that period. There was nobody like The Kinks. I was really on a tightrope then. I know the band weren't totally happy, but they went along with it. And we survived it. Maybe someone should have said don't make these records. But I'm glad we did, because it gave people a lot of fun. And we got a few good tunes."

The Kinks' American reinvention during their initial, ragged comeback shows also continued. "That's why I think America worked finally, in the eighties," Ray says. "Because *Preservation* helped the band change its personality from being the four mop-toppy guys in pink hunting jackets doing these quirky riff songs, and turned them into characters. All the characters in *Preservation* played by the drummer and the organist, the bassist and my brother, were drawn from the real people. You really had to be there to see it... but for the first time they had personalities, rather than being a band in suits.

I think that helped rejuvenate us. There was an acceptance of us as being something new."

The bandmates to whom Ray was giving personalities were bemused, at best. "When he steered into the concept things," Avory remembers, "we just wondered why we've gotta do it? Ray always steered the ship, because it was his writing that guided the group through. It would have taken too much time to do separately, so he involved the band with these low-budget theatre things. It saved him leaving us high and dry. Having to do the hits set as well was quite hard work. I remember we did a double show, and we were on stage six hours. But we were younger then. Being characters was quite amusing, I didn't really mind. But we lost our direction. We wanted to go out and be a big rock'n'roll band. We were hoping he'd get it out of his system eventually."

Did The Kinks still trust that Ray's songwriting would always pull them through in the end, no matter how rocky things seemed? "You felt secure in the fact that there was always material there. I never feel that secure about anything. Especially because Ray and Dave were brothers at the end of the day, and when Pete Quaife left, I was stuck in the middle. I've never really felt secure. It's something that bothers you. Not every day. You think about it sometimes, or something goes wrong and you think about it."

Dave was still recovering from the "psychic death" that had claimed him at that New York hotel window in 1972. He's barely present on *Preservation Act 2*. Unconvinced by the project, and feeling belittled by Ray in the studio, Dave did "what was required", he writes in *Kink*. "I went through a long period of time in the early part of the seventies thinking I wasn't helping him," he says, "because I was feeling so drained. I didn't mind the concept albums at first. You see, when Ray was having these nervous breakdowns, I was doing my internal work. I thought, 'There's got to be more to life than misery. If he wants to do that, that's great.' I wanted to investigate spiritual things, yoga – all the other things that really interested me. Maybe I'm not that interested in music in a way – not as a 'musician', it's a means of self-expression. Rock'n'roll's more than just physicality, it's about communication, spirituality, questioning everything. That's a thing I'm really pleased about in my life, that I've learned a lot. I found a lot of truth in science fiction, like Philip K. Dick, a great prophetic writer, who thought he was from the future. Time's not what it used to be..."

There's a shot of Dave then standing at Konk's mixing board in an extravagant sheepskin jacket, when his grin of devilish happiness from the sixties at last breaks out again. "The ideal way to help was to get the studio together," he says. "So if Ray's got all of these ideas, some of them I don't like – but with our own studio, we can do what we like to our heart's content. I used to do a lot of recording there, out of whack with what Ray was doing. The record company didn't know what the fuck we were doing either. So that was a good move."

Even before the *Preservation* tour, though, Dave's passive introspection was wearing off. His uncharacteristic patience was tested to snapping point by *Starmaker*, the Granada TV show The Kinks recorded in Manchester on July 25, 1974, the day before *Preservation Act 2*'s UK release. The band aren't mentioned in an opening which credits Ray twice before he appears, in a white jumpsuit doubtless inspired by a band trip to see Elvis in 1971. The musical play that follows is the peak of his band-abusing self-involvement, and a sharply self-aware satire of it. "I need a challenge to bring out my best work," he muses as "the Star". So he phones a suburban housewife (June Ritchie) who's watching him on TV, and tells her he'll be replacing her husband, Norman, for a week as research for his next song, about an ordinary man. Ray's all controlled camp as he primps and adores himself. Once in the wife's living room, he clutches his hand in awe at his creativity, marvelling: "I can feel a whole concept album coming on!" Bubble-haired groupies slide his striped pyjama bottoms on as he casually replaces Norman in bed. "Don't you think the background music's a bit loud?" the wife timidly asks. "Oh, is that all?" he sighs, silencing the other Kinks with the snap of a finger.

The rest springs from Ray's recurring nightmares. Rudely awoken at 7am, the crushing boredom of one day of office work has him hurrying to blot it out in the pub with his colleagues. Even the relief of his loving sympathy from his "wife" when he gets home finds workmates and wives going through the same motions behind him. Fear of recapture by this routine life grows as he struggles to write the song he's come for. "All you think about is your work," his wife chides, as rows with Rasa rise to the script's surface to play out before us. He feels himself becoming Norman, and his wife acts as if he always has been, his stardom just a fantasy falling away.

In a last hysterical bid to prove he's special, he opens his briefcase, where he carries actual Kinks reviews, and holds them up to her one by one, almost crying in frustration. "*Melody Maker* in 1970 said that I'm one of Britain's top songwriters. *Rolling Stone* said that my new album was a masterpiece! *The New York Times* – New York, America! – said that the concert I did at Carnegie Hall was the best thing there for years. Now what do you think of that?" The wife walks round the TV studio and looks at him through a camera, leaving him the wrong side of the lens. "Ever since 1965 you've had this fantasy of wanting to be a pop star," she explains, as if everything he thought he did with The Kinks was just a wistful dream, from which he must now wake. "You're just dull, ordinary and insignificant. What," she asks in the question haunting him, "are you trying to prove?"

Dave watched in mounting fury from the corner where The Kinks had been shunted, barely glimpsed throughout the whole show and treated like a house band with their leader "lost in a megalomaniacal trance", he wrote in *Kink*. He felt trapped in "the death scene of a once great British rock band". But Ray had written a different ending, grappling with how far out he'd gone, and falling back to earth. In the plaintive ballad to himself '(A) Face In The Crowd', he asks, "Mister can you tell me who I am?" and, with desperate hope, "Do you think I stand out?" Then he slips, resigned, into the audience of what is suddenly a Kinks gig. Dave leads the band through 'You Can't Stop The Music', a rock version of 'Celluloid Heroes' commemorating its strivers and stars, which the music itself will outshine and outlast. Ray in his accountant's suit dances in the crowd, leaving the band to his brother, finally able to enjoy The Kinks from the outside as he bows out, and admits he's nothing special.

Letting The Kinks and Dave go had long been a fantasy; absorption by the ordinary life he wrote about but feared when talent whose direction was now in question evaporated, a nightmare. Ray was as unhappy as Dave with the shoddiness of *Starmaker*'s production, slashed from his 50-minute script to 37, unwillingly worked on by Granada's Light Entertainment crew, and dumped in a late-night spot, which, like *The Long Distance Piano Player*, he couldn't bear to watch. But his helplessness as his psychodrama swallows him is a grippingly revealing performance.

Reviews of its September 4 broadcast, though, shared Ray's dismay. *NME*'s Charles Shaar Murray's savaging noted the show's glaring fault, down to Ray alone: the shortage of decent songs, "hole-filling" plot-movers by a writer losing his tussle with a musical's demands. Over a game of snooker with *Melody Maker*'s Allan Jones at Konk, ruthlessly won by Ray, he considered his situation. "A lot of people think I'm completely on the wrong track these days," he admitted. "They think I should never have stopped writing three-minute story songs like 'Waterloo Sunset'. But I've written so many of them...The formula begins to reveal itself. The magic goes. It did for me, anyway.

"I need to take [that talent] somewhere else, hence my little efforts like *Starmaker*. I know I'm upsetting a lot of people who want something else from me. Some of them are in my own band. One of them is my own brother... I wonder these days what my place is. Our band's never really fit in... I don't know what we are. I don't know who I am. Sometimes I feel I don't even exist... Right now, I don't even know if I'm winning or losing."

Ray still didn't switch course. The album of *Starmaker* – *(The Kinks Present) A Soap Opera* – was swiftly turned around by The Kinks before the *Preservation* tour. "I feared that *Soap Opera* might have become the last Kinks album," Dave said on its 1998 reissue. "I thought it was an exercise in Ray disappearing up his own arse, and that we should just get it done as efficiently and painlessly as possible." On its May 16, 1975 release it was the weakest Kinks album so far. Its B-side, though, fleshed out with three new songs, works. '(A) Face In The Crowd' is more affectingly melancholy, 'Underneath The Neon Sign' a new twist on Ray's horror of modern artificiality, as traffic lights replace stars and he sunbathes in neon. 'Holiday Romance' is a thirties pastiche tale with an archly acted, eventually addictive vocal. 'Ducks On The Wall', that cliché of seventies decor, is the funniest lyric as the sight of them wherever he goes makes the Star crazed, till the ducks can be heard quacking after him, a suburban variant on Hitchcock's birds. The latter two songs were ignored UK singles, the album sharing their fate.

In November 1974 Ray married Yvonne Gunner, a teacher surely represented in *X-Ray*'s closing pages by the young church schoolteacher he makes eye contact with soon after almost being killed by a lorry when cycling near Effingham, distraught after Rasa's divorce. "The sort of person you could depend on," he thinks. The wider world knew nothing of her till their own fraught divorce, years later.

Barrie Keeffe regularly saw the couple in their country retreat, after beginning writing work with Ray on the musical *Chorus Girls* in 1977. "I suddenly became a single parent of two sons," he remembers, "and we went down there often for weekends for the donkeys he had, and he was an absolutely fabulous uncle to Sam and Tom, the boys, they adore him." The gardens where they played had been bought in the disappointed hope of luring Ray's own, absent children. "We've had some wonderful laughs," Keeffe continues. "On one of my first times there, Ray as a wind-up got me totally pissed on calvados and took me to meet Yvonne, who was coming in from London where she worked in a school, and walking down a country lane, I collapsed. He left me there, met Yvonne, brought her to meet me, and said [airily], 'Oh, this is my collaborator, Barrie Keeffe,' as I lay there mud-spattered in a ditch!"

Ray's neighbours also found themselves on the receiving end of what Keeffe admiringly calls the "fucking destructive sense of humour" of 'A Well Respected Man''s always class-conscious writer. "Oh, it's a lovely spread in Effingham, like an estate," Keeffe says fondly. "It's near Guildford, very stockbroker belt. And I got the impression that some of the stockbrokers there were a bit snooty about, 'Who the fuck is this long-haired rock and roller in our midst?' They were playing cricket, and would clearly us much rather not be around to watch them. And Ray got the vibes of this snottiness and suddenly giggled and said, 'Ah, wait a minute. According to the deeds to my house, on the first Sunday of the month, I can graze my donkeys on the village green.' They were having tea, and they came out and there's suddenly these two donkeys planted in the middle of the wickets! He's a schoolboy as well - a schoolboy in disgrace, very often."

Keeffe observed a familiar duality in Ray. "I see him as half Max Miller and half Keats," he considers. "Max Miller, because he's a fabulous performer who I've seen really down, and then he walks on-stage and lights up the room. And I remember the first time I saw him in Konk, he was sitting by a window, looking rather like that famous painting of Keats, so still and quiet and wise. And having seen him the night before, rip-roaring with 'You Really Got Me', there's two people."

Ray had confused his sixties peers by staying in suburban Fortis Green to write. Keeffe saw a similarly contrasting attempt at peace in Effingham. "I'd seen him as the rock'n'roll star on a Saturday night, at one of those university things somewhere like Milton Keynes, where he wound them all up by coming on late so the mood was right, and he won 'em over totally. And after that wild night, the next day we went down to Sunday lunch with him and Yvonne, and it was the pinnacle of contented, ideal family life, it seemed. And I said, 'I can't get over it, Ray. Last night, you were the wild rock'n'roller, now you're going for a walk in the country, and talking about the flowers. It's like you've got two lives.' And he said, 'Yes, it's great, isn't it? You can have two lives. You don't have to settle for one.'"

In February and March 1975, Ray focused on another facet of his creative empire, producing the debut by Konk Records signing Cafe Society. The trio's subsequently famous member Tom Robinson had a less sunny time with Ray than Keeffe. He recalls the label's dysfunctional nature. "I think the larger record label that released Konk Records [ABC in the US] had come to him and said, 'Why don't you do some acts for us', because they wanted to nab The Kinks after they left RCA. They weren't really interested in what he might produce. I think The Kinks thought it might be an interesting challenge, and assembled Claire Hamill and Andy Desmond and March Hare, and Cafe Society. But Ray was playing at it. Any time we actually met with him, he'd make plausible suggestions. And then you'd come back at the agreed date, next Monday at 9 o'clock, and ring the doorbell at Konk and say, 'We're here.' And the girl would say,

'Who? Why are you here? The Kinks are in America.' He did set us up so we had 25 quid a week, which in those days was enough to live on and a great respite to write. But mostly he made me a professional musician by allowing us to support The Kinks a couple of times, and stand at the side of the stage watching him with the audience. I think, in the strange, distorted world in which he lives, he did the right thing by us. It was a great education. It came at a high cost, financially. But I'd do it again."

What was distorted about Ray's world?

"It's quite a paranoid world. He thinks the worst of people, rather than expecting the best. So that then sometimes leads the worst to happen. He had horrendous experiences with Eddie Kassner and those people earlier on, there's no question. In those early days of the music business, where it was just a blatant rip-off, their contract was an absolute disgrace. So I think he had big problems trusting people. And also I think being a working-class boy encountering the middle-class managers like Robert Wace gave him a good-sized chip on the shoulder, and having experienced a tiny fraction of the pressure that he must have sustained in the success of The Kinks, it's a miracle that he came out as normal as he did. He has enormous personal charm, huge charisma. If Ray wants you to like him, you'll like him. You're helpless, all your objections you were going to confront him with evaporate completely. 'Oh yes, Ray, no I understand completely...' You see everything from his viewpoint. But he was a difficult man for anyone to do business with. There was a flakiness in his dealings that made it very hard when you're the powerless recipient of those deals. There was always the weight of the world on his shoulders. He was juggling too many balls, of which Cafe Society was just one."

Things briefly looked up. "At one stage he had a bout of lucidity and said, 'Dave can produce the Cafe Society album.' And Dave said, 'Yeah, I can do that! Monday morning, 9 o'clock?' We turn up, there's Dave, we start recording. And after about three days, we'd got three or four tracks down, we were finally making this album. Then this shadowy figure in shades appears and sits at the back of the studio. And Dave starts to look more nervous in his chair, as this figure lurks behind him. And the next day, the shadowy figure's there again, and reaches forward and just moves one of the faders on the console. The day after that, Ray's in the producer's chair, Dave's in the back, and Ray's saying, 'Just try that one more time...' The fourth day, The Kinks are in America."

A second album fared little better. "Ray got in an outside production team. The songs never sounded so good, professionals at the controls, finally our luck's changed. It worked for a week-and-a-half like that. And then, 'The Kinks need the studio.' And it all got laid on a shelf, and ground to a halt. And by that point, I'd been to see the Sex Pistols, and had written 'Glad To Be Gay', and realised that what was going on out there was different from what was going on in here."

Robinson quit Cafe Society in November 1976, and their second album went unreleased. Ray wasn't pleased. "He was asserting, 'No, no, we've still got a contract, I am still your record company, let's talk, I'm sure we can do something with you.'" Things famously came to a head in December when Ray watched Robinson at London's Nashville Rooms. "As part of him asserting his rights as my label boss, he turned up to the gig. 'Tired Of Waiting' was in our set anyway, and we dedicated it to him. He threw a V-sign and walked out."

"It wasn't until I suppose the seventies that I produced a band that was gay, Cafe Society, with Tom Robinson," Ray muses one day, while discussing his own songs' ambivalent sexuality. "He wanted to leave the band, and I said, 'Well, let's see what you can write', and he wrote the song 'Glad To Be Gay'. I was pleased that I commissioned that. Then he went off and signed to EMI..."

"You cheeky git!" Robinson laughs at this radical rewriting of the song's history. "At the same time, 'He tried to be gay, but it just didn't pay, so he bought a motorbike instead', in 'Prince Of The Punks' [Ray's fuck-you to Robinson on a 1977 Kinks B-side]. So I think he's on the record there." Ray, it transpired, had learned a lot about publishing, since the days of Eddie Kassner. "He gets 40% of the money I received from 'Glad To Be Gay'. I got the legal minimum. So he gets a fairly hefty... he's done all right with that deal." ABC had pulled the plug on their deal, and the failed label was wound down.

★★★

The Kinks took their latest self-supporting, multimedia show *A Soap Opera* around the US, where *Starmaker* wasn't screened, in April and May 1975. Bad sound at many of the theatres they played showed the perils of taking rock into such places. *The Village Voice*'s Dave Hickey, though, found Davies again managing a rare union of the media. Applauding the show's lack of profundity, he wrote: "It was just *good*, and good-natured, and intelligent – a piece of very funny, humane musical entertainment, which along with *Preservation...* is one of the two really successful rock theatricals that I've seen... Davies doesn't introduce theatrical effects into rock and roll. He takes the theatrical aspects which are already in rock and roll and uses them to his advantage."

The Kinks were fully integrated into Ray's freak show now, as Ray leant not on reviews but on the playing of his old hits to prove his identity. Looking to his band to affirm it, Dave led the rejection of their errant leader. When *A Soap Opera*'s theatrical, role-playing conceit collapsed as Ray resumed his place in The Kinks to simply play rock music, "the effect on the audience was almost chemical – it was dramatic, funny, touching, and so goddamn smart it made you want to hit a wall". British reviewers were similarly impressed when *A Soap Opera* reached London's New Victoria Theatre in June. What leaps from tapes of that show is Dave's suddenly wailing guitar. The other brother was waking.

Ray and Dave's dad, Frederick, died suddenly on July 5 at Ray's Effingham home while Ray was in London, another hammer-blow to both sons, and what was left of their past. Frightened by the death he saw in Frederick's eyes a little earlier, Dave had avoided going for a last drink with him. Bitterly regretting it, he resolved to do better by their mum. Ray made his *X-Ray* alter ago kick absently, distracted and upset, as he remembered the day. "I don't care what people think," he once said, when accused of being old-fashioned. "I write songs for my dad." But that hadn't been true for a while.

Still Ray barely paused in writing yet another concept album, *Schoolboys In Disgrace*. In a phone call they must, by now, have dreaded, he told RCA to expect another record and show in November. Ray explained the six-and-a-half-day working week which allowed this to

Crawdaddy's Greg Mitchell. Waking at 8.30, by 10 he was timetabling the day's 30 tasks in his notebook, the stray verses and bridges of 30 songs needing writing. He'd pace around his empty house, muttering and laughing as ideas came, then settle at the piano or guitar. The pub at two for a pint of Guinness and cheese roll was his one break till seven. By August he was in Konk working up demos with the band. Mixing the album and cooking up another stage show ("Caveman outfit for Gosling. A-bomb footage...") occupied October. *Schoolboys In Disgrace* was released in the US on November 17. Four days later, The Kinks' latest production opened in Bethlehem, Pennsylvania. Support was Cockney Rebel, whose Steve Harley, it isn't commonly known, is Ray's cousin; predictable Davies clan conflict ensued.

Schoolboys In Disgrace was supposedly a *Preservation* prequel, outlining the harsh schooldays that formed Mr. Flash. But songs live and breathe inside a concept which draws on Ray's strength of knowing personal nostalgia. "We only remember what we choose to remember," he admits about 'Schooldays' where he bridled under authority, but now pines for their imagined simplicity and friendships. 'Education', a cod-profound epic summarising the educative impulse since pre-history, is outpunched by the outrageous dance routine 'Jack The Idiot Dunce'.

The second half is the most easily pleasurable, melodically hard-rocking side of Kinks music since the sixties. It was entirely based, though only the brothers knew it, on Dave's expulsion after impregnating Sue when he was 15. 'I'm In Disgrace', 'Headmaster' and 'The Hard Way' outline his fall, the latter song deepening Ray's observation to me that education then threw working-class children on the scrapheap, and ending with his unforgettable wail: "Please don't take my trousers down!" Avory got the nightly whacking at the gigs. The album is powered equally by Ray's rediscovery of tunes, and Dave's chopped, fuzzed, relentlessly right guitar chords, disinterred at the *Soap Opera* shows. Dave's voice, almost silent for three years, backs his brother. Drawing on their north London memories, they rebonded. Ray had tried to kill the old Kinks at White City, and Dave had watched helplessly as they seemed to expire under the Manchester TV lights making *Starmaker*. They were breathing again.

"*Schoolboys In Disgrace* was a rebirth of the band," Dave agrees. "As I was getting into my new internal, spiritual life, it wasn't as scary as I thought, it was empowering to find out about all this stuff, and I started to feel more confident in my playing."

How did Dave feel about Ray mining his traumatic past for comic songs? "Well isn't that what Ray does? Not as graphically as in this. If it had been about someone else, they would've sued him. But we worked so closely together, it was like, is it paying a homage to a very important point in my life? It worked in two ways – not only helping him with ideas, but my life is a backdrop for his own work. I'm his nearest raw material, if you like. That was the case on many, many occasions. But that was a cool album. The tour was so fun. A chance to be someone else again. That was cool about *Soap Opera* as well, although I wasn't as keen on the music, which was the height of Ray's dictatorship. I always feel urky about that. The live stuff with the characters was totally different."

Schoolboys tour footage of the school-uniformed Kinks has the Bash Street Kids comic anarchy referenced on the album's cartoon sleeve. It certainly looks more entertaining than that educative concept epic Ray so envies, *The Wall*. "*The Wall* was public school," he sniffs. "Ours was rebellious secondary modern."

Ray had intended *Schoolboys In Disgrace 2*. "It was just a start," he told *Crawdaddy*. "I wanted to say more about when Flash left school, and couldn't get a job because he never finished his classes. I had the whole story worked out. But it's too complicated. There's no point. That's rock'n'roll, isn't it?" Instead, *Schooldays'* best song, 'No More Looking Back', though it tramps streets filled with phantoms of Rasa or Sue, and typically does nothing but look back, symbolically drew a line from which The Kinks could move forward. Ray had walked his own path for three years, leaving the record industry, much of his audience and almost his own band behind. Did RCA ever try to stop him?

"Yeah. I did feel sorry for them. Because all they wanted was six albums like *Muswell Hillbillies*. They were confused by us. But you know, they'd signed David Bowie, and if we'd made a conventional album – if I'd wanted to, it would have been more of a struggle. Because they were trying to make you turn the company around, get it out of Nashville.

And look, they embraced what we did. To be fair, they gave us all the support, right to the end. One of us had to go, though."

On June 23, 1976, The Kinks signed with Arista Records, and resumed a conventional career.

Little survives of the madly ambitious vaudeville shows the sudden vanishing of Ray's wife and daughters drove him to. Like any theatrical experience they exist only as memories, for The Kinks and their most faithful middle-aged fans. Hit movies of *Tommy*, *Quadrophenia* and *The Wall* fleshed out and immortalised his peers' visions, which are frequently and lucratively restaged. The patchy soundtracks to Ray's biggest ideas, staged with such endearingly home-made ambition, lie largely forgotten.

One exception, Bobcat Goldthwait, was a working-class Catholic schoolboy in Syracuse, New York in 1975. Still best-known today as the strangulated-voiced cop in the *Police Academy* films, he is one of the 21st century's most blackly funny and honest writer-directors, responsible for *Sleeping Dogs Lie* (2006), about a woman's relationship problems after admitting an early sexual encounter with a dog, and *World's Greatest Dad* (2009), in which Robin Williams gains popularity by faking the circumstances of his obnoxious son's death. *Schoolboys In Disgrace* is his favourite album. "The idea of going to school and being oppressed, having authority tell you what to do and trying to mould you and fighting that – that's something I've always been fond of," he's said. Goldthwait is scheduled to film his script of a musical version in England in 2011. "It's something I've wanted to do all my life but never thought I'd get a chance to." Ray is executive producer. Almost 40 years late, maybe his most absolute music will find a home.

CHAPTER 11

Give The People What They Want

Ray rented a New York apartment in 1976. John Lennon lived next door at the Dakota building, the ominous Gothic landmark outside which he would be gunned down four years later. Mia Farrow, who had given birth to Satan in *Rosemary's Baby*, filmed at the Dakota, also lived on these Upper West Side streets, where she pushed a pram with her real baby. Ray's place was much more modest than the vast pad the former Beatle had just retired to as Yoko's house-husband, while she plotted their investment empire. His *Waterloo Sunset* stories about faded English rocker Les Mulligan, another doppelganger for himself, describe it as a homely bolt-hole, still with the same sofa and faded Indian rug 20 years later, lampshades from a sale, and a closet filled with old records and videos and cardboard boxes of unsorted memories: letters, diaries, contracts, newspapers. It was an old, high-rise building and Ray lived near the top, from where he observed the street. He left it to jog in nearby Central Park. The Dakota diner described in the book with its faded signed photos of ancient comedians, the nearest thing to a greasy spoon in this refined neighbourhood, sounds like the sort of place at which he'd eat, and take notes on customers. Arista Records, The Kinks' new home, was 15 blocks away on West 57th. Though Ray kept his Surrey house, he now had one foot in America.

"I realised at that point that compared to America we were being neglected in Europe, Britain particularly," he says. "And I thought, 'I'd like to pursue this thing, and find out what I'm writing about. I need to get some American experience, and find out about the culture.' But I went to New York, which is nothing like America. I learned a lot about Westsiders. That is a culture in itself. I only felt connected to New York. I'm still trying to get my head round America. I was very guarded about it. As events proved, it's a place where you have to be on your guard. I felt that I had some sort of community of people on the street, and friends, and a social relation with America when I stayed in New York. I felt at home there for a while. There was this longing, though, to come back."

The Kinks now made their final assault on the country that rejected them in 1965. Clive Davis, the maverick label boss who formed Arista after being sacked from a highly successful spell running Columbia, had personally courted them. Unlike RCA, which had simply been grateful to have an established rock act on an unfashionable label, Davis took a highly active role in The Kinks' American career. Ray listened to his advice, because they shared an interest in the band's commercial resurrection. Ray still burned with fury at the injustice of what had happened a decade before, and desperately wanted the success America had stolen from him. For the first time since Robert Wace was forced out he let himself be guided, taking demos to Davis, discussing and changing them. They plotted a strategy for The Kinks' final victory. Did Ray enjoy this collaboration?

"Look," he says, annoyed, "we were in a business together, and I wrote the songs, and that was the relationship, and I really enjoyed that. I've always enjoyed having feedback from people – while the work is in progress. When Clive started Arista it was kind of an indie. We found it a nice experience, and I thought he was very funny, in that New York way – he doesn't intend to be. And I made a conscious effort to sit down and say, 'I'm going to make 12 good songs here that we can tour with,' and no funny outfits and no character changes, and just be the band. And I think the band were relieved. Because I know it was pissing Dave off. And Mick, well, he just went along with everything, but I think he was a bit confused. I think Mick Avory was very pleased he could walk down the street dressed in his brown shoes and bad T-shirts again. So we went back with [next album] *Sleepwalker*, and started serious rebuilding."

"Why haven't The Kinks become super-big?" Ray was asked by *Circus'* Scott Cohen in 1974. "I think because they don't want to," he'd replied. "I think it isn't in them. Maybe they're selfish, they didn't want to sacrifice everything." Now he did.

"Even with Arista, I thought we made a record, and that's all you have to do," Ray says. "But I remember being in the Warwick Hotel on a Saturday off, and I got a phone call from Michael Kleffner, their promotions man. He said, 'Raymond, it's Michael. Do you wanna sell 250,000 units for the rest of your life?' I said, 'No'. He said, 'Well come to Boston with me and do some promotion.' We were stuck on that sales level – nowadays it would be incredible, and that was just in America. I think I'd been a little bit lazy. It was the constant touring that made The Kinks a major success in America. It was relentless, one after another. And we turned out an album every year or so, and the show kept moving, and the band were very into touring and wanted more records out so we could tour. It was a touring band that happened to have records."

The competitive instincts which had turned Ray into a singles-writing hit machine in the sixties seemed to grind back into gear, the 24-hour shop sign he had imagined working under lighting up. Did he discipline himself to become an American album hit machine now?

"I was trying not to be a hit machine – and we've certainly achieved that with a few albums. But we wanted to expand and find a new fan base – and hopefully, we'd still be excited by the music. Things like 'Misfits' and 'A Rock'n'Roll Fantasy' a bit later were attempts to do both: music we got a kick out of, and also improve the fan base. I never felt that we could get to the level we had reached. Because for a while, when we first started, we were just so successful. But I felt we were growing into a different type of band, with more depth to the music, possibly, which was more adult, interesting and sustainable. And certainly more fun to play live than popping out the old singles."

217

"When we were doing *Sleepwalker* and *Preservation*, they were two different bands," says Dave. "Ray wanted to get back from the place where he'd drifted off – to what on reflection was a good place to go, *Preservation* was very powerful. But he wanted to get back to some sort of semblance of what it was like when we started. You can never go back there actually. But at least *Sleepwalker* went part-way."

Konk reopened on June 24, 1976 as a state-of-the-art 24-track studio. The Kinks vanished into it till January 1977. Two weeks in, the air-conditioning failed, making it unusable in the sapping heat of a summer of drought. When they returned, Ray became lost in a studio where time was free and limitless. The Kinks were driven through endless, imperceptibly different takes of the new songs; finished versions were scrapped and started again. "Ray's not very good at choosing," Avory understates. "It could go on a bit. If you give him too much time then he goes on and on and does different takes, and he doesn't know which one to use." Gosling felt like a hired hand, which contractually, unlike Ray, Dave and Mick, he was. He thought Ray gave lip service to them all being a band again, inviting ideas he then ignored. "I find it interesting working in a team," Ray contends. "I suppose the best dictators know how to use the machinery. Not that I'm a dictator," he catches himself. "When you're in a band, the band dictates the music."

With the partial exception of Dave, the band were by now an unwieldy studio instrument Ray needed and used to precisely express his songs. There have been subsequent examples, such as Jerry Dammers' Specials, who eventually abandoned their perfectionist chief leaving him distraught, and coldly rejected him on a lucrative reunion; and Nashville Americana outfit Lambchop. Their leader Kurt Wagner's wandering muse has increasingly turned to music which almost silences the skills of his bandmates, yet they've stayed loyally beside him. "Having a sibling myself, imagining being in a band with him would be a challenge," Wagner tells me. "But the others in Lambchop are very independent, in most cases much more advanced musicians than myself, and I would of course try to feature the things that I thought were amazing in them. Songs don't quite work out the way I had in mind, because I'm willing to let them change beyond my preconception. If they are fulfilled as individuals and artists, that's the most important thing, whether it's within or outside Lambchop. If they're realised and satisfied as musicians then whatever they contribute will be all the better."

No one remembers The Kinks working this way after *Village Green*. The parts of Ray's five-man instrument inevitably began to buckle from the strain, as they were pushed to reconquer America in their thirties. John Dalton, a loyal, uncomplaining and quietly skilled presence since *Arthur*, decided he'd had enough of touring and the turgid Konk sessions. Diligently completing his bass parts for *Sleepwalker*, he quit on October 8. "He's really stable," Ray had told *Circus'* Janis Schact of the bassist. "He's good to have on tour. He holds things down because he doesn't change. He refuses to live in America; he's not here. His day is built around the things he does in London. He gets up at a certain time. He goes out and buys the English papers and he drinks tea." Dalton could do all that without The Kinks. Instead he fulfilled a long-time ambition to run a transport cafe.

The sessions continued. "When you produce your own stuff and you write it as well, it becomes like a mountain," Ray confessed to *Rolling Stone*. He seemed unsure of his identity as he left the concept characters behind. "I think what I do [playing Flash] in the musical [*Preservation*] is break down any of the barriers I've got as a person," he'd told *Circus'* Scott Cohen in 1974. Two years later to *Phonograph's* Barbara Charone, he made an about-turn. "I was trying to forget who I was for a bit, but the only things that are gonna work are me," he said. "Some of the performances particularly on that last album [*Schoolboys In Disgrace*] were not me singing... I was another character. But what I'm realising now is if I'm making Kinks records and writing Kinks songs, then I have to sing like Ray Davies." He contended he needed the band. "It's too lonely without a group... I could play all the instruments and have everything the way I want it, but it is a group. I want a group and I give them the benefit of the doubt. I need to see other people's inadequacies and their strong points to know mine." He apologised for concept albums he had been fully committed to earlier that year. "I've been trying to tell too much of a story... instead of trying to make each song work. The songs are better now without a concept."

Aged 32, Ray also looked nervously around at the changed musical landscape since he last tried to compete within it. Punk rock dominated the British music press in 1976, the Sex Pistols' 'Anarchy In The UK' coming out that November as his protégé Tom Robinson defected to it. Disco was an opposite, equal fashion. Inside Konk, meanwhile, what was he doing? "It's got to happen," he told Charone of the sessions. "But I don't feel desperate. If I was desperate I would have put out the first things we recorded in July... If I aimed songs for the masses they'd be totally different. I'd cover Barry White songs in a clown's outfit. I'd do that if I took my cue from what was happening outside."

Sleepwalker was finally released on February 12, 1977. In its inner sleeve photo, the band not only lack a bassist but look airbrushed, Dave at the centre, white-jacketed for a disco with sleek long hair. Listened to now, it seems a shame Ray trained himself to win, under Davis's tutelage, in one of the American chart's blandest eras. 'Stormy Sky' has the smooth, semi-funky luxury and carefully simplified sentiments of mid-seventies AOR. The wash of harmonies on 'Brother', for which Davis requested strings, mishearing it as a ballad with 'Bridge Over Troubled Water' potential, distract from its saccharine chorus. Though recorded by hard-pressed north Londoners, the music has the time's US studio sheen.

'Juke Box Music' is Ray telling himself that it's all right, letting Dave sing why the change had to be: "It's all because of that music that we started to drift apart/But it's there to dance to, so you shouldn't take it to heart." Dave's dirty fuzzed guitar is all over the track, continuing the brothers' rebalancing. 'Sleepless Night' is his first lead vocal since 1972. In the supposedly redemptive finale 'Life Goes On', Ray slips in a verse about failing to gas himself because he hasn't paid his bill. He pricelessly concludes: "No matter how hard I try, it seems I'm too young to die." And on *Sleepwalker*'s two strongest tracks, he uses his lifelong insomnia to suggest America's proudly hyped new chart hopeful is a maddened night-creeper, an unpleasant cross between a vampire and a werewolf. "Better close your window tight," he warns on 'Sleepwalker', "I might come in for a bite." Brooding major-key piano introduces 'Full Moon''s "truly broken man" who can't recognise his own face. Dave's layered guitars and pinpoint riffs on the former and banked harmonies on the latter still make them invitingly exciting.

"Ray definitely has a lot of vampire qualities," says Dave. "It's like having a big sucker on you. I noticed it when I didn't have a lot of energy myself. 'Sleepwalker' is very funny. Ray's very good at confronting things in songs. He is extremely manipulative. At the same time, if you have creative licence to do that, it might not be pleasant, but it might be part of the process, to get to the work. It's to be understood, not discarded completely. And it wasn't that bad with Ray. It wasn't a horror film. Although sometimes it felt like one. Maybe it'll be one. I should get [Dave's nineties soundtrack collaborator and horror auteur] John Carpenter to write the synopsis. It would be nice to think of it like that."

Primed by an Arista publicity blitz, reviewers largely welcomed the non-concept Kinks. *Sleepwalker* hit number 21 in the US, continuing the promising upward curve of their last two RCA releases (*Schoolboys...* made 45). The title track reached 48, a similar-sized hit single to their last in the US, 'Apeman', seven years before. The Kinks spent three months of 1977 touring America, building an audience there town by town, with Andy Pyle as their new bassist. There'd be no more seventies success in the UK, which made do with three shows at north London's Rainbow.

The band also showed punk, at its British high-water mark in 1977, hadn't outflanked them with their first non-LP 45 there since 'Plastic Man'. 'Father Christmas' (backed with Tom Robinson broadside 'Prince Of The Punks') is the great lost Christmas single, and a splendid Kinks 45. Ray as a department store Santa is mugged by working-class kids who sneeringly tell him to leave his presents for "the little rich boys". They want money, a job for their dad – and a machine gun to frighten everyone else. The sleigh-bells are interspersed with speeding buzz-saw guitar by Fortis Green's original punk. "I love the humour of it, and the aggression and bitterness," Dave told John Swenson. "I could see the faces of my parents when Christmas came around. They had to struggle to make ends meet. We kind of got what we needed, but there was something fake about the holiday." At one of the Rainbow shows, Ray was in full Father Christmas gear backstage ready for it as the encore, when Dave mischievously switched to the less appropriate 'You Really Got Me'. "I've never," he mused in *Kink*, "had a Santa Claus call me a fucking cunt before."

'Father Christmas''s spontaneous conviction was ignored as the next album's sessions ground on in grimly familiar fashion. John Gosling's frustration was increasingly plain to Ray, causing a frostily intimidating atmosphere. Gosling finally snapped in January, telling Ray to "do it yourself" after one take too many, and quitting with the equally recalcitrant Pyle. It was all somehow predictable. One year into The Kinks' slick professional comeback, Ray stood in the rubble of his band.

"Maybe I always expected too much," says Dave of the crisis. "That me and Ray could just get together and something would happen. Which it did, to be honest. Which I wouldn't be able to explain. I keep going back to *Misfits*. It took nearly a year to put that album together, a couple of band members left, and Mick didn't really want to do it. And we got together like we had so many times before, playing Chuck Berry records, having a laugh. And two songs came out of it, 'Rock'n'Roll Fantasy' and 'Trust Your Heart', which pulled the record together. That could very easily have been the end of it. But there was something not yet resolved. You know when it's over, don't you? Or I hope you do. I didn't feel like it was."

"'A Rock'n'Roll Fantasy' was a very personal song about Dave and I," Ray told John Swenson. As they had at the similarly fraught start of the seventies, they were talking to each other in songs. "Hello you, hello me, hello people we used to be," Ray begins, quiet and fragile. Predating the band-members' exits, its lyric suggests that it was Dave who was hankering to "break up the band, start a new life, be a new man," and rallies him for another round. "You might be through but I've just begun," Ray taunts. Then, summing up his mystifyingly ambiguous relationship to a band and brother he abused, suffered through yet refused to leave for over three decades, beyond all normal sense, he sings: "I feel free and I won't let go." Ray uses the needs of a Kinks fan clinging onto life with their music, and the death of rock's greatest hero Elvis Presley on August 16, 1977 as the song was written in New York, to justify their continuing.

In the story of the same name in *Waterloo Sunset*, Dan the fan is a suicidal romantic fantasist who has wrecked his life over records and a woman – not so different, on the other side of the studio glass, from Ray. He brushes past the book's Ray-substitute Les Mulligan going into Ray's building, and chats to Lennon, signing autographs outside the Dakota, as he would for Mark Chapman three years later. Hearing of Elvis's death and playing 'That's All Right, Mama' relieves the real world's encroaching chill for Dan. Ray concludes the song with a harder message to himself, to engage with life and leave his own rock fantasy. Its fan-revering, lighter-waving sentimentality, though, are what carried it onto American radio, and 30 in the charts. It's sappy and glib compared with earlier Kinks hits. But it reached new American fans unashamed of simple, heartfelt emotion.

Session men Clem Cattini and Nick Trevisick (drums) and Ron Lawrence and Zaine Griff (bass) were wheeled in for the Frankenstein patchwork which finally completed *Misfits* in April 1978. The lengthy, potentially catastrophic sessions didn't damage a record which, against the long odds on which Ray thrived, was nervier and weirder than *Sleepwalker*. The title song was another almost sickly AOR anthem for the tribe of losers and outsiders Arista suspected was The Kinks' demographic. 'Black Messiah' saw Ray switch voices between black and white bigots as he teased Middle America with the idea God was black, then, imagining himself beaten by black men as the only white on the block, confessed he wouldn't want a black messiah either.

'In A Foreign Land' found the tax-strapped bounder of 'Sunny Afternoon' successfully exiled across the sea where Ray now lived. Dave's 'Trust Your Heart' was an echo-drenched roar against politicians and for his new lover when in America, Nancy Evans. Ray's closing 'Live Life' had its most scathing verse, attacking slumming middle-class revolutionary "dedicated followers" and flag-saluting NF racists, edited out in America; a sign, perhaps, of his new willingness to compromise with Clive Davis' guidance. 'Out Of The Wardrobe' is a country song about a cross-dresser discovered by his wife who decides that, on reflection, "a change is as good as a rest", and is wonderful comic writing. Most of the songs rattle around a tinny New Wave echo chamber, and amount to a rough grab bag from Ray's fresh New York state of mind. Losing half his band barely broke his stride. It reached 40 in the US.

Avory returned, of course, for 1978's *Misfits* tours. Ex-Pretty Thing Gordon Edwards played keyboards and Jim Rodford, ex-Argent and a 1964 Kinks tourmate with The Mike Cotton Sound, became their faithful bassist for the rest of their career. Avory has said a return for Quaife was considered, but not pursued. David Melville-Quaife remembers contact was made. "That was when I first came to Denmark in 1978," he says. "At that time Pete knew he wanted to do something, he couldn't do it by himself and he loved music so much. And for him The Kinks was the easiest way to get back. There was some connection with Ray at that time, then it stopped. Any time Pete was ready to say, 'Yeah, OK, let's get back together,' one or the other brother would say no. Mick Avory even said no once."

Avory mourned the changed personnel, and balance in the band. "We'd knock around together," he remembers, "me and Nobby [Dalton], Gosling and [road manager and Avory's East Molesey mate] Scrap. We'd discovered all these different cocktails they had in America – there were hundreds. I bought a book, *Barnet's Bible*. I'd got all the ingredients and bottles of drink, and I'd put them in my store at home, and used to invite the family round at Christmas. 'What's that?' 'That's a Pink Squirrel, get it down, it's lovely.' There was one tour in particular where that was all we drank. It had to be a cocktail. And the road manager used to go mad, because he'd be trying to round us up to go on the plane and he knew he'd find us in the bar in the end. 'Take it easy, I haven't finished me drink!' Because we had John Dalton and John Gosling, it was mates going on a trip together really, except we were doing gigs. That's the other thing. Although I'm part of the original band, I fit half in with them – I'm always in between. But it's not always my fault. It's the way it evolved. Dave was with his girlfriend. Then Ray's knocking around with the management. So we were left, all mates in the bar.

"When the two Johns left, there was Andy Pyle for a while, but he never fitted in, because he was trying to be a clever musician. So then Jim Rodford came in, and he was all right. But you know the people I knock around with, they like having a good time. Pull a few birds, do the gig and enjoy it. I didn't worry about too much else. Jim wasn't fully in that mode. When Ian Gibbons became the keyboardist, I knocked around with him."

Did Ray and Dave find it hard to switch off to enjoy being in a band like he did? "They did other things I suppose. They weren't as down to earth."

Avory's isolation was exaggerated by his deteriorating relationship with Dave. Patched up since the Cardiff near-killing, it became more bruisingly hostile with each tour. "We got on pretty good for years," Avory remembers. "But as things moved on, circumstances changed for everyone. There was an incident at a show when Blondie were supporting that year where I stormed off, and kicked a chair through a window, and was throwing bottles everywhere, and wanted to kill him." He gives a small laugh. "They kept us separated. It's stupid, really. Especially when you're supposed to be there enjoying yourselves, playing the music."

Dave always maintains it was Avory's neutrality or siding with Ray in disputes which infuriated him. Avory believes the problem is more fundamental. He thinks Dave resented the band's legal fabric which, as Kinks Productions Limited, gave the three remaining founder members equal shares. "We'd been through that phase of all being together," he says. "Then Quaife had left, and John Dalton wasn't on an equal footing with everyone, they were hired musicians. So it was difficult to make it an equal band. Even though I was there from the beginning, Dave probably thought I was on the same level as John Dalton. I think his problem was Ray. I was in the middle. If I hadn't have been in the company, it probably wouldn't have mattered so much. But because I'm supposed to be reaping the same benefit as him, it went like that. Ray and Dave were the nucleus of the band. And I was only there because I was there in the beginning. But I wasn't on their level musically. But everything found its own balance, if you know what I mean. It didn't matter what was written on a piece of paper. I mean Ray controlled it, Dave opposed it. And I was left in the middle. I didn't really have the say of them."

It sounds a pretty lonely place to be for 20 years.

"Yeah. The thing is, I enjoyed a lot of it as well. It wasn't all... 'orrible!" he laughs. "There was a lot of elation in the good moments."

Learning the lessons of two band-breaking years at Konk, and perhaps wanting to bring The Kinks into his new American world, Ray moved them to New York to make *Low Budget*. They stayed in the Wellington Hotel in May 1979. A short distance from Arista's offices, it was in those days a classic Manhattan "shithole", Dave remembered, with mouldy walls, giant cockroaches and drunks shambling down its corridors. Gordon Edwards didn't make it and was fired, suddenly returning The Kinks to the rock four-piece they had been in the sixties. Ian Gibbons would become their new keyboard player in July. After a week's rehearsal, they blasted through a dozen songs in 10 days in something like their old style. Some first or second takes were the basis of tracks used on the album. "Doing it in America cost a few bob," Avory dryly explains. "So Ray did it quick."

The seediness of the then bankrupt, decaying, often stinking and ripely alive city suited the American songs Ray wrote there. Swinging London's satirist now applied his acuity to Jimmy Carter's USA. The Democrat President had, in the wake of Nixon's fall, been able to oversee a foreign policy which distanced America from fascist strong-man cronies such as Pinochet, and brokered peace between Egypt and Israel. His defining speech said that consumption for its own sake was immoral, and Americans must learn to live within limits, especially in their use of energy. The idea was initially popular. It sounds like a science-fiction dream of America now. But 1979's Iran Revolution wrecked Carter's hopes. The subsequent taking of hostages in Teheran's US embassy and petrol shortages after the new regime slashed oil exports, coming so soon after Vietnam and Watergate's shame, left Americans reeling. New York was one of the states which adopted gas (petrol) rationing, causing panicked queues. This was Ray's raw material.

'(Wish I Could Fly Like) Superman' was written in late 1978 after he saw *Superman – The Movie*. Ray crafted pumped-up beats and a ringingly full sound, successfully aimed at disco floors. An unimpressed Dave layered on electric guitar. But for all these steroid additions, Ray's lyric takes the part of an untransformed Clark Kent, scared by the relentless bad news on his radio. He wryly nods to *Saturday Night Fever*, planning on "staying alive", but also to an Animals hit he sometimes thought was the sixties' greatest and most pertinent record: "we've gotta get out of this place". The disco mix helped send it to 41 in the US chart in March 1979. "It was kind of a joke," Ray claimed, "taking the piss out of Clive wanting us to do a club-friendly record."

'Gallon Of Gas' is a heavy electric blues for the oil crisis. It revels in the situation's absurdities, as Ray lists all the drugs he can get before a drop of fuel. 'Apeman''s writer can't disguise his pleasure as, in his exaggerated vision, the sky empties of planes and highways are abandoned. "The air," he notes, "smells unnaturally clean."

'Catch Me Now I'm Falling' sums up the nation's mood with a brilliant broad stroke, intimately expressed. It could be a distress call from the last embattled radio station in an occupied land, murmured in your ear by Ray as a hushed communiqué: "This is Captain America calling..." The album's second superhero recalls the help America's given through the years, letting you think of the Marshall Plan's largesse to Europe at World War Two's end. Now the favour needs returning, "your secretary tells me... you've gone out of town". The music plundered Stones riffs and stiffly funky clubland beats, letting Dave's lean solo clash with a sax. Double the length of the concise wonder of old Kinks singles at six minutes, it proved Ray's adaptable sweep as a pop writer.

Less noticed was that the rest of *Low Budget* reacted to punk and Britain's "winter of discontent", as multiple strikes and creeping unemployment – British news which also informed 'Superman' – heralded Margaret Thatcher's May 1979 election. The album opened with Ray's gravel-throated howl on 'Attitude', a note to his band, he said, that: "The eighties are here, I know 'cause I'm staring right at them/ But you're still waiting for 1960 to happen." 'Pressure', the UK single, was a two-and-a-half minute, fast splicing of fifties rock and

Beach Boys beauty. 'Misery' combined personal and national pressure. The sound successfully cribbed from the New Wave elements of 1978 support acts Blondie, Tom Petty and The Cars. One of the songs Ray wrote first, 'Low Budget', found him the comic victim of straitened times, "a cut-price person in a low-budget land". The always financially "careful" Ray offered a practised, pitiful plea: "Don't think that I'm tight, because I don't buy a round." Clive Davis made it a radio-only single early in 1979. "It was brilliant marketing by Clive," Ray told John Swenson. "I went back to America and wrote the rest of the album. I used to get up at 8 o'clock, turn on the radio and hear the record, which gave me inspiration to work all day."

"I wrote it after the Arista guy in England turned down [financial] tour support for us if we didn't have a single," he tells me, "in the back of a Ford Fiesta driving up to the studio. White hot anger, totally, like 'A Well Respected Man'. It was still fairly insider, our music, even in the Arista days. That was sung with cockney rhyming slang, an east London accent and music-hall delivery, in a rock song. But it was one of our biggest records in America, so we didn't really abandon our Englishness. Songs like 'Attitude' say "Leave it out". We still kept our London humour. Like 'Come Dancing' later was one of our biggest singles, and it was about an East End spiv, sung in a London voice. So it knocks the theory that we'd become American completely out of the water. We were still making English music."

Ray's defensiveness springs from the hostility they now found in their homeland. The standard, cursory London show squeezed between US tours in 1978 was dismissed by *NME* as "second-rate heavy metal... living on past glories... a travesty of rock'n'roll." *Low Budget*, in fact, got good reviews though low sales. But punk's Year Zero doctrine and British suspicion of American success ensured their time was up. "It's a cheap shot," Ray complains. "You're doing well in America, so what are you doing back here? British DJs and reviewers thought we were making a fortune. We never made a lot of money in America. We worked really hard for it. Even in the eighties, when we were selling a lot of records, it was nothing in comparison to when we first started." Dave says: "I really liked *Low Budget*. But I don't think people liked us then in England. Probably because we deserted them for America. Americans really warmed to us. It could have gone horribly wrong, but we started playing bigger arenas. Life was very kind to us."

The Kinks' career uniquely splits in two here. With the exception of one hit Ray would soon write, The Kinks from now on were hardly successful at home. In America in the eighties, I met people who had no idea they were a sixties band. Those who condemned them for chasing mass US success were unfair. Ray did the bravest thing he could after 'Lola', following his muse to the point of destruction. The bravest thing after that was to hang on to it, and climb back to the top.

The Kinks at least found reflected glory from punk and its aftermath. They'd been around so long that another generation had learned from them. Alongside Van Halen's hit 1978 US cover of 'You Really Got Me', proving its proto-metal pedigree, The Jam got to number 25 in the UK the same year with *Something Else's* 'David Watts'. "The first time I saw Paul [Weller], on Marylebone High Street," Ray muses, "he was wearing the same scarf as I was, and we were both wearing Crombies. So he always had style." Says Dave: "I felt excited when punk came along, and The Jam, and they were screaming at the world, they didn't like the world, instead of dressing it up and making it more false."

Bigger, eventually traumatic, impact on Ray would come from The Pretenders' 1979 hit with 'Stop Your Sobbing'. Eddie Kassner would later offer Ray's unheard demo of 'I Go To Sleep' for a 1981 follow-up. "Living in the suburbs of Ohio aged 14," the band's leader Chrissie Hynde tells me of first hearing The Kinks in 1965, "anything English was really exotic. And then you get someone like Ray Davies, who was foppish, and it all looked pretty fucking strange from where we were sitting. And also he had that beautiful tender voice. When I finally got my band together in 1978, I did 'Stop Your Sobbing' as our first single. Then I was so, so excited when I heard The Kinks had started doing it at their stadium shows – and that just shows you what a nut this guy is, to lead his band from obscurity into that."

Low Budget was released in the US on July 10. When The Kinks' tour began the next day in Dallas, everything finally clicked. Ray's stupid fight with the union official in Hollywood when he was barely more than a boy, and all the indignities they had suffered since, were repaid in a year of unbroken triumph. The album cruised to number 11, their biggest non-hits LP there ever. In an arena filled with 16,000 Kinks fans, on July 28, Ray at last declared victory. "When we clawed our way back in America," he says, "we played a big gig at the Spectrum, Philadelphia. And I came off the stage and I said, 'Remember, fellas. This is a big moment. Treasure it, because we've fought for 10 years to get this. We've come back.' We played Madison Square Garden after that. But the big moment was the Spectrum, Philadelphia. To me, we'd finally made it. We'd redressed the balance. I do like moments like that, and I'm aware of them, and you treasure them much more, because we may not have been able to do that. It could have all ended on the 'Wonderboy' tour of 1968, with the bad suits."

"Oh, it was phenomenal, really phenomenal the power you felt you had," Dave remembers. "And it's funny, when we were playing the Philadelphia Spectrum, and Meadowlands, and these big gigs were starting to crop up, we had an engineer who used to work with Zeppelin years before. And he said some nights, waiting for us to go on, and then when we'd start playing, with the lights and the sounds and the energy and the people shouting and seeing us, it was frightening. He was in AA at the time, so it was a bit much. When you've got that many people in front of you, it does things to you. It makes you feel huge. Makes you feel that's what you're born for."

"I remember going back to that same stage, the Spectrum, Philadelphia," Ray reflects, "after we'd had three or four years of doing it successfully, and I was jogging up and down saying, 'Please let me get up for this gig.' It was packed for two nights. But the moment that had elated me had already become boring."

NME's Charles Shaar Murray, who'd given *Low Budget* one of its good reviews, saw the US tour's finish in October. He reassured his readers that a band previously prone to "the most shambolic live gigs since Dunkirk" now gave a "dynamic, energising rock show" standing comparison with The Clash's shows in New York the same week, led by their running, leaping singer. "Ray Davies," he wrote, "is Born Again."

In quieter moments, Murray had the privilege of watching Ray's by now legendary tightness in action. He almost missed the plane to the next gig, as an airport diner waitress drummed her fingers while he emptied his pockets of crumpled dollar bills and spare coppers, after grandly offering to buy the assembled company a round of milkshakes. "I'm... er... embarrassed," he mumbled to The Kinks' new US manager, Elliott Abbott, responsible as well for Randy Newman and Ry Cooder, and a valuable ally in their American adventure. Abbott paid.

Ray also gave Murray the clearest articulation of his political and personal philosophy. "I was a socialist," he said. "I was brought up to think that way, and then I had a success and it made a lie out of what I was. I made a gesture and it wasn't accepted so I left it physically and emotionally, but I didn't become a capitalist... I believe in anarchy with order." The explicit fear running through his words was that, having somehow become an established success again in his thirties, it would be his head on the pike when the barricades were stormed by the jobless working-class kids punk was deemed to speak to – the "slum kids" he and Dave once were. "Though I seem to be a moderate, I think the only way to have a revolution is to have a total revolution and change everything. The media says don't think about it and it'll go away, but one day it won't and I think somebody should be there before it happens... you've got to change art, change the way people think. Destroy all the pictures, all the music that's been written..."

Always a student of pop, he'd been listening to several challenging bands who rode the punk moment: The Residents, Devo, and David Thomas' Cleveland outsiders Pere Ubu. "It just needed one person to come along and articulate not just new ideas, but a new form as well," he said longingly. "An actual physical New Music, a new construction..." Echoing 'Attitude''s advice to face the future, he concluded: "I want to turn myself upside down now. I've started to do that. I'd like to do something more radical with our work. I'm accepting that things must change."

One For The Road, the live double album Ray assembled from that tour, cemented their US success, hitting number 14 on its June 4, 1980 release. It didn't sound like New Music, flattened by months of Ray's mixing into often stodgy rock. The 'Captain America' line from 'Catch Me Now I'm

Falling' gets a cheer, and 'All Day And All Of The Night' sounds like it's being played on a genetically modified, monstrous Green Amp. Given room to stretch, Dave's sound is still grimily personal. 'Where Have All The Good Times Gone' addresses new hard times straight after 'Catch Me Now I'm Falling', though Ray sings its heartfelt line about his parents who "always told the truth" with unfortunate irony. On '20th Century Man' he still sounds intimate and alone, smuggling Muswell Hillbillies and mention of Gainsborough into arenas. It's bland product, though, really. The video cassette of the same name, Ray now getting the visual aid he'd begged RCA, gives a better clue to why they were filling arenas. Ray is a bow-tied loon sprinting across the stage, face and shirt soaked in sweat. The camera watches the new Kinks fans file in as 'Celluloid Heroes' is played on the soundtrack. They look like a crowd of average Americans out for a stress-relieving rock night, dressed for the cold, not hipness. Later in the show you see them, out of their seats and hollering with excitement The Kinks' sound and Ray's new rock-star showmanship have created. The hit album was driven home with relentless 1980 tours.

Given room to breathe now the US beachhead was established, Ray spent early 1981 rewriting *Chorus Girls*, a musical he'd first worked on with Archway Tavern drinking companion and *The Long Good Friday* writer Barrie Keefe in 1977. This more sensible outlet for his theatrical ambitions opened at the Theatre Royal, Stratford East in April. *Melody Maker's* reviewer Patrick Humphries watched "Prince Charles falling through a trapdoor and held hostage at an East London theatre by a group of feminist dancers", in the year of his wedding to Diana. Ray's songs included one about dildos, 'Oh What A Glorious Sight', and were all "from a feminist standpoint, the most militant of which is 'All Men Are Fools'." It was a long way from Idaho arenas.

"It was based on Aristophanes' *The Poet And The Women*," Keeffe elaborates. "Ray was a very inventive collaborator." The theatre world wasn't so different from life in The Kinks. "Mike Elphick was playing one of the leads and drink wasn't his problem, it was his solution, and there was a lady in it who was on heroin at the time, so out of a cast of eight those two were casualties waiting to happen. The reviews were diabolical. It was a funny idea and Ray wrote such wonderful songs, but if I was in control of the movie, I'd reshoot it at a different time. I wanted to pull my weight but I couldn't. It was the worst time of my life. My lady at the time, Verity Bargate★, was dying of cancer that got worse and worse.

"I was in no fit state to be working," Keeffe continues, "but she was writing a last novel, which she stayed long enough to get published, and it was an absolute triumph and then she died, so I was determined to do this too. But every time the phone went I was dashing backwards and forwards to the hospital, and she had two young sons, Sam and Tom, aged about nine and seven, and their mum was so terribly ill and they were so young, so I was up most of the night with them. It was murderous. I feel very guilty that I wasn't the support for Ray that I should have been. He could have said, 'Fuck this, this is no way to work. Cancel it!' He didn't. He was incredibly sensitive, incredibly supportive. He was an absolute mensch."

Ray found himself collaborating with someone working feverishly through great pain, as he would do. In a way which was rarely evident in The Kinks, but he was capable of in the wider world and his writing, he put his visceral sensitivity to hurt at Keeffe's service. "I've seen Ray angry, I've had rows with him," Keeffe says. "I always think you can smell it coming - by God, you're in it now. I know he's a moody bugger, and he can be dangerous. But also, there's the kindness. When Verity was clearly dying I didn't want to be a nuisance, and I was very upset and it was painful, and he just phoned up to see how I was, and I was saying, 'Fine fine fine.' Putting on the face, putting on the face, not giving into the weakness. And he said [softly], 'Barrie, I wish you'd think of me as a friend.' And the way he said it, I was suddenly crying, and it all came out. And he came straight over, all the way from Effingham, to make sure I was okay."

Keith Altham counters with suspicion more typical of those who've worked with Ray in the music business. "Yeah, he could be kind, as

---

★ Verity Bargate is a legendary figure in London theatre for her productions at the Soho Theatre, where Keeffe is also a revered playwright long as it wasn't going to cost him money. He wasn't someone that you could make a friend of, or I thought would be worth making a friend of. He's a solitary man, and the people who get close to him tend not to be close to him for very long, because he doesn't seem able to maintain a relationship, whether with wives or others. He has charm. There's also still this deep-rooted paranoia that people are taking advantage of him in some way. He'll be very nice to you, and then he'll turn. And that's happened to a lot of people. They can have friendship and collaboration for some while, and then they're portrayed as Rasputin. Ray can turn on a sixpence". Altham could be describing the *Preservation* villain of "Here Comes Flash," part of himself, Ray's confessed, who "will smile at you, be a friend to you/ Then he's going to screw you, just like that." "I never had any problem with him, but I know other people that did. I saw the results of his scrap down *Top Of The Pops* with Slade's Dave Hill, which was unpleasant*. Something would snap in his head, and he would get spiteful. He was highly strung, and consequently little things could send him over the edge. Drink didn't help."

That's one, not uncommon perspective. But in a period of furious band activity, Ray's friendship with Keeffe is a rare glimpse into the life he has maintained wholly outside The Kinks, away from any spotlight. Away too from musical or fraternal competitiveness, his own fear of hurt when dealing with his family, and business and financial suspicions, Ray's charm and generosity could take flight. Wim Wenders would also see sickbed selflessness of the sort Keeffe describes here. But when Ray's own mum later needed it, he would flinch.

"One lovely thing was that for me to get the adoption of the kids, it seemed a very sensible idea to get married to Verity," says Keefe, "and Ray was the best man. He was a great support for Verity all the time. He spent a lot of time at the hospital as well. And we got married on Friday the 13th of February 1981 at Woolwich Town Hall. The registrar said, 'I've never in 45 years here married anyone on Friday the 13th.' Ray said, 'Well, it's my lucky day.' And then we had a big party

---

* On June 15, 1972, a Green Room altercation between Ray and Hill ended with Slade manager Chas Chandler's hands around Ray's throat, Altham reported in *NME*.

in the house, which was very bittersweet, and Verity went back to the hospital and died exactly five weeks later. Ray was smashing. He came back from being on tour, in Germany I think, and it was so strange having the wedding party and then the wake in the same place. But he's the loyallest friend you can have."

Keeffe would take his adopted children down to Effingham after that, playing and healing in the Surrey countryside. Losing touch after working on another musical, *80 Days*, in the late eighties, Keeffe recently found himself living a short walk down Highgate Hill from Ray. "I haven't seen him for 20 years, and within one minute it was hugging, and it was like yesterday," he says. "And Sam and Tom, God almighty. They met him again at my wedding in January 2012. They're 6′4″, 6′5″ now. But when they saw Ray again, they ran over and hugged him, almost climbing up, because he was always giving them great hugs – suddenly they were little boys again. He would hate to be called an uncle – older brother, he'd prefer! But Tom especially wanted to almost jump in his arms again, after all these years. I really do love him very, very much. I love him like the brother I never had. His kindness is everything."

Back on The Kinks' 1981 campaign, the title of their August album, *Give The People What They Want*, seemed to immediately announce both ironic resignation and repugnance at shows and crowds too big for subtle thought. These veteran self-destructive outsiders had somehow become a mainstream stadium act in what was now Reagan's America. Does Ray think he gave things up, to get that acceptance?

"Yeah. It's like, if you make a Hollywood blockbuster, you must remember not to put too much story in it. You lose to gain. You finesse a lot of things out of what you do. It was more, in a journalistic sense, written like a tabloid, than a... piece. And I was aware of making it an editorial. Easy to say now, I probably didn't think I was doing it then. You start thinking that way. Environment does have an impact. It was an achievement in a sense, because I made the record to be heard from Row 50. I went to great trouble to make the whole ambience louder and more aggressive – which is what those events tend to become."

This undervalues an excellent album which uses stadium dynamics to slam home attacks on mass culture, and includes the most sharply articulate and daring songs Ray had yet handed Arista. The title track attacks TV's servility to ratings from audiences who act like Romans at the arena, Kennedy's assassination reduced to endlessly rerun entertainment as they slump on their sofas. "Hey Ma!" he crows with dumb B-movie relish, "there goes a piece of the President's brain!" 'Killer's Eyes' is a disturbed near-ballad inspired by TV reports that year of the Pope's failed assassin Mehmet Ali Agca, and the Yorkshire Ripper, Peter Sutcliffe's, capture. Ray tries to understand their internal hell while condemning their actions, and the TV feeding on them. 'Entertainment', nearly the title song but held back till 1989's *UK Jive*, summed up his feelings: "Real life for entertainment/ cheapens my reality."

'Destroyer' toys with The Kinks' own mythology. Beginning with 'All Day And All Of The Night''s giant riff, it finds Ray "feeling kinda queer" in bed the next morning with Lola. Suspecting he's under surveillance, voices in his head confuse him as he roars, "paranoia, self-destroyer!" The warning might equally be aimed at himself or Dave, still working through the effects of his mental rattling. Drums, ramped up to crunching effect, drive the future mass crowd accompaniment anticipated in the song: "And it goes like this!"

'Yo-Yo' is about instability of emotion and character, as a marriage dissolves in boredom. "You think you knew me real well," Ray warns the wife. "With people like me, you never can tell." It might have been fair warning to his new audience too, yet the chants for this ambiguous song are arena-ready. 'A Little Bit Of Abuse', written, Ray said, at the request of *Chorus Girls'* female cast, wonders why a battered woman sticks around, its sympathy couched in approachable rock and harsh humour: "Huh, it's so uncouth/ excuse me, but is this your tooth?"

'Art Lover' is one of Ray's most memorably risky and successful songs. In it, he jogs through the park, then sits on a bench hidden by shades. It's all an excuse for watching little girls he longs to lure over and play with, reluctantly settling for appreciating their beauty. "I'm not gonna snatch you from your mother," he protests, "I'm an art lover." Kurt Wagner of Lambchop, who covered the song in 2002, laughs at the line. "You immediately go, 'Well, I wasn't quite thinking that – but now I am!'" Ray later explained that the song was inspired by his lack of access to his daughters from Rasa, and his wish for Sundays in the park with them. But he playfully shoves at the situation's boundary. Whether it's about Ray, or a paedophile on a bench who never acts, the song sympathises with such degrees of longing. It slips easily into *Give The People What They Want*'s stadium-rock Trojan horse.

This third hit album (number 15 in the US) moved The Kinks to even bigger venues, fulfilling its sound's prophecy. "When we did big auditoriums for it," Ray says, "the security guards are tougher, they're harder on people, and things are more mercenary. It's not always... fun. I particularly hated Detroit. I found that sort of audience got very ugly very easily. It's a bit worrying when you see a lot of people outside the arena on the street, in your T-shirts, fighting. They were our crowd, but the ones who came for the T-shirts, who only knew us as a stadium band and didn't know anything else about our music, and when you did 'Give The People What They Want', they'd be punching the air – it didn't feel like me. All these things bring out a different facet in the music. It becomes popcorn music. And in those big auditoriums, after a while you're on a treadmill. You can't judge the dynamics of the band. They became unreal events.

"There's a song on *Give The People What They Want*, actually, 'Back To Front'," he concludes, "with the line 'just came back where I came from', and that was written around the time Prince Charles married Diana. That's a record about someone being formed and transplanted into America. The whole album, in a sense. It's somebody who's made the transition, but is struggling to find a way back, to his origins. It's an interesting period."

During it, an old rival got in touch. "I was going onstage at a big open-air gig we'd sold out in San Francisco," Ray remembers, "and this guy handed me a phone. And it said, 'Ray, it's Bill [Wyman], I'm with Mick and Keith, we want you to come on tour with us.' I said, 'It's not a good time to call me right now. Can I get back to you?' He said, 'No, we've gotta have an answer.' 'Then it must be no.' I think it was just a momentary cocaine idea they had. Then Keith forgot about it. I didn't like the way it was presented to me. And there's a bit of history there. I'm still trying to work out how they got the *NME* Best Newcomers Award two years running [in 1965], and we got the runners-up in our year. Could somebody somewhere please explain?" Ray just won't let it lie. It must have been particularly sweet for The Kinks to finally be in a position to tell The Rolling Stones to fuck off.

CHAPTER 12

The Palais

The Kinks confirmed their ascendancy by playing New York's prestigious Madison Square Garden on October 3. "If we were booked into Madison Square Garden," Ray had said in 1975, when it seemed impossible, "I'd write a show to fill it. Everybody else can play there, why can't we?" But as this affirmation approached, Dave's feud with Avory took another worrying lurch. "I got pissed off with him the night before Madison Square Garden," Avory remembers. "We played at the Nassau Coliseum. He was making rude signs and spitting, and trying to knock the cymbal over. I threw the sticks at him, completely missed him and nearly took someone's eye out in the audience, and I stormed offstage. There was this big screen that Ray used to change his clothes behind. I marched through that, knocked that one over, through the dressing room, and Ray said: 'Excuse me a minute. Mick's just got to answer an important phone call.' And he's come and got me. I said, 'I ain't going back onstage with that dick.' And there was a 10-minute gap, and we carried on. But so did silly bollocks.

"That was one night. And then Dave thought he'd better speak to me, because we had Madison Square Garden. He said, 'Yeah, we've gotta stop all of this...' I said, 'I didn't start any of that. So don't blame

239

me for it. Whatever you think of me, let's just do the show and get it done, because it's embarrassing.' So we did that."

Ray was also entering another period of turmoil. In May 1980, against his better judgement, he had agreed to a request from Chrissie Hynde to meet. Hynde had been a Kinks fan since her teens, was fervently interested in the mythology of rock, and, in her brief career as an *NME* writer, had even given *Preservation Act 2*'s single 'Mirror Of Love' a good review. There was obviously an element of an acolyte meeting a presumed master. "I'd rather people just liked my songs from a distance than try to meet me," Ray later ruefully said of the approach. But as she asked to see him near his New York apartment, "I thought I'd take a stroll." In October 1981, he appeared on stage with The Pretenders in Santa Monica, making their romance public. Yvonne Gunner's divorce from the eventually unhappy marriage Ray perhaps drew on for 'Yo-yo' was successfully finalised then (the first most outside his intimate circle knew of her existence).

On May 21, 1982, he and Hynde tried to marry in Guildford Registry office, near his Effingham home. Infamously, the registrar was so appalled at their furious rowing, he refused to continue. In *Kink* Dave, who took a swing at Hynde with his guitar when she first trespassed on The Kinks' stage, remembers their tempestuous affair leaving whole flats trashed, and furniture splintered. This is exactly the scenario the musician Lucien wakes up to in Ray's short story 'Art Lover'. A door has been torn off its hinges, a bed overturned, a phone ripped from its socket. Hurled wine blotches the kitchen wall. Lucien inspects the bleeding cut above his eye, and his bruised knuckles. His lover's face and legs are bruised. Both post desperate notes saying "This has got to stop" around the wrecked home. Parallels to Ray's situation then are blurred, as Lucien's ex-wife is a rock singer made famous with "a cover of an old Sixties song", her bitter calls inflaming the new lovers' fights. But in one of the last two songs The Kinks ever recorded, 'Animal', Ray returns to such a scene. "It was not all wine on the wall... cuts and bruises/ or the pulling out of hair or the bloodying of nose," he reflects. "It cannot compare to times we cared" when there was "absolute compassion in the air." True love though, he concludes, painful as it may be, is animal and uncontrolled. 'Labour Of Love', on 1983's Kinks album *State Of Confusion*, offers a similar lesson, and Hynde's later song '977' touches positively on a violent affair. Neither has spoken directly about whether this did or didn't reflect their own situation.

The mentoring Hynde had originally sought brought its own problems. She and Ray travelled on each other's tours when they could. On The Pretenders' bus after a Brighton gig, Ray is said to have begun telling Hynde what she should be doing with her career, in an escalating exchange ending in furious scenes. When Hynde's road crew intervened, the mood was so deadly Ray stopped the bus, and untypically cracked open his wallet to buy everyone a fish supper.

The details of the relationship are off limits when I ring Hynde to discuss The Kinks' music. But her abiding love for a man she can no longer stand being around is plain. "His writing is distinctive because he sketches. Wherever he goes he carries a plastic bag with him and there's pencils and loose bits of paper and serviettes in it, and he's constantly making notes and drawing. And if you're sitting with him in a restaurant – and I spent a lot of time doing that, many years ago – if you're having a conversation, you'll notice that he's not listening to you at all, which can be incredibly annoying, actually. He's completely absorbed in the conversation at the next table. It's where he gets his inspiration. He has a real affinity for ordinary people. He's very working class. He is that traditional English phenomenon where all the culture comes from the working classes. He has a real love of classical music, and of fine art. The only person I've ever met who reminded me of him is Morrissey. Just their gestures, the way they walk and talk. Mind you, I haven't seen or spoken to him for over 20 years," she says, speaking before this subsequently, very briefly became untrue in 2008. "But I don't think a leopard changes his spots."

"She was someone who was on a journey that she found difficult to cope with and she thought that I could help her," Ray says. "Then she realised I was more difficult," he laughs, "than the journey she was on. But, nevertheless, "on reflection," he quotes 'Animal', "'it wasn't all wine on the wall'. You just stumble into that, I think. It's very difficult in relationships, particularly when it's people in two bands – the worst thing in the world. Not the two people themselves – but the people around you all have ambitions for their people."

Are the sort of bruisingly passionate relationships he describes in 'Labour Of Love' and 'Animal' the sort he finds himself in, more often than not? "I don't seek that sort of thing out. I sometimes stumble into it. I just want a quiet life. I just want all the excitement to happen in the music, but lately," he says, feeling his shot leg, "it's all been in the real world. I want to knock that on the head."

As Ray's wild affair continued, Dave's troubles were also returning. On that 1979 tour, Charles Shaar Murray asked Ray where the guitarist, whom he much admired but never managed to speak to, vanished between shows. "I don't know," Ray sympathised. "I never see him either." Dave spent every spare moment with his American lover Nancy Evans. "It was a relationship with a lot of give and take that really helped me," he says. He had confessed his double life to his wife, Lisbet. His sisters Peggy, Gwen and Joyce all descended disapprovingly on their little brother. Peggy relented when she saw how much Evans looked like Sue. In December 1980 Evans gave birth to their son Daniel, less than a year after Lisbet had to their son, Russell. In 1981, Lisbet had finally had enough, and Dave left the family home for a flat with Evans in Maida Vale, North London. "I went through the hell Ray went through with Rasa later," he says.

Dave had meanwhile gained enough confidence to finish his first solo album, *AFL1-3603*, after abortive sessions throughout the seventies. Used to almost telepathic music-making with his brother, he struggled to explain himself to other musicians. Did Ray's special connection spoil Dave for others? "It's like my mum used to say to me, 'If your aunt had balls, she'd be your uncle.' So we can reflect as much as we like about that. I feel quite happy for myself." The album, though not up to the great songs he left abandoned after 'Death Of A Clown', mixed open-hearted ballads somewhat in his sixties style with jagged, exciting guitar work layered by eighties technology. His spiritual convictions and love for Evans unobtrusively powered the lyrics. It cracked the US Top 50 in the slipstream of *One For The Road*, delighting Dave and his new label RCA. "That cast out a lot of demons I'd been holding in for years," he says, "and put them into songs and attitude and style. That was a really important period [for me] as a person, and in every other way."

The swift follow-up, *Glamour*, preceded *Give The People What They Want* by a month. Its cover, with Dave as a subtly zombified yuppie matinee idol, summed up his hostility to eighties greed. "I was feeling much more confident about the things that I believe in," he says. "That cover says it all, with the look of prosperity, aloof and confident. The eighties was all about that external world. But inside, people were falling apart. Some people didn't even have inner lives, because they thought that the outside was the only thing that mattered – the posh car and a good job. Not showing what we're feeling inside cheats life." The record, though, was rushed and weaker. It barely cracked the *Billboard* 150, dispiriting him.

Then on January 13, 1982, in the Sheraton Hotel before a gig in Hampton, Virginia, Dave had an experience as profoundly unsettling as his acid shock in 1969, and his near-suicide in another hotel in 1972. As soon as he stepped off the plane, he recalled in *Kink*, his brain felt as if a metal ring was squeezing it. In his room with Evans, he again became terrified he was going mad. Five voices started to communicate with him, through sensations of touch and smell as well as words. "Each separate intelligence had its own aroma," he told the *Independent On Sunday*'s Robert Chalmers. "One was similar to jasmine, but very deep. The smells would make me feel OK, as if they were saying, 'Everything is all right, you are not going insane.'" He saw his TV emit gassy blue tendrils. He was told this was a malleable substance which flowed through everything, "a sea of mind energy... full of thought and feeling." He was also told some of the intelligences were aliens, circling the earth.

Too much acid, you may reasonably say, the shock of his 1969 experience still turning hallucinatory keys in his brain. But however much you may dismiss Dave's latest perceived revelations, the lessons he took from them eventually made him feel more at peace (though, as those who worked with him later in The Kinks' career attest, spirituality barely lessened his hair-trigger rages). When you meet him, you realise Dave's at worst credulous, but not insane. "We may encounter madness," he told Chalmers, "but if we allow the madness to take over, that is when we get into problems."

Dave could see the absurdity of his situation even as the aliens communed with him. One of the things he shares with Ray, his irreverent humour, saves him from glazed piety. "Humour's so important," he agrees, "because it bridges the gap with spirituality – takes the piss, puts you in your place, but it's funny. And then you think, 'Oh, shit, let's just keep going.' That's why all the great comedians are philosophers, like Tony Hancock and Max Miller and Spike Milligan. The Kinks' path," he reasonably concludes, "is a spiritual one."

The initial aftershock, though, again left Dave mentally wrecked. He even blamed his anger at Avory on it to Matt Resnicoff: "I'd experienced a very profound change internally, and that's difficult when you're with people you've been close to for most of your adult life." Ray is always dryly scornful of his brother's beliefs.

The Kinks' three core members were once again in private agony, even at this new height of success. Typically, they responded with their last great album. And Ray heralded it with a single which suddenly returned them to the almost forgotten magic of Fortis Green, and his and Dave's family.

"I was around my sister's house one night, and she got some pictures out of the family when they had parties and dancing," he told John Swenson. "She used to go to the Palais, they'd see a big band and they'd dance. I wanted to write a song that evoked that era." It's a quirk of Ray's that he never specifies his sisters by name, as if he has only one. Rene, who died dancing, was in his mind as he wrote. His original demo of 'Come Dancing' is sung almost to himself, as if in a reverie.

On the record an acoustic guitar fades in, there's a drum roll and Ray begins. The first line peels back a place's past, from parking lot to supermarket to bowling alley, to the dance hall it was when he was young. A bloke waits frustrated at Denmark Terrace for Ray's sister, who leaves him that way once he's spent his wages on her. When the Palais is demolished and "part of my childhood died", Dave's serrated guitar punches in the switch to Ray's present in a band and his sister's, living on an estate. At the end, Ray shifts the lyrics' tense, and he and his middle-aged sister dance in the ghost Palais now, the song bringing their youth back to life. Along with the brass section used to conjure a fifties North London big band, the old-fashioned, cinema-style organ that is the single's hook is the last music you'd expect in 1983's chart. It sounds cheesy, till you register details, and perhaps find out about Rene. Then the poignancy of this perfectly constructed hit won't stop growing. "I wanted to regain some of the warmth that I thought we'd lost doing those stadium tours," says Ray. "'Come Dancing' was an attempt to get back to roots. To my sisters, and enduring remembrances."

The video which ensured 'Come Dancing''s success was directed by Julien Temple. He'd already starred Ray in a very funny clip for *Give The People What They Want*'s UK single, 'Predictable'. He's still filming him today. "You know when people said, 'Are you a Stones fan or a Beatles fan?'" he says. "When I was a child I said, 'No, I'm a Kinks fan.' I'm proud of that underdog status. The fact that they kept fucking up was what made it a badge of honour to be a fan. I saw the world through that music when I was very young. It made me feel there was another way of seeing things than what I was getting from my school and my parents. I heard 'You Really Got Me' and it freaked me out. It was a mystical song to me, because I heard it on pirate radio and couldn't find it again, and I wasn't sure what I'd heard. I was totally enlivened – not just by the sound, but also the weirdness of the person singing the song, who was not afraid to be fucked up. That was very different to The Beatles and pre-Beatles stuff I'd been used to. I responded to punk because I felt strongly that that was a continuation of what The Kinks had been doing in '64. So to work for them was a big deal for me."

At the dawn of the MTV age, Ray at last had a perfect visual accomplice. "I did click with him immediately," Temple agrees. "I had a huge reservoir of thoughts about the band. I seemed to have a shorthand with him, because of my obsessive love for the songs."

The key to the video is the spiv character Ray plays in pinstripe suit and slicked-back hair, selling dodgy nylons when he's not hanging round the dance hall: our guide to his lost world. "I was fascinated that Ray could write so powerfully about a period ostensibly before The

Kinks," Temple says. "It's such a narrative song, and so much to do with their family. So in that sense Ray is totally the author of the video. But I was beginning to think about *Absolute Beginners* at that time. I was deep into the post-war evolution of culture, and I always loved the spiv figure. I took it partly from the one in [1947's] *It Always Rains On Sunday*. I suggested that I wanted to do it as a dark Ealing thing like that. And Ray loved it. But then he took the notion of the spiv and made his own version. When he put that moustache on and slicked his hair back, he became that character. It was something he totally identified with. I was pleased he used the character in other videos I didn't direct. I got the feeling he must have been basing it on people he knew." Ray told John Swenson: "I remembered this character as a kid, he was a conductor on the local bus route, and his hair was slicked down and he had a little pencil-thin moustache. He always wore a carnation in his pocket and helped little old ladies onto the bus. I combined that character and my uncle Frankie."

When the video moves into the present, the camera pulls away from Ray playing in The Kinks to him as the spiv. He looks utterly out of place, his whole body frozen as his hands grip the balcony. Then his head creaks round to look at a modern girl with tragic contempt, as if he's the last of a proud race. "I was standing behind Scorsese at a bar, and he was going on about that shot, saying it was one of his favourites ever," says Temple. "There's a Buñuel film, *Simon Of The Desert*, where this guy who's been suffering on his pillar in the desert in BC whatever ends up in some weird club in Mexico City in '65. It's a bit like that. He did it beautifully, the fact he's so still and they're all heaving around him. I think Ray could have been more of an actor. He has a great, deep sense of film."

The video was filmed at the Ilford Palais, Essex's equivalent to the halls where the Davies sisters danced. Like the last line of a Kinks song, it was demolished in 2007 to make way for luxury flats. 'Come Dancing' was meant to reach out to The Kinks' lost British audience, and for its UK-only release in November 1982, they toured town halls and cinemas like the old days. The song had its London debut at the Lyceum, where Rene died. But British radio stations didn't play Kinks songs any more. Until, five months later, their return to London roots was reluctantly released in the US. "Clive Davis didn't want to put it out, because he thought it was too vaudevillian, too English," Ray remembers. "It was only the video that convinced him. It went on MTV when it first started, and they couldn't stop rotating it." It shot to number six, equalling 'Tired Of Waiting For You' as their biggest ever hit. When Jonathan King put the video on his BBC show about the US chart, it was re-released in the UK in July 1983. It made number 12, their first home smash since 'Apeman'.

"Woke up in a panic, like somebody fired a gun," are Ray's first words on the album that followed, just after he screams. It's the title song of *State Of Confusion*, one of The Kinks' most ferociously played, emotionally raw, witty and melodic records. The pain in the band's existence sharpened music that forcefully reached out to be heard. This was an eighties stadium-rock album written by a man about to turn 40 who has lost one wife, is losing her replacement and will be in a worse state if she stays, played by a band that's falling apart.

'Definite Maybe' is another complaint about the bureaucratic people in grey – "got a letter this morning that says I don't exist" – which becomes a Kafkaesque nightmare. 'Labour Of Love' introduces its marriage built on "bruises and tears" with Dave doing 'Here Comes The Bride' in the style of Hendrix's Vietnam-era immolation of 'The Star-Spangled Banner'. 'Property' picks over the useless, partitioned relics of a failed marriage, 'Picture Book''s author handing over photos falsely showing affection. 'Cliché's Of The World (B-Movie)' is a brooding eighties film noir about a beaten man looking down from a high-rise at a wasteland, perhaps writing a suicide note: "Dear world, feel so lonely and afraid..." The view of 'Waterloo Sunset''s voyeur has decidedly worsened. Backing vocals are deep and dark till they join synths in lulling him to sleep, where he dreams of aliens spiriting him to a happier place. This could be Ray taking the piss out of his brother. But he could be Dave as he keeps roaring, "It's just an illusion!" as squalling guitars wake his lonely man in a trapped life slipping uselessly away. Mostly composed from mundane irritants, the album continues Ray's conviction that we're stuck in a heartless world that's killing us.

The Kinks, though, sound brightly inspired. 'Young Conservatives' is a vivid satire of the eighties phenomenon of conservative US students rebelling against hippie parents with Reagan-voting wholesomeness, and the trainee Thatcherite young fogies back home. "Be a devil, join the young conservatives," Ray mockingly encourages. The Kinks' sixties cast of dubious poshos crowd back to join in, with the "fa-fa-fa" chorus from 'David Watts' and Ray's sneer at a new "well respected man", lounging in bed filtering his life through the *Sunday Times*. All the optimism for change his targets are missing is in this song by a man who doesn't know how to be satisfied, or give up.

"If anybody had lost any faith in us being real people," says Ray, "that record would restore it. Even a pompous love ballad like 'Don't Forget To Dance' had one of my favourite moments – a line, "a nice bit of old" [meaning middle-aged and sexy]. There's some nice writing in there. It had all the right ingredients, but it didn't work, in a brilliant way. And that's the real way to failure! To the realisation that this is just a normal working person making this record, that it has flaws.

"It's not a good idea to let people know what they're playing," he says, warming to his theme. "Just keep Mick Avory nervous, and you'll get great performances from him. He's responsible for some of the great comedy drum parts. His drum roll into 'Come Dancing', a really sharp click-click-click, then RA-AH! – it's totally a beat late. That's the brilliance of his playing. It's totally unplanned, and that's what was so magical about the band, when we were rolling. He forgot to put the snare drum on 'Well Respected Man'. He said, 'Shall I do it again?' I said, 'No, perfect.' That's what I'm finding difficult with musicians now. They're afraid of mistakes. I like them."

The struggles behind *State Of Confusion*, though, only got worse. "It was a difficult time – '83, '84," Ray says. "Songs like 'Definite Maybe', 'State Of Confusion', it's all got this concern about it. If you look at the album cover, everybody's going in different directions. And that was the last of... that band's records. And it had our biggest single on it. So there you go."

State Of Confusion was greeted as a crowning triumph in the US. "It cuts the competition to shreds," *Rolling Stone* declared. "Nobody but The Kinks could have made such a record in 1983, and no band deserves more to be at the very top – which is where this LP ought to place them." It made number 12 on its May 24 release, and the spring North American tour played to growing crowds. But Dave was becoming detached. In *Kink*, he recalls working on the album's songs with Ray in his Effingham home, as he had so many times before, and being promised credit for his work this time. He claims Ray rang Arista to personally remove any mention of him as co-writer or arranger in the liner notes the night before they were printed. It was almost instinctive sibling spite, if true, petty yet terrible. Dave was convinced by their manager Elliott Abbott to go through with the tour. But when his third solo album, *Chosen People*, was released in August, its commercial failure was compounded by the looks interviewers gave him as he explained the beliefs behind it. Feeling sane, he saw they thought he was mad. Ray had fulfilled a lifetime ambition by directing his first film, *Return To Waterloo*, in August, slightly delaying the scheduling of a US tour to drive home their latest success. On October 10, Dave, disillusioned and depressed, cancelled it. They were back playing New York by Christmas, hardly a major delay. But the ensuing chaos and bad publicity is now remembered as fatally wounding their seemingly unstoppable ascent. In the last rearranged show, in Cedar Rapids, Iowa, Dave and Avory had to be dragged apart. "'That's it, Mick,'" Dave remembers furiously deciding in *Kink*. "'"It's over."'"

"Dave didn't want to tour," says Ray bleakly. "We'd gone through such massive hard work to get to that point where we're in stadiums, claiming back some of our rights. We were right at the peak, the follow-up single ['Don't Forget To Dance'] was going in the charts. We'd sold out two dates at Madison Square Garden. It was the big return. The final summit. And we didn't climb it. And it was a devastating time for me. Because Dave just couldn't bring himself to tour any more, as the band was. Success can't make everybody better. It's as simple as that. And the feuds between Mick and Dave had reached a complete peak, and it was horrible to be on tour at that time. It was an ongoing nightly event, arguments over trivial stuff. The fights were so bad, it was so uncomfortable. There was a weird thing between Dave and Mick, and I'm curious to know what it was. I can understand with Dave and myself, it was sibling rivalry. But Mick and Dave still fascinates me, I don't know why? And I think all of us had had enough of it really – really, if we could have said what we felt."

Dave blames his antipathy on the "sloppy", "arrogant", "nonchalant" attitude of the "buffoon" Avory in *Kink*, and his "fence-sitting" in the brothers' rows to me. "Mick was good for Ray and me," he admits in a compliment which then abuses him, "because if he had been really creative, it would have been horrible."

When Avory talks about dealing with Dave in those days to me, this man of proverbial mild manners looks into the distance absently stamping a leg, and his face contorts, agonised. "I think he wanted to collaborate with Ray more," he says. "I was a barrier because I'd become closer to Ray. Jealousies come in, don't they? I was fairly laid-back. But there are limits to how laid-back I am. I get on with most people, but if they're not being friendly or considerate, I find it very difficult. That was a little bit selfish, really. But you get that with bands, don't you? You all start off fairly equal, then someone puts more into it than you [as Dave contends he did], and you just stay there and don't do anything different from what you've always done. Then it feels like you're a passenger.

"You could see it was going to come to an end," he reflects. "You can only take so much of an atmosphere. Dave was more and more separated from the band anyway. You never saw him on a day off. We used to have noisy get-togethers every now and again, even with Ray, but he was never present. He'd be sitting in his room with his girlfriend."

Did the bad blood stop Avory enjoying their American success?

"I enjoyed the success. And we made a couple of good albums. But we weren't a band any more, as far as I could see it. We'd see each other on stage, and it was like strangers, not thinking the same thing. Heads somewhere else."

There hardly seems any point playing music like that.

"No. I'd had enough."

In *State Of Confusion*'s appropriately chaotic aftermath, Ray finished editing *Return To Waterloo* in April 1984. Then with the schism between

Dave and Avory still yawning, another blow fell. On January 22, 1983, Hynde had given birth to their daughter, Natalie. On May 5, 1984, as The Pretenders toured the US with Simple Minds, she married their singer, Jim Kerr, in New York.

"Chrissie was in a bit of a fly by night situation," Simple Minds' drummer Mel Gaynor remembers. "I don't know the ins and outs. But I believe it had got quite physical in places. She upped and left because she'd had enough. And she had to go on tour, and then fell for Jim. It all happened in the States, within weeks. He was quite distraught, Ray Davies. Because obviously that was the love of his life. I believe they argued a lot. But I think he still loved her deeply. Ray was calling a lot, late pretty much every night. He wouldn't leave the situation alone. That went on for a month or so. She was pretty pissed off that he kept calling, and he was that insistent. She just wouldn't take any more phone calls in the end. I think he actually tried to fly over at one point. He was desperately trying to get her back, but to no avail. There was quite a heavy atmosphere. It wasn't a nice feeling to be around then. The wedding was a joyous occasion. Chrissie and Jim were ecstatic, they couldn't leave each other alone – although again it was quite short-lived.* I think Ray got the message then. But I think he was still deeply upset. Obviously with their daughter, it didn't help. He seemed very much in love."

As he had with Rasa, Dave helped pick up the pieces. But the brothers' own relationship was again fraying. "He was breaking up with Chrissie," Dave remembers, "and he was off his head. And we actually lived across the road from each other, virtually, in Maida Vale. He had this psychiatric nurse with him, because he was really crazy. I'd go down there to try and help, and all of a sudden Ray starts laying into me. 'It's your fucking fault, you bastard!' And I'm thinking, 'OK, if it's raining, it's my fault.' Part of me was thinking, 'Yeah, I've done good here, I'm putting up with this shit and it's not affecting me.' And this guy's jaw actually dropped. He said, 'Ray, you can't talk to your brother like that.' I thought it was normal."

* Hynde and Kerr divorced in 1990.

A month after the split with Hynde, Ray of course had The Kinks back at Konk, to start the final album in their Arista contract. A drum machine replaced Avory on one track, Dave's solo album drummer Bob Henrit, on another. "In the end I was the one who had to tell Mick that the band wasn't together any more, in that respect," Ray says. "In fact he was out. I remember taking him out for a drink one night, we had a few pints, and I said, 'Mick, you know you came to the audition in 1964?' He said, 'Yeah.' 'Well, we never actually told you that you'd got it. And you didn't get it.' It was the only way I could bring up the subject. And Mick is still my friend, and he always will be. He's still around. Just professionally, it couldn't go on."

This touching story is news to Avory. "I don't remember anything like that. I just rang up and said, 'I can't carry on like this. I'm unhappy. There's no point. You'd better carry on with Dave.' I wasn't sacked. It was made uncomfortable for me to be there. So I did the sensible thing, and got out. I don't think Ray wanted me to go. He likes to keep everything the same as it was. But I wasn't going to do anything I hadn't already done. We'd just had the biggest record we'd ever had in America. I thought, 'This is a good note to leave on.'" When I push for any memory of Ray's bittersweet goodbye, he allows, always wanting a quiet life: "I suppose if he said it, I suppose we did. There was a pub in Effingham we used to go to quite frequently, The Black Swan. We might have met there, if we did. I'd just had enough. It was a winning formula. It's a shame it couldn't have gone on a bit longer."

Ray had dragged The Kinks almost to the summit of his American dream. Then they'd stumbled. There was only one way left to go.

CHAPTER 13

Into The Machine

No one knew it, but The Kinks were in their final phase. Working through the late summer and autumn of 1984, they completed their last contracted album for Arista, *Word Of Mouth*. Ray's songs sifted through the wreckage of his relationship with Chrissie Hynde, and his band. 'Do It Again' opens with a ringing guitar chord echoing 1964's 'A Hard Day's Night''s declaration of intent, the year The Kinks began. The lyrics try to slap 40-year-old Ray in gear for another campaign, "now we're back where we started." 'Word Of Mouth' declares, "I've been trying to get a message to you/ But the operator can't put me through," as the switchboards of Hynde's hotels knew all too well. Matching Dave's gritty sandpaper guitar sound, here nodding heavily to the Stones' 'Start Me Up', he rails with raw anger at the (often true) tabloid rumours swirling round him: "The word of mouth says I've gone insane/ That wine and women have affected my brain... I'm round the bend/ It's all over/ This is the end."

'Good Day' finds him trying to get through to friends, wondering if he still has some, and an old flame whose name he claims he's forgotten. As when he serenaded Rasa with 'Sweet Lady Genevieve', he finds words to sum up his spurned devotion: "They can drop a small atom bomb on this city today/ But if you walk through that door, honey, you know it'll be a good day." Ray the resilient craftsman, though, lets the example of fifties British sex bomb Diana Dors, a trier like him, recently dead, draw him out of depression. He's tragicomically soaked to his shoes by English showers in 'Summer's Gone', a fool who "really blew it" with a girl. The song digs out lines which could be left over from 'Drivin'' in 1969, a snapshot of a childhood outing when eight of the Davies tribe would shoehorn into the family car: "Dad looked at us then he looked at his wife/ he must have wondered where we all came from..." He sings this with sudden vividness, summoning a vision to life from a world long before his troubles. Downbeat lyrics are generally buried in attractive, cleverly arranged rock clatter, the sound of a cornered band still fighting.

Word Of Mouth's most obvious change was its booming eighties drums, a dated distraction from the songs today, but undeniably powerful. Bob Henrit, an ex-bandmate of Kinks bassist Jim Rodford in Argent as well as Dave's solo session choice, had replaced Avory. "I was playing in a North London pub, the Torrington," he remembers, "and saw Ray in the audience. Afterwards he said, 'Would you be able to play some sessions?' So I turned up at Konk and played. I had no idea who this was for. Afterwards I was offered a tour by someone else, thought, 'I'd better ask Ray if he's finished with me,' and called him. He said, 'You can't do a tour, you're in The Kinks. Let's go for a beer.' My biggest problem in taking the gig was that Mick was my pal. Did he fall or was he pushed? I think he was pushed."

Henrit knew he was significantly changing The Kinks' sound. "I was into the technology of click tracks, electronic drums, and what American bands then were up to. I'd kept up and Mick hadn't, and Ray obviously wanted to go in that direction. I put in stuff appropriate to stadium rock – I wasn't coming from such an intimate musical situation as The Kinks. There was more attack and assurance to what I played. What Mick does is loose and great. I can only do that when I'm drunk. I hit heavier than Mick, I was louder than Mick, I was more bombastic than Mick, in my playing."

If Ray thought this was a good thing, he doesn't now. "The dynamic went," he says. "Mick's successor was a very great drummer, with a different technique. I'm not saying worse, some of the stuff on *Word Of Mouth* and the next album I'm really proud of. But he didn't have those happy accidents." He went further to John Swenson in 1998: "When The Kinks got together as a unit it was us against the world, and when you're not 'us' any more, the world starts to infiltrate. I think we got out of there [Arista] by the skin of our teeth. We still had our integrity... *Word Of Mouth* was Kinks music played by different people."

Henrit could, though, have been a Kink all along. "I was playing with Adam Faith at the Wimbledon Theatre in 1964," he remembers. "It was a week in variety, and I got a phone call from an American voice I didn't recognise. It said could I make IBC studios for a session, 10 o'clock start? I said sure, and told Adam. Even though I'd have finished half a day before he needed me, he wouldn't let me go. The American was Shel Talmy. The song was 'You Really Got Me'. I had no idea if anybody knew I'd been booked for the session. Then one day Dave said, 'Do you know if you'd played on 'You Really Got Me', you'd have hated me 20 years earlier.' I said, 'Surely not Dave...'"

Having ousted Avory, Dave didn't seem overjoyed at his replacement. "Dave is a mercurial character," Henrit says, picking his words. "He's unpredictable. I have no idea if he likes me. And I don't suppose I'm ever going to find out. I have every respect for him. What he did on 'You Really Got Me' is astonishing. I'm not going to suggest that he didn't have his angers. I never resorted to what Mick did in Cardiff." The guitarist, he discovered, had particular tastes. "Dave hated tom-toms. He also hated trumpets. There was a time when Dave decided I didn't need any monitors [considered crucial for musicians to hear themselves on modern stages]. He would just turn mine off."

Dave's moods, which broke Avory, could still be darker. "He's volatile, yes. Yes I have seen explosions. Didn't like them. But I've seen them. They could be frightening. We've had the odd confrontation. Which were completely unjustified. Head to head. Too close." He repeats the description with great care, flashing back to Dave with his fuse lit. "Heads too close together. But I survived them. And it wasn't just me. I just happened to be there. Often it was the tour manager."

Michael Farady also saw the last days of The Kinks' empire. On the road he was Henrit's drum technician at first, then Ray's guitar tech, road and then tour manager. At home, he became Ray's PA for the rest of the eighties, keeping close to him almost every day when he was in England. "Rick Graham was PA when I arrived," he remembers, "but he couldn't handle any more after Ray's post-Chrissie breakdown. After the next tour, he ran away from it all. My first day at Konk, [veteran Kinks tour manager] Ken Jones was running up and down the stairs, and his wife was running up and down after him shouting, 'Where is she?' because he had a girlfriend from Memphis hiding somewhere in the building. Maybe she climbed out of the window. This farce was my introduction. The atmosphere was always strained at Konk. It was quite an incestuous situation, with little power struggles, like a play – the Brian Rix or Terrence Rattigan type. I used to enjoy going there on Sundays, when Ray wasn't there."

Farady saw how his fellow new boy Bob Henrit was treated. "In somewhere like Kansas, he made the mistake of asking, 'Why do we have to have Indian food after every show? Why can't we have pizza?' In those days in America, the promoters sometimes had to drive hundreds of miles to get The Kinks the Indian takeaway they always demanded. They had to hold back Dave: 'You've only been in the band five fucking minutes!' They assumed he was a posh boy. He was never really accepted. Mick was like the clown and the animal. And Bob Henrit wasn't." In fact Henrit was from a similar North London background to the other Kinks. He gave up the chance of university to play with Adam Faith's backing group, The Roulettes. Faith provided Henrit with his higher education by quietly handing him a weekly reading list of the American literature he'd otherwise have studied. I talk to him in the rustic Middlesex house which, like Ray's Fortis Green semi, he always dreamed of owning. It's hard to imagine a better-fitting Kink.

Perhaps to compensate for these unfamiliar faces at an unstable time, Ray brought in his sixties *NME* Boswell Keith Altham, subsequently an important PR, to handle press. Almost unbelievably, he brought back Larry Page, unseen since their bitter 1968 court case, as The Kinks' UK manager. Ray reasoned that, with his relations with Dave again dysfunctional, someone they both knew might help. "He phoned me up out of the blue and said, 'Can we get together?'" Page told Johnny Black. "'I'd like you to look after us again.' And never once did he refer to anything that had happened before. Wace and Collins both phoned me up and said, 'What a brave man you are.' But Ray was as big an arsehole in the Eighties as he was in the Sixties."

Altham has his own theory about Page's return. "If you're looking for a manager, you'd look for someone who had produced the goods for you, who you maybe did an injustice to in the first place. He couldn't have been as bad as Ray said he was, or they wouldn't have gone back to him. During the year or so that I represented them, I don't think I saw Ray with Larry once. Larry just took care of business, at arm's length. It was a difficult relationship, but one based on mutual respect."

Avory, as a third of Kinks Productions Limited and Ray's friend and ally, was also kept on board, becoming Konk's manager. "Well Sarah [Lockwood]'s the manager really," he admits. "It was the only thing I could possibly do to still be in the company. I signed and checked out all the invoices. Necessary, but not terribly important. I just did that three days a week." One day when Avory was selling some of his old drumsticks, Farady asked him if he missed playing. "He said, [angrily] "Course I miss playing in the fucking band." Ray worried about that to *Rolling Stone*'s Anthony DeCurtis, "When we're rehearsing in the main studio, and you can hear the band playing, I often wonder what he thinks about. I just hope Mick doesn't drift into ordinariness."

Ray had been remarkably productive as 1984's chaos poleaxed him. *Return To Waterloo*, his debut film as writer-director which he finished days before Hynde left him, premiered on Britain's Channel 4 on November 4, a Sunday evening. Sharing the stubborn ambition of his concept albums, it uses fantasy music sequences to look inside the mind of a middle-aged estate agent (played by Ken Colley) who is also secretly the Surrey Rapist. He commutes endlessly between Guildford and Waterloo as if the line's a circle of hell. Ray's station, Effingham Junction, is on his journey. His home life is a shambles since seeing his newly sexual teenage daughter naked; discomfited, she's run away from home, where his suspicious wife carelessly blows cigarette smoke into his mouth in tired kisses goodbye each morning.

Colley's creased face, sunken eyes and weak smile perfectly catch the character's haunted anguish. For as long as Ray and cameraman Roger Deakins (Oscar-nominated for subsequent collaborations with the Coen Brothers) keep tight on his features, and fractured editing repeats his disturbed reaction to his daughter's naked back and empty marriage, the film fascinates. Musical sequences portraying the pressures of middle-class expectation which have replaced the happy boy he once was with a mediocre estate agent and rapist, are mostly effective. But Ray also overloads his first film with a favourite and dubious theme, England's betrayal by those who lost the Empire. Here it's somehow shoved into the mouths of a trio of punks led by a pop-eyed Tim Roth, singing 'Sold Me Out', Ray's attempt at a Sex Pistols rant.

Mixed reviews reflected his deeply flawed but memorable experiment. Wim Wenders and Martin Scorsese loved it; the latter thought it "very moving and very, very disturbing... I've never seen a movie quite like it." The important thing to Ray was that he'd managed it. "It was a hellish year and it cost me dearly in my personal life," he reflected. "But the point is I did what I wanted to do. That was the most unhappy yet most fulfilling time for me."

The soundtrack came out in the US only on July 1, 1985. It was billed as by "Ray Davies and members of The Kinks", because Dave refused to participate, or accept it as a band project. Three songs made it onto *Word Of Mouth*: 'Sold Me Out', 'Missing Persons' and 'Going Solo'. The latter two hinted at the fully realised Kinks album of suburban melancholy that might have been.

The Kinks convened on Brighton pier in October 1984, the sunny Sunday afternoon after an IRA bomb almost killed Margaret Thatcher at the town's Grand Hotel, to make Julien Temple's video for 'Do It Again'. Avory was given a cameo in a London sequence as a hapless busker Ray has to part ways with. *Word Of Mouth* was released on November 19. Halfway to New York that week to begin promotion on *Saturday Night Live*, the band looked out of their plane window to see an engine blazing. An emergency landing in Newfoundland was needed. It was a bad, accurate omen.

Word Of Mouth was their first flop since Ray and Clive Davis had carefully plotted The Kinks' comeback in 1976, limping to 57 in the charts. 'Do It Again' stalled at 41. They would never get so high again. Some thought it was because Ray's filming and Dave's tour blowout the year before had kept them away from America too long. The suspicion they would be leaving Arista, now their contract was fulfilled, didn't help. "Arista called it the Final Tap tour," Farady remembers of The Kinks' futile promotion of the album through 1985. "They stopped shipping the album at 450,000 copies so Ray couldn't get a gold record [for 500,000 sales]. Ray attacked the label for five minutes onstage the day he found out."

A song by Dave, 'Living On A Thin Line', came closest to success. Over an ominously skeletal bass-line and Henrit's eerie drum pattern, Dave's direct voice pierces cleanly home with ideas of national and individual betrayal. The track is driving yet ghostly as he mourns the 20th century's failed hopes, singing affectingly: "But there's no England now." It's a startlingly unique piece of music, picked years later to soundtrack several scenes in *The Sopranos*. DJs played it heavily, promo copies went out. But it was never released as a single. According to *Kink*, there was a contractual requirement that the first three from an album were always Ray's. If this is true, sibling rivalry killed The Kinks' last chance of a hit.

Farady recalls Ray's unimpressed reaction on tour. "He'd say, 'Here's Dave with his great new song,' and wander off. Then he'd climb up behind the screen where he'd change his clothes. He'd be silhouetted behind it, arms folded, looking down at Dave singing it, or else wander around. It was theatre. Unpleasant theatre. Contempt in mime!"

In November 1985, an MTV report prematurely announced The Kinks had signed with MCA, scotching any chance of remaining with Arista. Clive Davis, Ray's vital mentor in the band's commercial course, was now lost to him. They officially signed with MCA in January. "That was a catastrophe," Ray reflects. "Because Clive made a decent offer, and I was really happy. I think our management wanted for some reason to go to MCA. And I read about us being signed to them in the newspapers. Of course Clive reneged on his offer. Which I feel was total betrayal. They buried *Word Of Mouth*, with some difficulty."

"Clive Davis was a pal," Henrit says. "When me and Jim [Rodford] were with Argent, he guided us. He almost guaranteed us we would have American hits, and we did. MCA wasn't as friendly. And then record companies became successively less friendly. Not just to The Kinks, but to everybody. We didn't see the principals as often as we'd seen Clive."

The Kinks were now thrown from Arista's safe haven into the mincer of the eighties corporate music machine. "I don't think The Kinks would ever be a cog in a machine," Henrit protests. "It would be a very misshapen cog. But other stuff was coming along. It wasn't that we were dinosaurs. We just weren't flavour of the month any more. That happens to everybody in the end."

On October 23, 1985, Kinks Productions was replaced by Kinks 85 Ltd, with Ray and Dave now the sole principals receiving The Kinks' income (other band members remained on a wage). Dave writes in *Kink* that a contract was also signed to say neither brother could continue the band alone. Though Ray claims no memories of this, his frustrated attempts to do so in the 2010s suggest it's true.

Ray married for a third time, to Pat Crosbie, a red-haired Irish dancer, in Surrey on January 23. "For the first couple of years, when I was going out with a rather troublesome stripper," Farady muses, "I used to socialise with them. Pat was the absolute opposite of Chrissie Hynde – a sweet, mild-mannered ballerina whose father owned the *Cork Examiner*. He had a house overlooking the rocks of Cork Bay where they'd stay. When they were in New York, Pat said they were always getting chased out of restaurants because Ray's tips were so small. Around '85 and '86, he was pleading poverty to her because of the alimony he was paying, so he rented out the Effingham place, and lived in Ireland six months of the year, for tax reasons, in a beautiful Georgian townhouse in the middle of Kinsale. It was a break for him, and a break for us."

Though he's often typed as essentially English, and has dealt with the country more deeply than any other songwriter, Ray's paternal grandmother, Amy Kelly, was Irish. "It wasn't till I spent some time in Ireland that I realised I had so much of the islands in me," he considers. "People do under emphasise that part of me. But I'm not a diddly-doo-dah player. Some of those folk tunes, there's a reason why they're traditional, and they're inbred in our British, not just Irish and English selves. I call them the Northern Islands, I don't call it Britain. There's something in this land mass that most people grow up with. That's what is good about Irish music. Younger people mingle with older players. There's a willingness to accept what's gone before. I was always like that, with English folk music and everything else."

When Farady found himself chauffeuring Ray up and down the Cork to Kinsale road in 1988, he suddenly wished he'd stayed in England. "They were staunch Republican villages along there. They had the flags out. It was a bad time to be in the countryside. I didn't really feel safe. I was making excuses, hoping he wouldn't want the Bentley. Parked outside restaurants, it would make him such an obvious target. When I mentioned this in England, Ray said: 'Next time I come over, I'm wearing my Union Jack waistcoat.'"

Ray's journeys in bandit country inspired an unfilmed screenplay he wrote that year, *Man Of Aran*, about an ex-gunman on the run in southern Ireland, and 'The Informer', an icy little tale on The Kinks' *Phobia* (1993) about a drink between old comrades, which ends with one who's informed on the other being walked to his death.

Farady's drives with Ray in the Bentley back in London were also revealing. "The house he had in Highgate had been gutted – the pipes had burst and flooded it and it wasn't liveable. So he moved into Luxborough Street in Marylebone. It had been Chrissie's flat, she ran away, and he took over. When I used to drive him there, I went past Dave's house in Maida Vale on the way to pick his mail up off the floor while he was away, which Dave hated. Ray wouldn't let me stop to do it. He said, 'I never want to come this way again.' It was because Chrissie lived around there with their daughter. He didn't want to be reminded of the worst period of his life." When he was feeling sad, in the car or at home, particular music comforted Ray. "He'd always revert to Ray Charles in times of depression. 'Hallelujah I Love Her So' and songs like that. It reminded him of how he first started, playing them in Palais bands."

Ray's part in *Absolute Beginners*, Julien Temple's 1986 feature film based on Colin MacInnes' novel, had a similarly moving wistfulness. He played the cabbie dad of its bland hero Colin, his adventures long behind him as his son explores 1958's nascent youth culture. Ray wrote the song 'Quiet Life' for a dazzling set-piece in a cross-section of his house, showing how his slutty wife, lodgers and children all abuse him. Grey-templed and dancing with cleverly awkward grace, song and performance capture a man heroically keeping his lid on. Subduing an edge of mania amidst chaos, as Ray has had cause to, it's lovely work. "He is a reluctant actor, and there was always a sense that I'd pushed him into it," Temple reflects. "But he's a good actor, he gets it. I think he loves being someone else. Being himself might be more problematic. He has an affinity to singing through someone else's persona as well, which Dave always points out. When he was doing it, he was very natural. Except I'd cast him as a cab driver, and he hadn't told me he couldn't drive! That was a bit embarrassing with 100 people standing around. We had to get an angle where you couldn't see them pushing it. And then bizarrely I did a video with him a few years ago with Cathy Dennis singing 'Waterloo Sunset', where he could drive, and he drove a cab all round London."

Life on MCA was much less interesting for Ray, as The Kinks completed their next album, for November 1986 release. "I wanted *Think Visual* to be a concept record," Ray remembers. "I'd got this whole scenario about a man [the 'Come Dancing' spiv] who had a video shop, and dubbed illegal films in the back, and one night his satellite dish got hit by a thunderbolt, and gave him magical powers. But the people at the record company wanted us just to tour. To sell T-shirts. So I was already falling out with the corporate side. There was some good music afterwards..."

The opening song, 'Working At The Factory', sets out his dissatisfaction at where The Kinks and rock'n'roll find themselves in 1986, compared

262

... ave at the Dorchester, delighted The Kinks' concept album years are over. (DICK BARNATT/REDFERNS)

The Kinks sign with Arista boss Clive Davis, the Dorchester Hotel, 22nd June 1976. Ray and Davis would collaborate closely on the band's hugely successful American comeback. (DICK BARNATT/REDFERNS)

ick Avory. Ray jokes about Mick's "comedy drumming", but knows his
ot exactly metronomic, jazz-schooled style was crucial to the band's
ound. (VAL WILMER/REDFERNS)

Ray and Dave relive some of the worst years of their lives, for the
Schoolboys In Disgrace album in 1976. (MICHAEL PUTLAND/GETTY IMAGES)

he Kinks prepare to take America, 1978. Gordon Edwards (right) barely lasted the year on keyboards. (EBET ROBERTS/REDFERNS)

Have a cuppa tea. Ray with the Davies family cure-all. His and Dave's mum always had some brewing. Ray wrote two songs about his favourite drink. (MICHAEL PUTLAND/GETTY IMAGES)

Ray the rock monster leads The Kinks' eighties transformation into an aggressive, America-conquering stadium band. (IDOLS)

The Kinks during the video shoot for their single 'Come Dancing' at Essex's Ilford Palais, 1982. The hit song drew deeply on Ray and Dave's family story. (ESTATE OF KEITH MORRIS/REDFERNS/GETTY IMAGES)

in the 'Come Dancing' video, an early MTV favourite. He'd return several times to the "spiv" character he plays here. (ESTATE OF KEITH MORRIS/ FERNS/GETTY IMAGES)

Ray and Blur's Damon Albarn duet on 'Waterloo Sunset' at the height of Britpop, on *The White Room TV* show, 1995. "I was in love with him for that hour," said Damon. (LFI)

Ray looking ready for action, his famous gap-toothed smile clamped on a favourite cigar. (CHRIS GEORGE/CORBIS)

A Kink in his kingdom. Ray lingers in the up-for-sale Konk studios, 2010. (MICHAEL CLEMENT/IPCIMAGES)

and Dave at the opening of the Rock and Roll Hall of Fame, in Cleveland, Ohio, September 2, 1995. It would be The Kinks' final American show. (AL PRESTON/CORBIS)

Mick, Dave and Pete, inductees at the UK Music Hall of Fame in its only year, Alexandra Palace, 2005. The four original Kinks would never meet n. (LFI)

Dave and Ray in LA in 1993, publicising *Phobia*, The Kinks' last shot at success. (AARON RAPOPORT/CORBIS)

to his dreams of freedom when the band began in 1963. "Never wanted to be like everybody else," he sings, "but now there are so many like me sitting on the shelf." It's a crushing assessment, referencing then brushing aside the 1966 Kinks B-side 'I'm Not Like Everybody Else' which both Davies brothers took as a personal anthem. The liberty music once gave them just feels like clocking on now, alongside a thousand other identikit rockers. Thinking they'd escaped the constrictions laid out for their working-class lives, they've become another sort of factory fodder. The Kinks' first words on MCA tell their new paymasters they loathe them, and can't wait to leave.

Think Visual tries to rail against the idea of music as corporate product. But most of Ray's songs sound as if he's already succumbed. 'Welcome To Sleazy Town' is about a strip club being cleared for a parking lot, but he can't find anything new in his perennial preservation theme. 'Killing Time' hits on a more telling metaphor, finding stray phrases that successfully say the things he always tries to, as he wastes his life watching adverts for luxuries: "These lunatics will take my mind...why can't life be more sublime." Attempts at working-class anger sound spent, Ray's inspiration finally running dry. His production, meanwhile, tones down the stadium gestures to sometimes warm, mostly muffled effect, as if the album's half-submerged. Dave's 'When You Were A Child', a synth-choral song about regaining innocence, is again stronger and stranger.

Only two songs stand out. 'How Are You' is a more slight, middle-aged take on 'Do You Remember Walter', finding awkward humanity in a casual meeting. Ray uses his demo's vocal, which sounds alive. 'Lost And Found' draws on memories of Hurricane Gloria blowing through New York, an apocalyptically clearing wind which strengthens a wavering man's resolve. Soft synths and steel-drum percussion carry its pretty tune. Only "soaring" sax and other clutter meant to make it commercial sully its thoughtful beauty. It can't save the worst Kinks album so far. Ray and Dave promoted it hard. MCA seemed to, but *Think Visual* stalled at 81 in the US. All the band's Arista achievements were being washed away.

The Kinks pushed an album which was, they soon realised, already dead in the water for much of 1987. It was a gruelling, sometimes comical and inspiring process. "'Lost And Found' [released in the UK on April 3] had been reviewed by Charles Shaar Murray in *NME*," Farady remembers, "and he'd noted some similarities to the Four Tops' 'It's The Same Old Song'. It wasn't promoted properly by MCA because of that. We were in Holland around then, and Ray was interviewed by a young MTV-type presenter. He said, 'I knew I'd be interviewing someone like my father, but you're like my grandfather.' Ray said, 'A lot of people say I'm difficult. But so is Chuck Berry.' I was proud of him for that.

"We were in the Munich Park Hilton Hotel the next weekend [in May], after a German tour. Kool & The Gang were there too – they were on the same label, and champagne was flowing. Because a pint gets Ray drunk, he almost got into a fight with Kool, I presume, and was taken to bed. But he carried on arguing with Pat in their room. The next morning I was on the plane, relieved to be going home, counting the guitar cases going up into the hold. And suddenly they started going down again. Larry Page had called Lufthansa to stop me leaving. Pat was feeling shattered from the row the night before, and Ray felt awful for her. We had to stay behind to patch things up."

On June 27, the creative fatigue *Think Visual* suggested was confirmed when Ray met MCA executives before a gig in New York. "Ray didn't have any more songs," Farady states. "He had a $700,000 advance, and wanted to give them a double-live album and video instead of a new studio album. They told him to keep the money – we don't want your album." At the gig at Pier 84 that night, a frustrated Ray yelled: "C'mon MCA... *Beverly Hills Cop*, *Starlight Express* [all parts of their corporate entertainment portfolio]... Fuck you!"

The cursed live album's progress wasn't helped when the night before in Poughkeepsie their sound engineer, "a belligerent drunk" in Farady's memory, had been surly to the wrong Kink after the show. "How was it for you?" Dave asked him, a casual post-gig greeting. "As good as you're going to get," the engineer said with startling rudeness. One headbutt with following blows to the ground later, and he perhaps remembered which band he was working for. In New York the next night, the engineer agitated to get the sound crew to strike, but the show was recorded for Ray's intended LP. The next day, everyone travelled onto Columbia, Maryland. The Kinks' security man Terry Draper drove Ray and Pat, successfully reaching the right town, in entirely the wrong state. While they drove the extra 400 miles and six hours from Columbia, Pennsylvania, everyone else settled in at the hotel bar. As Ray finally entered, the engineer didn't entirely pick his moment to saunter up and say: "I'm leaving today." "OK," said Ray, bored. "Where's the tape from New York?" "I don't know. I think I threw it in the river." By this time Ray had had quite enough of his Sunday. Seconds later, the engineer found Ray's arm around his neck and fist in his face, on the way to being flattened by a second Davies. "I looked at the guests at the other end of the bar," Farady concludes, "and their glasses were frozen halfway to their mouths. I went over to Ray, raised his arm and said, 'The winner!' Ray went upstairs and told Ken Jones he'd beaten up the sound engineer, so there probably wouldn't be any sound tomorrow."

While most rock stars have a dozen heavies on standby to dive in once their charge has landed a swift sucker-punch, in their forties Ray and Dave still took care of things themselves, as if they were still at home. Showco, the sound company they'd used for years, soon quit, continuing The Kinks' 23-year history of offending the American music industry. Somehow a single live album, *The Road*, made it into the shops in 1988, reaching 110, not really worth the bruises behind it.

Ray was in New York mixing *The Road*, and working on a second theatrical musical, *80 Days*, when he received word in November that his mother was dying of cancer. In *Kink*, Dave remembers her looking out of the front room of 87 Fortis Green where she now lived with Gwen's family, hoping Ray would come down the path. Ray, in his story 'The Million-Pound Semi-Detached', imagines the magic in that room healing her heart. Dave also recalls the beautiful letter Ray wrote to her. Confronting emotions always confounded him. When she died on November 23, he flew back. Michael Farady drove him to see her body in the funeral parlour. This is where Ray's surrogate Les Mulligan goes in his story 'Scattered'. Looking at his mum's face, he almost faints. His guilt for not being with her grows. At the wake, looking at the changed, aged family he's grown apart from, he "knew all the faces, but somehow didn't know the people". The death inspires him to complete what would be the last Kinks studio album's last song, 'Scattered', on the old brown 'You Really Got Me' piano. It was a profound loss to the brothers, and the music they'd made.

"Ray's writing is drawn so heavily from our mum," Dave reflects. "I think Ray realised that before my mum died. I was with her for her last three weeks. And I think he really missed out big time not being with her when she was dying. It's quite profound that my mother was a big inspiration for a lot of Kinks songs – one of those people who lived through the war, and were confronted with so many topsy-turvy emotions about the world, and still trying to put on a happy face and trying to smile, in all this grim reality. A lot of that survival and positive although very upsetting emotional power that my mum had transmits itself to you. Every line on a face tells a story about something. And you can't avoid being affected by those sorts of people – people who aren't really here any more. By that whole working-class culture of London, not just cockneys, and how they learnt to survive, and then learnt to have a voice, in the sixties. That acceptance how ordinary people had ideas and inspiration and knowledge and wisdom, in *Saturday Night And Sunday Morning* and all the rest. All my friends were always saying, 'Oh, my parents won't let me play the guitar.' I think my mum was a smart old bird, because she knew that was how we could get out. I learned more from my parents and particularly my sisters than I ever did at school, about things that were cool, and emotion, and how to behave. That's where you learn proper stuff. And your friends you meet."

In January 1988, Ray's own always suspect health plummeted. "I remember taking him to a private clinic just by London Bridge," Farady says. "We were really worried. The next thing we knew, he'd had a heart bypass operation. Because he was still pleading poverty to Pat, he ended up convalescing in a home run by nuns in Cork. They didn't even have towels, he had to dry himself on bed sheets. Once he'd recovered, the band had to go to Ireland to rehearse – to prove he was fit enough to go through a show. Pretty soon after the operation, he did a half-show, to prove to himself that he was able to carry on. And his health improved. And we stopped calling him a hypochondriac."

80 Days started a fairly successful run at the La Jolla Playhouse in Santa Barbara, California in August. "Ray was doing it very much about the end of the British Empire, one of his obsessions," Barrie Keeffe says of a musical he bailed out from working on. The first five months of 1989 were spent back at Konk, trying to assemble another MCA album. Ray wanted to base it around his song 'The Million-Pound Semi-Detached', about the lives of a couple of his parents' generation and changing ideas of property. "Ray is a blotting paper," Henrit says, explaining its genesis. "You don't think he's listening, but he is. If Ray likes something, he'll remember it. I was sitting with Ray at breakfast reading the newspaper, and it said, 'Million Pound Semi-Detached.' I said, 'Look at this, Ray, a semi worth a million quid.' Nothing. Then later, there's this song."

This time Dave scotched Ray's ambition for the album. Dave found his own songs and ideas being excised, as their relationship became poisoned again. "He was editing out my guitar parts on *UK Jive*," Dave remembers, "and I just happened to come by the studio. And he said, 'Oh, it's too late'. I said, 'That's a load of bollocks.' He said, 'I can do what I like, I'm a genius'. I said, 'You're not a genius, you're a fucking arsehole.' We were arguing on the roof, and people in the office were crying. It's not a pleasant sight, when we have a... madness. We say terrible, awful things to each other. And then you get the knock on the door. 'Da-ave, my wife's left me...' I'm sure it's similar for Ray – there are parts of his personality that I can't stand. We're just very, very different people. I'd like to think that we're both going to come out of this more enlightened than we went in. He'd probably say that I love Dave, but I reserve the right to hate him."

"I don't think it's really hatred," says Ray. "I know I did a song called 'Hatred' [on *Phobia* (1993)], but it was tongue in cheek. It just annoyed me and I felt he could do better than what he was doing and doing to himself. That's all. I think if you care about anybody, you dislike them and you're angry with them when they let you down, or they let themselves down. I felt from time to time he did that."

Does he mean Dave's drinking, womanising and drugs, in earlier days? "All that stuff adds up, yeah. Dave is easy to provoke. Not that you try to manipulate it, because you wouldn't want such anger to spill out. It's too scary. I guess it's difficult to put aside all the things that have gone on before. And suddenly tension happens because it's latent. We just have our own opinions about how things should sound sometimes," he says of their studio conflicts. "And that was a hard period to go through."

"Never in the face," is Henrit's memory of the brothers' battles. At least drummers no longer had to take sides. "That would have been a breach of my position. If it happened we let it. It wasn't our business. We weren't Davies brothers. They were in their forties then. A fight would probably be caused by something that happened 35 years before, when they were growing up. And it's what propelled the band."

Dave and Ray reputedly came to blows several times making *UK Jive*, as Ray edited out two of Dave's songs (eventually tacked onto CD and cassette versions). Farady offers another reason in a year when, as Dave relates in *Kink*, errors by accountants left him with crippling back-tax. "Dave needed those two songs, or it could have resulted in his bankruptcy. The sisters were always pressuring Ray into not kicking Dave out of the band. There was pressure to treat the younger brother reasonably well. I drove him several times for that reason to one of them [probably Peggy], who lived just across Richmond Bridge. He'd come away looking sheepish."

The numbing repetition of *UK Jive*'s seemingly endless sessions, familiar to twitching veterans of *Sleepwalker* and *Misfits*, were another problem. Ian Gibbons quit after a decade as keyboardist in March 1989. "Ray sent me to Southend to ask him back," Farady remembers. "I just pretended to go. His wife told me, 'He's not coming back.' He was close to a nervous breakdown." Remembers Henrit: "At Konk, two digital tape machines were attached to the control room, towards the end. So you could make a hundred-track demo. Which is crazy. But we found ourselves doing it. We frequently did 14-hour sessions. The top bone of my vertebrae was red hot."

Was this just because Ray couldn't make up his mind?

"Well, he's got several minds, that's the point. Ray is quicksilver, and a genius, in the proper sense of the word. Ray, while he's thinking of one idea will be thinking of another idea at the same time. So that's something that we had to deal with. He changed his mind all the time, on everything. Musically, it was hugely exciting. We were always on our toes. And this is what Ray wanted." Farady adds a gem. "Around this time, Ray had a new analyst in Harley Street. He came out laughing and grinning. 'Apparently, I'm suffering from terminal creativity!'"

"It's the same as not knowing what song's coming next on stage," Henrit says. "There was a list on the floor, and if you were lucky the first song came first. Ray would see what was going on in the crowd, and often launch into a song, and I'd have no idea what it was. It was hugely risky, but it never worried him. Once he actually wrote a song on stage, in Cincinnati, at a thing called Regatta. Ray decided to play this song called 'Regatta My Arse'. And we all joined in. There were never any train wrecks, but there was the propensity for it. I always like a beer before I go on. In The Kinks, I quickly realised this was not a drunken man's gig. But the original guys I understand really liked a drink, so they couldn't possibly have followed Ray. Maybe it was more about anarchy then."

Ray's indecisiveness had other ramifications for those in his kingdom. "Everyone would call me," says Farady. "'What's Ray's final decision for tomorrow?' I'd tell them whether they could have the day off or not. Because I'd know Ray's last thoughts of the day."

When *UK Jive* arrived, it sounded flat, anaemic, artificial and superficial: previously unimaginable words for The Kinks. They had been through so much they always seemed indestructible. But Ray's draining illness and glimpse of mortality, a brother he could only communicate with in songs and punches, and months of attritional recording appeared to have beaten the life from them. There's a long, aimless complaint about traffic jams ('Aggravation'), a title song about the old Saturday night parties at Denmark Terrace that's impossible to dance or smile to, and another vague attempt at an English Eden ('Now And Then'). 'Looney Balloon''s giddy journey into space isn't bad. 'Down All The Days (Till 1992)' is a would-be European anthem most notable for a video shot at 87 Fortis Green, again harking back to their parents' parties. The single 'How Do I Get Close''s wish for feeling at least gets through its own barrier of stiff AOR style, as Ray sings, "I'm crying, I'm crying... darling, darling," hinting in the simplest terms at what he's been through. After an interview with *Rolling Stone*'s Anthony DeCurtis, once back in his New York apartment, he did weep. "I had a management that thought I was finished," he said, listing the blows he'd soaked up. "I had a record company that thought we'd peaked. I had an ex-girlfriend that thought I would top myself. But they were wrong. They underestimated me. I think I've finally come through all that. Nobody treats me the way those people did and gets away with it... everybody gets theirs eventually."

You can hardly hear Dave's backing vocals on the album, or remember his guitar, as if the band had already split up. "Dave let me know through someone else when I was in the hospital that if I wanted to quit he would understand and we could call it a day," Ray told Q's Charles Shaar Murray, after showing off the sunken knuckle where he'd punched Konk's wall, instead of his brother. "I think it's a combination of not wanting to pull the plug and realising why I wanted to be successful; because there was no other way for me. There's that double edge; you hate what you do but when you haven't got it any more you realise how lucky you were."

UK Jive sank without a trace. Larry Page left again in April, in a dispute over a commission for making the deal for Ray's autobiography, which would mercilessly lampoon him. Mark Haley replaced Gibbons. "The first thing he said to Dave was, 'Glad to see your hairstyle's improved in the last 30 years,'" laughs Farady. "So he didn't last long."

Farady himself jumped ship in the summer of 1989. Like Henrit, he remembers The Kinks' live splendour most, even at the late eighties low ebb. "At the Maple Leaf Auditorium in Toronto one night, Ray finished the set with Harry Belafonte's 'Daylight Come And I Want To Go Home' ['The Banana Boat Song']. And most of the 15,000 audience went down the street singing it. The arena shows were always wonderful. I've said all of my bad things. But most of the time, I was very proud to be there. I was proud to work for one of the greatest rock'n'roll bands. It wasn't as unpleasant as you might think. Most of the time, it was a pretty fucking happy affair."

The UK, though, was very different. "I always considered it a chore coming back to work in England. It was small theatres. We'd do half a dozen shows, and they could never do the great American songs, and they never got the respect they deserved. 'Waterloo Sunset' was only played on special occasions, when Ray thought they deserved it. I don't want to paint an entirely negative picture. It's all very well writing about 'Waterloo Sunset', but there's a lot more to their life than 'Waterloo Sunset'. Every time Ray used to climb the stairs to the stage, I could see there was a lot of pressure weighing down on his shoulders. 'Do I want to do this again?' Rather him than me. I wasn't brave enough."

Farady could also look back on Ray's whimsical dealings with the great and the good who rang Konk, wishing for songs. "Ray took an advance from Wim Wenders for a soundtrack," Farady says. "Wim called Konk every Sunday afternoon to try to get Ray to provide the songs he'd committed to. They never materialised."

"I don't remember any advance," Wenders tells me. "But in 1988 I did in fact ring Ray often. I was in London with my brother Klaus who was very sick then, and one of his dreams was to meet Ray. Ray did come to visit us and spent an hour talking to my brother, and that made Klaus very happy. It was amazing and very graceful that Ray did that. I remember I was hoping to involve Ray in the soundtrack for *Until The End Of The World* in 1990. It didn't work out, but I had 'Days' on the soundtrack after all, sung by Elvis Costello. And a couple of years later The Kinks contributed a song called 'Eternity' to a short film of mine. It had Dave singing. I dedicated my first long film [*Summer In The City* (1970)] to The Kinks. Their first albums had accompanied me through my early years. Ray's voice and lyrics made this music so special and personal. There was a fragility and a wit to it that I could strongly relate to. 'I'm Not Like Everybody Else' was a hymn of my generation."

Some of Ray's supposed peers had less luck. "I was standing outside Paul McCartney's offices in Soho Square when I saw Trevor Jones, who I knew and worked with Paul," says Farady. "The next day he called me to see if Ray was interested in talking to Paul about working together. Ray chuckled to himself. The next day Linda McCartney called Konk, and Ray wouldn't take the call. She called back once or twice after that. He just chuckled every time.

"For all I've said of Ray," Farady concludes, "I still think he's magnificent."

As The Kinks moved into the nineties, the limitations Ray had set as they punched their way back into the mainstream on Arista loosened. He'd been denied *Think Visual*'s concept album and 'The Million-Pound Semi-Detached'. But live, Pat Crosbie and a second woman performed silhouetted choreography during a couple of songs, adding ballet to the band's repertoire. Even the master of perverse rock performance, Bob Dylan, was impressed. "Only you could get away with that, Ray," he congratulated him after watching from the wings at a Bilbao festival. In 1985, Ray had refused to collaborate on a song with Dylan too and, almost uniquely among major sixties songwriters, has never admitted or exhibited his influence. Ray's unique stew of his post-war English family, blues and his own troubled head instead founded a school studied at by the likes of Ian Dury, Madness, Mark E. Smith and, later in the Nineties, a new, devoted generation.

Other stage schemes were contemplated. "Ray had lots of concepts," Henrit recalls. "We rehearsed as if we were a fifties lounge band in New York, playing Ray's stuff. That had to be a concept for something that was going to happen but didn't. Since I know Ray, it will perhaps, one day. We could all do it – because we sort of had. It was very subdued music, like you would get in the Peppermint Lounge. Dave felt it wasn't rock'n'roll. And at that time people came to The Kinks to hear the hits." This was probably for *The Kinks On Broadway*, which was planned but evaporated in 1990, in the wake of the band's January induction into the US Rock And Rock Hall Of Fame, at which Pete Quaife very briefly rejoined them.

In the summer of 1989, Ray was also becoming distracted by ideas outside of music. *Million Pound Semi*, also called *Breakfast In Berlin*, was announced as his next film, intended "to put Ray's current activities with The Kinks into historical perspective... It will reflect on his childhood and youth, probe into some of his past and present fears, and touch on some of his roles and responsibilities." The death of Annie Davies would be in there; all of *UK Jive* and the thematically crucial song thrown off that awful album, 'The Million Pound Semi-Detached', too.

Ray hawked this to the film division of PolyGram (whose London Records had the UK version of The Kinks' MCA deal). Their then head of production, who wishes to remain anonymous, remembers the scheme's odd reality. "It was very much him pushing us to consider financing an autobiographical sequel to *Return To Waterloo*. Once he found out where we were in Shepherds Bush, he would turn up, largely unannounced, and sit around my desk and other execs' desks. He was enthusiastic, genuinely up, whenever he came in. Very sardonic. Very determined to make a film of some sort. He talked a lot about his sister, a sister whose house he used to live in. And one of his principle ideas for this film was to rebuild that house – to have that house literally reconstructed, brick by brick [surely either the teenage paradise with Rosie from which he'd been cast out, or 87 Fortis Green, where he had recently filmed]. He was either in the middle or just post-therapy after a break-up. He made jokes about it himself. But we were all told to be wary of the deal, because he didn't involve a manager, and you can't structure business terms with the artist. It was just Ray, giving his ideas, and getting enthusiastic. And when he was with us, he barely mentioned albums at all. He barely mentioned songs, songwriting, the fact that he was in a band – it was all about his visual ideas, and he'd always wanted to be a film-maker. Perhaps it was a post-therapy project that he was attacking, to get himself into top gear."

Ray soon offered a startling gift. "I was shocked when he left me what he referred to as his diaries. I'd been introduced to him that day, and it was either the next day or soon after that he came in with them. They weren't diaries in format – printed pages with dates. They were the kind of sketchbooks that art students carry around, A4, maybe slightly bigger. He had them in a carrier bag, and he left them. He wanted to believe that from those books, a film would somehow emerge. I'm very familiar with working notes from film-makers, and what I was reading was too personal to be that. They were about the project, and his life, but inevitably weaving in The Kinks, because they're indivisible. They were in the drawer of my office for quite some time. Then I took them home for safe-keeping."

Finding out the executive lived a short walk up Crouch Hill from Konk helped Ray trust this stranger with his intimate thoughts. Then he tried to get closer. "On a couple of occasions, he rang from the studio and said, 'Hey, we're just finishing something off, and we're going over to Dick's Bar if you want to join us.' He'd ring the office, and if I wasn't there he'd ring the house. Even if I had been at home, I probably wouldn't have gone. There was something going on in his world. He was best left to his own devices."

On August 15 1989, The Kinks played Kentish Town's Town & Country Club (now the Forum) with guest Kirsty MacColl, then in the UK charts with her cover of 'Days'. Ray had it filmed, this too part, perhaps, of *Breakfast In Berlin*. "There was a separate project going on trying to enthuse London about a new recording deal," the executive recalls, "and they set up a one-off show. We all went to that, and it was a great show. And he did lots of talking in between the songs, lots of story-telling. I think that prompted the solo shows he'd do later. Then they went to America on another tour, and when he came back he'd forgotten about the film and the notebooks. I set up a final meeting at Konk, mostly to give them back."

Some of Ray's future was starting to brew, in the season he spent conjuring but never truly creating a film about himself. "I find all musicians of that generation hard to summarise," the executive considers of his time with Ray. "As a given, they're two or three people, because they've become famous very young, and so a mass of insecurity has been the best they can do in terms of a bedrock for personality and character. I think perhaps this whole film idea was part of the drive to recognise who he was, as opposed to what his famous identity was and who The Kinks were. He was driving himself into a space where he could be himself. The notebooks were like his conversations, quite confessional. At that time, we just thought he was telling stories about himself. Looking back on it now, that persona he had then has become by and large his public face. He's spokesman for himself. I think it was about five years later that he did his *An Evening with Ray Davies* solo shows. And now he's a national treasure..."

Ray did spend part of 1990 in New York working on a second film, *Weird Nightmare*, a documentary on the great jazz bassist and composer Charles Mingus, built around sessions for a tribute album. Interviewing Keith Richards, Charlie Watts and Elvis Costello among others, Ray focused on extreme close-ups of the musicians, studying their faces and bodies as they worked. They reminded him of his original, awkward band now almost 30 years ago, who had looked so offensively wrong to outsiders as they cut their revolutionary hits. "When you can do it, you don't think about those problems," he says. "'Is there a problem, that they don't understand?' When I was doing the Mingus film, I noticed a lot of those jazz players were not coordinated. But when it was time to get it right, they did it beautifully."

In November, The Kinks extracted themselves from MCA, to mutual relief. New manager Nigel Thomas helped them negotiate a deal with Columbia, signed on July 19, 1991. "Oh, the Columbia thing," Ray sighs. "You know, that could have been such a great record. But I allowed them to A&R me. Nice chap, but they A&Red the music out of us. It beats you up, really burns you out, working for the corporates. You couldn't just make a mad single and put it out the way we used to. You have to sell the idea not just to the band, but to marketing. It takes so bloody long, it takes years. I'm still waiting for the world to hear my song about the millennium..." Had he truly taken the Devil's coin now – joined the corporate Establishment? "Certainly the deal was put together like that. It's not the way I would have liked it."

The Kinks recorded the single 'Did Ya' as the deal was being finalised. The half-dead band on *UK Jive* rediscovered all their old spirit for one of their freshest and slyest songs. Quoting 'Sunny Afternoon''s descending bass-line, it examines what's left of the sixties, hilariously summed up as when "la-de-dahs drove mini-cars in the summertime". Unimpressed by the decade at the time, Ray is even more gleefully savage as he picks through its wreckage. Knocking on old addresses in Chelsea he finds them sold off to foreign buyers. The sixties chimera of a classless paradise has left "this green and pleasant land/ a dustbin full of promises and half-hearted plans", and the Cassandra who wrote 'Where Have All The Good Times Gone' and 'Dead End Street' can hardly keep from crowing. "Did you ever think when we was really fab," he inquires of his once-dazzling young peers, "that we'd be looking through a dustbin for a dog-end to drag?" Ray has the happy conviction he always finds in such fatalistic terrain, liberated because he knows the worst. The rousing chorus and simple, semi-acoustic arrangement recall The Kinks at the time this song merrily buries.

Released in the US in October leading a five-track "maxi-single" sampler of current work which included a new recording of 'Days', their new label could worryingly do little with it, and a UK release was pulled. The next two years were spent in Konk recording and re-recording what would become the final Kinks studio album, *Phobia*. Dave's move to LA, where he was getting Hollywood work on John Carpenter soundtracks, didn't help. The band sank hundreds of thousands of pounds into getting it right. In marked contrast to the concerted plans Ray had made with Clive Davis, Columbia reacted with confusion and inertia. The record was remixed and resequenced, half a dozen tracks were mulled over as singles, and release dates were pulled again and again. The stroke suffered in January 1993 by Nigel Thomas, the exuberant, trusted manager who'd got them signed, added to the chaos.

Against all the odds of the new record business culture in which it was made, *Phobia* splendidly returned The Kinks to form. 'Digital Assembly' is listed on the credits, and there are signs of Konk's 100-track tapes in its production's nearly radioactive nineties glow. But the apocalyptic theme suggested by Sue Coe's cover art of lynched animals hanging from burning high-rises is borne out in the opening two songs. 'Wall Of Fire' finds Ray energised by the ecological catastrophe then being glimpsed. "Lit the fuse/ now we can't retire," he notes of the human race who've caused it. Growling, "Let's have a real fire," he seems to imagine The Kinks' own bond tightening as they run into the face of disaster. 'Drift Away' sees him dreaming of escape to the island he's fantasised about in song since 1965, as civilisation crumbles, unmourned by The Kinks. "Wall Street's down, so what?" Ray snaps, as politicians hang from lamp posts and sixties phrases echo in a new context: "rivers of blood", "it's all over now". Giddy fairground keyboards by Ray and sweetly harmonised interludes break up ferocious playing and singing. The whole album might have been like this, a last grand concept piece. Nigel Thomas, knowing what Columbia would think, talked Ray down.

In 'Don't', a man teeters on the ledge of a New York high-rise. Ray knows how he feels (Dave describes his brother's White City overdose as his "first suicide attempt" to me), and his high voice in the chorus rises to meet the man looking down. 'Over The Edge' combines circus metaphors for frustrated orgasm ("once I start performing I can't really retire") with snapped jobless suburbanites land-mining their lawns. Though Dave was semi-detached again in LA, his high voice and committed guitar back his brother up. 'Hatred (A Duet)', entirely written by Ray, sends and sums up their relationship. "My hostility to you defies description," he hisses like Cruella De Vil. "Why don't you just drop dead and don't recover?" Dave sings at his brother, so recently operated on. They've rarely sounded so happy.

'Scattered' was begun in 1984, about Ray's break-up with Chrissie Hynde. The death of his mum catalysed its completion, making its sadness more profound: "I've been out of my mind ever since you've been gone... I feel older, I feel fatter..." He imagined her scattered in the stars, and him as ash in the ground. It also worked as an "end of career song", he said later: a farewell to and from his band. That was one goodbye. 'Did Ya', straight after it, with them sounding alive and ready for their future, was a second.

Phobia was finally released in the US on April 13, 1993 (two weeks after the UK). A US tour started four days later, and The Kinks played across the world for the rest of the year. It did them no good. The album made number 166 in the US, worse even than on MCA. "I asked to be let out of our contract halfway through a tour," Ray says, "because I thought they're not delivering what they said they would, and it was time the industry changed, and I knew there was a period when I'd have to get out of it. The Kinks were never an expensive act. You just have to look at 550 Madison Avenue, where [Columbia parent company]

Sony is, the real estate. Reprise was in a little shed at the back of the film lot in Los Angeles, now they've got these huge buildings, and you don't know who anybody is any more. The industry was at its most paranoid, and I could see the crash coming." *Phobia*'s failure could be simpler. No matter what they did, The Kinks' time may just have been up.

Ironically, in Britain the stock of the band they'd once been had rarely been higher. Blur's 1993 album *Modern Life Is Rubbish* used Ray's writing (and a touch of Small Faces) as its blueprint. The title was Davies' ethos reduced to crude graffiti, and songs on it and its all-conquering 1994 follow-up *Parklife* (such as 'This Is A Low', which mined pathos from a longing for Radio 4's shipping forecast while on a disastrous US tour) made a stand for English culture. 1995's *The Great Escape* descended to bad parody of Ray's old suburban vignettes, before Blur became their own band. The attendant Britpop phenomenon lasted through the mid-nineties. On March 13, 1995, their singer Damon Albarn symbolically duetted with the movement's new hero Ray on 'Waterloo Sunset' for Channel 4's *The White Room* TV show. The current Kinks stayed forgotten. 'Did Ya' had returned them to the sort of literate satire now back in vogue. But its demolition of the sixties myth Britpop unquestioningly bought left them as unfashionable as ever.

"Did Britpop do anybody any good?" Ray wonders. "I was amazed at how I particularly was called the Godfather of Britpop, or the Grandfather. I felt younger than the people citing me. It was all frightfully well-organised, they were good businessmen. The connection with me I could understand was that they were writing about the world they knew, in England. It inevitably was a Legoland version of the sixties. But the ones that had fun genuinely felt that they were reliving an important part of history. I could certainly hear my songwriting's influence on Blur. But whereas I was trying to be upwardly mobile but couldn't escape my roots, Damon was the other way round. I always felt that his songs came from a more privileged aspect. When I wrote 'Dead End Street', I really meant it. It was from my own fears and paranoia. With something like 'Girls And Boys', he was just visiting."

"I think hope springs eternal," Henrit says of The Kinks after *Phobia*. "You're a band and there's always, God willing, the chance to make another album. If this one hasn't happened, then the next one will. That's how a band goes on." There were signs though that perhaps, after 30 years, things were running down. "Ray turned to me onstage one night and said, 'Where have all the good times gone?' And I said, 'I don't know, Ray.' He meant for me to play the song. But he'd said it as a question. And not one I was surprised to hear."

In September 1994, Ray's extraordinary book *X-Ray: The Unauthorised Autobiography* was released. It radically exploded the traditional rock memoir, in one of his most brilliant and sustained works. Set in the then-future of the early 21st century, a ward of the Corporation which runs everything makes his way to Konk's decrepit ruins, to extract the facts from a life lived by a cantankerous 70-year-old rock star, R.D. This allows Ray to write a vividly emotional account of his life till the days after White City, while denying it's him at all. ("That's how devious he is," Larry Page moaned to Johnny Black. "I gave it to lawyers and they said there was no hope of suing him.") Alternately very funny and very painful, it tries to explain the true meaning of The Kinks' music through his early life. As Ray, who had just turned 50, probably already knew, creating R.D. also offered a hostage to the fortunes of his future self.

Coincidentally, out in LA Dave was just finishing his autobiography, *Kink*, published in February 1996. It was an equally exceptional piece of writing from an opposite personality, fearlessly and funnily laying out every sexual escapade, outer-space vision and contractual and violent row with Ray. Dave's love for his brother and his talent was just as plain. Ray didn't see the funny side of someone else exposing so much. A time bomb between them was perhaps set now.

X-Ray was a critical and commercial success. Ray at first publicised it with traditional public readings. Then in March 1995, he began the *An Evening With Ray Davies* tour. Accompanied by guitarist Peter Mathison, he interspersed readings and anecdotes with related songs. Subsequent tours were variously named *X-Ray*, *The Storyteller* and *20th Century Man*. This was the low-key start of the solo career he'd been considering since around 1966. "I was probably responsible for the demise of The Kinks," Henrit believes. "Again we were sitting at breakfast and I said, 'D'you know what, Ray, I think you're probably the Noël Coward of our generation.' He said, 'Why?' I said, 'I think your songs and Coward's strike a chord with the English psyche.' And then the next thing any of us knew, he had a showbiz agent and a showbiz manager, rather than rock'n'roll ones. And he went off and wrote *X-Ray*, and then he was on the road, thinking he could do a one-man show, and be a sort of vocal stand-up comedian." Robert Wace connected Ray to Coward long before, of course. But the tour's success meant The Kinks were less necessary.

In November 1993, then again in October and November 1994, The Kinks toured small British venues in rarely visited towns, rewinding to when they'd begun. They were even booed off stage in a working-men's club in Barnsley, as if they were still on the nightmarish cabaret tour of 1968. Michael Farady remembers the reaction of Ken Jones, who had quit as The Kinks' tour manager in 1992 after 24 loyal years, and was now dying of cancer. "He rose up from what was practically his death bed and said [referring to the new booking agents the band used from 1993], 'Those bastards have reduced The Kinks to an end-of-the-pier show.'"

On June 15, 1996, The Kinks played the Norwegian Wood music festival, near Oslo. "You never know it's the last gig," Henrit says. "It was the stadium where they did one of the first four-minute miles. Van Morrison was on before us. He had his back to the audience the whole time, then let Georgie Fame take over. So a perfect support act — because he's not interested. We had the girls with us, dancing. The band played full of spirit. We were better at being musicians than anything else. If Ray felt it was the end, he certainly never mentioned it. But then he wouldn't. He will make up his mind himself. If he asks other people, he'll keep a dog and bark himself. We assumed that there would be some more gigs. And there weren't."

The very last Kinks album, *To The Bone*, was a grander valediction. On April 11, 1994, they had recorded some favourite songs with basic instruments at Konk in front of a tiny audience. With tracks recorded on the recent tour, this became the basis of *To The Bone*, released independently in the UK on October 3. A US release needed a major label, and a vastly better double album was released there by

EMI two years later. It has room for every side of The Kinks playing at a peak. 'All Day And All Of The Night' is a huge noise to start with, then we fade in and out of Konk's intimacy, where Dave is grumbling at Ray's sudden desire for an accordion. "We're related," Ray confides. "Same mother – different fathers..." The home stretch could hardly be improved as a last hurrah. Dave takes the lead at 'Days" end, singing from inside its noble sadness. His guitar on 'You Really Got Me' sounds like some Gothic machine crunching through its gears, quite beautiful, while Ray still shouts, "Oh, no!" as he did falling away from the mic when The Kinks gave themselves a future in 1964.

The final songs they recorded, in Konk in March 1996, finish their final record. They sound almost as live as the rest, modern production's gloss removed at the last. 'Animal' has already been mentioned. 'To The Bone' is its companion piece, about "a guy who arrives home after a long tour", Ray wrote in the liner notes, to find his girlfriend has left, leaving only an old Kinks record. The lyric mentions a double album, so *Preservation Act 2* may be all the poor soul has for comfort. As he plays the record "the needle cut just like a nail", and visions rear up of a past when the music "covered up the screams" of arguments, and ecstasy too. A stalking bass-line and Indian-style guitar match 'Did Ya' as tremendous late work by a band about to vanish. In a wonderful video seen by almost no one for a single which was never released, Ray plays the song's subject as a moustached, worn-out old hippie, a convincing picture of a man of his age without his youth-preserving talent, looking back on life with his lover as a Kinks record spins. When this one ends, the band becomes a memory.

"*To The Bone*'s a good record. We made it here," Ray says, glancing around Konk. "I'd like to have made more Kinks records. But it became more difficult. And records are quite easy to make – when you've got a bunch of people who want to work together. I think the band had had enough. If I hadn't done so much with my solo tours, and come back a year or two afterwards, we might have given it another shot. Dave was living in America. Me and him were doing OK. And then I started my solo record, and that's where the trouble started."

To fulfil an obligation to EMI for one more album, Ray in fact tried to instigate a recording by the four original Kinks in 1997. Quaife, his brother David remembers, was desperate for it to happen. Dave wasn't, perhaps explained by what became the current Kinks' final meeting, symbolically held at the Clissold Arms on February 3, 1997. "The last time we were all together was at my 50th birthday party," Dave told the *Mail On Sunday*'s Rebecca Hardy. "Ray had the money and I didn't, so he offered to throw it for me. Just as I was about to cut the cake, Ray jumped on the table and made a speech about how wonderful he was. He then stamped on my cake."

"The idea of bands is a lot to do with love," Dave considers to me. "You do things you wouldn't normally do when that's there. And when it goes, that's when things go wrong. And that's what's happened to us."

CHAPTER 14

Two Brothers

The Kinks had been out of sight for so long, few people noticed that they had completely disappeared. Ray had a daughter, Eva, with Pat Crosbie, but they quietly divorced around the same time as his band. The 21st century arrived unmarked by Ray's song about the millennium, or the debut solo studio album he'd first announced in 1968. 1998's *The Storyteller* documented his live show, throwing in a couple of new songs – 'The Ballad Of Julie Finkle' and 'London Song'. He'd occasionally crop up on some daytime TV show, trying out the latter and other new work, all sounding too literal to expect he'd ever match The Kinks' magic. But gradually, his shows' stand-up singer reminiscences were abandoned. Still under the radar, Ray recruited a basic rock band to back him in often majestic tributes to his past. Suddenly, *Village Green Preservation Society* songs were placed at the show's heart, 'Celluloid Heroes' was greeted as the heartbreaking hit it should have been, and choice obscurities unplayed for decades showed the breadth of his achievement. At the Queen Elizabeth Hall on London's South Bank in 2002, I saw 'Waterloo Sunset' greeted by the crowd as a hymn of soul-clutching beauty, causing tears to pour. Ray ran across the stage shaking outstretched hands at the end, as if at a revival meeting for himself. Leaving The Kinks had, it seemed, let him realise what they'd done.

"Am I going to pursue this solo career, or shall I just go and live in Ireland where my daughter was?" is how Ray looks back on the fork in his road ten years on. "I chose the career. And in some respects I regret it. But that pivotal move was a big decision, because I had to reinvent myself. So there was a focus on it."

These shows would grow in size and strength throughout the decade, till Ray regularly played the Royal Albert Hall. New songs such as 'Stand Up Comic' and 'After The Fall' were tried each time, and not shamed by his classics. Sometime around the start of the century, Ray also quietly left London, for the third time, after his adventures in New York and Cork. He moved to the place where the American music he loved began, New Orleans. "Sometimes you get a quiet moment..." he told me of his city in the 2000s. "The rest of the time, it's being strangled. Too few people with too much wealth. It's becoming a place for the mega-rich, London. And I don't include me! When I left for New Orleans I was writing songs like 'Yours Truly, Confused, N10', 'London Song', 'Aggressive', 'What's Becoming Of My Country?' I wanted to keep some of the love I had for London, and the best way to do it was from afar. When they were doing the mayor thing [in 2000], I thought about getting a group of people together to be a mayor, rather than a dictator. I felt really strong about it. That's one of the reasons I moved."

But still there was no album, as record labels and years were burned through. ("I had a problem with Capitol Records," he told Peter Doggett of the latest contract casualty in 2002. "I didn't trust them.") The constitutional prevarication which gripped him in Konk with The Kinks had multiplied, now even they weren't there to answer to.

"Oh, Ray's such a drama queen, he really is," Dave laughs when I meet him in 2004 on the release of *Bug*, a diverse, melodic and humorous exploration of spiritual beliefs which are also radically political. Free of Ray, he reveals distrust not just of the authority his brother refuses, but the whole notion of objective reality, dismissed as media and government-enforced. And then, the simply affecting 'Fortis Green' matches memories of his childhood to a gorgeous brass band tune – a Kinks track only lacking the band. The album's rough around the edges and most other places but, unlike Ray's, it's out. "I wish he'd let me mix it," Dave says. "It would've been out two years ago. And he would have hated it."

In 2010 Dave brought up Ray stamping on his birthday cake as the catalyst in his total refusal to reform The Kinks. That day in 2004, he couldn't wait. "The end of last year, we got together, and we were writing some songs," he says. "He's got to get this solo album out. But there's this track on it, and he keeps asking me to play on it. And I say, 'I will, but why don't we use it as the start of a Kinks album?' If we're going to do it, we should do it. As time goes by, I think it'd be really silly and bad not to. And I thought, 'This is cool, maybe we really should.' And then the shooting happened. One of my sons showed me the headline in *The Sun*: 'You Really Shot Me'..."

"I was in a lift in New York City and wanted to go to the 50th floor," Ray had told an interviewer on his longed for return to America in 1969. "A woman came in and wanted to go to the basement and I said, 'I was here first, I want the 50th,' and she said, 'Sue me.' Great. I like that. A lot more casual, the Americans."

Sometimes they just shoot you, the interviewer told him.

"In England they just let you live," he laughed, unconcerned. "That's the best way to die. The deadest way."

On January 4, 2004, walking on Burgundy Street near New Orleans' French Quarter with his girlfriend, two young men snatched her purse at gunpoint. Ray, 59, but still acting instinctively as if he was at home and young, chased them. He was shot in the leg. He was treated at the Louisiana Medical Center and released the next day, it was announced. "The wound was quite clean," he had someone at Konk declare. "Luckily nothing was broken and they say he should be fine." The only truth in those sunny statements, it would gradually become clear, was the bullet that tore through his leg. He has yet to fully recover.

When I meet Ray at Konk six months later, days after talking to his brother, his hand keeps worrying at his leg, the way you might to a phantom, amputated limb. Talking earlier on the phone, he had sounded faded and weak. He has, I realise much later, only just left a New Orleans hospital where he might have died. Had he paused before giving chase? "All I'll say is, like everybody else, you never know what you'll do until you're in that situation. I wouldn't normally have thought I was the sort of person who'd have a death wish. I certainly don't have a death wish."

Had there been physical or psychic shock? "I haven't started thinking about that. I've made lots of notes. There are a lot of issues to deal with. It's put my life back, as well as the record. People don't realise how six months can take such a lump out of anything... not just me. Work, other people's lives around me. When I was in the hospital recovering, all these bloody songs were going round my head, like a documentary. I get wrapped up in my music, and it's never complete until the record's finished, and I can walk away from it. It's still tormenting me, saying, 'Get the bloody thing finished.' It's been," he says with understatement, "a troubled project."

When we next meet in 2006, in a cafe in Highgate which Ray enters in a manner as sideways as his smile, the album's done. *Other People's Lives* is his strongest set of songs since *State Of Confusion*, let down only by politeness in production and playing with no Kinks to rough it up. As Ray turns 62, his troubles, and refusal to bow to them, haven't changed. 'After The Fall' and 'All She Wrote' are among songs maybe mourning his latest marriage, often with rueful humour. 'The Getaway (Lonesome Train)' is a languid blues about the need to escape which took him to his fate in New Orleans. 'The Tourist', beginning in the crackle of police radios, has an interloper like him "checking out the slums with my plastic visa" as the night around him gets "restless". He looks diminished seen from the outside by unimpressed natives of New Orleans, or anywhere, as he searches for a new place to call home. 'Thanksgiving Day' is a more closely observed American song than those on *Low Budget*, watching a man "estranged in isolation at a truckstop" and a lonely, praying spinster on the country's day of family reunions. In 'Is There Life After Breakfast?' he's taking pills with his restorative tea now, steeling himself for another day. 'Stand Up Comic' allows him a crudely aggressive persona absent from the craft elsewhere, with which to mourn the loss of style and manners: "the little bit we had was all that we had", he movingly states of his working-class generation. 'Over My Head' recalls 'Quiet Life', asking the world to please let him alone as he tries to hide from it, and his friends to stick by him.

"With age, one becomes more innocent, and a little bit more vulnerable," he tells me of his changes. "But then that's when something happens to your chromosomes, like me, and you have complete inability to assess what your emotions are. I'm less cynical than I was when I was 25. I'm more innocent. The last year's been a rebirth. Any time you go into a hospital in a life-threatening situation, and unfortunately I've had that on three occasions on my life, so far – so I've got six to go – you always say to yourself, 'Now, it's a fresh start'. Then you gradually creep into all the old errors. But this is staying with me a lot longer, because I'm older and closer to mortality. And I was going through unbelievable personal changes before I was shot."

Most of *Other People's Lives*, though, was written before his New Orleans experiences. That, and the next album about it, fill his thoughts. "Being shot changes you," he says. "The care changed me, because it's frightening, the facilities are so bad there. It must be similar to being shot in a shanty town in Johannesburg. It's almost Third World conditions – and that was before Katrina. So that aspect scared me. And the fact that in New Orleans, witnesses get shot, it's not uncommon for people to go back and finish the job, when the police are involved, and there wasn't very good security at the hospital. And the lack of regard by the police, who gave me a really hard time, because I had the audacity to chase the person. It would've been easier if I'd been dead, then I could just be a statistic. It was not a very pleasant stay. I told the hospital to say it was a flesh wound, and I've gone back to England, and they did, and everyone believed it. I actually stayed incognito with some friends. I think I'm pretty well over it. I won't know till I go back. I'm not afraid of anyone or anything when I get there, except myself. And I can deal with that, I think. I'm not afraid of what I'll see [after 2005's Hurricane Katrina], because I think I know what I'll see. It's off the headlines of the world, and the same old crap's going on. And I'll be very disappointed if they haven't helped the poorer communities. We'll see about the culture.

"I went through a mad phase of having success in America," he considers of the country that is so central to The Kinks, in often awful ways. "But America always takes back everything it gives you. Maybe I should stick to going to Disneyland for my holidays like everybody else. That's what America's given us, entertainment – but at the same time it's trivialised our lives. It's turned us into a sitcom, 10-minute segments of life. Thank God soccer never gave in. It's still 45 minutes a half."

In 2007 the second album, *Working Man's Cafe*, is done. We meet again, in Ray's publicist's office in St. John's Wood. He has driven up from Cornwall that day. He's tired but his mind is happily restless. The light in the room isn't on when we begin. Evening dark falls around us as he talks in a carelessly exposed way he hasn't before. "If this album was a book," he says, "it would start off with Blair getting elected. I've never wanted to leave England, but I was going to. We'd just gone through all those years of Thatcher. But," Ray almost whispers, "I thought he was *worse*. And I really do feel bad about that, because I was brought up to admire Aneurin Bevan. When John Smith died, I was living in Surrey, and I went to Ockham parish church and said a prayer. Not because I was sad, but because I was concerned about what would happen. A certain kind of politics ended with him. Blair, he seemed to come from nowhere. Then what amazed me was a lot of people in my industry going to Downing Street. In that decade, I did get an award from the Queen [a CBE in 2004], but that was a day out for my sister and my daughter. What concerned me was everyone suddenly saying, 'It *will* be optimistic, it will be good, because there's nothing else.' So I made a half-hearted attempt to leave England, fucked it up royally, and ended up running off to America with this broad, and getting shot. And getting shot," he repeats grimly. "But there's nothing we could have done about it, it was inevitable."

'Morphine Song' on the album, sluggish as if under that drug with the beat of a heart that may stop, recounts his time in a "charity ward" afterwards, where "nobody visits, nobody grieves". "The lyric's the draft I wrote in hospital, as I saw it, on a notepad. I was in a ward with four other people. There was a poor, psychotic man next to me, I think a drug case. Brenda the alkie. She was giving me tips about which hospitals to get more morphine at. I hope it's not too self-pitying. It's a real instance. Even in that state, in the emergency room, my instinct to get something that half-worked down was still there. That kept my head together. I think what I've evolved at over the years is that my songwriting has become my ally through life. Because I ain't got much else. That sounds stupid to say. But basically, that's about it."

Jerome Barra, 28, was arrested and charged for armed robbery and aggravated battery. But the case was closed after Ray twice failed to appear at his trial as Louisiana law requires, in 2005 and July 2007. "I've cut two big songs about my anger with the New Orleans police department," he says. "Because I didn't turn up, because I was touring [court records show Ray was given two months' notice on the second occasion], the DA said, [in a Southern accent], 'Yeah, we've got a shooter, but we don't have a victim'. The guy had confessed already. They blamed me for getting shot. They prefer you to get shot, and get finished off. 'I'm A Victim' has been cut, and 'Angola', which is about being on the wrong side of the law. It was a hard song to write, because I wanted not to blame, but to write about a situation that ordinary people could get drawn into. And the law can go either way. I was in that predicament for a long time." Slipped onto *Working Man's Cafe*'s US vinyl release, 'Angola' finds Ray "lying in bed waiting for the drip to feed", but only uses four lines to rail against being left to "rot". The rest sympathises with the wrongfully accused – the fear which harried the dreams of Alfred Hitchcock, another brilliant working-class Londoner with a terror of authority. Ray too, it seems. His writer friend Barrie Keeffe remembers being stopped for possible speeding, with Ray in the car. The interrogation petered out, as the discomfited cops realised Ray had his own notebook out, and was recording every word they said.

'Working Man's Cafe' is by contrast an anthem for a lost British national culture. Ray again walks through a phantom London, buying designer trousers in the mall where he remembers a fruit-and-veg stall, seeing American consumerism and Internet cafe alienation everywhere. The working-class community of his youth, the gatherings in greasy spoons, has disappeared. He tries to understand the changes, but once more makes his stand on the other side of the line: "And if you forget my face," he sings as a challenge, "If you forget just who I am/ I'm the kid with the greasy spoon firmly held in my hand."

"A lot of that is from feeling alienated in America," he admits. "I used to go to a cafe like that with my brother where my mum worked. We'd have lunch there instead of school dinners. I was abroad, and looking for somewhere homely to have a cup of tea. And I was inspired by searching for my brother [to meet] this year – and the remembrance of going to that place when we were young, and having it all to look forward to. And now, after his illness, and me, on my constant quest for God knows what, I got on the mobile and said, 'I can't fucking find any fucking place to meet. There's not even a café here.' I said, 'I'll call you when I've found it.' I was looking for one that was a good place to meet when I was an art student. I was looking for a sign somewhere that I fit in."

When we spoke the year before, another sort of alienation and haunting came up: the way he was moving towards the time of life he imagined in *X-Ray*. The monstrous, decrepit 70-year-old doppelganger he created for himself, R.D., was now too close for comfort. His 1998 introduction to his book *Waterloo Sunset* also alludes to characters escaping their songs and overwhelming him. He said much the same in an interview with Barbara Charone in 1976. Dave has the reputation for supernatural beliefs, but Ray too sometimes feels he deals with literal demons. "I do feel closer to R.D. now," he said. "I do interviews sometimes in that room in Konk where I mix, as he does. It's becoming so uncannily close to reality it's not true. That's what's giving me a real problem over the record I'm writing now [referring to *Working Man's Cafe*]. I'm writing my own fate, and I just don't know what to do about it. My face doesn't frighten me now I'm older. I'm frightening me. My work is frightening me. Because it's gone beyond just writing songs. Something weird happened to me. I don't know who's driving what. I think it happened because I was writing a solo record, and I tried to write about me, rather than other people. It showed me how much about myself I don't deal with. I can't deal with it in the real world, I deal with it in my songs."

It's a fraught state not uncommon to many good fiction writers I know, otherwise rational people who've spoken of psychic dreams and characters living inside their minds. There's a reason the doppelganger, often a character hunting down his author, is so common in fiction. A song on *Working Man's Cafe*, 'Imaginary Man', tries to confront and explain Ray's fears, as well as his alienated state in America. The "imaginary man" is the imagination in his head which has taken him so far from where he began in Denmark Terrace, and let him do so many extraordinary things. There's also the sense that he has now become imaginary himself: a displaced phantom, the rootlessness he felt taking effect when he wrote *Muswell Hillbillies* in 1971 now total.

"I'm trying not to be so spooked out by art, and what it means," Ray says in 2007. "Because I believe in so much subtlety and nuance, innuendo, suspicion and superstition, and if you get carried away, it becomes overwhelming. I'm trying not to think that way. I'm trying to think it's just a song.

"'Imaginary Man' is not about someone who doesn't exist, it's someone who's forgotten his values, and me saying to myself that you've gone to New Orleans, yes, played with the Preservation Hall [jazz] band, it's all good. But you do exist, you don't have to go all this way to find yourself. And the more you seek, the more you become imaginary, trying so hard to exist in that culture. You try to escape, but where are you running to? It's like one of those horror movies where you're running away from the monster, and the door closes and it's in the next room. What are you running away from? When I was experiencing the 'Imaginary Man' moment, I didn't have John Dalton, The Kinks' old bass player, who didn't change his clock from UK time, to keep reminding me of who I was. I went to New Orleans to try and have a new life there. But people want to hear what you are, not what you want to become. The New Orleans thing started for me with the trad music at the Highgate jazz club. And in a way, that's what it always will be."

Was Ray ever able to simply enjoy a happy home? When he first moved into 87 Fortis Green with his young family, could he close the door, and be content?

"I wanted to. But I knew I couldn't. I really wish, later in life, that I could have that now. But I'm still living out of bags." He glances down at the one by his feet. "I really do respect them, with their homes, and their organised lives, and they make arrangements to have holidays together. You know, doing this record and touring this year, I've had no life, at all. I took the challenge on, and did it, for silly reasons, really. I wanted to show that I could do it. I was in terrible shape and I was told to take a year off, and ended up making another album. Because I would have been so tense after a year off. And I think if I hadn't made this record quickly, I'd never make another record. The speed coming into this project, it's like the body's not dead yet. I'm trying to slow down. That's why I went away for a few days to Cornwall.

"Tidy lives, and organised people – I would like that," he murmurs. "And I long for that. But if I got it, I'd get bored with it. What I'm finding sad now is that there aren't many reasons to hold me in that street I wrote about in 'Autumn Almanac'. I think I knew I'd never find my Shangri-La. So I'm looking for new horizons."

In the middle of his latest turmoil, and listening back to his album, Ray knew what he needed most of all in 2007: The Kinks. "In Nashville where I made *Working Man's Cafe*," he says, "I would tell musicians, I want you to play these chords as if you've never played them before. They didn't know what I was on about. The band understood everything I did. I miss the camaraderie and teamwork of The Kinks. It's like acting in a film. The session musicians get the script, and they're in it for that scene. The Kinks were all in the same movie all of the time. Whether they say it or not, we had virtually the same agenda. There was a sensibility: 'We wanna say this, regardless.' What's missing from the world now without The Kinks is realism. Even rawness can be manufactured, like the situation with Amy Winehouse recently, which got her on the front pages for a few more days. Regardless of the poor girl's situation, it's fake. With The Kinks, there'd always be something unexpected. There aren't too many bands like The Kinks around. Band records always seem more important. It's a lot to do with not being able to articulate what I want. Then The Kinks play it, and it sounds the way it should."

A few days after I spoke to Dave in 2004, he suffered his own physical cataclysm. On June 30, he was felled by a massive stroke. Dave's PR, Alan Robinson, picked him up at his son Christian's house near Fortis Green at 8am that day, with a packed schedule ahead. The first stop was Danny Baker's show, at Radio London in Marylebone High Street. Dave, though "carrying a bit of weight", was on "very good form", Robinson remembers. Next was Phil Jupitus's Radio 6 Music show at Broadcasting House in Great Portland Street. Robinson left Dave to it, and parked the car. Then he took the lift to the studio on the fifth floor. "The doors opened, and the first thing I saw was Dave, a couple of inches away, falling on top of me. He just kept saying, 'I've got to get out, I've got to get out, something's wrong.' Oh, Christ... he looked very, very pale. And his son Christian who was with him was obviously very concerned. It was rapidly apparent as we got out into the street that something was gravely wrong. He staggered round into Great Portland Street, and he was sat in the doorway of a pub called the Horse and Groom, and Christian said, 'Phone for an ambulance,' and I did. The stroke, the infarction, must have just kicked in during that interview. I did think when he collapsed, 'Fuck me, I've killed a Kink.' Because some people collapse in on themselves when they get really ill. And Dave literally looked about half his size."

In 2011, Dave remembers how he survived. "It was like my whole world was turned upside down. I thought that I'd already been through turmoil. But this was like nothing else. Because I had no control whatsoever over it. We pretend when we're doing OK that we have some control of our lives. We don't, on any level. But it's funny – at the weakest and most vulnerable I've ever felt, I felt the most helped. By the spiritual information that I'd gleaned. By the trees outside the ward, that made me feel great, and a certain male nurse who'd look round the door and smile at me. You'd see someone else walk by, and feel shit and saggy and grey. You're in a zone of hypersensitivity."

His guitar helped save Dave again. Playing the chords of songs such as 'You Really Got Me' as he'd done so often before became, like the lives of both brothers, a process of stubbornly sticking at it. "When I was in the hospital, I couldn't move my hand properly, and the therapy guy told me about muscle memory. So I'd take the guitar to bed with me, and put the hands on the strings, so I felt that when I slept, part of my mind would reconnect with the strings. It does. The subconscious can play havoc with our lives, but it can also be programmed to make them big and rich." Though he hasn't yet had medical permission to play live, *Fractured Mindz* (2007) began a fresh stream of albums.

Dave lives far from the old Village Green now, or perhaps all the way into it, in Devon's real countryside, where Julien Temple filmed him for his 2011 BBC documentary, *Dave Davies: Kinkdom Come*. "The reason I moved here in the first place is because it's so desolate," Dave says in it, a lone figure in the Exmoor wilds, thatched cottage on the horizon, a timeless English scene empty of other Englishmen to prick his tranquility. Temple can think of other reasons for his exile. "He had a lot of demons to get away from, didn't he? And he likes the distance between him and Ray."

"Here we go again," is how Ray remembered reacting to the news of the stroke. "I was very concerned. But when I knew he was safe and out of danger, I thought, 'This is a great opportunity for him to reassess and re-evaluate his life.' I'm not saying everyone should get shot, or everyone should have strokes. But now he's recovering he can address issues that I know have been haunting him. The world doesn't know it, but I know what he's been going through for the last ten years. Now he's recovered, I hope he's on the mend, physically and psychologically."

Dave's memory of staying with his brother immediately after his stroke, as Ray had with him when Rasa then Hynde left, is bitter. "I was ill in bed and could barely move," he told the *Mail On Sunday*'s Rebecca Hardy, "but he started screaming in pain from his stomach. A doctor from Harley Street came round at 3am and said, 'There's nothing wrong with your stomach.' He just wanted attention." Whether Dave's interpretation is true or not, this biliously hostile story shows sickness hadn't brought the brothers together. They met in 2008, to discuss Ray's plans for the Kinks reunion he pined for. Avory was acquiescent, Quaife again keen. Dave wasn't. They haven't seen each other since. They had privately sworn to themselves to look after each other when they were children in an already hostile world. Entering old age, they didn't even speak.

"They're both melancholy people," Bob Henrit says, pondering the differences which have become so intractable. "Ray is sardonic. Dave is cheerful. Depressed? I've been with Russ Ballard during his depression. We'd be walking round New York, and he just kept crying. I never saw that with Ray or Dave. If they were depressed, they kept it to themselves. Which is pretty difficult to do. Ray has more subterfuge about him. Dave wears his heart on his sleeve. A spade was worse than a spade with Dave, it was a cunt."

"They always used to work together, getting the best sounds for the records," Avory considers. "But as time went on, Dave thought, 'Everything's *Ray*, and I never get a look in.' But if you can't do it on your own, you've got to be part of something. Sometimes Ray probably just treated Dave like a normal, extra musician. Didn't mean to be that way, just because he was so absorbed in his music and getting it done."

"It's sad, because he's many times taken delight in keeping me under his thumb," Dave says, "or repressing certain creative inclinations I might have. Maybe there's still time for it all to get worked out. But so many times when he could have acted with more grace... but then, I might not have got interested in all the stuff I did. So who knows? Maybe that was part of the staging of the musical."

"I asked Ken Jones why Ray hated Dave so much," Michael Farady puts in. "He said Ray always thought Dave was romancing Chrissie, who lived nearby." There's absolutely no evidence or likelihood that such a thing ever happened. But it is exactly the sort of suspicion siblings have. It puts a new light on Ray raging, "It's all your fault!" at Dave after the break-up.

Both brothers carried literal wounds now. But the psychological ones of their teenage years were at least partially healed. Dave had finally been reunited with Sue in 1993, when she wrote to say his daughter Tracey, now 30, wished to see him. They spent as much time as they could together in subsequent weeks, crying and reminiscing. "We gave something back to each other," Dave wrote in *Kink*, "that had been missing in both of us for 30 years."

Ray lanced the trauma of his sister Rene's death when he was 13 (not seemingly an active hurt by now anyway) in his third musical, *Come Dancing*. It had been worked on almost since he wrote the song; Paul Sirett was his collaborator by the time it premiered on September 13,

2008 at the Theatre Royal, Stratford East. It's set in the nearby Ilford Palais in the late fifties, as rock music starts to replace the local dance bands. Ray sang and narrated each night. Rose and Arthur are among the characters. Its heroine, Julie, limps with polio, recalling Ray's sister Peggy's damaged arm. And like Rene, she dies on the dance floor. Ray's hand stretches towards her as she freezes in her tragic, dying fall, as if he can reach across time and touch his real lost sister right now. 'Come Dancing' in this context becomes agonisingly poignant. More even than in his Kinks songs (the others for this musical aren't his best), *Come Dancing* peoples the stage with his past. When I bump into Ray at the bar afterwards, he's delighted at the weeping wreck he's made of me.

He tells me he "didn't exactly research it, but drew on a well of experiences and stories I'd heard about the dance halls." Henrit believes this was Ray's blotting-paper mind, silently absorbing the world of The Kinks. "We had often spoken in the band about where we grew up," he says. "We were all from a certain part of North London, and around when Palais bands were at the top of the tree. We would if we were lucky be able to play at Gaumont cinemas during the interval, and we might find our way onto a Mecca ballroom stage. It was at the same time that fortunate people were leaving London for the garden cities. There were all these pressures on us when we were growing up, and Ray managed to incorporate every single one of them into *Come Dancing*."

Ray and Dave were damaged. Pete Quaife was the first Kink to die. He had lived in Canada since 1981, turning up at Kinks gigs when they were in town. He was diagnosed with end stage renal failure in 1998, requiring kidney dialysis, and moved back to Denmark in 2004. "He done his best," says David Melville-Quaife. "He just soldiered through. He knew he was dying, as soon as he started. He brought out the book *The Lighter Side Of Dialysis,* he was so bored with it. And you know as soon as you go in there – Oh, shit, I'm dying. How long's it going to take?"

Pete Quaife died on June 23, 2010, aged 66. In March 2011, the first volume of his novel *Veritas* was published in the UK. It confirms Ray's belief that The Kinks all had the same agenda; that the original band, anyway, fought the same battle. Quaife draws hugely on the background he shared with them, beginning with his parents' generation. It's a proud and angry compendium of working-class culture either side of the war, presented as a self-sufficient if penniless kingdom in which families gather over copious cups of tea in the kitchen. Middle-class interaction is restricted to medical emergencies and council snoopers. Quaife describes the musical development of his surrogate, Marcus, as he forms a group very like the early Kinks, with mystical intensity. This would surprise Ray, who seems firmly to believe his old bassist was mainly in it for swinging laughs.

Ray's tribute at the Glastonbury Festival four days after Quaife's death, though, could not have been more heartfelt. "Without Pete, I don't think I would have been here today," he said, dedicating 'See My Friends' to him. After 'Waterloo Sunset' is dedicated to Quaife and The Kinks, Ray mouths to the band that 'Days' is next. Then as he starts he finds his eyes misted with tears. Wiping his nose and shoving a hand in his pocket he bravely makes himself keep going. He glances at the sky, then inward, singing: "And though you're gone, you're with me every single day, believe me." He had written 'Days', he claimed, about the death of a friendship, and of the old band. Now it lent itself to the death of a friend, who had been bored to tears recording it. That didn't lessen Ray's goodbye.

"I looked at some footage of that period," says Dave, "and me and Pete were really bonded. Which I only realised after Pete died. We formed the nucleus of the band's energy, when Ray was still honing his craft. And without us being there, I don't think Ray would have had the inner strength to carve out those ideas. When Pete died I did a lot of reflection. And I played 'I'm Not Like Everybody Else' and Pete made lots of these little – not fluffs, they're colouration if you like. Him being nervous about a note throws you off, generates a different energy. They're perfect." Melville-Quaife's belief about the damage Dave may have unknowingly done to his brother doesn't dismiss this tribute, either.

Near the end of 2010, I was shocked to hear from someone who'd just had a meeting with him that Ray himself "didn't look long for this world". A US tour had just been cancelled on medical advice, but he was still scheduled to play London's Royal Festival Hall a few days later, on December 20. Watching that night, I was deeply relieved. "Trying to cut down on the meds," he says dryly after a small early slip, but it's a splendid, wide-ranging show, in which 'Imaginary Man' is transformed from an unexceptional record into a new anthem for Ray, and he looks as content and alive as someone can be when the crowd sing 'Sunny Afternoon'. It seems impossible to believe that he could have been any more than under the weather. It later becomes clear this was a Piaf-like effort of will. The gunshot was still trying to get him. "It's been pretty bad, actually," he told Q. "I got quite sick before Christmas from residue [of the bullet] that is still in the leg and which formed a clot. It made me quite ill and I was hospitalised for a bit. To put it politely, I don't think it was handled very well at the time... partly due to the nature of the gunshot wound. It was a zigzag bullet." To *Rolling Stone* he added: "It was scary... mortality flashed before me." This was perhaps the fourth of his nine lives.

Julien Temple filmed him during this illness, for the BBC documentary *Imaginary Man*. It's a character study of Ray, which Temple followed with his one on Dave; steps towards his most cherished project, a feature film on the brothers' relationship, and attack on post-war pop culture, to be called *You Really Got Me*. "He's one of those characters who when they get on stage pull it all together," Temple says. "He wasn't very well, and I was forcing him to do hours of interviews that he could have done without. But he broke through the pain barrier and really delivered."

Much of the film follows Ray's back, wrapped in long coat, hat and scarf, wandering through his patch. "I tried to get a Magritte-like sense of this figure in North London, gliding unseen through the dawn netherworld, because London is so different before the cars and people start moving. The first day, 6 am, I pulled up and he was already there in his costume. Then the next day: 'Nah, I'm not doing that again.' You never knew whether he'd be there, or whether he'd be into it. I took a lot of punishment to get to what he wants to say, because he's unique in his acuteness. His alienation from everyday life makes him pretty clear in his take on the world because he sees it from the outside. He's still really subversive, unlike most of his generation."

Temple thinks he understands Ray's failure to turn up for things and the attendant seeming hypochondria, even when lead isn't clogging his blood. "A lot of the problems are not unconnected with insomnia, and not being able to sleep. It's part of the make-up of his very, very active mind processes, where if you happen to wake up in the middle of the night thinking of those things, then you won't go back to sleep. In that state, people have all sorts of problems in the day. When I have that, I don't want to go the meetings, but I tend to. Ray might not."

Might it also go back to Ray's need for total freedom, and so control? To not do something because it's demanded? "Yeah. It's a personal state of anarchy."

Most of the shots of "Ray" wandering the North London wilds are actually Temple in Kink disguise. It's also him slipping in and out of 87 Fortis Green's front door. He waited with Ray's daughter Louisa one day, to film Ray in the house which had once meant the world to him. He didn't revisit that past, much to the disappointment of the current owner, who'd hoped to have a photo taken with him in their mutual home. By an odd coincidence, she works for breakfast TV, where Ray appeared a few days later, promoting his new album, *See My Friends*. With layers of 'Picture Book'-style absurdity only Ray can provide, she shows me a photo of him smiling with her and a photo of 87 Fortis Green.

When *Imaginary Man* was screened Ray popped into the Clissold Arms, either to see if anyone was watching, or to avoid seeing his performance. That's where I make my last visit to the neighbourhood, for the *Veritas* book launch on March 27, 2011. John Dalton is there, still looking like an entirely affable Paul McCartney. So is one of The Kinks' long-time backing singers, once a pregnant schoolgirl in *Schoolboys In Disgrace*. Pete Quaife and The Kinks' generation of North Londoners, their children and grandchildren, reclaim the now gentrified Davies local for the evening. After a while, there's a singalong to old Kinks songs. It's the first day of British Summer Time, and as they sing 'See My Friends' when the sun starts to set, I look through the big window at 6 Denmark Terrace, directly opposite. The blinds are down, so I can't see inside the front room. I think how astonishing the lives that led from there have been.

The next time I meet Ray, it's the winter of 2012. His long project to establish himself as a solo performer recently saw him sing 'Waterloo Sunset' to millions at the August 12 Closing Ceremony of London's hugely successful Olympics, a natural choice now for great national occasions. Still, petty regulations in London's grand St. Pancras Renaissance hotel leave us perched close together on a long seat in its lobby, alongside a dozen others. Ray isn't noticed. He keeps a plastic bag close, containing stiff-backed envelopes and scraps of projects. His eyes scan the crowd for song-subjects. Despite the hair that is probably dyed and finally thinning at age 68, with his curiosity and jumbled possessions he still acts like a teenage art student. "I'm the most unsettled I've ever been in my life," he says, "but creatively vibrant." He's living in a Highgate house he doesn't call a home, with bare, depersonalised walls concerned friends tried to cover with pictures, to his amusement. He's in the mood to look back at what he's done.

"Last night, I couldn't sleep, and I put on *Muswell Hillbillies*," he begins. "I really love the album, and there are gems on all those albums. It's great to have 'Sunny Afternoon' and 'You Really Got Me', but I'm discovering the value of the unheard work now. Good and bad. The Kinks failed more than any other group. We had our ups and downs, erratic chart success. But they were not failures. They were just either not mixed properly, or not in tune with what people wanted. But the body of work, anything from 'Creeping Jean' to 'Death Of A Clown', from 'Autumn Almanac' to 'Mick Avory's Underpants', deserves to be noted. A lot of what I've written, and a lot of what other people have written, not just The Kinks, they show the times. If anyone's interested in the sixties through to the present, this is part of it. It's part of how society works. And it's connected to a larger thing. It's this country we live in, and how some people survived it, and how we made our way through our career."

Ray's past is all around him at Konk and elsewhere, scattered across a chaos of unmarked tape-cans and hard-drives. "I don't have to write another song for the rest of my life," he admits. "I've got a back-log to be finished. Because I'm a bad sleeper, fast thinker, but I don't catalogue everything. I was in Konk yesterday, trying to find a demo I did around 2003, but I've lost the hard-drive. I'm still discovering songs that were momentary diversions between writing the big albums. There's a track called 'Affluent Despair' from the early eighties. That's the title on the box, because I hadn't worked out the song completely, and the engineer said, 'How do you want the band to play it?' I said, 'With a sort of affluent despair', and he wrote it down. It wasn't the title at all. You know, towards the end of his life, Anthony Burgess put the time and date on everything he wrote. I think I should start doing that. I want to still raid the archives and get some of these tracks down. But there's not enough time left in my life to play it all."

Still, more songs pour out of Ray, his latest insomniac bout caused not by *Muswell Hillbillies'* loveliness, but a new work that's still thrilling him when we meet.

"It's strange, yesterday, I got an idea for this song in Marks and Spencer's," he says, "and it brought back a chemical reaction – that's the way the brain works, I'm not a doctor – to something that happened 10 years ago. Then I went home, and a melody came, and I wrote words to it. And I thought, 'If I get this right, this'll be on the same sort of level as something like 'Oklahoma USA'.'"

He considers how creating such a song feels. "It is a feeling like, in really ridiculous terms, the moment you sip the first pint. You think, 'This is going down well, what's it going to end up like?' It's a moment of excessive emotion. I do get very emotional when I write, sometimes. And I had that last night. It's just a chill you get. You think, 'Ah, this is something somebody's never done quite this way before, and it's coming from me, and I have a voice.' When I had that idea last night I was meant to go to sleep, because I had an appointment earlier this morning – but no, I've got to put this down to tape and at least write an outline of it. I've done this for 48 years, and it's still a discovery to me. That's what I find disturbing, and a release."

When we spoke around the time of *Other People's Lives* in 2006, I remind him, he said he'd been reborn. Has that lasted into 2012?

"From when I got shot? I had a set of ambitions I wanted to achieve after that incident, and I've still got three of them to fulfil. A contemporary film drama, maybe a book I started 10 years ago that's all over the place, that puts everything in perspective. And an opera using some characters in *Come Dancing* that's due in two years. Now I've completed the cycle from when I pursued going solo in some respects, and I'm finishing off the things that I wanted to do along the way. But you know the future's very short, and maybe I should take on partners to help me. Maybe I should be like [Renaissance artist] Raphael, who employed people to paint the blue sky, and collaborate more. Maybe the reason things weren't finished is that I didn't have collaborators. In *X-Ray*, the grizzly old songwriter leaves the casket of work to the young boy to complete. I'd just hate all the little bits I'm working on to be unfulfilled in my lifetime."

There's a similar feeling of sands perceptibly running down when Ray talks about Konk, the sale price of which, £1.5 million, was slashed then quietly abandoned. "I was just making new plans for it yesterday," he says. "We're going to put on a little art exhibit in one of the rec rooms. And the bands there at the moment are all kids, all under 30, and they're just banging it out. So there's a creative society there. I'm passing the baton. Thinking of the Olympics, I was the last leg of the relay at school. And the sportsmaster said, 'You're going last. Not because you're the fastest, but because when you're in front, you don't let anyone overtake you.' But now I can pass the baton."

Ray's own Olympics saw him driven onto the Stratford stadium's stage in a black cab, and going straight into 'Waterloo Sunset' with an old stager's ease. That isn't how he remembers it. "That was a terrifying day," he shudders, "because I couldn't hear the vocal. I was having a problem with my hearing equipment, and it wasn't working when I was cued to go on, and I said, 'I'm not going on.' 'You've got to go.' 'This isn't fucking well working.' I could just hear this crackling in my ear. And I said, 'Excuse me, it's still not working.' And they slammed the door in my face and drove! I didn't know till I opened my mouth whether anything would come out."

Being kidnapped in a fast car for one of his most high-profile performances ever wasn't Ray's only reservation about the Olympics. *Olympicland*, a questioning look at its legacy, is another of his unfinished projects. And he sees the creep of corporate conformity and greed there and everywhere.

"What's scary is, look at the amount of suits around here," he says, glancing at the guests in the lobby. "These aren't real people. They're real people dressed up as other people. What's really frightening it it's harder for people who want to do things alternatively to this. These people have the right to exist," he says, his voice passionately straining to sympathise, "with their suits and their iPhones, they've got every right to do that. But what's frightening is, that's the only uniform that's accepted now. The Prime Minister wears it. And aspiring young accountants in Sussex wear it. I guess it's always been a uniform mentality. But it's frighteningly so now.

"The scariest thing in the Olympics was not going on-stage in a cab, not knowing whether my microphone was working. The scariest thing was driving from north London through to east London to get there. The amount of poverty in this country, and the growing under-class. All the pomp at the Olympics is wonderful. But I got out of there, and I was in the pub before closing time."

Though Ray's dream of reuniting all the old Kinks is gone, rumours have persisted since 2008 that the band may return. Ray's last two albums, *The Kinks Choral Collection* (2009), with North London's Crouch End Festival Chorus and a surprise, strictly-business cameo from Chrissie Hynde (Ray had wanted Vera Lynn, of course), and the duets album *See My Friends* (2011) revisit their songs. Dave has been apoplectically opposed, telling the *Mail On Sunday*: "The music is so beautiful it shouldn't be tainted. You don't want to see two silly old men in wheelchairs singing 'You Really Got Me'. Ray's an arsehole."

Even in 2012, Ray could imagine them still sparking. "It's possible," he insists. "I remember the last time the original band were all together, at that UK Music Hall of Fame show at the Alexandra Palace [The Kinks were inducted on November 16 2005], there was a chemistry.

And unfortunately we didn't play. If we'd picked up instruments, I'm sure that would've come back." Camden's Roundhouse on October 28, 2007 was the closest he and Dave have come to finding out. "We did the Electric Proms with the BBC's Mark Cooper, a great producer who's always looking for something new, and we nearly got Dave up for a song. But as time goes on, the more remote that possibility seems to be. Me and Dave don't fight at all now. We don't see each other... that's the secret."

In July 2011, Dave had told *NME*'s Matt Wilkinson how that distance could be bridged. "Why can't he just say, 'I would not have been where I am today without Dave?'" he pleaded, uncomprehending. "Could you imagine, even if he didn't mean it, how many cracks that would cover?"

Offered a last lifeline to the reunion he claimed to so want, Ray instinctively slashed it to shreds, unable to admit his dependence. "If I hadn't had Dave as my brother I would have found someone like him," he said with coolly destructive scorn. "He is important to me..." Mick Avory told me the situation, sitting in Konk in March 2011. "We all live separate lives now. I see Ray because I still do stuff down here. Dave buries himself out in the country. Seems to disagree with most things that are laid down. It's all like that at the moment. Ray keeps misleading people, saying we're all going to get together, because he likes to think that we could. But it's not going to happen because you need Dave. I make a little bit of difference, but Dave would make a lot. You could do something on record, we've got plans for that," he says tantalisingly, "but everything you try to do is hard work. It's one against the other all the time, there's *issues*," he says, suddenly boiling over with frustration. "Why can't we just *do it* like we used to, and sort out what we're going to do with it afterwards? If Dave and he don't agree with something, Ray knows in the end that he's his brother, and he's got to consider him. They've got to agree on it, and I'll fall in with it."

In a way it doesn't matter, because all The Kinks' music is still here: diligently crafted with fundamental emotions just below the surface; songs born in a hard world which insist on a better one, with an unusual capacity to blindside you with helpless tears at feelings you hadn't noticed were there. One even did so to its writer at Glastonbury. Dave considers his own relation to this sort of art.

"I look at things now I'm 64 that I saw when I was 16," he says, "and they're more illuminating to me. In that initial picking up of the guitar, you feel like the same person you were. When you feel good, you literally feel like that 16-year-old. You do things like playing 'You Really Got Me' that are done over and over again, but they sound fresh. You're playing that G chord – it's got such a lot of content in it, all the shit and all the great stuff, all the joy and all the misery. You get all of that at once. I think the blessing for me and Ray is that we grew up in a family that encouraged that newness. Seeing your kids discover a leaf falling out of a tree for the first time. That event has happened so often. But when a kid or someone you love notices it, the joy starts all over again. It's a continual job to look for those moments. I think the only thing that keeps me alive is looking for that purity. In a tree, or a thunderstorm. There's moments you can see it in Beethoven's music. Maybe three seconds when you're lost in the space that he must have been lost in. Which makes you think, 'That is what I've always been looking for.' Those moments of purity. Maybe this nothing, that we think is nothing, that is beyond our little lives, maybe it's really something."

Songs like 'Waterloo Sunset' and 'Days' let you directly into Ray's purest feelings. Dave now moves from Beethoven to another of his heroes, Tony Hancock, in his film *The Rebel* (1960), where Hancock's character's childish drawings are briefly taken up by pretentious art critics. "I've got a bit of rage about that," he says, not for the first time. "I keep going back to it. I actually liked those silly pictures. What's wrong with a fucking duck in a flat green background? Why can't it just be a scribble on a piece of paper, or a man walking ink across a piece of A4? Why does it have to be what everyone else thinks it should be? I think that The Kinks were never like everybody else. And I think 'I'm Not Like Everybody Else' really does sum up a lot of how Ray is, and how I feel I am."

Defiant?

"Yeah. Things are going to change and fall away and become something else. But passion and the love of creativity doesn't go away.

That's defiance. Defiance for the things that really are important, and not things that fall away. Because if you really think about things – really consider what the human body is, it's a bit scary, it's a weird fleshy robot. But the value of being in it, what you learn, are things to feel defiant about, or maintain, or stubbornly search for."

Talking to Ray about *Muswell Hillbillies* one day, and the relatives and culture it's about that are gone, he says much the same thing.

"I think the secret is knowing what you have is tangible, and understanding that change occurs, and not letting it upset you too much. Because music, great pop music, will endure, and accept that the change is there, but there is also great permanence."

The Kinks' songs are a lasting bulwark against everything they think is wrong in the world. After what they've been through to build it, they need someone to say: God bless The Kinks.

Acknowledgements

My interviews with Ray Davies were conducted between 2004 and 2012, and those with Dave Davies and Mick Avory between 2004 and 2011. Where the date of an interview is relevant, it is included in the text. Elements of some of these interviews were first published in *Uncut* magazine. My thanks to Paul Lester, Allan Jones, Michael Bonner and John Mulvey for commissioning them, and first letting me into The Kinks' remarkable world.

My greatest debt is to Ray, Dave and Mick for being such revealing and passionate witnesses and advocates of their unique story.

Thanks also to Johnny Black of www.rocksourcearchive.com for the generous use of the transcripts of his 2000 interviews with Ray, Dave, Larry Page and especially the late Pete Quaife for *Mojo* magazine, much of them unpublished till now. These are credited in the text, as are all quotes from other sources, where known.

Special thanks to: Stacey Shelley, who understands Waterloo sunsets; Deborah Nash, who saved me from a nasty accident in Highgate; Julien Temple, for Notting Hill insights; Michael Farady, for putting flesh and bone on The Kinks' last years over Sloane Square ciders; David Melville-Quaife, for telling his brother Pete's story; and to: Bob Henrit, Tom Robinson, Chrissie Hynde, Barrie Keeffe, Keith Altham,

Chris Johnson, Alan Robinson, Mel Gaynor, Wim Wenders, Adu, and Chris Carr, the contact king. And my brother Damian, for doing so much for our mum over the last few years.

Bibliography

Booth, Stanley. *Dance With The Devil: The Rolling Stones & Their Times* (aka *The True Adventures Of The Rolling Stones*) (Random House, 1984).

Davies, Dave. *Kink: An Autobiography* (Boxtree, 1996).

Davies, Ray. *X-Ray: The Unauthorised Autobiography* (Overlook Press, 1996).

Davies, Ray. *Waterloo Sunset* (Penguin, 1998).

Dawson, Julian. *And On Piano... Nicky Hopkins* (Desert Hearts, 2011).

Gilmore, Mikal. *Night Beat: A Shadow History Of Rock & Roll* (Picador, 1998).

Goodman, Fred. *The Mansion On The Hill* (Pimlico, 2003).

Hinman, Doug. *The Kinks: All Day And All Of The Night* (Backbeat, 2004). Every subsequent writer on The Kinks is indebted to Hinman's epically researched and thoughtfully annotated diary of their career.

McDonald, Ian. *Revolution In The Head: The Beatles' Records And The Sixties* (Fourth Estate, 1994).

Melly, George. *Revolt Into Style: The Pop Arts In Britain* (Penguin, 1972).

Miller, Andy. *The Kinks Are The Village Green Preservation Society* (Continuum, 2003).

Neill, Andy & Kent, Matt. *Anyway Anyhow Anywhere: The Complete Chronicle Of The Who 1958–1978* (Virgin 2005).

Oldham, Andrew Loog. *Stoned* (Secker & Warburg, 2000).

Orwell, George. *Coming Up For Air* (Penguin Classics edition, 2000).

Quaife, Peter. *Veritas Volume 1* (Hiren).

Rogan, Johnny. *The Complete Guide To The Music Of The Kinks* (Omnibus, 1998).

Sillitoe, Alan. *Saturday Night And Sunday Morning* (Pan, 1960).

The London A-Z (Geographers' A-Z Map Company, 2011).

Various music papers and magazines in the National Newspaper Library in Colindale, especially *Melody Maker, NME* and *Record Mirror* 1964–66. Dave Emlen's website www.kindakinks.net was another valuable resource.

Discography

(UK chart positions follow where applicable)

THE KINKS

ALBUMS

Pye Records

Kinks (1964)	3
Kinda Kinks (1965)	3
The Kink Kontroversy (1965)	9
Face To Face (1966)	12
Live At Kelvin Hall (1967)	
Something Else By The Kinks (1967)	35
The Kinks Are The Village Green Preservation Society (1968)	
Arthur (Or The Decline And Fall Of The British Empire) (1969)	
Lola Versus Powerman And The Moneygoround. Part One (1970)	
Percy (Soundtrack From The Film) (1971)	

RCA Records

Muswell Hillbillies (1971)
Everybody's In Show-biz (1972)
Preservation Act 1 (1973)
Preservation Act 2 (1974)

A Soap Opera (1975)
Schoolboys In Disgrace (1976)

Arista Records
Sleepwalker (1977)
Misfits (1978)
Low Budget (1979)
One For The Road (1980)
Give The People What They Want (1981)
State Of Confusion (1983)
Word Of Mouth (1984)

London Records [MCA in US]
Think Visual (1986)
The Road (1988)
UK Jive (1989)

In addition:
Phobia (Columbia 1993)
To The Bone (Konk/Grapevine 1994)
To The Bone [revised and expanded double-album] (Guardian 1997)

NOTABLE COMPILATIONS

Well Respected Kinks (Marble Arch 1966)	5
Sunny Afternoon (Marble Arch 1967)	9
The Kinks [aka *The Black Album*] (Pye 1970)	
Golden Hour Of The Kinks (Golden Hour 1971)	21
The Kinks' Greatest – Celluloid Heroes [RCA] (RCA 1976)	
Come Dancing With The Kinks [Arista] (Arista 1986)	
Picture Book [Six-CD box-set] (Universal 2008)	

The Kinks at the BBC (Sanctuary/Universal 2012) Available as a
5 CD plus 1 DVD box-set or a double-CD, superseding the
slimmer 2001 release *BBC Sessions 1964-1977*. The DVD
especially is essential.

NOTABLE US-ONLY COMPILATIONS

The Kinks Greatest Hits (Reprise, 1966)
The Kink Kronikles (Reprise 1972)
The Great Lost Kinks Album (Reprise 1973)

In 1998 all The Kinks' Pye albums were reissued by Castle (now Sanctuary) in the UK, and RCA and Arista albums by Koch/Velvel in the US, with significant, and in the case of the Pye albums extensive, extra tracks and liner notes.

The Kinks Are The Village Green Preservation Society was reissued by Sanctuary as a triple-CD set in 2004, including mono and stereo editions and contemporary out-takes previously only available on the withdrawn US compilation *The Great Lost Kinks Album*.

In 2011, *Kinks, Kinda Kinks, The Kink Kontroversy, Face To Face, Something Else By The Kinks, Arthur* and *Muswell Hillbillies* were all reissued again in even more extensive editions from Universal/Sanctuary.

SINGLES

Pye Records

Long Tall Sally/I Took My Baby Home (1964)	42
You Still Want Me/You Do Something To Me (1964)	
You Really Got Me/It's Alright (1964)	1
All Day And All Of The Night/I Gotta Move (1964)	2
Tired Of Waiting For You/Come On Now (1965)	1
Ev'rybody's Gonna Be Happy/	
Who'll Be The Next In Line (1965)	11
Set Me Free/I Need You (1965)	9
See My Friends/Never Met A Girl Like You Before (1965)	10
Till The End Of The Day/	
Where Have All The Good Times Gone (1965)	6
Dedicated Follower Of Fashion/Sittin' On My Sofa (1966)	4
Sunny Afternoon/I'm Not Like Everybody Else (1966)	1
Dead End Street/Big Black Smoke (1966)	5

Waterloo Sunset/Act Nice And Gentle (1967)   2
Autumn Almanac/Mr. Pleasant (1967)   3
Wonderboy/Polly (1968)   37
Days/She's Got Everything (1968)   12
Plastic Man/King Kong (1969)   31
Drivin'/Mindless Child Of Motherhood (1969)
Shangri-La/This Man He Weeps Tonight (1969)
Victoria/Mr. Churchill Says (1969)   33
Lola/Berkeley Mews (1970)   2
Apeman/Rats (1970)   5
God's Children/Moments (1971)

RCA Records

Supersonic Rocket Ship/You Don't Know My Name (1972)   16
Celluloid Heroes/Hot Potatoes (1972)
Sitting In The Midday Sun/One Of The Survivors (1973)
Sweet Lady Genevieve/Sitting In My Hotel (1973)
Mirror Of Love/Cricket (1974)
Mirror Of Love [second version]/He's Evil (1974)
Holiday Romance/Shepherds Of The Nation (1974)
Ducks On The Wall/Rush Hour Blues (1975)
You Can't Stop The Music/Have Another Drink (1975)
No More Looking Back/Jack The Idiot Dunce/
     The Hard Way (1976)

Arista Records

Sleepwalker/Full Moon (1977)
Juke Box Music/Sleepless Night (1977)
Father Christmas/Prince Of The Punks (1977)
A Rock'n'Roll Fantasy/Artificial Light (1978)
Live Life/In A Foreign Land (1978)
Black Messiah/Misfits (1978)
(Wish I Could Fly Like) Superman/Low Budget (1979)
Moving Pictures/In A Space (1979)
Pressure/National Health (1979)

Better Things/Massive Reductions (1981)   46
Predictable/Back To Front (1981)
Come Dancing/Noise (1982)   12
Don't Forget To Dance/Bernadette (1983)   58
State Of Confusion/Heart Of Gold (1984)
Good Day/Too Hot (1984)
Do It Again/Guilty (1985)

London Records

How Are You/Killing Time (1986)
Lost And Found/Killing Time (1987)
The Road/Art Lover (live) (1988)
Down All The Days (Till 1992)/You Really Got Me (live) (1989)
How Do I Get Close/Down All The Days (Till 1992) (1990)

Columbia Records

Scattered/Hatred (A Duet) (1993)
Only A Dream/Somebody Stole My Car (1993)

EPS

Kinksize Session (Pye 1964)   1
Kinksize Hits (Pye 1965)
Kwyet Kinks [includes A Well Respected Man] (Pye 1965)   1
Dedicated Kinks (1966)
The Kinks (1968)
The Kinks (from the soundtrack of the film *Percy)* (Pye 1971)
The Kinks Live (Arista 1980)
State Of Confusion (Arista 1984)
Waterloo Sunset '94 (Konk/Grapevine 1994)
Days (When! 1997)   35 (in singles chart)

NOTABLE US-ONLY EP

Did Ya (Columbia 1991)

RAY DAVIES

ALBUMS

The Storyteller (EMI 1998)
Other People's Lives (V2 2006)   36
Working Man's Cafe (V2 2007)
The Kinks Choral Collection (Universal/Decca 2009)   28
See My Friends (Universal 2010)   12

US-ONLY ALBUM

Return To Waterloo – soundtrack album by Ray Davies and members
    of The Kinks [not Dave Davies] (Arista 1985)

SINGLES

Quiet Life/Voices In The Dark (Virgin 1986)
Postcard From London (UMTV 2009)

EPS

The Tourist (V2 2005)

DAVE DAVIES

ALBUMS

PL 13603 [*AFLI-3603* in the US, both from catalogue number;
   aka *Dave Davies*] (RCA 1980)
Glamour (RCA 1981)
Chosen People (Warner 1983)
Rock Bottom – Live At The Bottom Line (Koch/MetaMedia 2000)
Bug (Angel Air 2002)
Fractured Mindz (MetaMedia 2007)

As Crystal Radio (with son Russell Davies):

Purusha And The Spiritual Planet (MetaMedia 1998)

As The Aschere Project (with Russell Davies):

Two Worlds (Modus 2010)

COMPILATIONS

Dave Davies – The Album That Never Was [compilation of Sixties
   material] (Pye 1988)
Unfinished Business [two-disc anthology of Kinks and solo work]
   (Castle 1998)
Hidden Treasures (Universal/Sanctuary 2011) The most complete
   reconstruction job yet of Dave's abandoned sixties album.

SINGLES

Death Of A Clown/Love Me Till The Sun Shines (Pye 1967)   3
Susannah's Still Alive/Funny Face (Pye 1967)   21
Lincoln County/There Is No Life Without Love (Pye 1968)
Hold My Hand/Creeping Jean (Pye 1969)
Doing The Best For You/Wild Man (RCA 1980)

EPS

Dave Davies Hits (Pye 1968)

Index